The publisher gratefully acknowledges the generous support of the

Philip E. Lilienthal Asian Studies Endowment Fund

of the University of California Press Foundation,

which was established by a major gift from Sally Lilienthal.

*Anyuan*

ASIA: LOCAL STUDIES/GLOBAL THEMES

*Jeffrey N. Wasserstrom, Kären Wigen, and Hue-Tam Ho Tai, Editors*

# Anyuan

*Mining China's Revolutionary Tradition*

ELIZABETH J. PERRY

*University of California Press*

BERKELEY    NEW YORK    LONDON

University of California Press, one of the most distinguished university presses in the United States, enriches lives around the world by
advancing scholarship in the humanities, social sciences, and natural
sciences. Its activities are supported by the UC Press Foundation and
by philanthropic contributions from individuals and institutions. For
more information, visit www.ucpress.edu.

University of California Press
Berkeley and Los Angeles, California

University of California Press, Ltd.
London, England

Library of Congress Cataloging-in-Publication Data

Perry, Elizabeth J.
  Anyuan : mining China's revolutionary tradition / Elizabeth J.
Perry.
    p.   cm. —(Asia : local studies/global themes ; 24)
  Includes bibliographical references and index.
  ISBN 978-0-520-27189-0 (cloth, alk. paper) —ISBN 978-0-520-
27190-6 (pbk., alk. paper)
    1. Anyuan (Jiangxi Sheng, China : West)—Politics and
government—20th century.   2. Anyuan (Jiangxi Sheng, China :
West)—Economic conditions—20th century.   3. Anyuan (Jiangxi
Sheng, China : West)—Social conditions—20th century.
4. Communism—China—Anyuan (Jiangxi Sheng : West)—History—
20th century.   5. Revolutions—Social aspects—China—Anyuan
(Jiangxi Sheng : West)—History—20th century.   6. Political
culture—China—Anyuan (Jiangxi Sheng : West)—History—20th
century.   7. Social change—China—Anyuan (Jiangxi Sheng : West)—
History—20th century.   8. Coal miners—China—Anyuan (Jiangxi
Sheng : West)—History—20th century.   9. Labor movement—
China—Anyuan (Jiangxi Sheng : West)—History—20th century.
10. Working class—China—Anyuan (Jiangxi Sheng : West)—
History—20th century.   I. Title.
DS797.57.A698P47   2012
951.2'22—dc23                                              2012003939

Manufactured in the United States of America

21  20  19  18  17  16  15  14  13  12
10  9  8  7  6  5  4  3  2  1

In keeping with its commitment to support environmentally
responsible and sustainable printing practices, UC Press has printed
this book on 50# Enterprise, a 30% post consumer waste, recycled,
de-inked fiber and processed chlorine free. It is acid-free, and meets
all ANSI/NISO (z 39.48) requirements.

*For Yu Jianrong, Cai Shaoqing, and the many other Chinese scholars who have shared so generously of their time and knowledge*

# Contents

# Illustrations

# Acknowledgments

The origins of this book can be traced to a conversation over dinner in the winter of 2003. Having just come across Professor Yu Jianrong's impressive articles on peasant protest in rural Hunan, I invited him to Harvard to speak on his research. Over dinner at a Chinese restaurant after the lecture, Professor Yu asked if I knew why he had come to Harvard. "Of course," I replied, "it's because I invited you here!" "No," he retorted, "it's because *I* want to invite *you* to the Anyuan coal mine!" Yu Jianrong explained that he had been conducting fieldwork at Anyuan for some five years in preparation for a study of the plight of the Chinese working class. Having read my book on the Shanghai labor movement, he asked me to join him in a collaborative project. I politely but firmly demurred, noting that I was in the midst of a book project on workers' militias and could not contemplate anything more. I assumed that would be the end of the story, but Professor Yu is not easily deterred. When he e-mailed from Beijing a few months later to say that all the arrangements for my "forthcoming" trip to Anyuan had already been made, I could no longer refuse.

My first visit to Anyuan, in July 2004, revealed the Jiangxi coal mining town to be everything that Professor Yu had promised it would be; it was a fascinating place whose complicated history exemplifies major themes of the Chinese revolutionary tradition. For someone interested in peasants as well as workers, the past as well as the present, leaders as well as followers, Anyuan has it all. I was instantly hooked. Follow-up fieldwork with Professor Yu and other Chinese colleagues in successive summers, capped by a longer stay on my own in the fall of 2009, yielded the core documentary, archival, and interview material on which this study is based. I am deeply indebted to Professor Yu Jianrong of the Chinese Academy of Social Sciences for his irresistible enthusiasm, warm friendship, keen sense of humor, and penetrating insight. Without him, this book never would have been written.

As I embarked on a study of Anyuan, my memory was jogged of conversations enjoyed many years earlier with Professor Cai Shaoqing of Nanjing University. As a visiting scholar at Nanda in 1979–80, I had the good fortune to conduct research on the history of Chinese secret societies under the direction of Professor Cai (as well as Professor Mao Jiaqi). Among the experiences that Professor Cai related during our frequent conversations that year were accounts of his early research on the Anyuan labor movement, conducted while he was still a student at Beijing University in the late 1950s and early 1960s. His animated descriptions of interviewing the charismatic Li Lisan in Beijing and venturing down into the Anyuan coal pits to chat with the miners were both entertaining and inspiring. It was a great pleasure to seek Professor Cai's advice yet again in connection with this study.

Individuals and institutions too numerous to mention have offered invaluable aid over the course of this project. I am grateful to them all, and I apologize to those whose names I have omitted, but I would like to single out a few for special acknowledgment. A succession of former and current graduate students contributed to the research effort; the assistance of Yan Xiaojun (now at the University of Hong Kong) and Ouyang Bin was especially critical. Repeated discussions with local party historian Huang Aiguo of the Pingxiang Communist Party School in Jiangxi played an important role in improving my understanding of Anyuan history. Harvard colleague Eugene Wang, a distinguished art historian, has consistently encouraged this political scientist's naïve efforts to trespass into unfamiliar cultural territory; he also helped obtain valuable Anyuan images, even taking a number of photographs himself. My assistant, Lindsay Strogatz, has provided a range of expert professional services, including locating obscure materials, commissioning maps, compiling the bibliography, and much more. Others who deserve special mention for key contributions to the final product include Nara Dillon, Feng Xiaocai, Cindy Fulton, Nancy Hearst, Liu Chunyang, Hannah Love, Lu Lei, Patricia Thornton, Ma Xiaohe, Reed Malcolm, Ren Jianghua, Victor Seow, Hue-Tam Ho Tai, Wang Xiaojing, Jeffrey Wasserstrom, Sharron Wood, and Yiching Wu. Many rare documents were supplied by the Harvard-Yenching Library, the Fairbank Center Library, Widener Library, the Anyuan Labor Movement Memorial Hall Archives, the Pingxiang Municipal Library, the Nanchang Municipal Archives, the Shanghai Municipal Archives, and the Shanghai Municipal Library.

The three reviewers for the University of California Press, all of whom graciously revealed their identities, offered exceptionally detailed and constructive (as well as critical!) comments. I am truly grateful to Joseph Esherick, Richard Kraus, and Steve Smith for their astute readings of an earlier draft. I also received many helpful ideas from discussants and audience members in the various academic forums where I presented parts of this work in progress: Harvard University, Princeton University, Yale University, the University of California at Berkeley, the University of Pennsylvania, Brown University, the University of Texas at Austin, Johns Hopkins University, the University of Hong Kong, the National University of Singapore, Fudan University, East China Normal University, Peking University, and the Association for Asian Studies.

Despite all of this welcome assistance and instruction, I alone am responsible for any remaining errors of fact or interpretation.

Material in this book was originally published as "Red Literati: Communist Educators at Anyuan, 1921–1925," *Twentieth Century China*, 32.3 (April 2007): 123–60. Reprinted by permission. The on-line version of this journal is at www.maney.co.uk/journals/tcc and www.ingentaconnect .com/content/many/tcc. Material is also reprinted, with permission, from "Reclaiming the Chinese Revolution," *The Journal of Asian Studies*, 67 (2008): 1147–1164.

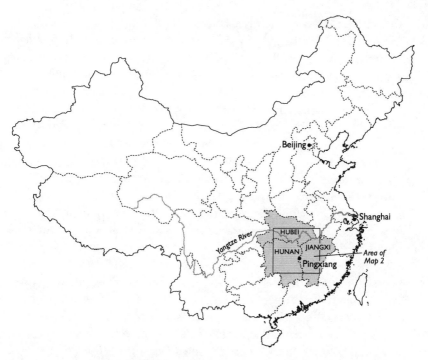

Map 1. Map of China, highlighting location of Pingxiang, Jiangxi.

Map 2. Map of Pingxiang County and surrounding area. The dotted line indicates Zhuping Railway.

# Introduction

The idea of a revolutionary tradition is inherently ironic. Revolutions are intended to overthrow traditions, not enshrine them. Yet nation-states born of revolution construct myths about their historical origins and political legacies that prove as powerful and persistent as they are contradictory and contested. Acrimonious debates surrounding the bicentennial of the French Revolution demonstrated that descendants of that epic event still grapple with its multiple meanings.[1] More recently, the rise of the Tea Party movement in the United States—named for the incident in Boston Harbor that helped ignite the American Revolution—has highlighted deep divisions in interpretations of this country's revolutionary inheritance.[2] Parties to these debates, although they present themselves as faithful defenders of their nation's historic revolutionary tradition, are primarily animated by contemporary concerns. Their claims not only alter narratives about the past; they also shape present and future political trajectories.

In no country is the challenge of confronting the revolutionary past in order to chart the political future more problematic or less predictable than in the People's Republic of China (PRC). The unfolding of that tortuous process is of great consequence not only for China, but for the whole world. Its direction, however, is far from clear. There are no obvious precedents or parallels that allow us to forecast with confidence the fate of the Chinese Communist system. In contrast to an earlier era—when it seemed that Chinese and Russian Communism had been cut from the same revolutionary cloth and were headed down a shared historical path—today the differences could hardly be starker. Perry Anderson observes:

> If the twentieth century was dominated, more than by any other
> single event, by the trajectory of the Russian Revolution, the twenty-
> first will be shaped by the outcome of the Chinese Revolution. The
> Soviet state . . . dissolved after seven decades with scarcely a shot, as
> swiftly as it had once arisen. . . . The outcome of the Chinese Revolu-
> tion offers an arresting contrast. As it enters its seventh decade, the
> People's Republic is an engine of the world economy . . . for a quarter
> of a century posting the fastest growth rates in per capita income, for
> the largest population, ever recorded. . . . In the character and scale
> of that achievement, of course, there is more than one—bitter—irony.
> But of the difference between the fate of the revolutions in China and
> Russia, there can be little doubt.[3]

Anderson writes at a time when, on the one hand, the collapse of the
Soviet Union (more than twenty years ago) has already relegated the
Russian revolution to a distant memory; and, on the other hand, China's
stunning economic ascendance—engineered by a Communist party-
state that continues to celebrate its revolutionary origins—has focused
renewed attention on the lessons and legacies of the Chinese revolution.

The paramount leader of that revolution, Mao Zedong, passed away
decades ago, yet his picture still hangs in the place of highest political
honor atop the Gate of Heavenly Peace (Tiananmen) in the center of
Beijing. "Mao Zedong Thought"—based on the pronouncements of a leader
whose chief concern was revolutionary struggle—is still recognized as a
centerpiece of the official ideology of the People's Republic of China. Mao's
mausoleum, located just across Tiananmen Square, continues to draw a
steady stream of visitors who pay respects to his embalmed corpse. The
fascination with Mao is not limited to the capital; nine hundred miles
inland, China's largest city of Chongqing recently held a massive "singing
red" campaign to revive Maoist revolutionary culture.[4] Admiration for
Mao and his revolution among Chinese citizens is far from universal, to
be sure.[5] Nevertheless, reverence for Mao Zedong extends well beyond
state-sponsored initiatives. A survey of popular religious beliefs, conducted in forty major Chinese cities, found that nearly 12 percent of urban
residents worship images of Chairman Mao in their homes, about the
same number as those who venerate ancestor tablets, and more than the
10 percent who pray to Buddhist images or the 9 percent who burn joss
sticks to the god of wealth.[6] In the rural countryside, respect for Mao's
revolutionary accomplishments is even more pronounced.[7]

Although the exact influence of Mao's radical policies on contemporary Chinese politics is open to debate, the importance of his revolution

in giving rise to a strong, unified country that is today a dynamo of the global economy is undeniable.[8] What explains the distinctive trajectory of the Chinese Communist revolutionary effort? How and why did the Chinese pattern diverge so dramatically from its Russian prototype? And what meanings does the revolutionary tradition hold for Chinese citizens today?

## MAO ZEDONG AND THE COMMUNIST REVOLUTION

Recent work by Western writers—scholars and journalists alike—paints a decidedly dark picture of Mao Zedong and his idiosyncratic brand of revolutionary change.[9] From his earliest days as a political organizer, Mao's best-selling biography tells us, the man was a vile and ruthless individual whose cynical machinations would bring terrible, needless hardship to the majority of his countrymen.[10] The poorest and most vulnerable members of Chinese society—the very people in whose name the Communist revolution was waged—would suffer more than anyone from Mao's eccentric follies.

There is ample evidence to support this grim conclusion.[11] And yet, were that the whole story, how do we explain Mao's remarkable ability to convince millions of his countrymen to sacrifice for his revolutionary crusade long before he possessed the coercive means to enforce compliance? And how do we account for the outpouring of nostalgia for Chairman Mao and his accomplishments so evident among many ordinary Chinese (especially the disadvantaged) even today, more than three decades after his death? Mao's charismatic appeal—then and now—is part of a larger revolutionary tradition that continues to reverberate in significant and sometimes surprising ways.

In contrast to Lenin's revolution, Mao's revolution was a protracted process.[12] Building upon the Republican Revolution of 1911 and the Nationalist Revolution of 1925–27, the Chinese Communist revolution took nearly three decades to achieve political victory, from the establishment of the Chinese Communist Party (CCP) in July 1921 until the founding of the People's Republic of China in October 1949. Having begun (like its Russian exemplar) as a movement directed toward the urban proletariat, the Chinese Communist revolution was later forced out of the cities into the countryside, where, under Mao Zedong's leadership, it grew into a powerful army capable of fighting first the Japanese (1937–45) and then the Nationalists (1946–49). But military victory in the civil war did not mark the end of the revolutionary process; Chairman Mao's call to "continue the revolution" found expression in a series of tumultuous mass campaigns stretching from the Land Reform and Marriage Law of the early 1950s through the turbulent decade of the Cultural Revolution (1966–76). Still incomplete at the time of his death in 1976, yet hardly insignificant in its impact, was Mao's lifelong attempt to invent and instill a new revolutionary culture.

The vicissitudes of the Chinese revolutionary process have posed exceptional challenges for social science explanations and popular interpretations alike. With successive phases having been guided by divergent policies, centered in disparate geographical locations and marked by differing degrees of success, the Chinese revolution has provided fertile ground for the formulation of competing hypotheses. For some, the Soviet connection was decisive.[13] For others, Mao Zedong's maverick mode of popular mobilization was critical.[14] In either case, a range of factors has been proposed to account for the eventual victory and lasting legacy of the Chinese Communist revolution: nationalism, class struggle, Leninist party organization, Maoist mass line, and more.[15]

## MAKING THE REVOLUTIONARY TRADITION: CULTURAL POSITIONING

This book does not gainsay the importance of any of these variables in a comprehensive explanation of the Chinese revolution. Ideological as well as organizational imitation and innovation were key ingredients in the CCP's rise to power and after. But still unanswered is the question of how the revolutionaries managed to introduce such radically new messages and methods in ways that resonated with their target audience, both then and now. How did the Communists get ordinary Chinese to understand, accept, and in some cases even embrace revolutionary authority?

Most of the early Communist leaders, Mao Zedong included, were educated intellectuals who brought to their organizing efforts substantial cultural capital and creativity. Central to this mobilization process, I argue, was the role of cultural positioning, or the strategic deployment of a range of symbolic resources (religion, ritual, rhetoric, dress, drama, art, and so on) for purposes of political persuasion. The supple methods of Mao and his fellow teachers-cum-revolutionaries not only enabled the transplantation of Soviet ideas and institutions onto Chinese soil; they further ensured that the Chinese revolutionary variant would grow into something quite different from its Russian prototype.

To stress the importance of cultural positioning in generating a

Chinese species of Communism is not to suggest some essential continuity from imperial days to the present that preordained any particular or predictable outcome. It should be made clear from the outset that the concept of culture employed in this study presumes neither an unchanging Chinese national character or ethos nor an internally consistent system of symbols and meanings. Rather, in keeping with recent theorizing across the social sciences, culture is treated here as a realm of fluid and often contradictory semiotic practices.[16] This is not to say, however, that culture is either arbitrary or infinitely malleable. To assume such a position would be to rob culture of any independent explanatory power. By the same token, cultural positioning—while evident to some degree in any social movement—is not always effective. In order to be convincing, cultural positioning demands intimate familiarity with prevailing norms and habits as well as a keen eye for the possibilities of meaningful invention within tradition. Social protests (and protest leaders) vary considerably in their success at meeting this common challenge.

Although the "cultural turn" in the social sciences has been underway for over a generation, it is often conducted as discourse analysis in which writings, speeches, films, festivals, and other communicative materials are treated for the most part as disembodied texts whose meaning emerges through the process of scholarly deconstruction. The analytical approach adopted in this study is somewhat different. Cultural positioning requires active effort that can be understood only by serious attention to the particular people who undertake it. Success in generating new commitments and identities hinges as much upon the skills of the messenger as on the substance and syntax of the message itself.

This is therefore also a study about political leaders. Cultural positioning is certainly not the only dimension of revolutionary leadership, but it is a crucial one.[17] Mao Zedong and his colleagues in the Chinese Communist Party were aware of the attraction and adaptability of symbolic resources in their quest to recruit and mobilize a mass following. Although deeply influenced by Soviet models of agitprop, they brought a distinctive Chinese sensibility to this process. Still, individual Chinese revolutionary leaders differed notably in the style and success of these efforts. And such differences became magnified over time.

The use of cultural assets for purposes of mass mobilization is not unique to China, of course. Students of the French Revolution have long emphasized the cultural dimensions of that historic event.[18] Nor is cultural positioning found only in revolutionary movements; any sustained protest requires the adaptation of familiar cultural resources to new collective purposes. Sociologist Alberto Melucci pointed out years ago that the cultural construction of novel group identities that captured the commitment of their emergent constituencies was central to the development of "new social movements" (for example, the peace movement, environmental movement, women's movement, and so on) in twentieth-century Europe and America.[19] Despite such cross-national commonalities, the special appreciation for cultural power that has for millennia marked the exercise of political authority in China renders this a particularly promising vein to mine in the Chinese context.[20] Moreover, given the acknowledged significance of ritual and public performance in Chinese protest culture, continuities and discontinuities are arguably more readily observable in that country than in many other political settings.[21]

Tracing the means by which both familiar and foreign symbolic resources have been employed and imbued with radically new content and connotation affords considerable insight into China's revolutionary trajectory. It also illuminates ways in which Chinese culture has itself been transformed through this dynamic process. As political scientist Richard Kraus noted in his study of calligraphy in modern Chinese politics, *Brushes with Power*, " the long reign of calligraphy as the premier art of imperial China can be explained by reference to its social utility to the ruling bureaucratic class. But the recent status of calligraphy must be explained by the new meanings it has assumed in this century of social revolution."[22] Kraus explored the changing political uses of one distinctive Chinese art form, calligraphy, while this study touches (in less depth) upon a broader range of cultural media: painting, poetry, drama, dance, film, literature, music, and more. In contrast to Kraus's national perspective, however, the focus here is decidedly local.

## THE CASE OF ANYUAN

This book traces the course of China's revolutionary tradition as it related to one small, yet surprisingly eventful and influential, place over the span of a century. The long time period under consideration distinguishes this effort from the handful of other works that have investigated the culture of the Chinese revolution.[23] As a diachronic study based upon a single locale, and crossing the 1949 divide, the approach bears some similarities to the few existing microhistories of the Chinese Communist revolution, most notably William Hinton's two-volume study of Long Bow Village in Shanxi Province; Jan Myrdal's two-volume study of Liuling Village in northern Shaanxi Province; and Edward Friedman, Paul Pickowicz, and

Mark Selden's two-volume study of Wugong Village in Hebei Province.[24] It differs from these works, however, in several respects.

The focus of this study, the Anyuan coal mine, is not an agricultural village on the arid North China Plain, but an industrial enterprise situated amid the lush mountains of south-central China. Thanks to its strategic geographical location and special economic significance, Anyuan experienced Mao's revolution earlier and more intensely than most places in China. The formative lessons that Mao Zedong and his comrades drew from their pioneering and prolonged experiments at Anyuan were later applied widely across the country. Moreover, because Anyuan was not only a cradle of the labor movement (1921–25) but also a springboard for the organization of peasant associations (1926–27) and a recruiting ground for Red Army soldiers (1928–30), the Anyuan experience played an influential part in the subsequent development of the Communist revolution when its leaders redirected their primary mobilizing energies from workers toward peasants and soldiers. Anyuan was by no means a "typical" Chinese enterprise or town, if such an entity can be said to exist. Nevertheless, to understand what happened at Anyuan in the 1920s and its aftermath is to grasp much of the direction of the Chinese revolution.

A study of Anyuan offers insight into the methods and appeals of Chinese revolutionaries from their earliest days forward. Anyuan's long history of rebellion also opens a revealing window onto differences between the Communists and previous insurgents. More than a decade before Mao's initial investigation of the coal mine, Anyuan had been involved in the first in a series of insurrections that prefigured the 1911 Revolution—the Ping-Liu-Li Uprising of 1906. It thus constitutes an instructive site for comparing China's Republican and Communist revolutions. Although progressively minded intellectuals played leadership roles in both events, only in the latter case did they succeed in bridging the cultural chasm that separated them from their putative constituency among the peasant-workers.

Mao Zedong's maiden visit to the town of Anyuan, which took place only a few months after the founding of the Chinese Communist Party in the summer of 1921, was part of a concerted Communist Party program of targeting promising industrial enterprises for proletarian revolution.[25] The comprehensive "red education" that Mao's comrades subsequently carried out at Anyuan produced a remarkable cohort of committed worker activists dedicated to improving the plight of the poor. Several years later, when CCP strategy shifted from labor organizing toward peasant associations and military struggle, Anyuan workers provided a critical source of manpower and leadership for these endeavors as well. The peasant associations established across Hunan and Jiangxi provinces in the mid-1920s, made famous by Mao Zedong's influential "Report on an Investigation of the Peasant Movement in Hunan," were largely founded and directed by former Anyuan workers. The Autumn Harvest Uprising in September 1927, which propelled Mao down the path of peasant revolution, was planned and launched from Anyuan with the participation of hundreds of coal miners. By the fall of 1930, thousands of Anyuan workers had enlisted as soldiers in the Red Army. Due to its close connection to these formative events, Anyuan affords a revealing vantage point for examining the origins and evolution of the Chinese revolution.

The success of the Anyuan mobilization effort, we will discover, was closely related to the ability of the young Communist cadres to convert cultural capital into valuable revolutionary currency. Formal education (at schools for workers) played a key role in the process of constructing a new proletarian ethos, but so too did the innovative deployment of classical phrases, folk practices, clothing, ritual, and other elite and mass cultural resources. Over the years, moreover, the symbolic power of Anyuan, reflected in a full range of cultural media, grew apace.

Three of the most important leaders of the early Chinese Communist Party, Mao Zedong, Liu Shaoqi, and Li Lisan, were active at Anyuan in the 1920s. All three were educated intellectuals who had grown up in nearby Hunan counties, anxious to take advantage of their cultural intimacy along with their superior social status to effect radical social and political change.[26] At Anyuan, Mao and his fellow "red literati" used the pedagogical authority long associated with the Confucian elite of imperial China to forge new revolutionary inroads.[27] At the same time, they recognized the contribution that the local secret society and martial arts tradition—once tamed and redirected—could make to their revolutionary enterprise.

In drawing liberally upon both literary and military sources of power, the Communists demonstrated a grasp of the fundamentals of Chinese cultural authority. The parallel pull of *wen* (literary attainment) and *wu* (martial prowess) to the target constituency of male coal miners and railway workers was a magnetic force that Mao and his comrades redirected to their own advantage. In part this was a gendered appeal to the dual ideals of Chinese manhood.[28] But it also bespoke an instinctive appreciation for the twin pillars of cultural and political authority more broadly conceived, one grounded in the literary arts *(wenyi)* and the other in the martial arts *(wuyi)*. Political legitimacy in the Chinese context required an ambidextrous deployment of both types of power: *wenwu shuangquan*.

The impressive achievements of the Communist labor movement at Anyuan evidenced a knack for enlisting conventional sources of authority in service to new political purposes. Among the most potent of these familiar resources were religious and quasi-religious rituals, drawn eclectically but effectively from folk festivals, ancestor and spirit worship, secret societies, and the like. Such practices had long reflected and reinforced the civilian and military governance structures of imperial China. As Emily Martin Ahern argues, popular religion in China mirrored the traditional bureaucratic political system "with uncanny sociological accuracy," offering to ordinary people an instructive guide to understanding, accessing, and opposing political power.[29] Although hardly a road map for overturning the extant political order, ritual practices constituted a valuable vehicle for activists with revolutionary ambitions.

The decision of Mao Zedong, a native of Hunan, to target nearby Anyuan as a site for revolutionary mobilization was more than a matter of geographic convenience. Thanks to Anyuan's well-established reputation for rebelliousness, as well as its concentration of industrial workers, the coal mine was a promising candidate for proletarian struggle. Moreover, the fact that several of the most dedicated and determined early leaders of the CCP were cultural insiders, familiar with local customs and capable of communicating with the majority of miners in their own dialect on the basis of shared symbolic meanings, greatly facilitated their efforts. Building on this insider advantage, in September 1922 Mao Zedong, Liu Shaoqi, and Li Lisan cooperated in launching a hugely successful nonviolent strike at Anyuan that came to be seen as one of the early milestones of the Communist revolution.

The revolutionaries from Hunan tapped into common cultural understandings to mobilize a mass movement based on a fundamental claim to human dignity. The slogan of the 1922 Anyuan strike, coined by Li Lisan in response to guiding instructions from Mao Zedong, captured this spirit brilliantly: "Once beasts of burden, now we will be men!" Framed as a morally compelling cry for social justice, the five-day strike of thirteen thousand miners and railway workers won the sympathies of the entire Anyuan workforce as well as key members of the local elite. The result was a stunning victory, secured without property damage or personal injury, which brought major improvements in workers' economic and social position together with official recognition and substantial financial support for their Communist-controlled labor union, the Anyuan "workers' club."

After the successful conclusion of the strike, Anyuan served as a national center of Communist organizing for the next three years. Known as "China's Little Moscow," the mining town garnered attention from across the country (and abroad) as a standard-bearer of the nascent revolutionary movement. The site of China's first Communist party branch (composed almost entirely of industrial workers), the biggest and most active enterprise union, the first party-sponsored consumer cooperative, and the largest network of Communist-operated schools for workers and peasants, as well as the first school for party cadres, Anyuan in the 1920s became a magnet for progressive intellectuals and organizers. Its workers' club, which enrolled more than ten thousand members and (as part of the strike settlement) enjoyed hefty subsidies from the mining company, served as a wellspring of proletarian revolutionary culture.

The creative use of folk religion and other elements of popular and elite practice in the repertoire of the Anyuan workers' club was part of a fluid and flexible effort to cultivate a new class consciousness. Through participation in mass education, didactic dramas, and other Communist-sponsored activities, many workers acquired an unprecedented appreciation of the economic importance and political potential of the Chinese proletariat. As a result, miners gradually transferred their loyalties from the local secret society (a Triad offshoot known as the Elder Brothers Society or Red Gang, which was behind much of the well-deserved reputation for rebelliousness of this region) to the workers' club. The growing participation in schools, literacy and vocational training classes, reading rooms, libraries, consumer cooperatives, labor unions, drama and lecture troupes, peasant associations, and other grassroots organizations developed under close Communist supervision during this period was a concrete expression of the shift in collective identity. The transference was not total, to be sure. Miners sometimes exhibited greater loyalty to charismatic leaders than to socialist ideals. And the violent inclinations of the many martial arts adepts among the former secret-society members of the workers' club were never fully tamed by the educational efforts of young Communist teachers. Nevertheless, for the most part "Little Moscow" was a society that valorized the *wen* of culture and education over the *wu* of violence and war.

Most of the sizable budget of the Anyuan workers' club went toward literacy classes and other forms of proletarian education and expression. The textbooks, dramas, songs, lectures, and other mobilizing materials developed for these pedagogical purposes constituted a cultural template that was later disseminated to the Jiangxi Soviet and then, during the wartime period, to Communist base areas across the country. Furthermore, the workers who had been educated at Anyuan assumed key leadership roles—as heads of peasant associations and political commissars in the Red Army—when the focus of the revolutionary movement shifted from proletarian mobilization to peasant militarization.[30]

During its heyday, "China's Little Moscow"—a coal mining town of fewer than eighty thousand inhabitants—harbored more than a fifth of the national membership of the Chinese Communist Party. Extinguished by overwhelming military opposition in September 1925, the Anyuan experiment nevertheless retained a special significance in the annals of the Chinese Communist revolution. As the training ground of three of the most influential revolutionary pioneers, the breeding ground of some five thousand worker-recruits to the Red Army, and the building ground for grassroots organizations of peasantry and proletariat alike, Anyuan and its events were closely connected to the subsequent direction of the Communist revolution. Not surprisingly, then, members of future generations would vie for the right to claim Anyuan's revolutionary legacy as their own.

## MINING THE REVOLUTIONARY TRADITION: CULTURAL PATRONAGE

The "glorious Anyuan revolutionary tradition," as it came to be known, was not, however, an unproblematic source of guidance and inspiration for later generations. Although its formative influence on subsequent policy is widely acknowledged, both its history and the evaluation and representation of that history have undergone repeated revision to serve a number of shifting and conflicting agendas. In the "mining" of Anyuan's revolutionary tradition, facts were conveniently forgotten or consciously fabricated by influential institutions and individuals to advance conflicting personal and political ambitions. Memories of revolutionary actions and ideals were both stretched and shrunk as a result.

Like any complex and protracted event, the Chinese revolution has been understood differently by competing claimants to its legacy.[31] The construction of collective memories of the Chinese revolution is, as sociologists Ching Kwan Lee and Guobin Yang emphasize, "a highly political process. Equally important, it is a cultural process involving a 'poetics' of memory, that is, the use of cultural tools and resources for the constitution and articulation of memory."[32] Motivated by intensely political conflicts and concerns, the "poetic" reconstruction of the Anyuan revolutionary tradition became embroiled in polemical leadership struggles.

After the establishment of a Communist party-state, influential government agencies—most notably the Department of Propaganda and the Ministry of Culture—spearheaded concerted efforts to rewrite the revolutionary record on behalf of powerful political patrons. In this historical reconstruction, cultural positioning was superseded by cultural patronage, as local and national officials leveraged bureaucratic resources to capitalize on Anyuan connections for purposes very different from those that had animated revolutionary mobilization in earlier years. During the 1920s, cultural positioning had enabled the communication of foreign concepts through familiar conduits in the making of the Anyuan labor movement; after 1949, cultural patronage elevated the history of that movement to an authoritative touchstone of political legitimation, conveyed through official media and designed to strengthen the standing of individual leaders as well as the Communist Party as a whole.

The early Communist organizers had not shied away from exploiting personal charismatic authority to pursue their mission, yet such efforts were directed toward the goal of a collective awakening on the part of the proletariat and peasantry rather than a cult of personality to enhance the power of the political elite. In later years, however, the "glorious Anyuan revolutionary tradition" was resurrected and reconstructed by official propaganda organs to serve very different ends. Under the Communist state, devotion (to the party and its leaders) came to replace dignity (of the proletariat and peasantry) as the primary objective. This process was most obvious during the Cultural Revolution, when the ascendance of Mao Zedong to the role of sole protagonist of the Chinese revolution was exemplified by the famous oil painting of the young Mao arriving at the coal mine in 1921, *Chairman Mao Goes to Anyuan*. Completed in 1967 by a student Red Guard artist, the painting—reproduced in some nine hundred million posters and countless other formats—became a sacred icon in the deification of Mao Zedong that underpinned his growing cult of personality. Although Mao's actual contribution to the Anyuan revolutionary movement had not matched that of either Liu Shaoqi or Li Lisan, he alone was now credited with its entire success. The full force of the Communist state was harnessed behind a quasi-religious revival that sought to rescue the one and only "savior" (*dajiuxing*) of the revolution and his "correct revolutionary line" from the alleged dangers of Soviet "revisionism." Military as well as literary sources of authority were brought to bear in the construction of a new revolutionary theology featuring Chairman Mao's spiritual leadership of the Anyuan workers. But, egregious though the excesses of the Cultural Revolution were, the rewriting of Anyuan's history neither began nor ended there.

Cultural patronage to highlight the Anyuan connections of particular party leaders was already clearly observable in the early years of the PRC, when clients of Vice-Chairman Liu Shaoqi at various levels of the political system used both visual and literary media to burnish his image as leader of the Chinese proletariat. Modeled on Stalin's earlier cult of personality, the cult of Liu featured his alleged heroism at Anyuan through a flurry of paintings, dramas, short stories, films, museum displays, and other artistic representations. The Cultural Revolution deification of Mao's Anyuan experience was a spectacular redirection and escalation of this prior exercise in cultural patronage. During the Cultural Revolution, moreover, the reinterpretation of the Anyuan story was infused with a decidedly militant bent in which for a time the rampages of Red Guards, bolstered by the iron fist of the People's Liberation Army, took center stage. Liu Shaoqi was attacked for having pursued a nonviolent strategy at Anyuan that denied the necessity of class struggle; his "revisionist" transgressions, committed more than forty years earlier, were highlighted as part of the pretext for his brutal purge. The Cultural Revolution, which in some respects resembled a militant religious crusade, esteemed the violent impulses of the revolutionary tradition above the more restrained organizational and educational efforts that had in fact—with Mao's own blessing—once been so essential to the success of the Anyuan experiment. Temporarily, at least, the way of the soldier *(wuren)* trumped that of the scholar *(wenren)*. Today, competing claimants to the legacy of Anyuan—within state and society alike—struggle with this complicated and contradictory heritage.

## THE ANYUAN CHALLENGE

The process of making and mining the Anyuan revolutionary tradition, from its origins to the present day, is the subject of this book. The first four chapters highlight the role of cultural positioning in revolutionary mobilization; subsequent chapters consider the power of cultural patronage in appropriating and reinterpreting that complex heritage. The case of Anyuan invites us to explore the multiple meanings and uses of China's revolutionary tradition—as a conduit of mass mobilization, a foundation for elite authority, a core subject of state education and propaganda, and an enduring encumbrance as well as inspiration to officials, intellectuals, and ordinary people alike.

The pages to follow focus as much attention on the process of recovering and reinventing the Anyuan tradition as on the initial revolutionary period itself. My intention is not simply to expose distortion and deception in the development of the Chinese revolution, but also to better explain dedication and devotion—then and now. The extraordinary sacrifices made by millions of people over the past century, along with the continuing attraction of revolutionary personalities and places for many Chinese today, are part of an interwoven and ambiguous fabric of events and memories that—although often engendered by self-interested motives—are nonetheless deeply invested with cultural and political significance. The facility of Mao Zedong (and a number of other CCP leaders) for introducing and adapting Soviet concepts in such a way as to render them culturally resonant, and therefore resilient, should not be overlooked in assessing the establishment and endurance of a Leninist party-state in China.

If the divergence in outcomes of the Chinese and Russian revolutions stems to some degree from their differential success in nurturing and normalizing a credible political culture, then unraveling the Anyuan thread in the complex tapestry of Mao's revolution also lays bare one of the key challenges facing contemporary China. On the one hand, the steady outpouring of literary and artistic works to commemorate (and critique) "Anyuan's glorious revolutionary tradition" attests to its persistent emotive power and underscores the enduring allure of Mao's revolutionary quest in the Chinese political imaginary. On the other hand, the glaring discordance between the dismal plight of the actual Anyuan coal miners (now as a century ago) and the romanticized images they have inspired speaks to the unfinished agenda of the Chinese revolution. The demand for human dignity and social justice by the dispossessed, so poignantly captured in the watchword of the Anyuan strike—"Once beasts of burden, now we will be men!"—remains a central issue in contemporary Chinese political debate.[33] In the end, the survival of the Communist party-state may ultimately hinge upon its ability to satisfy this unfulfilled promise of the Chinese revolutionary tradition.

# 1  Rehearsing Revolution

Revolution does not take place in a cultural vacuum. Although the ultimate aim of revolution is a radical break with tradition and a wholesale reconfiguration of the political and social landscape, its objectives must be conveyed in terms sufficiently intelligible and attractive to engage a mass following. When the blueprint for revolution is borrowed from abroad, the difficulty in communicating the new message is especially daunting. Impressed by the Russian Revolution though the founders of the Chinese Communist Party were, they recognized from the outset that their own revolution would demand a degree of adaptation and alteration of the Soviet model in order to garner widespread allegiance among their fellow countrymen.

Mao Zedong, raised in a rural household in the heartland of agrarian China and unexposed to overseas education, was better attuned to the cultural requirements of popular mobilization than some of his more cosmopolitan colleagues. Convinced from a young age of the exhaustion of the Confucian tradition and the need to develop a new revolutionary consciousness, Mao nonetheless evinced an instinctive appreciation for the critical role that indigenous culture could play in this transformation. When Mao returned to his native province of Hunan shortly after the establishment of the CCP to take charge of the labor secretariat there, his search for a mass constituency led him almost immediately to the Anyuan coal mine in nearby Pingxiang County. As Mao was quick to discern, the Pingxiang area offered a would-be revolutionary from Hunan the advantage of cultural accessibility combined with a local populace well schooled in the practice of protest. It was, however, also a place known for hostility to foreign ideas; introducing unfamiliar ways would not be easy.

Nestled amid the verdant mountainous terrain that spans the Jiangxi-Hunan border, Pingxiang County was in many respects closer to Hunan than to the province of Jiangxi, which governed it administratively (see map 1).[1] The rivers that crisscross the county flowed westward toward Hunan; its urban food supply came primarily from rural Hunan; and the distance to Hunan's capital of Changsha (80 miles) was less than half the distance to its own provincial capital of Nanchang (170 miles). Dialect, religion, opera, and other markers of local culture also showed strong Hunan influence.[2] Just as alluring to Mao as Pingxiang's familiar culture was the area's claim to a celebrated history of antistate rebellion. For centuries, this rugged borderland—dotted with hundreds of makeshift coal mines amid its densely wooded hills—had harbored a variety of sectarian and secret-society outfits whose members proved to be ready recruits for insurgency. Armed feuds among rival lineages competing for the rich coal resources contributed to an unusual degree of militarization and mobilization, blurring the distinction between everyday resistance and outright rebellion. A pattern of violence and lawlessness infused the local institutions of this region. In both imperial and republican periods, private militias and secret-society criminal networks were the main enforcers of order (as well as engines of disorder) in Pingxiang; state control was notoriously lax.[3]

To cite but a few notable examples of this rebellious heritage: In the mid-fourteenth century, Pingxiang County contributed more than five thousand soldiers to the millenarian Red Turban Army, which helped to rout the Mongols and establish the Ming dynasty. Five hundred years later, Triad-affiliated miners from this area constituted a significant source of recruits for the Taiping Rebellion. In 1892, twenty years before the overthrow of the imperial system, more than nine thousand members of the Pingxiang Elder Brothers Society (known locally as the Red Gang)—again drawn largely from Anyuan miners—launched an abortive insurgency against the dynasty.[4] A local history textbook for middle school students boasts, with some justification, "The people of Pingxiang have a glorious revolutionary tradition . . . virtually every one of the successive revolutionary movements and political struggles in Chinese history has a connection to Pingxiang . . . The history of Pingxiang is a microcosm of China's revolutionary struggle."[5]

Many of the earlier conflicts were at best distant memories by the time that Mao appeared on the scene in 1921. The more recent protests, however, figured centrally in the local lore of Anyuan and its environs.[6] Mao's interest in this area as a target of mobilization was sparked not only by its large and concentrated industrial proletariat, which included railway workers as well as coal miners, but also by Pingxiang's ongoing pageant of rebellion. In September 1920, a year prior to Mao's first visit to the coal mine, large-scale riots had broken out in the nearby villages, with thousands of hungry peasants pilfering surplus grain and staging raucous "eat-ins" at landlords' homes. Mao Zedong wrote glowingly about these events in the journal *Communist Party*.[7] The next month railway workers at Anyuan went on strike to protest a wage reduction.[8] Instigated by the powerful secret societies that oversaw lucrative gambling and opium rings operating across the Hunan-Jiangxi border, the endemic unrest bespoke a deeply ingrained local pattern of protest that would present both opportunities and obstacles to Mao and his comrades.

## THE ANYUAN COAL MINE

Like most counties in imperial China, Pingxiang was predominantly agricultural. For hundreds of years, primitive coal mines and fireworks mills had constituted the only form of local industry.[9] The Self-Strengthening Movement of the late nineteenth century brought major change, however. Although coal mining had been practiced in this region since before the Tang dynasty, a transformation in scale and technology occurred after the establishment of the Pingxiang Mining Company at Anyuan in 1898. Initiated by the foremost bureaucratic capitalist of his day, Sheng Xuanhuai (acting at the behest of the reformist governor-general Zhang Zhidong), the Anyuan mine was developed for the purpose of supplying the recently opened Hanyang ironworks in Hubei with an accessible and economical source of coal. With most of the country's coal mines concentrated in the distant northern and northeastern provinces, the prohibitive cost of transport to Hubei dictated the need for a more conveniently located coal supply. Sheng Xuanhuai engaged the expert assistance of two German engineers who, after scouring several provinces in central China, recommended Anyuan as the headquarters for a new mine. Pingxiang's extensive reserves of exceptionally high quality coking coal (required for smelting iron), together with its relative proximity to Hubei, rendered it both geologically and geographically suitable as an affordable supply source for the Hanyang ironworks.[10]

The first director of the Pingxiang coal mine, personally commissioned by Zhang Zhidong and Sheng Xuanhuai, was a Jiangsu man by the name of Zhang Zanchen. Zhang actively assisted Sheng in securing financing for the new enterprise during a series of fund-raising trips to Hankou and

Figure 1. Original headquarters of the Anyuan mining company, established in 1898. Photo by the author.

Shanghai. Equally important for the future development of the mine was Zhang's recruitment of a forward-looking deputy director, an intellectual and fellow Jiangsu native named Li Shouquan.[11] While a young teacher in Yangzhou during the late 1880s, Li had become convinced that the future of China required the adoption of advanced Western technology. Anxious for an opportunity to translate his reformist ideals into reality, Li readily accepted Zhang's invitation to join him at Anyuan. As deputy director, Li was charged with overseeing the construction of the mine and railroad and managing (not always smoothly) the delicate relations with the local gentry.

In the past, the mines in this region had been run as small, scattered concerns owned and managed for the most part by the various lineages in Pingxiang County. Sheng Xuanhuai, acting through Deputy Director Li Shouquan, paid over five hundred thousand yuan to buy out the private mines in the area, consolidating them into his new modern venture.[12] It took eight years to purchase all of the 321 private mines that had been operating in the Anyuan area, but by July of 1908 every one of the formerly independent enterprises had fallen under the control of the

Pingxiang Mining Company, whose jurisdiction now spanned a sizable territory of more than 250 square kilometers.

The inroads made by the new mining company were facilitated by the fact that the dominant lineage in Pingxiang, the Wens, initially cooperated with Sheng Xuanhuai's state-backed modernization plans. Led by several prominent Confucian degree holders known for their reformist sympathies, the Wen lineage—ignoring the objections of other gentry in Pingxiang—provided crucial information and assistance to Sheng Xuanhuai and his colleagues. However, once it became clear that the drastic transformation in technology and management envisioned for the modern Anyuan coal mine threatened to exclude local notables from the mining business altogether, even the Wens withdrew their support.[13]

Fanning the flames of local resentment was the role of foreigners and foreign know-how in the establishment of the Pingxiang Mine. At Sheng's invitation, more than thirty German engineers were hired to help introduce an impressive package of advanced methods of production: "Mechanized power replaced human labor, as Western drills and explosives extracted coal from the walls of the vertical mines, and electric winches hauled it out of the pits. In 1904, two horizontal adits went into operation, equipped with German-built electric trains to haul out the coal. Coal from the Pingxiang mines was sent to one of the modern scrubbing plants housed in multistory buildings near the adits. After purification, it was coked in one of about three hundred new German coking ovens."[14]

Unwelcome as the foreign intrusion was to the local elite, it proved economically successful. Within the space of a decade, the Pingxiang Mining Company at Anyuan had amalgamated with Sheng Xuanhuai's two major concerns in Hubei Province, the Hanyang ironworks and the Daye iron mine, to become the largest Chinese-owned industrial conglomerate in the country, the Hanyeping Coal and Iron Company, headquartered in Shanghai. A railroad, known as the Zhuping railway because it connected Pingxiang to Zhuzhou, was built to transport the coal from Anyuan to Hunan—and then by river to Hubei (see map 2). The Pingxiang Railway and Mining Company, as the colliery was now formally known, was also outfitted with its own machine shop, foundry, repair shop, and coking stations.[15] As a comprehensive embodiment of the late imperial self-strengthening reform project, the mining company opened a savings bank in 1899, and in 1904 it opened a fully equipped hospital whose staff soon included more than twenty Chinese and foreign doctors.[16] The modern complex even boasted a Western-style public garden, complete with dining facilities and a small zoo, on one of the hills just above the main entrance to the mine.[17]

The development of such an ambitious industrial enterprise, stocked with state-of-the-art machinery from Germany, required substantial capital. Funding came in part from money borrowed from Sheng Xuan-huai's other enterprises and in part from loans by German and Japanese financiers. Despite this foreign financial assistance, ownership and overall management of the Anyuan mine (like that of its parent, the Hanyeping Coal and Iron Company) remained in Chinese hands. In 1908, Sheng registered the Hanyeping Coal and Iron Company with the Ministry of Commerce as a limited liability joint-stock company in a bid to attract additional private Chinese capital. Economic historian Albert Feuerwerker characterizes the Hanyeping conglomerate as "the most ambitious industrial enterprise attempted in late-Ch'ing [Qing] China."[18]

By 1909 the Pingxiang Mining Company was producing more than one thousand tons of coal a day, enough to meet the needs of the Hanyang ironworks. Two years later, the daily output had soared to over 2,200 tons per day, making Anyuan the largest Chinese-owned coal mine in the country (in terms of both the tonnage of coal produced and the size of the labor force).[19] The high quality (low sulfur content) of its coke, which was equivalent to the finest English product, rendered Pingxiang coal particularly suitable for use in steamships and in the manufacture of heavy industrial products. The coal was so prized on the international market that Japan included a demand for control of the Pingxiang coal mine as part of its notorious, but in the end unsuccessful, Twenty-One Demands.[20] By the end of World War I, coal from Anyuan had replaced Japanese coal as the primary supplier for both industrial use and house-hold consumption throughout the Yangzi valley.[21]

The modern coal mine brought a sudden influx of new residents to the once small town of Anyuan and its surrounding county.[22] The basic labor force, recruited primarily from among peasant families in Pingxiang and the nearby Hunan countryside, soon numbered well over ten thou-sand miners and over a thousand railway workers.[23] Initially Pingxiang locals comprised the majority of miners, but before long they had been overtaken by Hunanese, contributing to a certain tension between the two groups despite similarities in language and customs. The most back-breaking and dangerous underground work of digging and hauling was relegated to laborers from the Hunan counties of Xiangtan and Liling (the native places of Mao Zedong and Li Lisan, respectively). These workers— known for a fondness for betel nut as well as for hot chili peppers—maintained close connections with their home villages, returning regularly for holidays and to recuperate from injuries, illness, and exhaustion. Many of the railway workers, who also hailed predominantly from Hunan, enjoyed a level of education and training that set them apart from the illiterate and unskilled miners. But their common dialect and local identity facilitated communication and collective action across occupational lines. By contrast, the railway workers and miners did not interact easily with the hundreds of relatively well-paid mechanics recruited from distant cities in Zhejiang, Jiangsu and Guangdong. The skilled technicians, whose native tongue was Shanghainese or Cantonese, were accustomed to the amenities of urban living and considered themselves a cut above the local rubes. Further complicating interpersonal relations were the several dozen highly paid German engineers employed to maintain the imported machinery.[24] As a mark of their cultural separation, neither the Germans nor the Chinese technicians from afar deigned to take part in the rowdy folk festivals that enlivened public holidays in this part of China, preferring to pass such occasions indoors listening to music or playing mah-jongg.[25]

The rapid industrialization and attendant demographic diversification at Anyuan aroused concern on the part of many local residents, who saw the developments as a threat to their traditional way of life. Mistrust of the alien machinery sparked widespread apprehension. A native of Pingxiang recalled, "A weird variety of rumors circulated throughout the county seat and countryside. Some contended that the railroad destroyed the *fengshui* (the mystic balance of nature), thereby disturbing ancestral graves. Others insisted that a child had to be fed into the locomotive's smokestack each day before it would run, and the same was reportedly true of the chimney at the coal mine. There was deep-seated hatred for such new monsters as trains and mechanized coal mines."[26] Locals regarded the mysterious movements of the trains and blast furnaces as a menace to the prevailing cosmic order. That these "new monsters" were tended by foreign overseers was an additional irritant. The Germans, who resided in "elaborate foreign living quarters with tennis courts and beer halls," presented a visible target for xenophobic animosity.[27]

The arrival of Gustavus Leinung, chief engineer at the mine during its first two decades of operation, generated considerable commotion in this area of the Chinese heartland where the local gentry had a reputation for antiforeign hostility. Even before Leinung made his first appearance, notices were posted around the county accusing the foreigner of intending to "suck out Pingxiang's marrow" and calling upon every household in the county to "send forth one armed person to attack him in the alleys or kill him in the fields."[28] The animosity was due not simply to raw xenophobia, or even to the fear of foreign technology and machinery, but also to a pragmatic interest in protecting the lifeblood of the Pingxiang gentry, who for centuries had benefited from the hundreds of private coal mines dotting the Anyuan landscape. In January 1898, instructions from a worried Sheng Xuanhuai warned Leinung of the ferocity of the local populace and cautioned him never to venture out without the express permission of the factory director in order to ensure ample protection.[29] Antipathy to the foreigner may have been strongest at the outset of Leinung's tenure, but it never entirely subsided:

> Upon his first arrival at Pingsiang [Pingxiang] he was the object of awe and amazement to the natives who had never seen a European. All sorts of beliefs were held about him. He was said to have three eyes, one at the back of his head, and it was believed that he could see deep into the bowels of the earth and detect the treasures there. When he entered Pingsiang for the first time in 1896 the natives were sitting on the roofs of houses to see him. He was put into a small room in an ancestral hall in which there was a grated window, and the people were allowed to come along in squads of 10 or 12 to have a look at him, as though he were a rare zoological specimen. . . . During the first year there were always 200 soldiers around Mr. Leinung. . . . At this time there was very strong anti-foreign feeling in Hunan. . . . Two years later he had to leave due to riots and murders of missionaries.[30]

Antiforeign incidents, often led by the secret-society lodges in the surrounding area, were a continuing and escalating issue at Anyuan.

In the spring of 1901, stimulated by the Boxer Uprising in North China, members of the Elder Brothers Society (or Red Gang) posted notices across Pingxiang County calling for the destruction of the railroad and other "foreign" machines. Coming only a decade after major anti-Christian riots—attributed to the Elder Brothers in concert with the Hunan literati—had swept throughout the Yangzi delta, the resurgence of xenophobic sentiment was taken seriously.[31] Sheng Xuanhuai, concerned about the safety of his German engineers at Anyuan, cabled from company headquarters in Shanghai to the provincial authorities in Jiangxi and Hunan to request military intervention. The Pingxiang Mining Company took the precaution of sending all its German employees and their families to a temporary refuge in Hunan, and the unrest was quelled when provincial troops arrested two Red Gang ringleaders at the mine.[32]

Opposition to the foreign presence did not diminish, however. Four years later the Elder Brothers organized a strike of several thousand miners in protest against a newly arrived German supervisor who had docked workers' wages as a punishment for shoddy performance. The angry workers trashed the mining company offices and the residences of the German engineers and beat up the supervisor in question. Once again the company packed off its foreign employees to a secure location in Hunan, and once again provincial soldiers were dispatched to suppress the turmoil. This time, however, the workers refused to be intimidated, and in the end the mining company agreed to repay all withheld wages.[33]

### THE PING-LIU-LI UPRISING

The Elder Brothers at Anyuan did not confine their protests to work-related issues. Although the origins of the secret society lay, it seems, in a search for protection in local feuds rather than in wider political objectives, by the late nineteenth and early twentieth centuries many of its members (like the Triads, to which the Elder Brothers were ritually connected) were also involved in anti-Manchu agitation.[34] In 1904, the Elder Brothers at Anyuan conspired with confederates in other parts of western Jiangxi and Hunan to attack imperial forces in Changsha.[35] The uprising was discovered and crushed before it could get off the ground, but two years later an even more audacious effort was undertaken.

In 1906 the Anyuan Red Gang again linked up with like-minded secret societies in the region to launch the historic Ping-Liu-Li Uprising, the first in a series of insurrections that presaged the Revolution of 1911. Conducted under the aegis of Sun Yat-sen's newly founded revolutionary party, the Tongmeng hui, the Ping-Liu-Li Uprising brought together some thirty thousand secret-society members in three contiguous counties: Pingxiang (in Jiangxi) together with Liuyang and Liling (both in Hunan). More than six thousand of the participants in this cross-border undertaking were Anyuan miners affiliated with the Elder Brothers Society. Their leader, Xiao Kechang, was a foreman at the mine. Originally from Xiangtan in Hunan (the native place of Mao Zedong), he was a revered chieftain among the Elder Brothers and was known respectfully as the "old dragon king."[36]

To unite the disparate secret-society constituency behind the uprising, the Tongmeng hui leaders formed a new secret society named the Hongjiang hui. Although the name was novel, the actual structure of the Hongjiang hui was closely modeled on that of the Elder Brothers Society, with its eight inner temples (representing departments in charge of finance, communications, and training, for example) and eight outer temples (representing affiliated branches in other nearby areas). The new society also enlisted millenarian religious authority, persuading monks at a Pingxiang temple to issue a proclamation that "the world is about to undergo great chaos; heroes will take from the rich to assist the poor." The prophecy was publicized among local residents at an October temple fair to mark the midautumn festival, which drew crowds of nearly ten thousand a day. Although nominally commanded by Red Gang chieftain Xiao Kechang, the Hongjiang hui leadership was composed largely of students who had joined the revolutionary Tongmeng hui at its founding in Tokyo the year before. Their hybrid secret society, which soon boasted a membership of some two hundred thousand across the Hunan-Jiangxi border region, retained the traditional Triad-style rooster blood and wine initiation ritual but introduced a new revolutionary slogan: "Establish a republic, equalize land rights."[37] Although the proclamation issued at the time of the uprising drew an explicit connection to the Taiping Rebellion of a half century earlier, it also reflected the new political ambitions of the student contingent: "We must establish a republican nation of the people and give our 400 million brothers the benefit of equality and the blessings of freedom. As for social problems, it is particularly appropriate to study new laws which will cause land rights to be given to the people equally."[38]

The Hongjiang hui embodied Sun Yat-sen's recommended recipe for revolution, combining progressive leadership by young intellectuals with popular participation by mass-based secret societies.[39] On paper, the decimal organization created by the Hongjiang hui was impressive, with a hierarchy of hundred-man and thousand-man combat units comprising a force called the Revolutionary Vanguard of the Southern Army of the Republic of China.[40] But the lack of coordination among constituent elements proved fatal. The Anyuan Elder Brothers were the first to defect from the Hongjiang hui coalition. Their society had for some years been depositing its substantial revenues into an account with the savings bank operated by the Pingxiang Mining Company. When the director of the mine set a trap for the Elder Brother chieftain by announcing that the company bank was going out of business and that all accounts would be frozen unless claimed within three days, the unsuspecting Xiao Kechang rushed to the bank, where he was immediately apprehended. He was executed soon thereafter. The demise of the "old dragon king" spelled the end of the Anyuan miners' involvement in the planned insurgency.[41]

Individual leaders, not abstract causes, were the primary basis of secret-society members' allegiance.

The problem, however, went deeper than the downfall of a single leader. The dismal failure of the Ping-Liu-Li Uprising, which collapsed within a matter of days from internal contradictions, bespoke a fundamental flaw in Sun's optimistic vision of a revolutionary alliance: "The basic weakness of this theory, as became devastatingly evident in 1906, was that the leaders and followers were from two different segments of society, each with their own goals. . . . Unable to exercise leadership, the young students were riding the crest of a wave—totally unable to control the direction of events, and apparently with very little understanding of the factors motivating the rural masses."[42] Here, in a nutshell, was precisely the challenge that would face Mao Zedong and his young intellectual comrades when they attempted to mobilize at Anyuan just a few years later. On the one hand, the pervasive secret societies—accustomed to antistate rebellion and committed to the protection of their members' livelihood—provided a ready-made vehicle for popular mobilization. On the other hand, the methods and objectives of these indigenous outfits fell far short of what their idealistic allies had in mind. To bridge the abyss would require a more sophisticated and sustained effort at cultural positioning than the student revolutionaries of 1906 were able to muster.

The distance that separated the secret societies from their would-be organizers in the Ping-Liu-Li Uprising can be seen in an autobiographical account by Zhang Guotao, the scion of an elite family in Pingxiang County who later became a founding member of the Chinese Communist Party. A frightened schoolboy at the time of the uprising, Zhang described the Hongjiang hui rebels—who very nearly chopped off his head—as "a crowd of hefty drunken men carrying sabers."[43] Zhang acknowledged that the secret society provided mutual aid and protection to its members, most of whom were impoverished and vulnerable peasants, miners, handicraft workers, peddlers, and coolies. His own, comparatively well-to-do family was not treated kindly by the rebels, however. During the course of the uprising, hungry insurgents helped themselves to the Zhangs' pigs, which they gleefully devoured on the spot, leaving his home "a shambles." One of Zhang Guotao's uncles was kidnapped for ransom.[44] Noting that the Hongjiang hui "obviously did receive encouragement from the revolutionaries," Zhang nonetheless described the resultant uprising as exhibiting "a far stronger heritage of old Hung Men [i.e., Triad] Society traditions than of modern revolutionary techniques."[45] Historians of the Ping-Liu-Li Uprising have reached a similar verdict. Joseph Esherick concludes that in 1906 "the revolutionary students were little more than catalysts who helped to organize and trigger a popular uprising which was really responding to an internal dynamic of its own."[46]

Like previous rebellions in this area, the Ping-Liu-Li Uprising devolved into an extremely violent affair on the part of rebels and government authorities alike. The suppression of the abortive insurrection resulted in a terrifying bloodbath in which thousands of Red Gang secret-society members lost their lives.[47] With so many Anyuan employees implicated in the failed rebellion, its repressive aftermath exacted a serious toll on operations at the coal mine. Miners from Xiangtan, the native place of their Elder Brother leader, were especially singled out for reprisals.[48]

The Ping-Liu-Li Uprising also sowed discord within the upper management of the mining company. Deputy Director Li Shouquan, having alienated members of the Pingxiang gentry by his aggressive acquisition of the hundreds of local coal mines previously under their control, had nevertheless gained important allies across the provincial border in Hunan. Welcomed into the circle of pro-Western reformers, Li was an active participant in the progressive literary society Nan she, through which he developed connections to prominent Hunanese scholars and politicians.[49] The most famous of these associates was Huang Xing, soon to become Sun Yat-sen's chief coconspirator in the Revolution of 1911. In the winter of 1904 Huang Xing had paid an unannounced visit to Anyuan for the purpose of recruiting Li Shouquan to Huang's newly organized revolutionary party, the Huaxing hui. After listening to Huang's explanation of the Huaxing hui as a patriotic association dedicated to the revolutionary overthrow of the Manchus, Li agreed to join. Huang Xing thereupon presented him with a contraband copy of Zou Rong's tract *Revolutionary Army*, which Li read over and over again. According to his diary, this pamphlet convinced Li Shouquan that China's only hope for the future lay in revolution. The following year, when Huang Xing incorporated his association under the umbrella of Sun Yat-sen's revolutionary Tongmeng hui, Li—thanks to Huang's introduction—transferred his allegiance to the new organization. During the Ping-Liu-Li Uprising of 1906, Li Shouquan displayed his revolutionary leanings by encouraging a number of the skilled mechanics at Anyuan to join the insurrection. Director Zhang Zanchen did not share Li's progressive sentiments, however, and it was due to Zhang's intervention that the Hongjiang hui chieftain, Xiao Kechang, was captured and beheaded.[50]

## LABOR AND LIVING CONDITIONS

The devastation and division wrought by the Ping-Liu-Li Uprising resulted in a harsher managerial regime at the mine. In the aftermath of the conflagration, the Pingxiang Mining Company established its own police bureau in an effort to forestall future unrest. The new bureau, which soon employed nearly nine hundred armed policemen, oversaw a court for determining punishments and a jail for enforcing them.[51] Police operations were generously funded from the proceeds of two vegetable markets that the mining company had established, as well as from fines collected by the police themselves. Before long police work had become so lucrative that the miners referred to policemen sarcastically as "gods of wealth."[52] Equipped with Mausers and uniformed, the mine police were stationed at posts around the area to ensure local order. They also conducted luggage searches at the Anyuan train station to guard against outside troublemakers.[53] Although some of the mine police were northerners, with connections to the Beiyang warlord forces, most were local thugs who were also active members of the Red Gang. Thus, despite the brutal suppression of the Ping-Liu-Li Uprising and the mining company's subsequent attempt to gain the upper hand, the grip of the secret societies on the Anyuan workforce remained firm.

Over the next several years the miners engaged in a number of protests instigated by the Red Gang. The growing size and prosperity of the Pingxiang Mining Company during World War I encouraged the labor contractor–cum–gangsters, who received a sizable slice of the wages of the workers they recruited, to launch strikes calling for pay hikes. In this era of nascent Chinese nationalism, the visible presence of privileged foreigners at the mine was also a protest trigger for a secret society associated with patriotic causes. In May 1913 the Anyuan workers lodged a complaint about wages. That October they walked off the job to protest the beating of a miner by a German overseer, returning to work only after the offender issued a formal apology. Two years later, complaining that the Germans encouraged brutality by the Chinese foremen, miners again went on strike.[54] These confrontations were accompanied by muggings and death threats against the German engineers, and in the summer of 1919—in the nationalistic climate of the May Fourth Movement—all the foreign employees were forced to leave Anyuan permanently. Their departure did not result in a noticeable improvement in working conditions, however. Under the despotic rule of the labor contractors and their henchmen, arbitrary fines and corporal punishment continued to be imposed.[55]

The plight of the workers deteriorated notably with the abrupt economic decline that the Pingxiang colliery experienced after the end of World War I, when the price of iron and steel plummeted and the coal mine suffered major losses in production and personnel. The dismal situation was exacerbated in 1920–21 (just before Mao's maiden visit) by successive incursions of rival warlord armies fighting for control of the critical Zhuping rail line.[56]

The violence of everyday life at Anyuan mirrored the inhumane conditions that prevailed underground. Temperatures in the pits hovered around 100 degrees Fahrenheit and ventilation was poor.[57] Miners worked with no safety equipment and no clothing aside from a three-foot-long piece of blue cloth that they tied around their head as a turban to reduce head injuries. The same piece of cloth was retied as a loincloth to provide a modicum of modesty when exiting the pits and was subsequently converted into a washcloth and towel for bathhouse use. During gas explosions the cloth had yet another application, serving as a makeshift mask to shield the miner's mouth and nose from the deadly fumes.[58]

Gas explosions occurred frequently and loss of life was alarmingly common. A summary survey of accident statistics at Anyuan offers sobering evidence of these perils. In 1905 more than ninety workers died during a gas explosion. Three years later, more than two hundred Anyuan miners perished in an underground fire. In 1917, ninety-two workers burned to death from a gas explosion in the central pit that closed down the entire mine for a week. Three years later, thirty-nine workers lost their lives in yet another gas explosion. The following year, forty miners were killed and twenty injured in fires caused by dynamiting.[59] In other words, in just the fifteen years preceding Mao Zedong's arrival at Anyuan, some 450 workers had died in a steady string of major disasters at the mine. Disease was also a serious problem. In 1918 a physician at Anyuan reported that 90 percent of the miners suffered from the debilitating effects of hookworm.[60] Black lung disease, which culminated in an excruciating death, was rampant among the miners as well.

The inherent dangers of underground coal mining were made even more formidable by harsh treatment at the hands of callous overseers. By most accounts, German supervisors—although an easy target for the wrath of the secret societies—were not the worst offenders. A general foreman from Hubei by the name of Wang Hongqing (known colloquially as Bearded Wang the Third) was widely regarded as the cruelest overseer at the Anyuan mine. Having assumed his post soon after the coal mine opened, Wang's power derived not only from his own lengthy tenure, but also from his close personal connection to two other local strongmen in the area. One was fellow Hubei native and classmate Fang Benren, the longtime commander of the western Jiangxi military garrison. The other was Wang's older brother, an important Red Gang chieftain in Pingxiang.[61] Thanks in large measure to the coercive clout that these ties afforded him, Wang functioned as the despot of underground production operations at Anyuan for nearly three decades before fleeing for his life under the changed political climate of the Northern Expedition (see chapter 4). During his many years at the mine, Bearded Wang supplemented his regular salary by selling labor contractor posts to the highest bidder. Wang's contractors seldom ventured into the pits without a leather whip in their hands, ready to impose their authority whenever the urge struck. The arbitrary and excessive punishments liberally dispensed by Bearded Wang and his contractor cronies added an extra element of uncertainty and danger to what was already a perilous work situation.[62]

Living conditions at Anyuan were hardly better than labor conditions. Four dormitory districts, each housing several thousand workers, surrounded the mine. The dormitories were cramped, dark, and squalid huts where workers slept and ate before and after their grueling twelve-hour shifts.[63] A placard bearing the name of the labor contractor responsible for the particular group of workers residing within was hung at the door of each hut. Three and a half meters wide by seven meters long, the huts were designed to sleep forty-eight workers in two rows, three levels high, of crude two-person bunk beds, separated down the middle by a long table for eating meals. The number of workers accommodated within each hut was actually twice the number of bunks, which were shared in rotation by day and night shifts. Meals consisted of low-grade rice and pickled vegetables. The dorms were infested with insects and vermin and reeked from poor sanitation.[64] The contrast between the gloomy, grimy workers' dormitories and the sunny, spacious housing provided for the company staff (technicians and managers) was, according to one observer, "as far apart as high heaven and the deep sea."[65] Needless to say, the foreign advisors, until they were forced to leave the area, occupied the finest residences of all: large, wooden frame houses situated amid the refreshing greenery of the surrounding hills.[66]

## POPULAR RELIGION AND SECRET SOCIETIES

The stark differences between the haves and have-nots, as well as between underground and aboveground activities, fostered a Manicheancum-millenarian mentality among residents of the mining district.[67] As the revolutionary writer Wu Yunduo, who grew up at Anyuan (and was educated at a Communist school there), recollected in his famous autobiography, "We lived in a shanty near a pit-head at the foot of the hill. As a boy, I looked upon the mine as a mysterious place. I heard all sorts of tales about it. The older people said that there was treasure hidden in it—happy would be those who could get it. Others said that down the mine perpetual darkness reigned; the day when the sun shed its luster into those dark caverns would see an end to the sufferings of the poor."[68] In view of the extraordinary hardships and inequities that coal mining entailed, it is not surprising that supernatural beliefs and rituals occupied a central place in the local culture. Before venturing underground each day, miners at Anyuan burned joss sticks and prayed for protection to a bodhisattva statue, purchased by the director of the mine and placed on a large altar adjacent to the main entrance to the pits. The altar was also the site of an annual festival—sponsored by the mining company—in honor of the patron deity of mining, Patriarch Wang (Wangye), in which chickens were sacrificed and pungent incense and paper money were burned to secure divine protection in the year ahead.[69]

Mine safety was not the only purpose of religious observances. Large-scale collective exorcism rituals, which featured a statue of the Daoist Celestial Master Xu paraded through the streets in an open palanquin, were an important form of religious observance in this region. Religion and recreation were closely connected; colorfully costumed and ornately masked exorcist dancers were appreciated for providing a form of popular entertainment in addition to whatever curative benefits they might bestow by expelling evil spirits from the assembled crowd. As a major center of fireworks production, Pingxiang's religious festivals were marked by brilliant nighttime displays. Loud clanging cymbals, elaborate carved wooden masks, fragrant incense, ornate lanterns, the beating of drums, and the deafening sound of firecrackers drew throngs of observers to these lively spectacles, which were often complemented by performances of local operas and acrobats as well as by lion and dragon dancing.[70] The largest annual religious observance in the Pingxiang-Hunan border area was the spring Lantern Festival, when temples and market streets were festooned with elaborate lanterns fashioned in the shape of lions, dragons, and other creatures. The major form of local opera in Pingxiang, popular since at least the eighteenth century, was known as tea-picking opera *(caichaxi)*. Strongly influenced by Hunan's flower-drum opera, the tea-picking opera was performed during Lantern Festival cel-

Figure 2. Original entrance to the Anyuan coal mine. The building on the right, now empty, once contained bodhisattva images before which workers burned incense before entering the coal pits. Photo by the author.

ebrations, augmenting the colorful lantern displays with lively song and dance routines.[71]

In addition to invoking supernatural assistance, the miners observed various taboos believed to forestall industrial disasters. While underground, miners were not permitted to utter "unlucky" words associated with catastrophe, such as fire, flood, gas, or ghost. If anyone broke the taboo, the director or general manager of the mine would set off firecrackers to expel the bad omen, after which the culprit was required to buy four slices of bean curd (paid for out of his withheld wages) for each fellow worker who had witnessed the indiscretion. Since miners generally worked in large groups, an infraction of this sort might result in the loss of one or two months' wages. It was also taboo to harm the many rats to be found milling about the pits. The rodents were believed to serve as a valuable early warning system, scurrying out of the shaft (sometimes nipping at the miners' bare toes in the process) shortly before a flood or gas explosion was about to occur.[72]

The place to which workers might most effectively turn for help in surviving the many hazards of this forbidding environment was often their local secret-society lodge. By the early twentieth century, the great majority of Anyuan miners belonged to the Elder Brothers Society, having undergone a clandestine nighttime initiation rite in which they drank wine mixed with the blood of a rooster and swore a solemn oath to safeguard the secrets of the society and to show loyalty and mutual aid to fellow members. Bonds among initiates were strengthened by fictive kinship nomenclature that designated all recruits as "brothers" of a single family. The internal organization of the local lodge was hierarchical, with ordinary members required strictly to obey the dictates of their lodge "teacher." The clientelistic relationship between "students" and "teacher" involved dense ties of allegiance and obligation. By contrast, external connections to lodges in other places were tenuous and fleeting.[73]

Details on the origins and development of the Elder Brothers Society, in Anyuan as elsewhere, are frustratingly fragmentary. The Anyuan branch was part of a loose network of sworn brotherhood associations, with no single headquarters or commander. Individual lodges "shared a quasi-religious heritage drawn from Chinese folklore, rich in moral and ethical idealism and in clandestine ritual."[74] Whether the Elder Brothers Society originated from Triad, White Lotus, or (most likely) syncretistic roots is uncertain.[75] Whatever their beginnings, by the end of the nineteenth century the Elder Brothers had become the predominant secret society in central China and were closely akin to, if not indistinguishable from, the Triads. They were major instigators of banditry and organized crime in the region.

The rapid spread of the Elder Brothers Society in the latter half of the nineteenth century was in large part the doing of demobilized soldiers from Zeng Guofan's Hunan Army, who had joined the brotherhood during their period of military service. When the Hunan Army began to disband in 1864 (its campaign against the Taiping Rebellion having ended), more than a hundred thousand former "braves" suddenly found themselves out of work. Hardened by battle and accustomed to mobility, the still-young veterans—most of whom were now members of the Elder Brothers Society—fanned out from Hunan across central China in search of an alternative livelihood. Aside from brute physical strength, however, they had few skills to offer prospective employers. The best chance for a new job was through the introduction of the Elder Brothers Society, which held a virtual monopoly on opportunities in gambling, smuggling, mining, and other unskilled occupations. Although individual lodges were territorially bounded, mobile members could circulate in and out of different lodges when they moved from one location to another.[76]

Unsurprisingly, information on the inner workings of the Elder Brothers Society is hard to come by. The society's rituals were by most accounts quite similar to, yet somewhat simpler than, the elaborate ceremonies traditionally associated with the Triad (or Heaven and Earth) Society.[77] As was true for the Triads, initiations generally took place late at night, in a rite known as "opening a mountain lodge" (kai shantang). New members were introduced by a guarantor, who vouched for their trustworthiness. After some pro forma questioning by the lodge leaders, initiates swore a solemn oath of loyalty to the society's regulations, lit sticks of incense before an altar holding ancestral tablets of the "five patriarchs," who were revered as the society's founders, and drank a rooster's blood (mixed with liquor) to signify brotherhood with other members. Payment of an initiation fee was usually required. A lavish, often raucous banquet then sealed the bond between old and new members. Each lodge had its own mottos, secret passwords, rhymes, and hand signals in which new inductees were instructed by the lodge teacher once they had paid their entry fee.[78] As in other Chinese secret societies and sworn brotherhoods, these code phrases and gestures reflected a fascination with numerology; the numbers three and five were considered especially felicitous. Glyphomancy (the deconstruction and recombination of Chinese characters as a means of fortune telling) was a common practice among lodge masters. New members were given charms or amulets (e.g., a piece of red cloth or a small replica of the lodge banner containing the magical characters) to carry on their persons to provide supernatural protection. Lodges offered instruction in martial arts techniques to new inductees as well. The violence that characterized everyday life in Anyuan—both inside and outside the mines—made such skills particularly valuable.

Market fairs and popular religious festivals (especially the springtime Lantern Festival) were prime opportunities for exhibiting martial arts abilities and enlisting new followers. As a recruitment incentive, secret-society members handed out small cloth amulets to prospective members among the crowd, a gesture known as "issuing vouchers" (fangpiao). Spirited lion and dragon dances were performed by martial arts masters to the accompaniment of loud drums and cymbals in order to attract new students. "Invitations" were sent to local notables, who were expected to welcome the dancers with firecrackers and red envelopes of money.[79] Such occasions, with thousands of people milling about the town to enjoy the colorful lantern displays and lively operas and dances, also offered a convenient cover for Elder Brother uprisings—which were often timed to coincide with these events.[80] Before directing their followers to engage in risky collective action (whether a nighttime raid on a local granary or a bold assault on the county government offices), lodge masters would reinforce the bonds among members by reenacting the rooster-blood oath and raising battle banners.[81]

In the Hunan-Jiangxi border region, the Elder Brothers oversaw large, lucrative gambling operations. Each morning the lodges (which were generally located in market towns) sent out men to collect bets from residents in the surrounding villages for the evening's drawing. Known locally as "opening a voucher" (*kaipiao*), the betting required players to select any of thirty-six Chinese characters—one of which would be drawn that evening—with the winning character paying thirty times the bet. The gambling was immensely popular with wealthy landlord and gentry families in the region as well as with the workers and marginal elements who made up the core of Elder Brother members.[82] These gambling operations afforded the society the financial means to underwrite its sumptuous banquets and to provide assistance to members in need. On paydays at the mine, the first and fifteenth of every month, when workers had the day off from work, the gambling houses (and brothels) of Anyuan overflowed with customers. Administrative staff participated in the gambling activities as well. On one occasion a company staff member hanged himself by the side of the road when his gambling debt of over one thousand yuan proved too much for his monthly salary of fifty yuan to cover.[83]

It may be that the term Elder Brothers Society (*gelaohui*) was a generic label applied to the secret-society lodges by official and literati commentators rather than a self-appellation used by society members themselves. In Jiangxi, at least, members generally referred to their organization as the Red Gang (*hongbang*) or Red Family (*hongjia*). As homophones of common appellations for the Triads (*hongbang or hongjia*), with which they were used interchangeably, the terms created confusion between overlapping and yet apparently once-distinct secret-society traditions. Even so, it is clear that by the early twentieth century the numerous groups across central China denoted by the Elder Brother label shared common patterns of organization and ritual behavior.[84] Equally clear is the fact that these secret-society networks exercised considerable economic and political control within their local spheres of influence.[85] In areas under the domination of the Elder Brothers, everything from personal disputes to public markets was regulated by the lodges.

As its name implies, the Elder Brothers Society was overwhelmingly—if not exclusively—a male institution.[86] Its masculine camaraderie and promise of fraternal protection proved especially appealing to single men—soldiers and miners, for example—who lived in austere bachelors' barracks and engaged in life-threatening occupations. In some instances, the lodges may have provided a setting for same-sex liaisons.[87] In any case, opulent banquets, heavy drinking, opium smoking, and clandestine nighttime ceremonies surely helped to enliven an otherwise often drab and difficult existence and to forge closer bonds with fellow members. Regular martial arts practice sessions strengthened the basis for collective militancy. Group discipline was encouraged by strict regulations known as the "ten red rules" (*hong shitiao*), which all members were required to follow. In the eyes of the society, the worst offense that a member might commit was to engage in extramarital relations with a female relative (wife, sister, or daughter) of another member. This infraction, called "wearing red shoes" (*chuan hongxiezi*), was punishable by death.[88]

Although there was considerable geographical differentiation, the internal structure of the Elder Brothers Society was invariably clientelistic and hierarchical. Lodges were generally comprised of eight tiers of leaders, known as "temples" or "palaces" (*gong*), each charged with discrete functions. At the apex stood the "dragon head" (*longtou*), the grand master to whom all lodge members swore absolute obedience. Revered for his quasi-supernatural capacities (ranging from superior martial arts skills to reputed invulnerability to swords and bullets), the dragon head had the final say on all lodge decisions. On ceremonial occasions, the dragon head often donned a long gown adorned with a special talisman to indicate his magical powers. Under him were seven additional levels of leaders, with standard titles (e.g., "red flag," "whirlwind," and the like) and separate responsibilities ranging from recruitment of new members to liaison with the local authorities. Lodges also operated their own patrols (*zhencha*) and communications (*tongxun*) networks, which provided protection for society leaders and gathered intelligence on plundering opportunities, enemy troop strength, and so forth.[89]

By the late nineteenth century, if not earlier, some leaders in the Elder Brothers Society subscribed to an anti-Manchu sentiment that rendered them receptive to revolutionary initiatives aimed at toppling the Qing dynasty. It is unclear just how broadly such orientations extended across the leadership, let alone how far they may have filtered down to the rank-and-file membership. As the ill-fated Ping-Liu-Li Uprising demonstrated, the secret societies were not entirely reliable allies in the revolutionary enterprise. Nevertheless, the fact that ordinary members (who often numbered in the thousands per lodge) were sworn to obey the commands of their lodge teachers meant that alliances with secret-society leaders came to be regarded as extremely useful by revolutionary cadres, Nationalist and Communist alike. For radical intellectuals in search of a popular constituency, a pact with the local dragon head offered an immediate (if inconstant) mass base for wider political action.

Although the great majority of violent incidents involving the Elder Brothers Society during the nineteenth century were confined to predatory behavior such as banditry and smuggling, by the 1890s there was growing evidence of overtly antiforeign and anti-Christian activity. Originally sparked by hostility toward the missionaries and their converts, these confrontations helped prepare the ground for another form of antiforeignism directed against the ruling Manchus. Calls for overthrowing the alien Qing dynasty and restoring the (Han Chinese) Ming dynasty began to make an appearance in Elder Brother slogans and banners. Interpreted by turn-of-the-century revolutionaries as welcome signs of budding nationalism, these expressions of anti-Manchu sentiment—tentative and scattered though they were—paved the way for an alliance between radical intellectuals and the secret societies.[90] Both the promise and the perils of this coalition were graphically demonstrated by the rise and demise of the Ping-Liu-Li Uprising. When, fifteen years later, Mao Zedong and his comrades extended their own overtures to the Elder Brothers at Anyuan, they were the beneficiaries of this cumulative experience.

## LOCAL STRONGMEN: GANGSTERS, CLERGY, GENTRY, AND CAPITALISTS

Thanks to its control over both labor and leisure, the Elder Brothers Society, or Red Gang, was the dominant power holder in early twentieth-century Anyuan. By this period Anyuan had acquired the nickname of "Little Shanghai" and—like its more illustrious namesake (where the Green Gang held sway)—was a booming industrial center populated largely by rural migrants who had obtained work through labor contractors connected to a secret society.[91] The dragon head of the Red Gang in Pingxiang served as a paid "advisor" to the management of the Anyuan coal mine, and most of the labor contractors at the mine were his sworn followers. The contractors, who enlisted workers from their native places in return for a hefty percentage of their wages, exercised tight control over their recruits. A worker recalled,

> Workers had to send gifts whenever there were weddings, funerals, or births in the labor contractor's family. We also had to gather at the labor contractor's home to gamble. Naturally, the labor contractor was in charge. This provided considerable income for the contractor. It was considered an insult not to send gifts. If your contractor was somewhat kindhearted, he would just rough you up until you offered him proper respect. But if he wasn't so kind he'd fire you. In those days it was easy to fire a worker. A labor contractor or staff member simply needed to say the word and you were gone.[92]

With hiring and firing so dependent upon patron-client relations with labor contractors (who had long ceased to work in the pits themselves), workers were more attuned to signals from their gang bosses than amenable to supervision by on-the-job mine staff. The dependency was deepened by the fact that most miners lived and ate in dormitories and mess halls owned and operated by the Red Gang.

Despite the dragon head's position as "advisor" to the mining company, upper management viewed the gangster-contractors as a major obstacle to labor discipline. Frustrated by the contractors' power, Chief Engineer Leinung at one point attempted to undermine their hold over the miners by providing directly for worker welfare. As a contemporary account chronicled the conflict:

> These gang leaders only visited the mine on the first of the month to make contracts and on the fifteenth, pay day, when they appeared in gorgeous silk attire, being carried from Pingsiang [Pingxiang] city in sedan chairs. The rest of the month they spent enjoying themselves in the city, letting the men work for them. This did not please Mr. Leinung at all and he realized that he now had to break the power of these labor contractors. The only way in which the power of the contractors over their men could be broken was by quartering the miners in houses belonging to the mine and feeding them at the cost of the mine. . . .
> The quarters were almost completed by the next Chinese New Year and the miners were informed that every one should get his pay according to the work done, and that no man would have the right to squeeze other men. Early in the New Year [Leinung] received a written protest from the 63 gang leaders in which they told him that all the miners protested against the innovation. . . . [I]t leaked out that on the fifth day of the New Year the miners had been assembled at a

temple nearby and that one of the gang leaders had addressed them telling them that the proposed innovation was against their interests and that they should combine to protest against it. The usual thing happened; the crowd went with the agitator and the aid of a *literati* had been invoked to draw up the protest. They all swore not to betray each other.[93]

In this instance, Gustavus Leinung was able to pay off the ringleader and successfully install the workers in their new quarters. But it was not long before the gangsters reasserted their stranglehold over the labor force. As outsiders to the area, the mine managers could not effectively recruit or retain new workers without the assistance of the labor contractors. The gangsters' influence, moreover, extended well beyond the confines of the mine itself. In the surrounding towns, the main commercial establishments—gambling and opium dens, brothels, and pawnshops—were all under Red Gang control.[94]

Despite the considerable reach of the Red Gang, secret societies were not the only power holders in Anyuan. More orthodox institutions— government agencies, chambers of commerce, lineage halls, temples, churches, and schools—were also influential.[95] And, as the above example in which gangsters gathered at a nearby temple and enlisted the aid of a literatus suggests, local elites and institutions interacted in complex and overlapping ways.

By the early twentieth century, one of the largest and most important organizations in Anyuan was the St. James Episcopal Church.[96] In 1898, a Chinese Episcopal priest by the name of Wu Hongjing arrived in Pingxiang with plans to establish a church there. Finding that he was unable to make much headway in the county seat itself, he traveled the five additional miles to Anyuan, where the recently opened coal mine was attracting a large and diverse group of both Chinese and foreign residents. The burgeoning population of this boomtown struck the minister as an ideal target for evangelism. The Reverend Wu applied to the Episcopal Diocese of Hubei and Hunan (located in Hankou) for approval of his plan to build a church at Anyuan and was granted funding to purchase 2,800 square meters of land—situated prominently on a hilltop overlooking the coal mine—on which to erect a substantial complex. Construction of a large church, able to accommodate a congregation of more than two thousand people, was finally completed with local funding in 1915, and it was followed by the building of a rectory, church offices, and a chapel. The Reverend Wu was amply rewarded for his pioneering efforts by a congregation that soon filled the pews of his capacious

church. Every Sunday the loud peals of a bell in St. James's steeple rever-
berated across the mountainous terrain, calling worshippers to service.
The church membership drew predominantly from the administrative
staff and technicians at the Pingxiang mine, along with their families,
who for the most part hailed from towns and cities in Zhejiang, Jiangsu,
and Guangdong.

As alien transplants in the western Jiangxi highlands, the Chinese
Episcopal Church and the Hanyeping Coal and Iron Company shared certain characteristics and concerns. Both organizations were headquartered
in cosmopolitan Shanghai, with subsidiary operations managed out of
Hankou, inclining those who were responsible for running their Anyuan
branches to think of themselves as representatives of a much larger modernizing and civilizing mission rather than beholden to local interests.[97]
The ties between St. James Episcopal Church and the Pingxiang Mining
Company were further strengthened by a mutual interest in promoting
modern education. In 1906 the mining company had decided to open its
own elementary school for the children of its employees, to be financed
by a fixed percentage of company profits. With enrollment soaring, in
1912 the company expanded the school into a lower and upper elementary
school and began to charge tuition. The fees were well beyond the reach
of ordinary miners and, even though the company agreed to provide
scholarships for a few talented students from indigent families, the great
majority of the several hundred pupils were the children of electrical
engineers and other highly skilled workers able to afford the steep fees. In
July of 1920, having decided that it was too much trouble to manage the
schools on its own, the mining company offered the Episcopal Church in
Anyuan an annual subsidy of eight hundred yuan in return for assuming
these educational responsibilities. Seeing the schools as an ideal vehicle
to further its evangelical effort, St. James readily accepted the proposal.
A new school board, which included the director, vice-director, and
comptroller of the colliery along with the school principal and the rector of St. James Church, was formed. Over the next few years the board
oversaw the opening of several additional schools in the town of Anyuan,
enabling an enrollment of nearly five hundred students. As the Reverend
Wu had anticipated, these schools were an excellent means of expanding
church membership. The curriculum featured a heavy dose of Christian
doctrine, and soon more than half of the students were attending Sunday
school classes as well.[98]

The remarkable growth of the Anyuan flock convinced the Episcopal Diocese of Hunan-Hubei (where the left-leaning bishop, the Right

Reverend Logan Roots, was in charge) to assign additional clergy from Hankou to the St. James parish. Accordingly, a recent seminary graduate, the Reverend Long Yongjian, took over as school principal, and he soon replaced the aging Wu Hongjing as rector of the church. Known for combining sound theology with effective pedagogy, Long injected new energy into both the evangelical and educational dimensions of his mission.[99] Under Long Yongjian's dynamic leadership, additional schools and ancillary chapels were opened around the Anyuan area.

Although the Pingxiang Mining Company appreciated the contribution that the church was making toward the education of its employees' children, other members of the local elite—Confucian gentry as well as secret-society chieftains—reacted somewhat differently. In their eyes, both the colliery and the church were intruders who upset the traditional balance of power. Education in Pingxiang had previously been the purview of the so-called Six Halls, a group of charitable institutions operated by the major lineages in the area.[100] Local gentry were not pleased to have their pedagogical monopoly challenged by outsiders offering a form of instruction that departed in both content and style from Confucian standards.

Resentment of the mining company was heightened by the imperious manner in which the industrialist Sheng Xuanhuai and his lieutenants had restructured mining operations soon after identifying Anyuan as the location for their new enterprise. Even the once-sympathetic Wen lineage had grown disenchanted. In the end, however, the state patronage that Sheng Xuanhuai enjoyed from his connections to Zhang Zhidong and other highly placed government officials rendered local resistance futile. As a historian of this process concludes, "When it came to coal mining, the state's interests edged the Pingxiang gentry out of all decision-making positions in their county. . . . Because the Wens and other gentry families could not integrate into the modern economy, the new industrial order rendered them superfluous."[101] The mining company headquarters replaced the Wen lineage hall as the economic nerve center of Pingxiang County.

Shortly after the 1911 Revolution, the uncertain political climate encouraged Jiangxi authorities to try to seize control of the mine on behalf of local interests. Deputy director Li Shouquan (with help from his friends across the border in Hunan) was elected director at an all-employees assembly convened for the purpose of preventing the colliery from falling into the hands of local gentry and officials. At this time the Hunanese revolutionary leader Huang Xing, who eight years earlier had recruited Li

Shouquan to the revolutionary cause, made a special trip to Pingxiang to honor its role in the Ping-Liu-Li Uprising. During the trip, Huang—who held the position of national superintendent for mining under the new Republican government—made a high-profile visit to Anyuan to boost the authority of the recently elected director, Li Shouquan.[102]

While serving as director of the Anyuan coal mine, Li Shouquan became known for a number of charitable public works that underscored his loyalty to people and places beyond Pingxiang. He commissioned the construction of two imposing buildings to honor his fellow Jiangsu provincials, the founder (Sheng Xuanhuai) and first director (Zhang Zanchen) of the mine, upon their deaths. He also did not forget his Hunanese friends. In 1921, when a severe drought struck nearby Liling County (located just across the provincial border in Hunan), Li Shouquan traveled to Shanghai to raise over thirty thousand yuan in relief funds for the victims. Despite his interest in foreign technology, Li was an unabashed patriot. As director of the coal mine, Li Shouquan intervened on the side of the workers in several cases involving altercations with German supervisors, and in 1919 it was his decision to replace all of the foreign staff at the colliery with Chinese nationals.[103] Although Li Shouquan would later be demonized in official Communist party histories as a heartless capitalist and imperialist toady, he was in fact no enemy of progressive causes. Indeed, Li's own revolutionary leanings would play a crucial role in facilitating inroads at the mine by Hunanese Communists.

By the 1920s, interactions among the Anyuan elite exhibited a complicated and fluctuating combination of conflict and cooperation. Members of the Pingxiang gentry, initially cheered by the prospect of economic prosperity that the substantial influx of bureaucratic capital promised to bring to their struggling county, had grown resentful of the aggrandizing tactics of the mine management. The mining company's relentless land acquisitions, as well as its heavy reliance upon foreign expertise and its chummy connections to the Episcopal Church, aroused animosity. That both the Pingxiang Mining Company and St. James Church were culturally and administratively more closely attached to Hunan and Hubei (and even Shanghai) than to the province in which they were actually located, was a further source of irritation for the Jiangxi gentry. With old and new elites at odds, the role of pivotal powerbroker fell to the chieftains of the Red Gang. This was the complex local political context that Mao Zedong and his comrades were required to navigate when they selected the Anyuan coal mine as the launching pad for a revolutionary labor movement.

## ROOTS OF REVOLUTION

Anyuan was in many respects an exceptionally promising setting for organizing a revolutionary labor movement. Its more than ten thousand miners and railway workers, heirs to a long and illustrious history of rebellion, formed a receptive audience for a movement aiming to elevate the status of the proletariat. From the perspective of social science theory, the choice of Anyuan was auspicious. Sociologists Clark Kerr and Abraham Siegel, in their classic cross-national study of labor strife, point to coal mining and railroads as the two most strike-prone industries; the Pingxiang Railway and Mining Company was a combustible combination of the two.[104] That the company just prior to Mao Zedong's arrival had suffered a sharp economic downturn after more than two decades of steady expansion was another source of volatility.[105] Further fueling feelings of "relative deprivation" among the miners was the string of terrible industrial disasters that had recently afflicted the Pingxiang coal mine.

Yet even under the most explosive of circumstances, labor protests seldom occur entirely spontaneously. And in early twentieth-century Anyuan the spark plug igniting such incidents was the Elder Brothers secret society. As the major criminal syndicate in the region, the society possessed ample coercive clout to encourage compliance from its large and diverse membership. But the secret society did not operate by force or fear alone. Control was also exercised through a variety of symbolic codes: initiation rituals, loyalty oaths, magical charms, martial arts routines, passwords, and secret codes. An integral component of local folk culture, these quasi-religious practices played an important role in securing obedience to the commands of secret-society chieftains, as well as strengthening fraternal bonds of association and mutual assistance among rank-and-file members.

Thanks to its hold over the unskilled labor force, the Elder Brothers Society served as the main instigator of rebellion and collective violence in the Pingxiang area from the mid-nineteenth through the early twentieth century. It was a catalyst in most of the antiforeign incidents as well as the periodic workplace protests that punctuated life at Anyuan. And it constituted a crucial ally for revolutionary movements keen on recruiting miners to their insurgencies, Taipings and Tongmeng hui alike. Yet secret-society allegiances were often fickle, as the Ping-Liu-Li Uprising demonstrated.

The stark differences in outcome between the Ping-Liu-Li Uprising of 1906 and the Communist-instigated Great Strike of 1922 (the subject of the next chapter) offer telling clues to the Chinese Communists' success in mass mobilization. Initially the young intellectuals who pioneered the Communist effort at Anyuan, whose modern political party was headquartered in distant Shanghai, seemed at least as far removed from their putative constituency in the Jiangxi highlands as their Tongmeng hui forerunners. In sharp contrast to their predecessors, however, the Communists would manage to find common (and more stable) ground with elites and workers alike. The secret society constituted an important stepping-stone toward that end, but it was not the only means that the Communists would employ. A wide array of cultural resources—elite as well as popular—would figure in their efforts.

Unlike earlier generations of insurgents, Mao and his fellow revolutionaries were committed to building innovative local institutions—worker schools, labor unions, consumer cooperatives, armed patrols, and a Socialist Youth League branch and Communist Party cell—that would eventually prove capable of challenging and supplanting preexisting networks. Yet they approached this task cautiously and deliberately, reaching out to key members of the local elite on the basis of family and native-place connections. Only after gaining the confidence of influential local notables were they ready to proceed. Although initially the Communists framed their activities squarely within familiar practices, their ambition was not simply to take advantage of Anyuan's rebellious tradition, but to transform it. The ultimate aim was a radical reconfiguration of the social and political system.

In the overwhelmingly male society of Anyuan, successful leadership was inevitably intertwined with standards of manly superiority. Kam Louie has pointed out the dual importance of literary arts *(wen)* and martial arts *(wu)* in the cultural construction of Chinese masculinity.[106] As Louie stresses, however, in China the balance between these two ideal types of authority had long favored the former: "Right from the beginning of Chinese philosophical thought, *wen* was considered superior to *wu*."[107] According to Louie, unlike classical Western conceptions of masculinity, which privileged the macho male, the Confucian tradition valorized the cultivated scholar over the warrior. In such a cultural context, even the formidable muscle of Red Gang dragon heads would not render them immune to challenges from claimants to a higher form of authority. The special status of the refined literati in Chinese society was a critical resource upon which the young Communist intellectuals drew liberally in their attempt to reshape and redirect the endemic violence of the Anyuan miners.

The Communists' stunning success in their radical mission would derive in large part from their skillful deployment of elite social capital. Drawing upon a deep reservoir of reverence for the Confucian scholar, the well-educated young Communists parlayed their academic credentials and connections into revolutionary power. It was as respected teachers that the Communists first entered, and then fundamentally altered, Anyuan society. Their transformative project hinged upon imbuing the workers of Anyuan with a new revolutionary culture, largely imported from the Soviet Union and instilled both inside and outside the classroom. Yet in order to accomplish this alien agenda, Mao and his comrades initially presented themselves as members of the literati establishment.

The shared esteem that both elites and masses placed upon education was crucial to the mobilization process. But so too was the willingness of the Communists to reach, much more aggressively than had their Tongmeng hui predecessors, across the cultural chasm that normally separated educated intellectuals from illiterate workers in order to render their new revolutionary message intelligible in terms of prevailing conventions. Ideologically opposed as they were to the "feudal superstition" of Chinese folk tradition, the early Communists would nevertheless draw creatively on the practices of popular religious ritual for their own political purposes. Members of the Red Gang were actively recruited to the Communists' workers club and only gradually urged to abandon their previous affiliation in favor a new identity.

Anthropologist June Nash writes of miners' militancy in a very different cultural setting: "Resistance takes many forms, but it is always strengthened by the self-determination of a people who have not yet lost their self-identity. The rituals and belief combine to reinforce the myths which encompass their history, and . . . prepare the people for a time when they can shape their own destiny. Sectarian political leaders usually reject ritual protest as deviance. However, if one thinks of it as a rehearsal that keeps alive the sentiment of rebellion until a historically appropriate moment, it may reinforce political movements."[108] In Nash's terms, the series of Elder Brothers' uprisings that punctuated Anyuan life for more than a century prior to the arrival of the Communists served as a kind of dress rehearsal for the political drama to come. As she notes, revolutionaries are generally inclined to dismiss such quasi-religious ritual protest as "deviance"—or, in Communist parlance, as "feudal superstition." To be sure, official Chinese Communist doctrine disparaged these practices, and idealistic young Chinese Communist activists—Mao Zedong included—were deeply suspicious of secret-society power and other "feudal remnants." Yet Mao and certain of his Hunanese comrades—who were themselves intimately familiar with the local folkways of this region—also evinced an astute appreciation of the value and convertibility of Anyuan's protest tradition to their new revolutionary movement. There was nothing automatic or inevitable about the transition from Red Gang rebellion to Red Army revolution.[109] Intentional and inventive cultural positioning on the part of committed Communist cadres, aided by the crucial intervention of local elites, would be required in order to enable an otherwise elusive objective.

# 2 Teaching Revolution

## *The Strike of 1922*

Despite an accumulation of excellent scholarship on the Chinese Communist revolution, we are still hard-pressed to offer a compelling answer to a question that goes to the heart of explaining the revolution's success: How did the intellectuals who founded the Chinese Communist Party (CCP) manage to cultivate a large and loyal following among illiterate and impoverished peasants and workers, a stratum of the populace so distant from themselves?

One might ask a similar question of many revolutions, of course, in light of the leadership role that intellectuals have typically played in nationalist and Communist movements around the world.[1] It seems especially perplexing in the case of China, however, where Confucian precepts had long fostered a stark distinction between mental and manual labor. The superior status of the literati, celebrated in Mencius's dictum that "those who labor with their brains rule over those who labor with their brawn," contributed to a huge social and political distance between the "cultured" and "uncultured." Moreover, although the iconoclastic New Culture Movement of the early twentieth century inspired many progressive Chinese intellectuals, Mao Zedong among them, to repudiate Confucianism in favor first of anarchism and then of Marxism-Leninism, among ordinary workers and peasants these radical new ideas had made few inroads. Nationalism (as opposed to xenophobia) was also initially an ideology largely confined to the educated elite.[2] For most Chinese, both the nation-state and the social classes that supposedly comprised it were still unfamiliar concepts.

As we saw in the case of the failed Ping-Liu-Li Uprising (chapter 1), an alliance between would-be revolutionaries and their purported followers was far from a foregone conclusion. Fertile ground as Anyuan

46

was for collective protest, preexisting solidarities and mentalities were not easily converted to alternative political purposes. Furthermore, the Communists were determined from the start to introduce new modes of grassroots organization. The founding resolution of the Chinese Communist Party, adopted in Shanghai in July 1921, began as follows: "The basic mission of this party is to establish industrial unions."[3] The resolution went on to explain the means by which this mission was to be accomplished, stressing the key role of education: "Because workers' schools are a stage in the process of organizing industrial unions, these sorts of schools must be established in every industrial sector. . . . The main task of the workers' schools is to raise workers' consciousness, so that they recognize the need to establish a union."[4]

In emphasizing proletarian education, CCP policy drew both upon the precedent of the Russian Revolution (where schooling for workers was an element of Bolshevik strategy) and upon contemporary experiments within China.[5] At the time, Y. C. James Yen's Mass Education Movement, Huang Yanpei's Vocational Education Campaign, and Liang Shumin's Rural Reconstruction Movement were part of a growing number of high-profile initiatives, intended to foster popular literacy and provide practical training, which had captured the imaginations of many concerned young Chinese intellectuals, including a number of future Communists.[6] Equally significant for the ultimate success of the Chinese Communists' pedagogical effort was the central place that education had long occupied in Chinese popular and political culture. A belief in the educability of all human beings, and an attendant obligation on the part of the intelligentsia to provide moral instruction to those with less education, were deeply ingrained precepts of both ancient and modern Chinese thought.[7] In the late imperial period, the civil service examination system, which rewarded outstanding scholars with official government position as well as responsibility for the moral cultivation of those living under their rule, was the institutionalized expression of this philosophy.[8] Seen as the surest path to political and economic success for families who could afford it, education for centuries had been highly prized as a means of upward mobility.[9] In this particular context, "teaching revolution" would prove to be an unusually persuasive mode of popular mobilization.

When Communist study groups first formed in Beijing and Shanghai in the wake of the 1919 May Fourth Movement, their members dedicated themselves to the project of educating workers. More than a year before the formal founding of the CCP in July of 1921, Communist students from Beijing had already established a school for workers at Changxindian, a terminus along the Jing-Han Railway. Within a few months, the railroad worker-students organized a labor union that they euphemistically called a "workers' club" (*gongren julebu*) to avoid arousing suspicion among the local authorities. Soon Communist activists in Shanghai followed the Changxindian model, introducing first schools and then unions among textile workers in the city.[10] This linkage between mass education and grassroots organization was critical to the success of the Communist revolutionary effort.

## TARGETING ANYUAN

Mao Zedong, having attended the founding congress of the Chinese Communist Party in Shanghai before returning to his native Hunan province to head a branch of the CCP-sponsored Labor Secretariat in Changsha, was eager to follow the party's prescribed recipe for proletarian mobilization. At the time, however, factories in Hunan were generally small and scattered, and the nascent labor movement was under strong anarchist influence.[11] The nearby site of Anyuan, located just across the border in Jiangxi's Pingxiang County, was virgin territory. Its coal mine and railroad had a combined and concentrated labor force of over ten thousand workers, making it the largest industrial enterprise in the area. The region's reputation for rebelliousness rendered it of particular interest.

In fact, Mao Zedong had been attracted to the revolutionary potential of Pingxiang even before the first CCP congress. In November 1920 he traveled there for a week to enjoy the refreshing mountain scenery and investigate local conditions. At the time, Mao was teaching Chinese literature at the First Normal School in Changsha to make ends meet, but most of his energy was already directed toward social activism. Although Mao seems not to have visited the Anyuan coal mine on his initial trip to Pingxiang, he was clearly taken by the possibilities for popular mobilization in this area. A few months earlier, thousands of Pingxiang peasants had engaged in a series of rowdy "eat-ins" at landlords' homes; in one instance, the peasants set fire to a landlord's house, incinerating several of his family members. Shortly after his Pingxiang journey, Mao wrote a stirring piece entitled "Open Letter to the Peasants of China" for the journal *Communist Party* in which he enthusiastically referred to the recent uprising: "This year's events in Pingxiang are inklings of dawn for the awakening of the Chinese peasantry. . . . It is exactly like the first rays of sunshine from the east after a pitch black night. . . . From birth you have had to work like beasts of burden. . . . You just need to imitate the peasants of Pingxiang. . . . Of course Communism will come to your aid. . . . So long as you follow the lead of the peasants of Pingxiang, Communism will release you from all suffering so that you may enjoy unprecedented good fortune."[12]

Mao's budding interest in the power of the peasantry notwithstanding, at this early stage in its history the newly established Chinese Communist Party was oriented toward proletarian—rather than peasant—mobilization. Shortly after returning from the founding party congress, Mao Zedong made another trip to Pingxiang, this time for the express purpose of investigating conditions at the Anyuan coal mine.[13] Mao embarked on his fact-finding mission in a period, in the fall of 1921, when the mine was experiencing severe economic difficulties as a result of a dramatic drop in demand for coal at the end of the First World War. To make matters worse, battling warlords had cut the critical Zhuping rail line and exacted a toll on the labor force through the forcible conscription of miners into their makeshift armies.[14] That the moment was ripe for agitation was clear from the fact that several educated Hunanese railroad workers had taken it upon themselves to write to the Communist Labor Secretariat, requesting that it send someone to Anyuan to help organize a labor movement.[15]

To make contact with the miners, however, required a proper introduction. On his initial visit, Mao stayed at the home of a man from his home county of Xiangtan, a distant relative by the name of Mao Ziyun, who happened to be employed as a supervisor at the coal mine. Renowned for his skill in using Chinese herbal medicine to heal the painful throat ailments that afflicted many miners, Mao Ziyun had befriended a good number of Anyuan workers in the course of practicing his curative techniques. Living in a comfortable house just outside the main entrance to the mine, Mao Ziyun was well situated to assist his visiting relative from Hunan. After being introduced to several miners at his kinsman's home, Mao Zedong ventured down into the coal pits.

According to later interviews conducted with miners who encountered Mao Zedong during this visit, Mao arrived at Anyuan carrying a Hunan umbrella made of oiled paper and dressed in a long blue Mandarin gown of the sort worn by teachers at the time.[16] Mao's scholarly demeanor left a deep impression upon the workers, who recalled being surprised by the peculiar sight of a privileged intellectual anxious to interact with lowly coal miners. The Confucian separation between mental and manual labor rendered such a cross-class encounter unusual, to say the least. The miners were not the only ones struck by the cultural distance between themselves and the young teacher from Changsha. More than thirty years later, when Mao Zedong hosted a banquet for newly appointed members of the Central Military Affairs Commission, several of whom were former Anyuan workers, he reminisced about his first visit to the coal mine. A participant at the 1954 banquet later reported:

> Chairman Mao recalled his youthful effort to develop the labor movement in Anyuan, Pingxiang. Chairman Mao said, "In those years, after receiving some education in Marxism, I imagined I was a revolutionary. But as it turned out, when I got to the coal mine and began to interact with the workers, because I was still a student at heart and a teacher in style, the workers wouldn't buy it. We didn't know how to proceed. Looking back now, it was pretty amusing. I spent the whole day just walking back and forth along the railroad tracks trying to figure out what to do. . . . Only when we dropped our pretentious airs and respected the workers as our teachers did things change. Later we chatted with the workers, sharing our genuine feelings, and the worker comrades gradually began to get close to us, telling us what was really on their minds."[17]

Despite the initial cultural gulf that separated him from his targeted constituency, Mao, thanks to his rural upbringing and colloquial dialect, was able to converse easily with the workers—most of whom shared his Hunan origins—and by week's end he had shed his scholar's gown in favor of a pair of trousers, which were more suitable for forays down into the mining pits.

In his exploratory conversations with the Anyuan workers, after a few inquiries about their difficult working and living conditions, Mao Zedong turned to the topic of education. Since Mao was supporting his revolutionary activities by teaching in the mass education movement in Hunan, it must have seemed quite natural for him to direct the discussion toward this issue. Although the establishment of schools was official CCP policy, in accordance with the Russian revolutionary recipe, it resonated especially strongly in a cultural milieu where education had long been valued as the pathway to social mobility. A miner who met with Mao Zedong on his maiden visit to Anyuan later recalled Mao's introduction of this topic (referring, anachronistically, to Mao as "Chairman"):

> The Chairman asked us whether we went to school. I answered that we weren't even able to afford to eat, so how could we possibly manage to take classes. The Chairman asked: what if education were free? I said that if it didn't require any money of course people would want to study. I asked the Chairman when we could get started. He pointed out that the year was almost over, but promised that the next year he

would send someone to open a school. The following day I ran into the Chairman again and he repeated that he would send somebody in the new year to open a school for us.[18]

In December 1921 Mao Zedong returned to Anyuan to make concrete plans for establishing a school at the mine.[19] He took with him three other educational activists from Hunan, including the energetic Li Lisan, who had recently returned from two years of studies in France and had joined the Communist Party in Shanghai before heading home to Hunan. In addition to Mao and Li Lisan, the advance team was composed of Song Yousheng, a teacher at a Hunan elementary school, and Zhang Liquan, a cadre in the Liaison Department of the Hunan Labor Secretariat who edited the secretariat journal, *Labor Weekly,* while teaching at the Hunan Jiazhong Industrial School in Changsha. The four young men stayed for several days in a small inn near the mine, inviting workers to drop by for a chat as soon as they got off work.[20]

Initially, the members of the Anyuan workforce most receptive to Communist overtures were railway workers, whose own educational and cultural backgrounds facilitated communication with the young intellectuals from across the border. Among the most enthusiastic was the chief engineer of the Zhuping railway, a fellow Hunanese by the name of Zhu Shaolian, who had graduated from the railroad academy in Hubei before being assigned to the job at Anyuan. When quizzed by the visitors from Hunan about their most pressing concerns, Zhu and his fellow workers reiterated what the miners had previously told Mao Zedong, complaining that their children were unable to attend school because of the prohibitive expense. Mao reportedly replied, "Suffering is caused by lack of knowledge. We are not only going to open a school for workers' children. We will also open a school to educate workers."[21]

## EDUCATING ANYUAN

Soon after the group had returned to Hunan, Mao Zedong informed Li Lisan of his decision to send Li back to Anyuan to make good on his pedagogical pledge. Mao impressed upon Li Lisan the importance of dealing sensitively with prevailing conditions and customs. In particular, he cautioned Li about the power of the Red Gang in light of the secret society's formidable grip on the workers. Stressing that the "reactionary ruling forces" and "dark social environment" at the mine made it impossible to undertake open revolutionary mobilization, Mao suggested a more oblique approach. First on Li's agenda would be to establish schools for workers and their children. Only after having earned the miners' trust as a respected teacher would Li be in a position to organize them for overtly political purposes.[22]

The first resolution of the newly founded CCP, as we have seen, gave the official party stamp of approval to workers' education as a stepping-stone toward unionization. Mao's specific instructions to Li Lisan reiterated these guiding principles. Li recalled many years later that, although Mao Zedong had chosen Anyuan because of its exceptional revolutionary potential, he warned the impatient young firebrand against premature radicalism. Instead Li was to proceed by stages, beginning with a focus on public education:

> In November 1921, when Comrade Mao Zedong sent me to Anyuan to undertake the labor movement, he already had a clear idea of how to begin work among the workers, how to gradually organize so as to advance toward struggle. He told us . . . that it wouldn't be easy to launch a revolutionary movement, and he said we must first take advantage of all legal opportunities and focus on open activities to get close to the labor movement and identify outstanding elements among the workers, gradually disciplining and organizing them before establishing a [Communist] party branch. He wanted us to operate under the banner of mass education, going to Anyuan with an introduction from the Hunan branch of the Mass Education Society.[23]

Only twenty-two years of age at the time, Li Lisan was an ideal choice to assume the role of Anyuan schoolteacher. His father was an imperial degree holder from nearby Liling County (less than thirty miles due west of Anyuan, in Hunan Province) who offered instruction in the Confucian classics, and Li Lisan himself—at his father's insistence—had taught at an elementary school in his native Liling before heading off to Beijing and France for additional studies. Within weeks of his return from Lyons in late 1921, Li Lisan traveled to Beijing to see one of his old middle school classmates from Hunan, Luo Zhanglong, who was then directing the new Communist-sponsored school for railroad workers at the Changxindian station on the Jing-Han Railway. Impressed by what he witnessed, Li was anxious to replicate Luo's pioneering efforts in another industrial setting. The fact that many of the Anyuan miners hailed from Li Lisan's home county of Liling (as well as from Mao Zedong's home county of Xiangtan) was an additional attraction for the would-be labor organizer.

Armed, at Mao Zedong's suggestion, with a letter attesting to his educational credentials written by Li Liuru, the deputy director of the Hunan branch of the Mass Education Society, Li Lisan returned to Anyuan under the guise of an aspiring schoolmaster. Although the idea of worker schools derived from the Russian experience, Li's method of implementation drew self-consciously on his own cultural traditions. Upon learning that the magistrate of Pingxiang County was a top-ranked Confucian degree holder who adamantly opposed written vernacular language, Li Lisan put his own classical training to use by composing in his best literary Chinese a flowery petition requesting official permission to open a school at Anyuan.

Like Mao Zedong before him, Li Lisan relied upon the introductions of relatives to gain local access. Thanks to the help of a friend of Li Lisan's father, a Liling man by the name of Xie Lanfang who happened to be the director of the Anyuan chamber of commerce, Li Lisan's petition was delivered directly to the county magistrate. Delighted by the classical style and fluid calligraphy of Li's writing, the Pingxiang magistrate invited the young scholar from Liling to meet in person to discuss his pedagogical proposal. So pleased was the conservative magistrate by Li Lisan's Confucian-sounding pronouncements about the contribution of education to the improvement of public ethics that he immediately agreed to issue an official proclamation in support of the proposed new school. The proclamation quoted verbatim from Li's petition: "helping workers to increase their knowledge in order to promote virtue."[24] Unbeknownst to the magistrate, Confucian rhetoric would pave the way toward Communist revolution.

The moralistic magistrate, who hailed from Hubei, hoped that Li Lisan's pedagogical efforts might help to improve public civility in the notoriously roughneck town of Anyuan, where brothels, opium dens, and gambling halls far outnumbered schools. In this town of eighty thousand inhabitants, the only functioning school, -- which was operated by St. James Episcopal Church with some assistance from the mining company (see chapter 1), charged steep tuition fees in return for a strongly religious regimen of instruction. Enrollment at the church school was largely limited to the children of high-level staff; the sons and daughters of electrical engineers from Shanghai and Guangzhou were especially well represented among the few hundred children fortunate enough to attend. Ordinary workers at Anyuan had little prospect of educational advancement for either themselves or their children.[25] From the magistrate's (mistaken) perspective, Li Lisan's proposed school could serve as a Confucian counterweight to the Christian education being dispensed by the local church.

With assistance from Zhuping railway chief engineer Zhu Shaolian and a couple of fellow Hunanese railway workers to whom Mao had previously introduced him, Li Lisan rented the top floor (three rooms) of a house in town for his school, prominently posting the magistrate's supportive proclamation above the front door. He also put up several announcements around town advertising the new tuition-free educational opportunity. Thirty or forty students, almost all of them the children of railway workers, soon enrolled.[26] Li Lisan took advantage of his position as teacher to pay home visits to the children's parents, thereby becoming acquainted with a number of the workers. Wearing his long Mandarin gown and striding ostentatiously from house to house to drum up additional pupils for his classes, Li acquired the moniker of "itinerant scholar-teacher" (*youxue xiansheng*) among the locals.[27]

Although his literati dress and obvious erudition allowed Li Lisan to win the approval of local officials, a crucial first step toward realizing his educational ambitions, he soon revealed that he was no ordinary Confucian teacher. Despite his Mandarin bearing, Li Lisan on evening visits to his students' families engaged his hosts in animated discussions about the possibility of improving labor conditions through workers' education, organization, and struggle. Railway workers—who generally had some education—initially proved much more receptive to Li's message than did the illiterate miners. A group of Hunanese railway mechanics, including Hubei Railway Academy alumnus Zhu Shaolian (at whose house Li Lisan was living) along with several recent graduates of the progressive Jiazhong Industrial School in Changsha, formed the nucleus of Li Lisan's coterie. Within a couple of weeks, Li had identified eight potential activists—all but one of them railway workers—whom he persuaded to join him in forming an Anyuan branch of the Socialist Youth League. At Li Lisan's prompting, the league members (six of whom Li soon tapped to constitute a Communist Party cell) focused on educating fellow workers as their first priority. They converted the rented classrooms, occupied by the workers' children during the day, into a school for workers at night.[28]

Starting with a handful of students drawn from the railway machine shop, the night school quickly expanded to enroll several dozen workers. Li Lisan's dynamic teaching style—which combined basic literacy instruction with revolutionary messages—proved immensely popular. Employing the art of glyphomancy (the deconstruction and recombination of Chinese characters) familiar from secret-society fortune telling, Li Lisan showed how the two characters that combined horizontally to form the term for "worker" (*gongren*) could be repositioned vertically into a single character meaning "Heaven" (*tian*). When the workers stood up, he explained, they would enjoy the blessing of Heaven. Li also had a knack for translating abstract concepts into mundane metaphors. Many years later, one of his Anyuan students still recalled the memorable way in which Li had conveyed the importance of proletarian unity: "Once, when Comrade Li Lisan was lecturing about how the workers needed to unite in order to have enough power to struggle against the capitalists, he grabbed a single chopstick along with a bundle of chopsticks as an illustration. A single chopstick, he demonstrated, could be broken with one flick of the wrist. When bundled together, however, no single chopstick could easily be broken. This simple example left a profound impression on our thinking."[29] Soon the CCP assigned another young teacher from Hunan, Jiang Xianyun, to handle the classes for children, so that Li Lisan could devote himself to the workers full-time.[30] The initial eight or nine worker-students, like the founding members of the Anyuan Socialist Youth League and Communist Party, were predominantly railway mechanics from Hunan who had attended the Jiazhong Industrial School.

The receptivity of Hunanese engineers and mechanics to Communist appeals was not an Anyuan anomaly; in other parts of China as well shared native-place origins and educational backgrounds rendered skilled male workers especially responsive to Communist initiatives.[31] But whereas in many Chinese industrial enterprises occupational skill was closely aligned with gender and native-place origin, the situation at Anyuan was rather more complicated. Unlike textile mills or tobacco factories, where unskilled labor was often performed by women migrants who did not speak the local dialect, the Anyuan coal mine was an all-male operation that recruited its haulers and diggers as well as its railway engineers from within the local dialect region. The majority of unskilled miners shared with skilled railway workers a common Hunan provenance. In this they differed markedly from upper-level staff and electrical engineers, who hailed from distant urban centers in Guangdong, Jiangsu, and Zhejiang. The Hunan miners were distinct as well from those miners (a minority, but a significant minority nonetheless) who came from nearby villages in Pingxiang County itself. Despite the strong similarity in language and customs between Pingxiang and Hunan, many locals harbored resentment toward Hunanese incursions into their economy and politics that dated back to the founding of the modern coal mine.

It was obvious to Li Lisan from the outset that success at Anyuan would require substantial support from coal miners, who outnumbered railway workers by nearly ten to one. Despite the railway workers' educational advantage over miners, their shared dialect and culture facilitated communication and cooperation. Li therefore encouraged the railroad workers—some of whom had Red Gang connections—to reach out to their sworn brothers among the miners. Although he imagined that new Communist-sponsored institutions would eventually supplant the Red Gang's hold over the workers, Li Lisan realized (as Mao Zedong had warned) that a direct clash with the secret society would be disastrous at this preliminary stage. In order to enroll in Li's school, therefore, miners were required first to obtain permission from their labor contractors, virtually all of whom were Elder Brother chieftains.[32]

When Li Lisan first headed into the coal pits to enjoin miners to attend his classes, this bizarre behavior on the part of an intellectual was greeted with sarcastic incredulity: "Is this the Episcopal Church or the Catholic Church? The Red Gang or the Green Gang? Come to spread the gospel or to enlist soldiers?"[33] But Li was undeterred by the tendency to interpret his revolutionary efforts in terms of more familiar institutions. He persisted, prevailing upon each new student at his night school to recruit several friends, and soon the coterie of worker-students had expanded in both number and diversity. When the sixty enrollees could no longer be accommodated within the space that Li had originally rented, he formed the Educational Affairs Committee—composed of himself and his fellow teacher together with railway engineer Zhu Shaolian and one miner—to oversee the move to a larger facility. Both the school for children and the workers' night school were relocated to a more spacious building, which housed a newly opened reading room stocked with left-wing periodicals in addition to several classrooms.[34]

Besides the issue of space, Li faced the problem of securing appropriate instructional materials for his educational activities. The classes for children could make use of basic textbooks that had been compiled previously by the Mass Education Society with the help of the YMCA. These contained beginning lessons in reading and arithmetic. More challenging, however, were the textbooks for workers, whose education was intended ultimately to instill revolutionary class consciousness in addition to functional literacy. Li Lisan later recounted how he gradually introduced subversive ideas under the cover of an officially approved curriculum: "The workers' classes used two types of textbooks. Openly we used the textbooks prepared for mass education. But actually we used materials that we ourselves had edited. At every class we dispensed a bit of basic Marxist-Leninist knowledge, emphasizing that all the world's wealth had been produced by the working class."[35] The first lesson in the approved thousand-character mass education reader began with the innocuous sentence "One person has two hands; two hands have ten fingers." The unauthorized materials, by contrast, included lessons in class conflict with telling titles such as "Workers and Capitalists."[36] The combination of conventional textbooks together with unorthodox handouts called for some subterfuge on the part of the students. As one of them recalled, "When Li Lisan first opened the school, I joined. Our text was the thousand-character reader. But his lectures stressed the exploitation and oppression of the workers. Someone stood guard at the classroom door to keep outsiders from eavesdropping. Later on, stencils of Marx's ideas were handed out for us to study. If outsiders happened to come by, we covered the stencils with the thousand-character reader."[37] Aware of the pressing need for teaching materials, Mao Zedong sent the deputy director of the Hunan branch of the Mass Education Society, Li Liuru (whose letter of introduction had opened official doors for Li Lisan and whom Mao had just recruited into the CCP) to Anyuan in the spring of 1922 for the express purpose of editing textbooks appropriate for the workers' school there. After touring the coal pits and dormitories to observe labor and living conditions firsthand, Li Liuru compiled a four-volume series, known as *Mass Reader (Pingmin Duben)*, which introduced students to a rudimentary understanding of Marxism-Leninism.[38]

Renting classrooms and printing and purchasing textbooks all took money, of course, and obtaining enough funding to underwrite these educational activities posed another challenge for Li Lisan. At first the Anyuan school was financed by the Labor Secretariat in Shanghai and the Hunan branch of the Mass Education Society in Changsha.[39] But this dependence upon distant benefactors with more pressing priorities presented obvious disadvantages, and Li again employed Confucian logic on local notables to remind them of the moral benefits of education. Soon the classes were supported by philanthropic contributions from members of the local elite, augmented by nominal fees from the workers themselves. The foreman for construction at the coal mine, a skilled artisan by the name of Chen Shengfang who hailed from Li Lisan's own native county of Liling, was a particularly generous source of financial assistance.[40]

## UNIONIZING ANYUAN

Just as party policy prescribed, the Anyuan workers' school served as a springboard for other modes of labor organization. One evening, some of the workers came across a journal article in their school reading room about Shanghai textile workers having recently formed a "club" (a euphemism for a labor union) to advance their collective interests. The workers asked Li Lisan whether they might do something similar at Anyuan, a proposal that of course delighted the eager young Communist organizer. After two preparatory meetings, Li Lisan, Zhu Shaolian, and several other workers submitted a petition to the Pingxiang County government requesting official approval to establish a "workers' club," which would be restricted to railway workers and miners (and explicitly exclude the company staff). Satisfied with the club's seemingly innocent motto of "forge friendships, nurture virtue, provide unity and mutual aid, and seek common happiness," the county magistrate—without consulting the Pingxiang Railway and Mining Company—readily approved the request.[41] The new Anyuan workers' club preparatory committee, with Li Lisan as its director and railroad engineer Zhu Shaolian as its deputy director, was headquartered in rented space at the Hubei Guild Hall, and the night school classes were moved to this more capacious site.[42]

Although the introduction of a labor union was a novel development, its organization and operations were evocative of local precedents. As in the Hongjiang hui of the Ping-Liu-Li Uprising (see chapter 1), club members were organized according to a decimal system. Groups of ten (*shirentuan*) were established in every workshop, with one leader from each workshop responsible for all of the ten-person groups in his department.[43] Like Red Gang lodges, the Anyuan workers' club had its own clandestine code phrases. Although the public motto was sufficiently innocuous to win the instant support of the magistrate, the internal maxim—which new members pledged to keep confidential—was more revealing of the proto–labor union's actual aspirations: "protect workers' interests and relieve the oppression and suffering of the workers." As was true for secret societies, membership demanded an entrance fee. New initiates, after swearing a solemn oath of unity and a pledge of mutual aid, were required to contribute the equivalent of one day's wages. Thereafter, a modest monthly fee was charged to underwrite basic operating expenses.[44] Even so, finances remained an issue, and for the initial six months of its existence nearly half the income of the workers' club (90 yuan out of a total revenue of 206 yuan) came in the form of a loan from Li Lisan himself.[45]

The reliance on recognizable secret-society conventions to build new revolutionary organizations was not unique to Li Lisan and the fledgling Anyuan workers' club. At this same time, peasant movement activist Peng Pai borrowed liberally from Triad traditions to establish a radical peasant union in his native county of Haifeng, Guangdong. As Fernando Galbiati writes of the former Triads who flocked to Peng's new peasant union, "they saw no contradiction between the two."[46]

Figure 3. The Anyuan Workers' Club Preparatory Committee. Li Lisan stands in the central row from the engine head, fifth from the right. Zhu Shaolian is looking out the window of the engineer's booth.

Secret societies were not the only local institution whose practices the Communists found serviceable in the process of constructing new associations. Li Lisan's efforts at cultural positioning drew upon a broad range of familiar rituals. For example, to stir up greater interest in the workers' club, Li decided that the night school should host a lion dance at the time of the annual Lantern Festival. In this region of China, the Lantern Festival was customarily an occasion when the local elite sponsored exhibitions by martial arts masters, who displayed their skills and thereby attracted new disciples in the course of performing spirited lion dances. One of Li's new recruits to the workers' club, a highly adept performer by the name of You Congnai, was persuaded to take the lead. You was a low-level chieftain in the Red Gang whose martial arts skills were second to none. He dutifully donned a resplendent lion's costume, tailor-made for this occasion by local artisans, and—to the loud accompaniment of cymbals and firecrackers—gamely pranced from the coal mine to the railway station, stopping along the way at the general headquarters of the company, the chamber of commerce, St. James Episcopal Church, the Hunan and Hubei native-place associations, and the homes of the gang chieftains to pay his respects. As intended, the performance attracted a large and appreciative crowd, which followed the sprightly dancer back to the workers' club to learn how to enlist as his disciples. Contrary to popular expectation, however, the martial arts master announced to the assembled audience, "Teacher Li of the night school has instructed us that, starting tonight, we should no longer study martial arts. Instead, we should all study diligently at the night school. Anyone interested in studying, come with us."[47]

It soon became clear that the Communists had in mind something altogether different from traditional pedagogy—whether of the Confucian literary (*wen*) or the martial arts (*wu*) variety. As lion dancer You Congnai put it to the throngs of would-be disciples, "Our teacher's home is in Liling [Li Lisan's native county, just across the provincial border in Hunan], but the ancestral founder of our school lives far, far away. To find him one must cross the seven seas. He's now more than a hundred years old and his name is Teacher Ma [Marx], a bearded grandpa."[48]

Li Lisan's imaginative recruitment drive resulted in a large influx of new members to the workers' club, but the festivities did not end there. On May Day in 1922 the Anyuan Railway and Mining Workers' Club was publicly inaugurated with a gala parade in which hundreds of workers carrying red flags marched behind Li Lisan shouting revolutionary slogans: "Workers of the World, Unite!" "Long Live Labor!" "Long Live the Club!" "Down with Warlords!" "Long Live the Communist Party!" Once again Li Lisan's ingenuity in reworking traditional practices for new mobilizing purposes was on brilliant display. Martial arts adepts among the crowd carried an open palanquin of the sort that was normally used to transport statues of deities during religious festivals (see chapter 1), but the honored passenger this day was none other than a bust of that "bearded grandpa" from across the seven seas, Karl Marx.[49] Li Lisan's innovative cultural positioning was converting familiar folk rituals into vehicles for revolutionary recruitment.

A few weeks after this boisterous public celebration of the new workers' club, Mao Zedong returned to Anyuan to evaluate the progress of the labor movement. Expressing overall satisfaction with recent developments, Mao nevertheless bluntly criticized the inclusion of "Long Live the Communist Party" among the slogans shouted in the inaugural parade. At a meeting of the recently established Communist party cell, Mao stressed the importance of strict secrecy in party affairs and the need for strengthening the organizational foundation of the labor movement before making such public declarations about the role of the Communist

Party. Mao reiterated his earlier directive that mobilization must proceed gradually, avoiding any unnecessary and premature radicalism.[50]

Mao Zedong's stern admonition to the Anyuan activists was an early harbinger of the Chinese Communist Party's unease about Li Lisan's freewheeling approach to mass mobilization. Contemporary CCP leader Zhang Guotao would later write of Li Lisan, "Completely a man of action, he looked only for results, and he was unaccustomed to restrictions from the organization . . . he always insisted that he 'had to have an immediate solution.'"[51]

Impetuous and uninhibited in both personality and work style, Li Lisan's flamboyant manner was as captivating to ordinary workers as it was disturbing to his party superiors. Li sashayed ostentatiously around the grimy coal mining town of Anyuan, dressed either in long Mandarin gown or in stylish Western coat and tie, in a fashion designed to attract attention. When the shiny metal badge (acquired in France) that he sported on his chest generated persistent rumors of Li Lisan's invulnerability to swords and bullets, he did nothing to dispel them. On the contrary, taking a cue from Elder Brother dragon heads whose authority rested upon their reputation for supernatural powers, Li Lisan actively encouraged the belief that he enjoyed the magical protection of "five foreign countries" bestowed during his travels abroad.[52] In this overwhelmingly male environment, where female companionship was in short supply, even Li Lisan's reputation for womanizing may have contributed to his charismatic aura.[53] But surely what most endeared Li Lisan to the workers of Anyuan was the tireless dedication that he devoted to their cause, whether as a schoolteacher or as a union organizer.

Although the hundreds who had joined Li Lisan's workers' club still comprised but a small percentage of the total Anyuan workforce, which stood at over thirteen thousand, their enthusiasm and organization were seen by the mining company as a serious and growing threat. One of the more worrisome initiatives of the workers' club from the perspective of the company was the establishment of a consumers' cooperative. In July 1922 the club opened a cooperative store that offered its members low-interest loans, attractive rates for converting silver to copper currency, and basic necessities (oil, salt, cloth, rice, and the like) at below-market prices. Starting with only thirty or so members and a mere one hundred yuan in capital, the new co-op was initially a small-scale operation that conducted its activities out of the workers' school. Modest as this beginning was, however, the company recognized that the cooperative—whose first general manager was Li Lisan—presented a challenge to its own monopolistic control over the workers' livelihood. Li publicized the new venture with a simple yet appealing slogan: "cheap goods for sale." The concrete economic benefits that resulted from co-op membership, which was restricted to those who had already joined the workers' club, attracted a surge of new club members.[54]

An additional concern for the mining company was that the workers' club (like the Red Gang whose structure it resembled) had organized its own militia. Called a "patrol team" (jianchadui), the force was recruited primarily from among Red Gang members known for their martial arts skills. Responsible for providing security for the workers' club and its Communist leadership and for gathering intelligence on company management, the patrols carried wooden staves and drilled regularly at the night school. Their captain, Zhou Huaide, was a notoriously combative miner who hailed from Mao's native county of Xiangtan in Hunan and had been active in the Elder Brothers Society for nearly two decades before his association with the Communists. Zhou was a veteran of the Ping-Liu-Li Uprising, having served as a petty chieftain in the Hongjiang hui in 1906. Zhou also had a history of directing his pugilistic skills against the foreign staff at the mine, spearheading a series of assaults on German advisors and engineers until their departure en masse in 1919. Thanks to his martial prowess, Zhou was often called upon to settle disputes among his fellow workers. Because of his truculence and his standing among the workers, Zhou—like fellow gang members You Congnai (the lion dancer) and Xie Huaide (who became vice-captain of the patrols)—was specifically targeted by Li Lisan for recruitment, first to the night school and eventually to the Communist Party.[55] A similar pattern obtained in the case of Yuan Pin'gao, a young miner from Li Lisan's native place of Liling who was also known for exceptional martial arts skills. Yuan was persuaded by Li to study at the workers' night school, then to join the workers' club, then the Socialist Youth League, and eventually the Communist Party. He became a key member of the patrol team and later served as Liu Shaoqi's trusted bodyguard after Liu's arrival at Anyuan.[56]

Once prospective members had been identified and recruited, initiation into the Communist Party was a fairly simple affair. An inductee recalled,

> Li Lisan operated a school for workers. I studied at that school. I entered the party before the strike, introduced by Li Lisan. I was inducted together with Yi Shaoqin, a supervisor on the railway. The oath swearing took place in a rented upstairs room on the walls of

which there were pictures of Marx, Engels, Rosa Luxemburg, and Karl Liebknecht. The words of the oath were "Sacrifice the individual for the interests of the masses, strictly maintain secrecy, say nothing to fathers, mothers, wives, or children, observe discipline, struggle to the end for revolution!"[57]

For many of Li Lisan's recruits, previous experience with Red Gang induction rituals must have lent the party initiation process a certain air of déjà vu. The qualifications for party membership were in fact quite similar to those for gang membership. When joining the Communist Party, Anyuan workers were not expected to demonstrate any particular knowledge of or commitment to Marxist theory. Instead, as one of them later reported when asked about the criteria for membership, "the requirements were to keep secrets, promote mass interests, and sacrifice oneself."[58]

Even if party membership did not mark a qualitative ideational break with previous secret-society beliefs and practices, rumors of the party's rapid growth raised the disturbing specter of a militant proletariat in the eyes of the Pingxiang Mining Company. As had been the case during the Ping-Liu-Li Uprising fifteen years earlier, the challenge presented by restive workers generated a rift within the upper managerial ranks of the coal mine. Faced with the prospect of an increasingly organized and unruly workforce at just the time that a massive strike wave was sweeping much of industrial China,[59] the directors of the mining company disagreed on how to respond. Whereas Director Li Shouquan's revolutionary sympathies (see chapter 1) inclined him toward compromise, Deputy Director Shu Xiutai was intransigent. The result was vacillation between clumsy attempts to buy out the workers' club leadership followed by hollow threats of repression. When these efforts failed to entice or intimidate either Li Lisan or Zhu Shaolian, the company petitioned the county magistrate and the garrison commander for military assistance to forcibly close down the workers' club.[60]

## THE GREAT STRIKE OF 1922

At this critical juncture, Mao Zedong paid another visit to Anyuan. Noting the further progress that Li Lisan had made in educating and mobilizing railway workers and miners alike, including the organization of a Communist Party cell that now had more than thirty members and was firmly in charge of the rapidly growing workers' club, Mao concluded that conditions at Anyuan were ripe for a major strike. The fact that the

Pingxiang Railway and Mining Company (responding to the drop in the price of coal) was several months in arrears on wage payments had angered the entire workforce. Moreover, its bungled efforts to suppress the workers' club presented a perfect provocation for a walkout. After returning to Changsha, Mao summed up his recommendations in a letter to Li Lisan, who happened to be home in Liling at the time, calling on him to return to Anyuan immediately to carry out an orderly strike designed to elicit widespread public sympathy. Drawing on an idea from the legendary Daoist thinker Laozi that "an army burning with righteous indignation will surely win" *(aibing bisheng)*, Mao proposed as the guiding philosophy behind the strike a literary phrase of his own: "Move the people through righteous indignation" *(ai er dongren)*.[61]

In keeping with Mao's instructions, Li Lisan hurried back to Anyuan to mobilize his followers for a general walkout. At the same time, he emphasized the importance of protecting the basic infrastructure of the mine so as to avoid damaging its productive capacity. One of the participants remembered, "Two days before the strike started, I was called to a meeting at the workers' club at which Li Lisan presided. It was held at night, and over one hundred people attended. We were all students at the night school. Li explained that we were all going on strike, except for the electricity room, the boiler room, and the ventilation room."[62] The boiler and ventilation rooms remaining open would ensure that the pumps and fans designed to prevent flooding and gas explosions in the mine pits would continue to operate. The electricity room, which provided illumination and running water to the entire town of Anyuan, would also stay open in order to avoid plunging the community into darkness and inciting public anger and disorder.[63] That these critical workshops were staffed by technicians from Jiangnan and Guangdong—the segment of the workforce among which the Hunan-born Communists had made the fewest inroads—was perhaps also a consideration in exempting them from the strike action. In any event, aside from a skeleton crew to maintain the basic infrastructure, the whole workforce of over ten thousand miners and railway men was expected to participate.

Worried about maintaining order in this place renowned for its history of violence, Mao Zedong decided at the eleventh hour to dispatch another comrade from Hunan, Liu Shaoqi, to provide supervision and impose restraint during the impending strike.[64] Liu had attended the same school as Mao in Changsha before going to the Soviet Union to study at the University of the Toilers of the East in 1921. Just returned from his year in Moscow, Liu was already known for a disciplined Leninist work style that

Mao believed could serve to temper Li Lisan's more impulsive inclinations.[65] Together, Li and Liu worked to ensure that the impending strike would proceed under party command. A miner involved in the preparations explained,

> The night before the strike got underway, the leaders and members of the workers' club convened a meeting that lasted the entire night to decide upon the strike resolution and to figure out various strike-related measures. At that time management regarded the club as a pain in the neck and the immensely popular Li Lisan as a thorn in the flesh. So they threatened to harm him. At the meeting, everyone agreed that Li Lisan should not go out in public for the period of the strike. But then who should be in charge of the negotiations? This led to a very spirited debate. . . . In the end, Comrade Li Lisan made the decision, "The strike is led by the party. Comrade Liu Shaoqi was sent by the party to undertake a leadership role. Naturally he must serve as the negotiator." Finally, the meeting decided that Li Lisan would serve as supreme commander of the strike while Liu Shaoqi would serve as top negotiator. Next on the agenda were the strike demands to be negotiated. This issue also generated considerable disagreement. Some workers raised unrealistic demands. Only after patient persuasion and explanation by Li Lisan and Liu Shaoqi did these workers agree to drop their radical demands.[66]

Under the combined leadership of Li Lisan and Liu Shaoqi, the Anyuan strikers presented the railway and mining company with a set of demands that they considered ambitious yet attainable: payment of back wages, improvement in working conditions, reform of the labor contract system, and—most important of all from the perspective of the Communist leaders—a guarantee of recognition and financial support for their newly established workers' club.

In the spirit of Mao's classical admonition to move the people through righteous indignation, Li Lisan came up with a stirring colloquial slogan for the strike: "Once beasts of burden, now we will be men!" (*congqian shi niuma, xianzai yao zuoren*). Referring to unskilled laborers as "beasts of burden" (*niuma*) was a familiar trope, but the call for these "cattle and horses" to stand up as men was fresh and arresting.[67] This cri de coeur was elaborated in a strike manifesto (also composed by Li Lisan) intended to elicit widespread public sympathy for the workers' cause.[68] In the centuries-old tradition of protest petitions,[69] the manifesto emphasized the desperate defensive motivations of the participants. Significantly, the argument was framed not in terms of class struggle but as a plea for human dignity:

Our work is so difficult; our pay so meager. We are often beaten and cursed, robbing us of our humanity. The oppression we suffer has already reached the extreme limit so we are seeking "better treatment," "higher wages," and an "organized association—a club." . . . We want to live! We want to eat! We are hungry. Our lives are in danger. In the midst of death we seek life. Forced to the breaking point, we have no choice but to go on strike as our last resort. . . . Our demands are extremely reasonable. We are willing to give our lives to reach our goals . . . Everyone, strictly maintain order! Carry through to the end![70]

As the manifesto implied, public support depended upon the ability of the strikers to ensure order. With some five thousand unemployed laborers milling about the town of Anyuan at the time, the possibility of violent confrontations between strikers and strikebreakers was of particular concern.

Both Li Lisan and Liu Shaoqi, like Mao before them, recognized that the key to maintaining order was the cooperation of the Red Gang. Accordingly, they agreed that Li Lisan—accompanied by workers' club patrolmen and gang members Zhou Huaide and You Congnai—should visit the local dragon head to secure his assistance. Bearing a bottle of liquor and a rooster, the basic elements of a Triad-type initiation rite, Li and his companions went to the society lodge on a night when they knew that the top leaders of the Red Gang had been planning to hold an induction ceremony. Li strode brazenly into the main hall, plunked his gifts on the altar, and—using Elder Brother code language that his associates had taught him—indicated his desire to enter the fraternity. When the Red Gang leaders expressed some doubts about Li Lisan's sincerity, Zhou Huaide rushed to his defense: "I won't deceive my brothers. Mr. Li has traveled all over China, to cities large and small. He has also gone overseas to many countries. He has taken 'Ma the Bearded' [Marx] and 'En the Bearded' [Engels] as his teachers, and his person is protected by these two foreign worthies." You Congnai added, "Whoever makes friends with Mr. Li enjoys good fortune." Persuaded by this character reference from his underlings, the dragon head accepted Li Lisan's presents and invited him to state his concerns.[71] Li made three requests—the suspension of gambling operations, opium dens, and looting incidents for the duration of the strike. When the Red Gang leader beat his breast three times to indicate his assurance that all three demands would be met, the strike was called.

Li Lisan later acknowledged the signal importance of this diplomatic mission to the Red Gang in facilitating the success of the Anyuan strike, explaining how he had won the dragon head's acquiescence by framing his request in a manner congruent with secret-society precepts:

> We paid a great deal of attention to working with the Red Gang. Many of the workers had joined the Red Gang, and the Red Gang leader was an advisor to the mining company. The great majority of labor contractors were his followers, and the capitalists at the mine relied on them to oppress the workers. They used concepts such as "honor," "protecting the poor," "seeking happiness for the poor," and so on to trick the workers. Thanks to our efforts, several of the lower-level Red Gang chieftains joined the party. Before the strike, our biggest fear was that the Red Gang would break the strike. So Liu Shaoqi instructed me to have a couple of gang chieftains under our influence take me to see the Red Gang leader. I bought some presents and went there. The head of the Red Gang was very pleased that I had come. He called me Director Li (as workers' club director), and after we had drunk the rooster blood (I had brought along a rooster), I told him we were planning to go on strike. I also explained that the strike was intended to help our impoverished brothers "seek happiness," "protect the poor," and so forth. I asked that he do the "honorable" thing by helping out. He slapped his chest and said, "I will definitely help." I immediately raised three demands for the period of the strike: 1) close the opium dens, 2) suspend street gambling, 3) prevent looting. He slapped his chest three times in a row: "The first point, I guarantee, the second point I guarantee, and the third point I also guarantee." He even wrote the first and second points into a public notice. The implementation of these three provisions had a dramatic effect on [Anyuan] society. Even some capitalists and intellectuals thought the workers' club was pretty amazing (because for so many years these problems could not be solved, but the strike completely resolved them).[72]

Having secured this critical guarantee of Red Gang cooperation, the strike commenced at two o'clock in the morning on September 14, 1922, among the most reliable base of Communist support, the railway workers. Within two hours, however, the walkout had spread—by careful prearrangement—to the rest of the workforce. At each of the more than forty workstations, yellow triangular flags—bearing the characters for "strike"—were unfurled and patrols were stationed to ensure that no one entered the premises. Workers were told to return to their homes or dormitories to reduce the potential for public disorder.[73] Notices were posted on the streets, in all the residential districts, in the workers' dormitories, at the train station, and at the entrances to the pits urging full cooperation: "Wait for an announcement from the club before resuming work!" "Everyone return home!" "No disorderly conduct!"[74]

With virtually the entire workforce idled, a group of labor contractors—fearing an end to their lucrative livelihood should the strikers win their demands—attempted to intervene. The general foreman, Bearded Wang the Third (see chapter 1), led this opposition. As Liu Shaoqi and Zhu Shaolian described Wang's unsuccessful effort,

> The labor contractors were deeply upset by the strike. They tried by every means possible to destroy it in order to protect themselves. The worst offender was General Foreman Wang Hongqing (from Hubei), who received thousands of yuan each month from the sale of labor contractor positions. After the strike began, Wang convened a meeting of all the labor contractors for underground operations to discuss methods for breaking the strike. They decided that every contractor would offer some of the workers under his control full pay simply for entering the pits without doing any work. Some of the workers, either because of family pressure or greed, wanted to take advantage of this invitation. But the workers' patrols were very strict and did not allow them to enter the pits.[75]

To carry out its enlarged responsibility for combating scabs, the patrol team of the workers' club was expanded in both size and scope. In addition to guarding against strikebreakers, a major duty of the patrols was to conduct nightly inspections of the workers' dormitories to ensure that the idled workers remained indoors and refrained from gambling or other activities deemed corrosive of strike discipline. For the duration of the strike, by eight or nine o'clock at night the normally bustling streets of Anyuan were entirely empty except for the workers' patrols. Wearing red armbands, waving white flags, and armed with wooden staves and metal bars, the patrols also provided protection—and the threat of an iron fist—for Liu Shaoqi and Li Lisan during their negotiating sessions with the railway and mining company management. When word of an assassination plot aimed at Li Lisan reached the strikers (via Li's fellow Liling native, mine construction foreman Chen Shengfang), a special contingent of pickets was deployed as round-the-clock bodyguards. On more than one occasion, threats from the workers' club patrols to destroy company property if management were to reject the strike demands served to expedite the negotiation process.[76]

Despite the social tensions that the work stoppage inevitably generated, the strikers continued to stress the defensive motivations that underpinned their struggle. Halfway into the strike, the Anyuan workers' club, with Li Lisan's guidance, issued a second manifesto, addressed to "fathers and brothers in all social circles": "The life we have lived in the past is not the life of a human being; it is the life of a beast of burden or a slave. Working for a dozen hours a day, day after day in the depths of darkness, we suffer beatings and curses. We definitely do not want to continue this nonhuman sort of life. . . . Fathers and brothers! Twenty thousand of us workers are on the verge of death! Can you bear to watch death without offering assistance?"[77] The consistent demand for human dignity, presented as a plea for sympathy from fellow kinsmen, ultimately proved persuasive. After five days off the job, with no injuries or major property damage, the strikers won agreement to nearly all of their demands. This impressive outcome, at a time when the labor movement was being suppressed in other parts of China, contributed to the iconic status of the Anyuan strike in the annals of the Chinese Communist revolution. CCP labor organizer Deng Zhongxia wrote of Anyuan in his influential history of the Chinese labor movement, "The strike demonstrated the great enthusiasm and courage of the masses. After five days, the company caved in and accepted the workers' thirteen demands, the most important of which were the recognition of the authority of the workers' club to represent the workers and a wage increase. It was a complete victory."[78] Even a labor historian hostile to the Communist cause acknowledged the strike's importance: "The most notorious strike in the annals of the Chinese labor movement was the strike in the Anyuang [Anyuan] and Chuping [Zhuping] Railroad in September, involving an overwhelming body of 20,000 miners and 1,500 railway workers. . . . [T]he workers in Anyuang and Chuping started to organize themselves and built a clubhouse which was only another name for a union."[79]

Historians and activists alike attributed the Anyuan victory to the power of a united, militant workforce. But leadership was also a critical factor. As Mao Zedong had calculated, Li Lisan's penchant for creativity and Liu Shaoqi's tempering concern for control were a winning combination. Because of the threat of assassination, Li Lisan was forced to spend part of the strike period in hiding and to cede much of the day-to-day responsibility for negotiating to Liu Shaoqi. Li Lisan remained secretary of the Anyuan party committee as well as director of the workers' club, however, and it was he who crafted the strike manifestos, signed the final agreement on behalf of the workers, and presided over the jubilant victory celebration at the conclusion of the strike action.[80] Li's cultural positioning—a blend of old and new that augmented prevailing notions of invulnerability and master-disciple relations, for example, with novel

Figure 4. Celebrating the victory of the Anyuan Great Strike on September 18, 1922.

claims to overseas sources of power—contributed to a leadership style that was both appealing and effective. Liu's obsession with order was also instrumental in forestalling violence and winning widespread public support for the walkout.

As soon as the strike settlement was signed in the chamber of commerce offices, Li Lisan convened a massive outdoor celebration in the open field in the center of town. To thunderous applause, Li ascended a makeshift stage. When he began to speak, a hush fell over the assembled multitude, who hung on his every word: "The victory of this strike was entirely due to our singleness of purpose. I hope everyone will forever maintain this spirit."[81] Li concluded his remarks with a rousing cheer— "Once beasts of burden, now we will be men!"—a mantra that the crowd echoed with a deafening roar.[82] A jubilant march through the streets of Anyuan to the accompaniment of firecrackers was followed by the promulgation of a triumphant work resumption manifesto, drafted by Li Lisan: "The strike has been victorious! . . . In the past, workers were 'beasts of burden' but now it's 'Long Live the Workers!' . . . We have received the support of the garrison commander and the martial law command post as well as negotiators from among the gentry, merchant, and educational circles, allowing our demands to be entirely satisfied. We thank them profoundly. . . . This strike was the first time that the workers of Anyuan lifted up their heads, exposing the dark side of Anyuan. From today forward we are closely united, of one mind, in the struggle for our own rights. We now wish to declare 'Long Live the Workers!' 'Long Live the Workers' Club!'"[83]

More prosaically, in keeping with his controlled Leninist approach, Liu Shaoqi summed up the achievements of the strike this way: "The Great Strike lasted, altogether, five days. Discipline was extremely good and organization was very strict. The workers did a fine job of obeying orders. It cost the workers' club only a total of some 120 yuan in expenses; not a single person was injured and no property was damaged. Yet a complete victory was won. This truly was a unique event in the experience of the young Chinese labor movement."[84]

ELITE INVOLVEMENT

The Anyuan strike is portrayed in CCP legend as a shining example of pure proletarian prowess. The actual story was considerably more complicated. Intellectuals, local gentry, military officers, merchants, Red Gang dragon heads, and church clergy also contributed to its success. As we have seen, the strike of 1922 was launched and led by outside intellectuals; moreover, its nonviolent, swift, and generous settlement was enabled only by the sympathetic involvement of a wide array of local elites. At this stage in the Chinese revolution, Li Lisan would later recall, it was still possible to elicit the gentry's cooperation by a policy of "education for national salvation."[85] The ready acquiescence of the Pingxiang County magistrate to Li's pedagogical proposal had indeed set the stage for the entire mobilization effort. When the strike erupted, moreover, the head of the most powerful lineage in Pingxiang, Wen Zhongbo, was vocal in pressing for a swift settlement that would meet most of the workers' demands.[86] Wen's position was quite possibly a product of the longstanding resentment of the modern mining company on the part of the local gentry, but elite involvement was not limited to the gentry. Even "capitalists" seemed willing to betray their class status. As Li Lisan acknowledged, "The family members of mine director Li [Shouquan] all joined the workers' club at the time of the strike."[87]

A powerful element of the local elite whose sympathetic stance facilitated the peaceful resolution of the strike was the military. At the outset of the strike the mining company had persuaded the garrison commander of western Jiangxi, who received a generous monthly stipend from the mine, to declare martial law in Anyuan. However, the officer in charge of the martial law command post, Li Hongcheng, was so impressed by the effectiveness of the workers' club patrols—whose discipline was noticeably superior to that of his own motley crew of soldiers—that he ordered his troops not to interfere with the strike. The soldiers, having heard the pervasive rumors of Li Lisan's magical invulnerability, were happy to comply.[88] Liu Shaoqi expressed appreciation for the military's accommodation: "Brigadier Li understood that the workers were demanding an improvement in their livelihood, which could not be settled by military force. Over time he even became an active advocate of the strike, making a huge contribution."[89]

When the workers' club delivered its list of strike demands to the company management (with copies sent to the county magistrate as well as the garrison command), an addendum was attached: "If you wish to negotiate, please send formal representatives designated by the chamber of commerce to meet with Liu Shaoqi."[90] Initially, the company was represented in the strike negotiations by its newly appointed deputy director, Shu Xiutai, who hoped that his unbending stance would so ingratiate himself with the upper echelons of the Hanyeping Coal and Iron Company that he might be tapped to succeed Director Li Shouquan. But, after repeated importuning from the chamber of commerce and local gentry, Director Li himself helped broker a peaceful resolution.[91]

The head of the Anyuan chamber of commerce, Xie Lanfang (the same friend of Li Lisan's father who had delivered Li's initial petition to the county magistrate), played a major role in convincing the railway and mining company to accede to the strikers' demands.[92] Li Lisan explained, "The negotiations . . . were mediated by the chamber of commerce. . . . We had good relations with the chamber of commerce. I used a friend of my father's named Xie."[93] Xie Lanfang was hardly a disinterested arbiter; Anyuan workers and their families were the main customers for his many grocery stores dotted across western Jiangxi, and the businessman no doubt appreciated that a hike in workers' wages would bring him increased sales. In serving as intermediary between strikers and management, Xie was joined by craftsman, landlord, and capitalist Chen Shengfang, from Li Lisan's native county of Liling, who enjoyed close relations with the strike commander as well as with company management. At a crucial juncture, Chen Shengfang, who was hosting the negotiations at his Anyuan home, expedited the process by warning mine director Li Shouquan that unless the company were willing to accept the strikers' demands, Li Lisan would feel compelled to give in to the workers' desire for a violent resolution.[94] Even the rector of the St. James Episcopal Church, in his role as principal of the mining company's school, volunteered his services as mediator. Many of his parishioners were active in the strike, and the warden of his church vestry was a professional photographer who, at the invitation of the workers' club, shot the only surviving photos of the victory celebration following the strike.[95]

The Anyuan strike of 1922 stands as one of the major accomplishments of the early Chinese Communist Party. In less than a year's time, Li Lisan and his comrades had managed to mobilize a remarkably successful protest among a large, unruly, and initially mostly uneducated workforce. Although Anyuan proved exceptionally amenable to revolutionary initiatives (due to a combination of its rebellious heritage, concentrated living and working conditions, Hunan connections, cooperative local elite, and above all the brilliant organizing efforts of Li Lisan), the basic model that the Communists followed at Anyuan was standard operating procedure for the day.

The recipe was copied in part from Russian revolutionary experience, but it also displayed a distinctly Chinese flavor. The Communists took special advantage of the cultural capital that Confucianism bestowed upon educators to "teach revolution" to their worker-pupils. Sporting literati attire and spouting literary adages, cadres drew from a deep reservoir of both elite and popular respect for intellectuals to pioneer a highly successful nonviolent movement. Martial arts traditions and underworld Triad connections were crucial to the mobilization effort, but these "heterodox" ties were subsumed within a broader "orthodox" pedagogical strategy. Li Lisan's masterful mix of literary and military—*wen* and *wu*—authority was a winning combination that established his own leadership credentials within the all-male community of miners and railway workers while at the same time garnering support from a wide spectrum of the local elite.

Framing the strike as a plea for fundamental human dignity was a masterstroke conceived by Mao Zedong (who presented it in literary language) and executed by Li Lisan (who translated the concept colloquially into a stirring slogan that promised to make "men" out of former "beasts of burden"). As John Fitzgerald argues in his study of Chinese nationalism, a demand for dignity has been at the heart of twentieth-century Chinese political discourse, fueling the outrage that has erupted repeatedly in protests against international humiliation.[96] Similarly, Steve Smith's study of the Shanghai labor movement locates the nexus between working-class protest and nationalism in a new stress on human dignity that nevertheless echoed much older values: "The discursive link between national and [working-] class identities was forged, above all, around the issue of humane treatment. Workers' refusal to be treated 'like cattle and horses' derived from a new but powerfully felt sense of dignity, albeit one that resonated with traditional notions of 'face.'"[97] Presenting strike demands as a defensive cry for human dignity was a unifying strategy as reassuring to the local elite as it was appealing to aggrieved coal miners. The concerted efforts of various local power holders were critical to the swift and smooth resolution of the conflict.[98]

Mao's periodic interventions were vitally important, but they were fully in line with official party policy. Workers' schools, elite alliances, secret-society cooptation, and orderly strikes enforced by worker patrols were staple ingredients in CCP-sponsored labor agitation around the country during this period. In recognizing that the mobilization of the Anyuan workers required the complicity of power holders who had long wielded effective cultural control over the labor force, Mao and his comrades avoided the dismal failure that so frequently greets attempts by outside radicals to organize among coal miners. In the case of America's Appalachian Valley, for example, repeated efforts by committed activists to unionize the miners were frustrated by the powers that be. As John Gaventa explains, "Those who sought to alter the oppression of the miner—the northern liberal and the Marxist radical—failed partly because they did not understand fully the power situation they sought to change. . . . The radical sought to develop a revolutionary class consciousness, but he misunderstood the prior role of power in shaping the consciousness which he encountered. It was the local mountain elite, who knew best the uses of power for control within their culture, who effectively capitalized on the mistakes of the others."[99] The case of Anyuan presents a dramatic contrast to this familiar scenario. As cultural insiders, Mao Zedong, Li Lisan, and Liu Shaoqi were keenly aware of the need to engage and thereby neutralize the control of local power holders. Working within the existing power structure, and using familiar symbolic tropes to gain widespread support, the young Communists succeeded in mobilizing a spectacularly successful strike that opened the door to a new industrial order at Anyuan.

By all accounts, the Great Strike of 1922 resulted in notable gains for the workers of Anyuan. One participant remembered,

The victory of the strike greatly boosted the workers' confidence. My strongest memory is of the huge differences before and after the strike. The workers' livelihood improved markedly and the organizational work of the club was much expanded. Unlike before, the foremen and staff were no longer arrogant and didn't dare to beat or curse the workers at will. The workers gained some political rights and some economic rights. There was a general wage hike. Before the strike, my monthly wage was three dollars. After the strike, it was immediately increased to four and a half dollars. The food in the miners' cafeteria improved; we were no longer served moldy red rice and withered vegetables.[100]

The perceptible improvement in material conditions fostered a more self-assured mentality on the part of many workers, who themselves became active participants in creating a new revolutionary culture.

The changed climate was reflected in a narrative folksong, composed in the poetic style of the "spring gong" (*chunluo*), a rhymed doggerel verse chanted to the beat of a gong and traditionally popular in the Jiangxi-Hunan border area as a means of announcing the spring planting, which began to circulate among the workers of Anyuan soon after the victory of the 1922 strike. Although the three surviving versions of the song, all of which were transcribed in 1925 and all of which are hundreds of stanzas in length, differ slightly in substance and sequence, they concur in lavishing praise upon Li Lisan as the beloved leader of the strike who brought education and organization to the miners of Anyuan and whose innovative instruction convinced the workers to take action to ameliorate their lot. Brief mention is made in the song of both Liu Shaoqi and Zhu Shaolian, but the narrative makes clear that "Teacher Li" was regarded as the true hero of the Anyuan labor movement.[101] It is Li whose resolve does not falter in the face of threats from capitalists and militarists. It is Li whose metal badge of invulnerability, bestowed by the five foreign powers, frightens the garrison commander into submission. It is Li who tells Liu Shaoqi how best to offer assistance. Thanks to Li Lisan's energetic instigation and direction, the song explains, the workers won a significant political victory that dramatically elevated their social status as well as their economic livelihood. Above all, Li is credited with restoring a sense of dignity and self-esteem to the workers of Anyuan:

> Teacher Li, just twenty-four,
> From Liling County, right next door.
>
> Taught us miners how to read;
> Attended to our every need.

Called upon workers to unite;
Helped us strike for what was right.

Teacher urged workers, "Repeat after me:
Long live thy union and long live thee!"

Workers echoed, with joyful glee:
"Long live our club and long live we!"[102]

The popularity of this vernacular folksong, known variously as "Labor Record" *(Laogong Ji)* or "Strike Song" *(Bagong Ge)* and written and sung joyfully by groups of miners in the months and years following the strike of 1922, suggests that Li Lisan's skillful cultural positioning had progressed from an elite preoccupation to a process actively embraced and advanced by the workers themselves. Faith in their charismatic leader had instilled confidence in their own capacities.

The Communists' success at Anyuan in converting traditional sources of cultural power to new revolutionary purposes was not without parallel elsewhere in the country. At this same time, the rural organizer Peng Pai—addressed by the peasants of his native Haifeng as "Bodhisattva Peng"—was the center of a cult, "bordering on idolatry," that greatly facilitated his efforts to build a peasant union. As Peng later justified his approach to skeptical fellow cadres, "When we work in the villages, the first step is to gain the confidence of the peasants. . . . And you can't gain their trust if you attack their belief in gods. There are times when we must not only not insult their gods, but must even worship along with them. This doesn't mean that we capitulate to religious superstition, but only that some concessions are necessary to even begin to do our work."[103]

Popular as this flexible approach proved to be among workers and peasants alike, it was not easily sustained in the inhospitable political circumstances of the period. In a matter of months after the victorious Anyuan strike—on February 7, 1923, to be exact—the Communist movement would enter a new and much more difficult phase. Warlord Wu Peifu's bloody suppression that day of a strike by railway workers at Changxindian and other stations along the Jing-Han railroad signaled a major setback. All across the country Communist activists were rounded up and executed, and the workers' clubs and unions that they had established were unceremoniously shut down.

Anyuan, thanks to its relatively remote mountainous location and the forbearance of the local elite, was spared the devastation that befell other hotbeds of labor organizing at this time. Both the warlord who controlled Hunan Province, Zhao Hengti, and the head of the western Jiangxi military garrison, Yue Zhaolin, indicated that they did not oppose the socialism advocated by the Anyuan workers' club. Their real concern at the time was the Nationalist Party, not the Communists.[104] Moreover, the impressive educational efforts being carried out by the Anyuan workers' club were widely viewed as a source of social stability rather than a threat to the political order. Such tolerance on the part of local power holders afforded critical space within which the Communist experiment could grow. Alone among previous centers of labor mobilization, Anyuan in the years immediately following the February Seventh Massacre not only survived but thrived. The remarkable victory of the 1922 strike strengthened the hand of the Communists, who, under the direction of Liu Shaoqi, began to express openly their Marxist-Leninist allegiance and aspirations.

Unlike Li Lisan, Liu Shaoqi had been trained in the Soviet Union. When he succeeded Li as head of Communist activities at the coal mine, Liu did his best to put a clear Leninist stamp on operations. Under Liu Shaoqi's guidance, Anyuan would come to be known in progressive circles as "China's Little Moscow," a place where the Soviet Union was touted as a model of emulation for everything from political organization to architectural style. Despite the declared devotion to Russian ways, however, the Anyuan revolutionary tradition continued to reflect the imprint of indigenous patterns of mass mobilization. The workers' club, although impressively reconstructed by Liu Shaoqi in a fashion that he deemed reminiscent of the Bolshoi Theater in Moscow, would still serve as a classroom for popularizing new revolutionary messages by recourse to familiar cultural media.

# 3   China's Little Moscow

In the aftermath of the victorious 1922 strike, Anyuan shed its "Little Shanghai" moniker in favor of the new sobriquet of "China's Little Moscow." The notable successes of Li Lisan, Liu Shaoqi, and their comrades at Anyuan, together with the crushing defeats suffered by Communists elsewhere in China (epitomized by the February Seventh Massacre along the Jing-Han Railroad), turned the coal mining town into a prominent stronghold of Bolshevik-inspired labor organizing. For three years (September 1922 to August 1925) Anyuan served as the paramount center of the Chinese Communist labor movement. The special importance attached to Little Moscow was reflected in central party references to Anyuan as "the great fortress of the proletariat."[1] The first worker to join the Central Committee of the CCP, and one of only nine members of its Standing Committee in this period, was railway engineer Zhu Shaolian, Li Lisan's initial convert at Anyuan.[2] The coal mine exerted a magnetic pull on left-wing activists from around the country and abroad, with countless progressives making the pilgrimage to Anyuan to observe and absorb the lessons that it offered in revolutionary mobilization.[3]

As its new nickname made clear, Anyuan was now closely identified with the Russian revolutionary model. Many of the Communist activists at Little Moscow had received training in the USSR, and other party cadres who showed outstanding potential in the course of their assignment at the coal mine were rewarded with a ticket to the Soviet Union for further study. Liu Shaoqi, recently returned from Moscow himself, was especially eager to introduce the Soviet experience. And yet, over the course of three years as head of Anyuan operations, Liu would face frequent frustration in his efforts to achieve that aspiration.[4] Leninist discipline did not always sit well with Anyuan miners, and in later years

China's Little Moscow would be remembered less for its replication of Soviet patterns than for its contributions to a distinctively Chinese revolutionary tradition. The educational programs of the Anyuan workers' club, effected through an innovative course of drama, lectures, songs, films, and other cultural media (in addition to formal classroom instruction), constituted the core of this achievement.

## REORGANIZING AND REBUILDING THE WORKERS' CLUB

The favorable terms of the 1922 strike settlement—while enabled by the sympathetic intervention of local notables—permitted the Communists to attenuate their elite connections in favor of greater attention to building grassroots organizations at Anyuan and the surrounding region. Among the provisions of the strike settlement was a generous monthly subsidy (of 1,100 yuan) from the Pingxiang Railway and Mining Company to underwrite the operations of the workers' club. When this sizable sum was added to the initiation fees and monthly dues collected from the club's burgeoning membership, which now included virtually every worker at Anyuan, the result was an enviable balance sheet.[5] By the summer of 1923, the regular annual income of the workers' club (exclusive of donations earmarked for crisis relief) amounted to more than twenty thousand yuan.[6] This impressive revenue stream made the club an important source of financing, not only for activities at Anyuan but for the wider Communist effort as well. As the national party treasurer, Luo Zhanglong (Li Lisan's former classmate who had founded the railway workers' club at Changxindian), explained:

> After the Third Party Congress of 1923, I assumed the post of central treasurer, in charge of finances for all the party's activities. At that time, besides the periodic payments that we received from the Communist International, the main sources of support for party activities were the national railway union in the north and Anyuan in the south. After the victory of the strike at Anyuan, it accumulated substantial union funds. In addition to underwriting its own large-scale workers' consumer cooperative and educational activities for workers, it often provided crucial financial assistance to other places.[7]

To manage its enlarged coffers and responsibilities, the workers' club launched a fundamental reorganization soon after the 1922 strike. While retaining the neutral name of "club," the reconstituted labor union was actually a powerful economic, cultural, and political entity that in effect served as the ruling authority of Anyuan during the entire Little Moscow period. As Li Lisan later explained, "To call it an embryonic soviet would be appropriate. . . . The union actually did constitute a quasi-regime."[8] Conflicts and other pressing matters that previously had been mediated by the local elite were now brought before the workers' club for settlement. Ostensibly modeled on the workers' soviets of the Russian Revolution, the reorganized labor union drew upon a range of domestic exemplars as well.

The basic building blocks remained the "groups of ten" that had structured the Anyuan workers' club since its inception (see chapter 2), and which were now expanded into higher-order units. This decimal hierarchy replicated that of the Petrograd Soviet of 1917, which had also been organized into layered units of first ten, then one hundred, and finally one thousand factory workers.[9] But the configuration had substantial homegrown precedent as well. A similar arrangement provided the organizational backbone for such apparently disparate Chinese precursors as, on the one hand, the imperial *baojia* system (which, for purposes of mutual surveillance, grouped households into units of ten at the basic level, one hundred at the intermediate level, and one thousand at the tertiary level); and, on the other hand, the ranks of secret-society rebels during the Ping-Liu-Li Uprising of 1906 and student protesters in the May Fourth Movement of 1919, both of which (at least in principle) organized their followers into nested decimal groupings.[10] Administratively as well, the configuration of the Anyuan workers' club was consistent with indigenous practices. The club was initially managed by eight departments, whose division of labor was similar to that of the eight inner temples of a Red Gang lodge, with responsibilities for education, mutual aid, accounts, documents, general affairs, lectures, entertainment, and liaison.[11] Territorially reminiscent of the outer temples of a Red Gang lodge, the Anyuan workers' club set up affiliated branches in the surrounding towns and counties of western Jiangxi and eastern Hunan, including Zijiachong, Xiangdong, Liling, Zhuzhou, and so on.[12]

If the form of the reorganized workers' club was recognizable enough, its purpose was much less so. The Communist organizers broke sharply with Chinese tradition in importing from the Soviet (and Paris Commune) experience a commitment to proletarian governance. In the month after the strike, members of the Anyuan workers' club (now more than thirteen thousand strong) participated in the first of a series of direct elections to select their representatives. Each of the 1,382 ten-person units in the club elected one representative, known as a "ten representative" (*shi daibiao*); every hundred-person grouping (approximately 140 in all) elected one "hundred representative" (*bai daibiao*); and each workstation in the railway and mining company (forty-five total) elected its own "general representative" (*zong daibiao*). The assembly of general representatives, which met twice a month, constituted the highest deliberative body (equivalent to a supreme soviet), but its decisions required approval by the monthly assembly of hundred representatives, of which Li Lisan was chosen as the first general director. The ratified decisions were then communicated to the assembly of ten representatives, which gathered every three months.[13]

Annual elections, scheduled to take place in the summer shortly before the anniversary of the Great Strike, were conducted for all levels of representatives. The fourth and final round occurred in August 1925, just a few weeks prior to the demise of Little Moscow.[14] At various points during the existence of this electoral institution, reforms were proposed to strengthen the powers of the most basic level of representation, namely the ten representatives, on grounds that "aside from collecting the monthly fee, they are completely useless, merely listening to reports and wielding no actual power to speak of."[15] The proposals were never implemented, however, due to concerns among the top Communist leadership that an assemblage of more than a thousand untrained and undisciplined workers was not an appropriate forum for debating or deciding major issues.[16]

Liu Shaoqi's own Leninist predilections were made clear in a series of essays that he wrote on the topic of the Anyuan workers' club during his tenure there. As he put it in one such essay, "The organization of the labor union must be extremely tight and highly systematized, as in the military; only in this way can it accomplish its work mission."[17] Yet Liu went on to acknowledge that, despite his strong preference for "democratic centralism," in fact the Anyuan workers' club fell far short of this standard: "Although the organization of the club was originally based for the most part on the precedent of Soviet Russia, due to the restrictions imposed by actual difficulties, there have had to be compromises and adaptations on many levels. Thus while the club organization is at present relatively advanced, tight, and systematic when compared to all other unions in China, nevertheless it is still quite immature, loose, and unsystematic when contrasted with the motherland of the proletariat—Soviet Russia!"[18] Anxious as Liu was to follow a Russian blueprint, indigenous realities made fulfilling such an ambition elusive. As Mao Zedong had warned Li Lisan when Mao first identified the Anyuan coal mine as a promising site for revolutionary mobilization, local complexities would demand patience and flexibility on the part of a would-be organizer.

One of the concessions to local custom that even Liu Shaoqi seemed willing to condone was that of favoritism toward fellow provincials. Although condemned in official party directives as an outmoded expression of "feudalism," native-place ties played a key role in the Communist mobilization effort, at Anyuan as elsewhere.[19] Among the thirty top leaders of Liu's reorganized workers' club, twenty-five hailed from eastern Hunan—where Mao Zedong, Li Lisan, and Liu Shaoqi all had grown up—and five came from the neighboring province of Hubei. Not one was a local Jiangxi native.[20] This pattern of leadership, recruited on the basis of native-place connections, persisted throughout the duration of Little Moscow and contributed to resentment on the part of locals. Although the majority of Anyuan workers were from Hunan, a substantial minority had been recruited from surrounding villages. The Pingxiang locals, who at this time accounted for some 30 to 40 percent of the total Anyuan labor force, surely noticed their exclusion from the leadership of the Communists' workers' club. That there was a certain degree of tension between insiders and outsiders was indicated by the frequent melees that pitted Pingxiang workers against those from Hunan. After resolving one such brawl in the spring of 1923, Liu Shaoqi vowed to tighten the workers' club organization and strengthen its educational mission in order "to overcome native-place factionalism."[21]

The Anyuan workers' club may not have fully satisfied Liu Shaoqi's Leninist aspirations, but its handsome revenues supported a remarkable array of activities nonetheless. Convinced that these ever-expanding programs called for grander accommodations, Liu proposed that each worker contribute seven and a half days' pay (deducted from the half month's annual bonus that the workers had gained as part of the strike settlement) to construct new quarters for the workers' club.[22] This compulsory "donation" provided a tidy sum of thirty thousand yuan that constituted the core funding for an ambitious construction project. Work began in the fall of 1923 and was completed—thanks to volunteer labor from club members during their off-work hours—in time for a gala inauguration ceremony on May Day of the following year.[23] The result was an imposing new four-story building that was seventeen meters in height.

The architectural design for the renovated workers' club, like the club's organization and operations, reflected a blend of Russian and Chinese inspiration. The main hall (which could seat eight hundred people on the ground floor and an additional five hundred fifty people in each of

Figure 5. Contemporary view of the Anyuan workers' club, with a statue of Liu Shaoqi on the right. Photo by the author.

three balconies) was modeled on the Bolshoi Theater in Moscow, but the curled roof was unmistakably Chinese. The interior decor made clear the Marxist-Leninist philosophy of the Anyuan workers' club. A large plaque above the stage proclaimed, "Workers of the World, Unite!" Directly across from the stage loomed gigantic portraits of Marx and Lenin. The side walls were festooned with banners containing traditional-style couplets written in bold black Chinese characters on red cloth with progressive slogans such as, "The spirit of unity and class consciousness are labor's security and mankind's salvation." Besides serving the functions of a conventional labor union, the club's splendid facilities allowed for public performances of revolutionary dramas, films, art shows, and lectures. Offices in the complex provided space for the staff and patrol team as well as rooms where members could enjoy recreational activities or convene small meetings.[24]

The renovated workers' club replaced the St. James Episcopal Church as the largest public building at Anyuan. Indeed, its size and grandeur were suggestive of the club's intention to serve as the new spiritual center of Little Moscow. When the refurbished club opened in the spring of 1924, Anyuan witnessed an exponential increase in both Youth League and party membership. By December 1924, the Communist Party branch at Anyuan numbered approximately two hundred members, up 350 percent from six months earlier, making it both the largest and also the most proletarian of any CCP branch in China. The Anyuan branch in fact accounted for more than one-fifth of all the Communists in the country (who at this time totaled fewer than a thousand). Youth League membership at Anyuan stood at 245 by the end of 1924. Although this figure represented only 10 percent of national membership, the Anyuan Youth League was nevertheless—like its party counterpart—both the largest and the most proletarian of any local branch in the country.[25]

Impressive as these developments were, they did not necessarily bespeak a qualitative break with the previous mentality of Anyuan workers. Cultural positioning that relied upon familiar rhetoric and rituals to ease the transition to a new collective identity could come at the expense of full comprehension by participants. Among workers whose earlier experience with outside organizers had been limited to Elder Brother chieftains and Episcopal clergymen, Communist practices, from the swearing of loyalty oaths to the display of sacred symbols, were often mistaken for those of their competitors. Even the act of joining the Communist Party could be confusing for an inductee. A worker who had previously studied martial arts under five masters and was widely respected for his fighting skills recalled,

> Li Lisan and Liu Shaoqi introduced me into the party. There were nine other workers who joined when I did, all from either the coal-washing department or the coking department. When we swore an oath in front of the coal-washing stand, I saw the party emblem and mistook it for a cross. I was very unhappy. They asked what the matter was and I said this must be a Christian organization. They patiently explained that this was actually a party emblem made out of a hammer and sickle because the Communist Party represented the interests of peasants and workers.[26]

Much of Li Lisan's and Liu Shaoqi's attention during their years at Anyuan would be devoted to adapting previous practices to new ends, while at the same time they tried to clarify the distinction between their own revolutionary message and those of the more familiar missionaries (whether of Triad or Christian persuasion) who had preceded them. The confusion of new converts was understandable. After all, the Soviet model from which the Chinese Communists drew inspiration had in turn been heavily influenced by Russian Orthodox iconography.[27]

## REVOLUTIONARY LEADERSHIP

Although Li Lisan left Anyuan a few months after the strike victory to share the successful techniques he had pioneered there with labor activists in the major industrial centers of Wuhan and Shanghai, Liu Shaoqi remained at the coal mine for nearly three more years as director of the workers' club. (Li's other position, as secretary of the Communist Party branch at Anyuan, was inherited by his first convert among the workers, Zhu Shaolian.) Thanks to the immense popularity that the outgoing Li Lisan enjoyed among the workers, it proved hard for the uptight Liu Shaoqi, with his constant calls for discipline and restraint, to fill the vacuum created by the departure of his charismatic predecessor. These two revolutionary pioneers, although equally committed to the goal of mobilizing a radical labor movement, approached their common leadership task quite differently. Han Wei, an Anyuan miner who later became a lieutenant general in the People's Liberation Army (PLA), remembered Li Lisan's extraordinary appeal among the workers:

> The workers fervently insisted: Director Li enjoys the protection of the five foreign countries; he is invulnerable to swords and spears. This was because he had returned from studying abroad and usually wore a long gown with a metal badge on his chest that made him look awesome. The rumor that he was invulnerable to weapons expressed the workers' love and esteem toward their own leader and their belittling of the reactionary powers. Because of the tight unity of the more than ten thousand workers, and their obedience to his command, the mining company could do nothing and had to agree to negotiate with the workers' club.[28]

In contrast to the freewheeling Li Lisan, who was bold in making use of folk religion and martial arts traditions and brazen in brokering deals with secret-society chieftains, Liu Shaoqi practiced a more controlled—and less popular—mode of cultural positioning. Committed to Leninist discipline, Liu longed to replace the "immature, loose, and unsystematic" tendencies of Chinese workers with what he regarded as a superior Soviet organizational form.

The difficulties Liu Shaoqi faced in following in Li Lisan's footsteps stemmed more from differences in temperament and style than from any fundamental philosophical disagreement. Li Lisan's charm and imagination had endeared him to the miners. By contrast, Liu Shaoqi was "a compulsive character," with an annoying proclivity for "red tape rather than creative achievement."[29] Zhang Guotao, who had been Liu's class-mate during his studies in Moscow, recalled how the young Liu Shaoqi differed from his peers: "In 1922, the Communists were passionate and full of verve; but he [Liu Shaoqi] seldom displayed any excitement. . . . Some people . . . found him a bit too glum and devoid of youthfulness."[30] Another former classmate remembered that Liu's performance during his Moscow days in the role of a worker in a student-scripted drama about a strike at a Chinese factory came off as "rather wooden" despite his "seriousness of purpose."[31]

Having been captivated by Li Lisan's charisma, the workers of Anyuan were dispirited by his departure and loath to transfer their allegiance to a new authority, especially someone as emotionally distant as Liu Shaoqi. Painfully aware of his own unpopularity, Liu turned to Li for help in persuading the workers to accept his leadership. In response, a few months after Li Lisan had left the coal mining town he wrote an open letter to the workers of Anyuan, urging them to put their faith in socialism rather than in his own person. Li explained the importance of his new assignment in Wuhan and emphasized that he would "definitely" not be returning to Anyuan in the future. He concluded, "I am someone who believes in socialism. Socialism is workerism. Those who are now in charge of the workers' club all believe in socialism and strive for the unity and interests of the proletariat. Workers need only to recognize social-ism; they need not recognize any single individual."[32] Shortly thereafter, Liu Shaoqi followed up with a speech to the coal miners that conveyed a similar message: "Only because we all believe in socialism—workerism— did we come to Anyuan to help everyone out. . . . It is very dangerous for workers to put their trust in a single individual because one person can-not protect everyone for decades or centuries. . . . You can't rely forever on a single individual. I hope you workers will believe in socialism, believe in your own organization."[33]

The workers' reluctance to shift their loyalty to a new leader or orga-nization was not only a product of Liu Shaoqi's bland personality. It was also symptomatic of a pervasive clientelist culture (reflected in the prac-tice of labor contracting as well as in secret-society networks) in which primary devotion was owed to individual patrons rather than to abstract ideas or institutions. As the founder of the workers' club, Li Lisan enjoyed a special claim on its members' allegiance. But Li's continuing hold over the workers was due to more than his head start over Liu Shaoqi as a labor organizer. The workers' unwillingness to attenuate their attach-ment to him attested also to Li's appealing mode of labor mobilization, which had so ingeniously harnessed a wide range of cultural codes and customs in the construction of new political identities.

By contrast, Liu Shaoqi was a conventional Leninist in both temperament and leadership style. Politically correct to a fault, he exemplified his overriding commitment to the workers' club and its socialist principles though both his personal and professional life. But such disciplined dedication was sometimes misinterpreted by the workers, to whom Liu's stoic devotion to the Anyuan workers' club and its revolutionary cause could appear unfeeling and alienating. Once the new club building was erected, Liu moved out of the place where he had been living since his arrival at the coal mine to take up residence in the club itself.[34] Soon thereafter Liu's own wedding was also held at the workers' club, a further indication of his personal identification with the organization. Yet rather than seal his camaraderie with the community, Liu's frugal wedding ceremony ended up having precisely the opposite effect. When Liu Shaoqi married He Baozhen, a fellow Hunanese and the first woman to teach in the Communist schools at Anyuan, his insistence on dispensing with the lavish banquet, bridal sedan chair, and other costly trappings of a traditional ceremony in favor of a bare-bones "civilized wedding" (*wenming hunli*) provoked grumbling from disappointed members of the workers' club who had been looking forward to the occasion as an excuse for a more festive celebration.[35]

Liu Shaoqi made no secret of the fact that his goal at Anyuan was to promote socialism among the workers. In September 1923, in a widely circulated essay entitled "On Past Problems and Future Plans for the Club," he advertised his ideological vision for the Anyuan workers' club with the opening sentence: "We embrace and affirm socialist thought."[36] That same month, to commemorate the first anniversary of the Great Strike, the workers' club distributed a handbill that elaborated on this theme. The cover of the handbill featured the new logo of the Anyuan workers' club, a crossed sledgehammer and pickax superimposed upon a train wheel, which was intended to symbolize the unity of the miners and railway workers.[37] The contents of the handbill spelled out Liu's understanding of socialism:

> What is socialism? Socialism is an ideology that protects the interests
> of the entire working class, urging workers to unite to attack war-
> lords and capitalists, to strike down the bourgeoisie and implement
> a proletarian dictatorship so that all the productive relations in the
> world—land, factories, railroads, steamships, mines, etc.—are then
> taken over by the proletariat as public property and a proletarian state

is established that implements a law according to which "no one who doesn't work may eat." This will make the entire world a place where equal and free workers produce and consume for themselves. This is called socialism. This is the true aim and ultimate victory for us workers. . . . Workers must believe in socialism and must strive and struggle for socialism.[38]

To underscore the egalitarianism of his socialist ideals, Liu insisted—on the model of the Paris Commune—that all cadres, himself included, adhere to an abstemious regimen. One of his contemporaries later recalled the material sacrifices that this entailed:

> We comrades who worked at the Anyuan workers' club, according to the organizational principles of the Paris Commune, limited our monthly wage to that of an average worker, about five yuan. After paying for food, there wasn't much left over. At that time we were all very clear that we were really working for the liberation of the working class and no one was concerned about compensation or lifestyle. Comrade Shaoqi's wife, He Baozhen, was also at Anyuan at that time. She had just given birth, and she and Shaoqi lived in an upstairs room in the workers' club. They also led a very frugal existence.[39]

This recollection exaggerated somewhat the voluntary poverty of the Communists. Most memoirs say that Liu and his fellow cadres allowed themselves fifteen yuan per month, equivalent to the wage of a skilled worker rather than an ordinary miner, and the account books of the workers' club bear out this more generous figure.[40] Liu Shaoqi's sizable medical expenses were also covered by the workers' club (as was a partial repayment for Li Lisan's loan, more than a year after he had left Anyuan).[41] Even so, the basic point is correct. At Liu Shaoqi's insistence, the leaders of the workers' club—who for the most part came from comfortable family backgrounds—lived in humble circumstances intended to demonstrate their identity and solidarity with the working class.

Liu's painstaking efforts to reduce the economic distance between the leaders and the led sometimes backfired, however. More attuned to the carefree manner of the colorful Li Lisan than the dour demeanor of his successor, the workers initially suspected Liu of harboring ulterior motives behind his drab display of frugality. Liu later recalled,

> After the strike victory, the workers elected me as general director of the club and wanted to pay me two hundred silver dollars a month. At that time I was content to get by on only fifteen dollars in living expenses, causing a debate among the workers. Some said I sought neither fame nor fortune and wondered whether my lack

of ambition was because I wasn't getting paid enough. They wanted to give me a raise of one hundred dollars. When I still declined, the workers suspected me of some hidden motive. I had to convene a meeting of activists both inside and outside the party to give them a clear explanation that we were carrying out a revolution for the sake of liberating all of China, constructing socialism, implementing Communism.[42]

In part because of his austere style, Liu Shaoqi found himself waging a constant battle against the predilections and objections of the workers. In one frank self-criticism, Liu admitted that his inherent aversion to interacting closely with the workers had provoked their "misunderstanding."[43] Unlike the genial Li Lisan, for whom connecting with the workers was both easy and gratifying, Liu Shaoqi's reserved personality posed a barrier to his activist aspirations.

Despite stark differences in aptitude and approach between these two Anyuan pioneers, Liu continued Li Lisan's stress on workers' education as the core element of their socialist experiment. Periodic calls to "strike down the bourgeoisie" and "implement a proletarian dictatorship" notwithstanding, Liu's actual mobilizing strategy remained firmly fixed on classroom study rather than on class struggle.

## REVOLUTIONARY EDUCATION

The extraordinary educational efforts sponsored by the workers' club during the years when Anyuan served as China's Little Moscow attracted both national and international notice. The American journalist Nym Wales, who later interviewed a number of former Anyuan workers in Yan'an, observed in her general history of the Chinese labor movement, "The most active center was the An-yuang [Anyuan] Mines, on the Hunan-Kiangsi [Jiangxi] border, where 20,000 miners had won a big strike in 1922. Here the organization of the workers was very strong. Schools were founded, even for the miners' children, and educational work at the mines was carried on all during the 1923–1925 period."[44]

In early 1923, two additional workers' schools were opened at Anyuan. That year, more than three hundred workers and nearly five hundred of their children were enrolled at the three schools. Children's enrollment varied considerably according to their parents' work. Although railway workers (who were mostly mechanics and white-collar workers) were a mere 8 percent of the Anyuan labor force, their children comprised 14 percent of the enrollees. The mine workers who labored aboveground (primarily as mechanics) made up only 32 percent of the workforce, yet their children comprised 50 percent of the enrollees. The least fortunate of the Anyuan workers, the coal miners who labored underground in the pits, constituted fully 60 percent of the company's workforce, but their children comprised only 36 percent of the students. It is possible that the apparent imbalance, rather than indicating differential access among the children of different types of workers, simply reflected the higher percentage of bachelors among unskilled miners. In any event, there was also a noticeable gender imbalance; nearly 70 percent of the schoolchildren were boys.[45]

In November 1924 the standing committee of the Communist Youth League dispatched a special emissary to Anyuan to investigate the education situation. An important result of this visit was a report intended to serve as a road map for revolutionary organizers in other parts of China. The report summarized the four goals of the Anyuan pedagogical effort as literacy, general knowledge, class consciousness, and struggle capacity; class consciousness was highlighted as "the lifeline of our education."[46] Although the primary goal of adult education was to inculcate some grasp of Marxism-Leninism, the Anyuan curriculum also stressed basic reading skills. Entry-level students were expected to master one thousand characters; intermediate students learned an additional one thousand characters; and the advanced students were required to learn enough characters to be able to write simple essays.[47] By the end of 1924, the workers' club reported that three-fourths of the Anyuan workforce had attained rudimentary literacy. Not satisfied that a quarter of the workers were still illiterate, however, the workers' club vowed to make education more accessible by opening additional schools and reading rooms located closer to the miners' workstations and living quarters.[48]

By 1925, the number of schools operating under the aegis of the Anyuan workers' club had increased to seven, with an enrollment of some fifteen hundred workers and two thousand children. Two hours of classes for workers were offered every night except on Sundays at all seven schools. Both the textbooks and the in-class instruction at these nighttime classes were designed to deliver a strong dose of Marxist-Leninist ideas. Public speaking was another critical area of attention, with workers required to give extemporaneous speeches each week on such topics as the evils of private property and the class system, how the proletariat should throw off oppression and seize political power, and the like. In the children's classes, emphasis was placed upon cultivating a sense of public civility and responsibility in addition to the instruction in basic reading and arithmetic skills. No examinations were given in order to avoid generating competition among the youngsters.[49]

The seven schools were augmented by thirteen reading rooms, all of which provided literacy classes, and a library.[50] To involve the women of Anyuan, vocational sewing classes were introduced in all of the schools.[51] The seamstresses produced both Chinese- and Western-style clothing that they then sold through the consumers' cooperative.[52] The sewing classes were part of a larger effort to mobilize the female population for participation in an Anyuan branch of the Women's Federation, which at its height claimed more than a hundred members.[53] Although most residents clearly welcomed the opportunities afforded by this educational expansion, the young coal miners who performed the backbreaking work of digging and hauling were less interested in attending class, often preferring to while away their limited leisure hours gambling or engaging in other unsavory activities.[54] In the case of workers who refused to study voluntarily, Liu Shaoqi—following Leninist prescriptions—directed the workers' club patrols to use force to compel class attendance.[55]

These pedagogical developments, even if occasionally imposed upon recalcitrant recipients, resonated with a general thirst for education in rural China. Moreover, the impact on those who benefited from the experience was often profound. A worker from an impoverished peasant family in a nearby village who began to work at the mine's furnace room in 1924 as a nine-year-old child laborer recalled his excitement at the educational opportunity provided by the Anyuan workers' club:

> At that time the club called on the workers to study at night school in order to gain a revolutionary education. I was overjoyed by that. Although I worked all day and was tired at night, it was important that I gain some cultural knowledge as well as a revolutionary education. . . . One didn't have to undergo any kind of procedures to study at the night school. The teacher just asked my name, which workshop I worked in, and where I lived—and then issued me a textbook. . . . We studied every night for two hours, from seven to nine. The conditions were not good—the light was dim—but everyone was very diligent and seldom did anyone skip class. I studied for three years at the night school, and I could recognize some characters and came to understand some revolutionary principles. I was very happy and very enthusiastic.[56]

As primitive as the school facilities were, they still cost money to operate. Since the workers' club was committed to providing free education for all workers, it was responsible for covering the costs. As a result, the lion's share of the club's monthly expenses (which averaged 1,500 yuan in total) went to support these educational activities. Over 950 yuan per month (equivalent to two-thirds of the club's total expenditures) was designated for this purpose, spent on salaries and livelihood subsidies (450 yuan and 205 yuan, respectively) for the thirty teachers; on wages (55 yuan) for the eleven workers employed at the seven schools; and on basic operating expenses and supplies (200 yuan on rent for classrooms, kerosene for lamps, teaching materials, notebooks, postage, etc.).[57]

The rapidly expanding pedagogical effort required a steady supply of new teachers. To meet the need, a teachers' training class, with forty students, was inaugurated. Because the initial enrollees were all from student backgrounds, and had little if any firsthand knowledge of working-class problems, the club also decided to open a special four-month teacher training class for thirty handpicked workers who demonstrated high aptitude. Those selected were offered small monetary incentives to enroll and were promised teaching jobs at worker schools in the area upon successfully completing the program.

To satisfy the curricular demands of this impressive educational outreach, the Anyuan workers' club began to publish its own textbooks for the use of workers and their children. In 1924 the club edited a textbook series for elementary school students called *Elementary Chinese Primer (Xiaoxue guoyu jiaokeshu)*. The lessons introduced basic Marxist-Leninist concepts in readings that covered everything from poetry and philosophy to natural science. The textbooks also made clear the cultural values that the Communists believed were essential for nurturing a new revolutionary generation. Equality of the sexes was emphasized; the woman warrior of Chinese legend, Mulan, was prominently featured, for example. Significantly, the traditional Confucian privileging of the literary *(wen)* above the military *(wu)* was reiterated and reinforced: "The weapon of the warrior *[wuren]* is the gun; the weapon of the scholar *[wenren]* is the pen. Guns can kill people, but their range is very limited. . . . Pens can strike people's hearts, stimulate their potential, and strengthen their character! . . . The written word has no spatial limits. The gun is always ruled by the pen; the pen is never ruled by the gun."[58] Many of the graduates of the Anyuan elementary school curriculum went on to play important roles in the Chinese revolution. The celebrated worker-writer Wu Yunduo, known as "China's Pavel Korchagin," was among them.[59]

For the workers themselves, two new lines of textbooks—both designed to combine rudimentary reading skills with Marxist-Leninist ideology—were published in 1925. The more basic of the two, known as the *Workers'*

*Reader (Gongren duben)*, was comprised of three volumes, each of which progressed from simpler to more complex characters and concepts. The first volume began, "Living in this world, everyone must study, everyone must work. Without studying, one is a know-nothing. Without working, one is a good-for-nothing." The opening lessons repeatedly stressed the dignity and value of labor: "Workers and peasants are the most honorable; without workers and peasants there would be no world." Within a few lessons, however, the message advanced to the question of class exploitation: "Capitalists don't work, yet they dress well and eat well. From where does their food and clothing come? It comes from the blood and sweat of the workers." A few lessons later, class struggle was introduced: "Marx called for proletarian revolution to overthrow capitalist class society. Lenin carried out proletarian revolution and established a worker-peasant government." The reader offered elementary instruction in Chinese history and geography and inveighed against the wastefulness of popular religion and the evils of imperialism. Again and again it returned to its main theme: only a workers' revolution could save China from the twin scourges of capitalism and imperialism.[60]

The second series, entitled *Textbook for the Workers' School of the Anyuan Railway and Mine Workers' Club (Anyuan lukuang gongren julebu gongren buxi xuexiao buxi jiaokeshu)*, consisted of four volumes, each with twenty-five lessons. Although the first volume concentrated on vocabulary and basic knowledge, it did not shy away from blunt political messages. Midway through this volume, in lesson nineteen, workers were informed about why revolution was necessary: "Revolution is 'blood-letting terrorism.' When people hear the word 'revolution,' they are usually afraid. So why do we advocate revolution? It is because the suffering of mankind can only be relieved through revolution. As Marx said in 1848, 'There is only one way to reduce suffering, and that is by the terrorism of revolution.'"[61] The second volume provided a history of the international labor movement, centering on the Russian Revolution. The third volume offered an overview of China's contemporary economic and political situation, again stressing the importance of proletarian revolution. The fourth volume focused on Marxism and the state of the Communist Party in various countries around the world. The terms used to characterize Marx, "founding priest" (*kaishanzu*), and Lenin, "seer" (*xianshi*), derived from familiar religious and secret-society parlance, but the objective was clearly to instill a new revolutionary Marxist-Leninist ideology.

In addition to promoting literacy and raising revolutionary consciousness, workers' education had the more pragmatic goal of identifying and cultivating Socialist Youth League and Communist Party members. Teachers regularly reported to the workers' club on the study habits and "demeanor" (*biaoxian*) of their students, the more promising of whom would then be tapped for recruitment to league and party membership.[62] The notion of *biaoxian*, which would loom large in the assessment and treatment of both students and workers in the People's Republic of China, had no obvious Soviet equivalent and was evidently reflective of a deep-seated Confucian belief in the behavioral manifestation of virtue.[63] But Liu Shaoqi also put to good use the lessons he had learned in the Soviet Union about training party operatives. Prospective Communist Party and Youth League cadres from around the country were sent to Anyuan for instruction before being assigned to posts elsewhere.[64] The CCP's first regional party school was opened at Anyuan, with Liu Shaoqi as its founding principal. The curriculum included an introduction to the principles of political economy, the history of the Russian Communist Party, and the international youth movement. A major theme in the teaching materials at the party school was the proper relationship between the labor movement and the nationalist movement; cadres were urged to ensure that the labor movement provided proper leadership so that the nationalist movement would be amply "revolutionized." Outstanding graduates from the Anyuan party school were rewarded with a ticket to the Soviet Union for further education.[65]

## CULTURAL MOBILIZATION

In addition to formal classes, the workers' club organized a large number of other educational and quasi-educational activities designed to disseminate revolutionary ideas among the populace. The education department of the Anyuan workers' club functioned like a proto–propaganda department, with overall responsibility for coordinating the various formal and informal pedagogical programs. Although it would be another twenty-five years before they controlled a national state, the Chinese Communists were already gaining valuable experience in the construction of a political culture that, although strongly influenced by Soviet precedents, would come to seem very much their own.

Newspaper reading boards were placed in all the schools and at all work sites so that newly literate workers could easily keep abreast of current events. The latest editions of leftist publications such as *Worker Weekly (Gongren zhoukan)* and *Labor Weekly (Laogong zhoubao)* were posted at these venues. The consumers' cooperative also sold these and other progressive publications, including *Guide (Xiangdao), New Youth (Xin qingnian), Vanguard (Xianfeng),* and the like.[66] For the further edification of the workers, the club operated both a regular and a special lecture series. Locals (workers as well as teachers) were responsible for giving the regular lectures, whereas the special lectures were delivered by visiting notables. The talks were coordinated by a lecture department whose official mission was to "directly instruct the workers . . . so that they grasp the meaning of every program and initiative of the club; and rectify the mistaken thinking of the workers so that they follow the correct road."[67] As was standard Soviet practice at the time, statistics were compiled on popular participation in party-sponsored "agitprop."[68] From August 1923 to July 1924, the lecture department reported having convened 129 regular lectures attended by more than ten thousand people.[69] The titles of these talks—"What Is the National Revolution?" "What Is Class?" "What Is a Union?" "What Is the Communist Party?" and so on— make clear the lessons that the Anyuan workers' club sought to convey.[70]

Ideologically orthodox articles and lectures, however, were not always the best way to capture the workers' attention, especially when it came to the younger workers, who comprised a large percentage of the unskilled labor force at the coal mine. Much of the energy of the Anyuan workers' club was thus directed toward inventing livelier forms of cultural communication. The head of the entertainment department from 1924 to 1925 explained,

> During the year I worked at Anyuan, the main focus was propaganda work targeted at younger workers. We often organized younger workers in the workers' club through singing, dramatic performances, cultural studies, and various recreational activities. We instilled revolutionary thinking so as to unite the young workers under the party to become the backbone force of the labor movement. At that time the renovated Anyuan workers' club had just been opened, and every week we held evening gatherings and staged plays there. Our plays had no set scripts but were self-written and self-performed. . . . The content included opposing the exploitation of workers by capitalists, overcoming imperialism, and defeating warlordism. . . . These plays drew large audiences, not only workers but also peasants from the surrounding areas. The propaganda effects were very good.[71]

A child worker who witnessed these performances at the age of ten remembered them vividly many decades later:

> The entertainment department [of the Anyuan workers' club] organized the young people to produce and perform "civilized plays" [wen-

*ming xi]*. Whenever these were staged, the main hall of the club was packed. Gas lamps were lit. Many of the plays reflected the laboring life of the workers in the mine pits. I remember one night watching a new play inside the club about the terrible treatment of workers under the leather whips of the capitalists. It also showed how the Bearded Marx had engaged in revolutionary activity, and how the Russian working class had taken up arms to struggle against the capitalists. The plot of this drama deeply moved us all. I admired the working class for its fearless spirit of struggle. It gave us a Marxist education and the hope that one day we too would be able to take up guns and struggle against the capitalists of the mine.[72]

More creatively still, the workers' club oversaw the writing and staging of thirty-one "costume lectures" *(huazhuang jiangyan)*, a hybrid form of didactic entertainment that was part drama and part lecture. With moralistic titles such as "The Road to Awakening," "The Evils of Prostitution and Gambling," "The Patriotic Bandit," and "Our Victory," the costume lectures were presented in evening performances in the worker's club auditorium to enthusiastic audiences numbering a thousand or more.[73] As one worker recalled, "At that time the Anyuan labor movement was developing quite dramatically. It operated many workers' schools. I studied in the Number Three School and participated in the costume lecture team organized at the school, with twenty-three members. We performed "The Evils of Prostitution and Gambling," aimed at eliminating these vices. We also staged some dramas intended to unite the workers and peasants. I played a comic role—the American devil. The costume lecture teams performed not only at Anyuan, but also in Zhuzhou, Liling, and other places."[74]

The forms of cultural mobilization developed by the Anyuan workers' club were heavily influenced by those developed in the Soviet Union, where labor unions also sought to rouse "the unorganized part of the population with worker-activists, traveling theatrical groups, and lecturers."[75] But the immense popularity that local opera had long enjoyed among Chinese villagers rendered the "costume lectures"—which appear to have been a Chinese Communist adaptation of the original Soviet model—particularly appealing. A former Anyuan worker recalled of these "costume lectures,"

In order to gain the sympathy and support of the peasants for the labor movement, the head of the workers' club's recreation and arts department every Sunday led us to nearby villages to perform. Whenever we arrived someplace, the band members would beat drums and play trumpets and flutes to attract a crowd. Then we would perform a program after which there would be a lecture on how the capitalists exploited the workers and how the landlords exploited the peasants, how we should strike down imperialism and militarism, and so on. It was warmly welcomed by the peasants.[76]

The traveling costume lectures, like local operas in rural China, were performed in the open spaces in front of temples where religious festivals and market fairs were customarily held.

On major holidays and anniversaries to mark milestones in the history of both the international and the Chinese labor movements (e.g., Labor Day, the birthdays of Marx and Lenin, the anniversaries of the founding of the Paris Commune, the death of Rosa Luxemburg, the Anyuan strike, the Jing-Han Railway massacre, and so on), large-scale demonstrations were organized for the entire workforce. Political posters were plastered on the walls of public buildings, marches were held, street lectures were staged, and thousands of handbills were distributed. A high point of this collective action came with "Propaganda Week" in May of 1925. During ten days of frenetic activity, the workers' club organized five major demonstrations—to honor Labor Day on May 1, the sixth anniversary of the May Fourth Movement on May 4, the 107th birthday of Karl Marx on May 5, and the national humiliation days of May 7 and 9. The Labor Day demonstration alone drew more than fifteen thousand marchers to its ranks.[77]

Music was an important part of these events, with bands and choral groups organized by the workers' club and workers' schools adding a festive note. The singing of "The Internationale" was a staple feature at parades and demonstrations.[78] The workers' club also had its own theme song, with lyrics written by Li Lisan as part of his effort to foster pride and confidence among the membership.[79] A worker recalled, "Soon after I started working at Anyuan I joined the workers' club. I distinctly remember my first club activity: learning to sing the club song (known as 'The Laborers' Song'). It began, 'The world was created by us laborers. We laborers are the oppressed and the exploited. We have created the world and we can eliminate oppression.'"[80]

Large-scale protests were certainly not unprecedented in Chinese history,[81] but the recurring public celebration of anniversaries associated with revolutionary milestones that punctuated life at Anyuan during this period was clearly modeled on Soviet practice. In the case of the Soviet Union, Peter Kenez argues that the commemorations were part of a deliberate effort on the part of the Bolsheviks to construct a new civil religion that would replace the church calendar. A centerpiece of the emerging Soviet religion was "the ever-increasing Lenin cult."[82] In China's Little Moscow, by contrast, veneration was directed toward the workers and their club. Li Lisan's own popularity notwithstanding, the state-promoted leadership cults of personality that would in time become so closely linked to the Anyuan revolutionary tradition were not yet part of the pattern.

Despite the lack of a personality cult, Communist political rituals at Anyuan—drawing upon both Republican and Soviet models—showed signs of an emerging civil religion.[83] On the second anniversary of the strike victory, in September 1924, the mining company declared a holiday to permit all employees to attend a celebration in the workers' club. The ceremony, which began at 10 o'clock in the morning with the ringing of a bell, had a distinctly religious air. After singing the club song and the strike song, the several thousand attendees bowed solemnly three times to the club banner. Speeches followed, and the service concluded with a group chant that was repeated three times in unison: "Long live the memory of the strike victory! Long live the unity of the international proletariat! Long live the club!" The newspaper article reporting on this event observed that the workers showed "great faith" (*shifen xinyang*) in their club.[84]

The Anyuan workers' club served as the central node for a growing network of political activism that extended across the western Jiangxi and eastern Hunan countryside. To spread their radical message into the surrounding countryside, teachers from Anyuan made frequent visits to the Pingxiang High School, thereby inspiring a sizable number of students in the county seat to volunteer as rural organizers. By early 1925, seven "costume lecture" teams with more than fifty members each—composed entirely of high school students—were making regular visits to villages throughout the region. Often hundreds of peasants gathered to observe the melodramatic performances and pepper the performers with questions about such pressing concerns as how to avert warfare and evade military conscription.[85]

Patriotic resistance to foreign imperialism was an important theme in these rural lectures. In 1924–25, several Korean nationalists arrived at Anyuan to share grim tales of life under Japanese occupation. One such Korean lived for a time at the Pingxiang High School, where he mobilized students to launch a local boycott of Japanese goods.[86] The Pingxiang boycott was part of a larger movement gaining ground across the country at the time, in which consumers were enjoined to buy domestic products as an expression of patriotic pride.[87] The explosive synergy between nationalism and labor unrest would soon erupt in Shanghai's May Thirtieth Movement of 1925, in which the dynamic duo of Li Lisan and Liu Shaoqi joined forces again to play a critical leadership role in a massive industrial strike wave of historic proportions.[88]

## ECONOMIC MOBILIZATION

At Anyuan, consumer nationalism found institutionalized expression in the flourishing cooperative founded by Li Lisan, which sold only goods made in China. Two months after the victory of the 1922 strike, Mao Zedong sent his younger brother, Mao Zemin, to Anyuan to help oversee the operations and expansion of the cooperative. As Mao Zemin reported soon after his arrival,

> When the Anyuan workers organized a workers' club last year, they took steps to operate a workers' consumer cooperative. At that time it was organized by very few people, with barely one hundred yuan in capital. It couldn't operate independently and was located instead inside the workers' school. Although small in scale, the meaning and benefit of the cooperative became deeply ingrained in the workers' minds.
>
> Following the victory of last September's strike, the club leaders realized that in order to reduce the workers' cost of living burden they would need to expand the operations of the cooperative. So they proposed increasing the capital investment. Understanding that this was closely linked to their own material interests, the workers contributed enthusiastically. In addition to investing a part of their year-end bonuses, they each purchased vouchers so that now the cooperative had over ten thousand yuan in capital. China's only workers' consumer cooperative was officially open for business on February 7 [1923].[89]

The consumer cooperative, which sold domestically produced goods at low prices to workers' club members, embodied the Communists' dual commitment to nation and proletariat. Novel as this particular institution was, it drew upon familiar mobilizing modes. Just as Red Gang lodges had once "issued vouchers" *(fangpiao)* for secret-society membership and gambling stakes, so now the workers' club issued vouchers that allowed its constituents to make purchases, take out loans, and exchange cash and coins at favorable rates. The cooperative was also willing to accept at face value the "mine vouchers" *(kuangpiao)* that workers received as wage payments, in contrast to other stores in the area, which required that the workers convert the vouchers to cash at a substantial loss.[90]

Figure 6. Anyuan workers' consumer cooperative building, opened in 1922 as a means of attracting new members to the Communist-sponsored workers' club. Photo by the author.

The cooperative was the financial mainstay of the workers' club. As the first commercial institution that the Chinese Communists had ever attempted to run, however, it encountered predictable problems. On the recommendation of the ever-vigilant Liu Shaoqi, in 1923 the workers' club undertook a thorough investigation of the cooperative's accounts, which revealed that the director of the goods and services department had embezzled more than one thousand yuan and that several workers' club cadres had taken out loans from the cooperative that were long overdue. In addition to dismissing the department chief and meting out various fines and punishments to the guilty cadres, the workers' club leadership insisted that both the embezzled funds and the outstanding loans be fully repaid. More important for the long-term financial health of the cooperative, a new regime of accountability and transparency was imposed. Henceforth every co-op employee would need a guarantor, who was required to put down five hundred yuan as collateral to help ensure the employee's good behavior. The account books became subject to monthly review by the club's audit department, which, after affixing an official stamp of approval, posted its findings at the door of the workers' club to render the co-op's transactions fully visible to the membership at large. By late 1924, popular confidence in the consumer cooperative had permitted an expansion from one to three stores that collectively employed some forty clerks and other personnel.[91]

In addition to the consumer cooperative, the club established a labor introduction office whose primary mission was to aid unemployed members in finding new jobs. According to the terms of the 1922 strike settlement, the mining company agreed that all future hires would require the approval of the workers' club. In theory, this gave the club substantial power over personnel. In practice, however, securing work for the unemployed in this company town was by no means easy. And the fact that labor contractors continued to exercise control over the workforce, despite the shared interest of the mining company and the workers' club in eliminating them, made the work of the labor introduction office that much more difficult. At one point more than 140 club members demanding immediate job placements were expelled following two weeks of continuous protests at both the club and company headquarters, staged at the behest of their labor contractors.[92] By August 1923 the labor introduction office had received applications from 197 unemployed workers, only 36 of whom it was able to place successfully in new jobs. Over the next sixteen months, the success rate improved marginally, with 46 of 154 applicants taking up new jobs on the recommendation of the office. Despite this rather disappointing placement record, the labor introduction office—which gave priority to longtime members of the workers' club—was a visible symbol of the club's commitment to worker welfare.[93]

Further reflecting commitment to the economic well-being of the workers was the establishment of support groups to provide for the victims of industrial accidents and their dependents. Although at first the workers' club harbored hopes of setting up an enterprise-wide organization for this purpose, it soon became clear that the uneven distribution of work-related accidents and illnesses among the labor force made it impossible to convince those who worked under less dangerous conditions to underwrite the costs of those most at risk. Only six workstations—the coking plant, cafeteria, electrical machine shop, coal-washing plant, business office, and repair shop—agreed to set up support groups, leaving the great majority of miners unprotected. Within these six (relatively safe) work units, compensation for fatalities from work-related causes was raised by means of all other workers in the unit contributing the equivalent of one day's wage. Accidents were treated on a case-by-case basis after careful investigation and recommendation by the support group.

Although for a brief period this type of coverage was extended to eight work units, even at its height the arrangement left some three-quarters of the workforce unprotected, among them the most vulnerable underground coal miners.[94]

## THE CCP AS LOCAL POWER BROKER

Thanks to its growing influence across the region, the Anyuan workers' club threatened to eclipse the authority of the local elite. Fearful of just such a development, a delegation of gentry from Li Lisan's home county of Liling had visited Anyuan shortly after the 1922 strike to offer apologies for the trouble that their obstreperous native son had caused to Pingxiang mine director Li Shouquan (who had, after all, raised over thirty thousand yuan in famine relief for their county just the year before) and to try to convince Li Lisan to return home. But of course the young Communist agitator, flushed with the recent strike victory, was not about to abandon his revolutionary mission at this historic juncture.[95] The cultural and economic power of the workers' club was augmented by substantial coercive power. Although immediately after the victory of the 1922 strike the club had optimistically disbanded its armed pickets, it soon reinstated them. In the interim, several labor contractors had conspired to create a counterweight to the Communists by recruiting unemployed workers and other local toughs to a new association that they dubbed a "recreation club" (*youle bu*). When the workers' club learned that its new rival was plotting an assassination attempt against Li Lisan, the patrols were quickly reactivated and dispatched on a successful mission to close down the competition.[96]

The revamped workers' club patrols had a dual charge: "internally, to monitor club members' activities; externally, to investigate and prevent plots and activities harmful to the club."[97] Each workstation in Anyuan was required to designate one or more workers to serve on the patrol team, which included more than one hundred pickets stationed at Anyuan itself and an additional one hundred in three ancillary branches. Although they served without pay, the pickets were uniformed and armed with iron bars and spears. When the new workers' club was being built, pickets guarded the construction site to prevent the theft of materials. At times of large-scale gatherings or other major events that called for enhanced public security, temporary pickets from among the workforce were mobilized for short-term service to supplement the regulars, swelling the total size of the patrol force to as large as 1,600. For most of the duration of Little

Moscow, a dozen or more pickets were posted every night to the workers' club, with responsibility for patrolling the dormitory districts to discourage gambling, brawls, and other forms of "improper behavior" among the workforce. Needless to say, not all workers appreciated this moralistic monitoring of their activity while they were off work. Even more irksome to some than the nighttime patrols were the daytime pickets who stood guard at entrances to the coal pits in order to prevent miners from attempting to leave work early.[98]

The ascendance of the Communists was facilitated by a commensurate decline in secret-society control. At the conclusion of the 1922 strike, Li Lisan paid off the local Red Gang boss in return for his agreement to leave the area. Li later recalled, "After the victory of the strike, the capitalists wanted to use the Triads as a pretext for destroying the workers' club. I gave [the Triad chieftain] some travel money and sent him packing. As the labor movement flourished, the Triads disintegrated. Otherwise the workers' organization could not have been consolidated."[99] With the departure of the Red Gang dragon head, Li and his fellow Communists became the pivotal power brokers at Anyuan.

Growing power brought increased responsibilities. Overwhelmed by the number of disputes and disruptions that it was now expected to resolve, the workers' club in May 1923 established an arbitration committee composed of seven members of the highest representative assembly. The committee's charge was to settle conflicts among club members as well as between members and nonmembers. In its first two months of operation the committee handled 98 cases; in the nine months from December 1923 to September 1924, the caseload more than quadrupled to 432. These cases reflected a range of misdemeanors, including infractions of club regulations, brawls, financial impropriety, theft, shoddy work, gambling, disturbance of the peace, and failure to follow factory rules.[100] The workers' club had replaced the local elite as the primary arbiter of conflict.

Aware that the coal mine was the lifeblood of the labor force, Li Lisan and Liu Shaoqi proceeded to take advantage of their newfound authority to work directly with company management to develop a plan for implementing the terms of the strike without destroying the solvency of the mine. In the six-month period between the end of the strike and Li's departure for Wuhan, Director Li Shouquan's diary records no fewer than thirty-five lengthy meetings with Li Lisan about matters ranging from company construction projects to workers' discipline. After Li Lisan's own departure, Liu Shaoqi continued this practice. In the ten days from

June 11 to June 20, 1923, for example, Director Li Shouquan's diary makes note of eight lengthy meetings with Liu Shaoqi, most of which revolved around the question of how to reconcile workers' demands for wage hikes with the company's growing financial difficulties.[101] The frequency and substance of these meetings not only pointed to the enhanced status of the CCP, whose economic and political clout overshadowed that of the local elite; they also reflected the shared interest of capitalists and communists in the continued viability of the Anyuan coal mine.

As all the parties recognized, the economic situation was serious. The parent company of the Pingxiang Railway and Mining Company, the Hanyeping Coal and Iron Company, tottered on the verge of bankruptcy as a result of the sudden drop in demand for iron and steel products following the end of World War I. With its principal buyer, the Hanyang ironworks, on the ropes, the Anyuan coal mine faced a decrease in demand at the same time that its emboldened workers were insisting on increased wages. As the major supplier of both household and industrial coal throughout the Yangzi delta, Anyuan was in a situation that was not quite as dire as that of its parent company. Nonetheless, it suffered a steady decline in annual production over the period of Little Moscow, from 827,870 tons of coal in 1922, to 666,939 tons in 1923, to 648,527 tons in 1924, to 512,300 tons in 1925.[102] Profits plummeted even faster than production, and a desperate ploy by the deputy director of the coal mine, Shu Xiutai, to meet payroll demand by printing up more mine vouchers did not prevent the company from having to seek loans from local merchants and gentry.[103] Even more worrisome, the mine was now in the awkward position of relying upon the workers' club to mollify its restive employees. By June of 1925 the situation had grown so desperate than an acting director of the mine proposed in a confidential communication to Hanyeping general manager Sheng Enyi (son of the founder Sheng Xuanhuai) that management be handed over to the workers.[104]

## Conflicts with Workers

Even at the height of Little Moscow's glory, however, the Communist leaders were not able to carry out their activities unopposed. Ironically, in the immediate aftermath of the Great Strike the thorniest challenges to Communist designs issued not from the local elite—whose authority had been largely supplanted by the workers' club—but from the workers themselves. The strike victory gave the workers both a heady awareness of their own power and a hearty appetite for more. With the tables turned, miners felt free to flex their muscles against the now subdued staff.[105] Memoirs from this period recall that after the strike the workers of Anyuan were routinely addressed by chastened members of the local elite and the mining company administration with the exalted salutation of *wansui* ("long life," or ten thousand years), a call for immortality that had once been reserved for emperors.[106] Signs of the workers' newfound status were evident in their improved food and dress as well. The bonuses that workers received as part of the strike settlement allowed many of them to enjoy the taste of sausage (which they gratefully referred to as "strike meat") for the very first time in the 1923 lunar new year celebrations.[107] On that same occasion, some younger workers used their bonuses to affect a student image, complete with newly purchased blue uniforms and leather shoes.[108] The increase in workers' disposable income came at the expense of labor contractors. Although the labor contract system was not abolished by the strike, it was curtailed. Contractors' "squeeze" was henceforth limited to 15 percent of the workers' bonuses.[109]

The heightened expectations of the workers, emboldened by their meteoric rise in status, sometimes exceeded the party's ability to deliver. As Liu Shaoqi noted, "After the strike, the workers' livelihood was much improved and their status was also greatly elevated. Everyone addressed them with 'long life,' . . . but even so, the workers weren't satisfied and wanted more."[110] The workers' appetite for additional gains ran afoul of prevailing party policy. In this time of national crisis for the labor movement and economic duress for the Anyuan coal mine, the Communist Party adopted a cautious stance aimed at consolidating previous gains rather than risking further military provocation. Immediately after the February Seventh Massacre, in which hundreds of strikers on the Jing-Han Railway were killed by warlord Wu Peifu, Li Lisan went to Changsha to seek instructions from Mao Zedong. Mao, quoting a classical line of Tang poetry by Han Yu, stressed the necessity for temporary restraint: "The bent bow must await release" *(wangong daifa).*[111] In late April, when Li Lisan had just been transferred to Wuhan to rebuild a party branch decimated by the February Seventh Massacre, Mao returned to Anyuan to deliver several lectures at the workers' club. He emphasized the importance of strengthening defenses in order to protect the workers' club against a possible military assault.[112]

Mao Zedong's admonitions were consistent with the inclinations of the congenitally cautious Liu Shaoqi, but not everyone at Anyuan was so willing to exercise restraint. With expectations having been raised by the gains of the 1922 strike, many club members wanted to press for further concessions from the mining company. A cadre later recalled,

I remember that after the victory of the Anyuan Great Strike there developed among some workers' leaders and party comrades a certain "leftist" orientation. They believed that the higher the demands placed on the capitalists the better. . . . At that time the party's policy was to . . . maintain production at the Anyuan coal mine to prevent unemployment and protect the basic interests of the workers. The legal status of the union was to be fully utilized to preserve strength and cultivate and send forth cadres to engage in union work all around the country.

Comrade Shaoqi steadfastly followed the party policy and responded to this leftism with persuasion and education. But some of the leftists mistook this as rightism. At that time the deputy director of the workers' club, Lu Chen, opposed Comrade Shaoqi's approach. There was also a worker named Xie Huaide, a big burly fellow, who was the head of the workers' patrols and who was very aggressive. He had considerable influence among the workers but he was pretty leftist. For a time, because of this leftist orientation, he raised unrealistic and excessive demands and organized the workers for strikes, marches, and demonstrations that imperiled mining operations and resulted in some workers being fired. Opinions within the workers' club were divided and Comrade Shaoqi was very upset.[113]

In June 1923, a group of workers instigated by Xie Huaide, the deputy director of the pickets and a hotheaded former secret-society member recruited by Li Lisan, threatened to go on strike—in direct defiance of Liu Shaoqi's orders—if they were not granted a generous wage hike. The situation was made more volatile when Xie, who was known among the workers as "Xie the Fierce" (*Xie mengzi*), delivered a sound thrashing to the chief of the Anyuan railway station, accusing the stationmaster of having caused a rise in the price of rice by exporting local grain to distant locales.[114] In the midst of this tumultuous state of affairs, Xie's supporters contacted Li Lisan, calling upon the hero of 1922 to return to Anyuan to lead them in another strike. At Liu Shaoqi's urging, Li Lisan (whose salary was still being paid by the Anyuan workers' club despite his transfer to Wuhan) rushed back to the mine in an attempt to calm the storm. Adhering to party policy, he advised the workers to abandon their struggle in favor of protecting production. This was not the message the disgruntled workers had anticipated, and the more militant among them refused to be mollified even by as respected a leader as Li Lisan. When words proved unpersuasive, Li reluctantly resorted to force.[115] As Liu Shaoqi later recalled, "Li Lisan personally led the pickets to repress the workers, who wanted to beat him up. I cautioned the workers not to be so extreme, and the workers then wanted to beat me up, saying I had been bought off by the capitalists."[116] The conflict was clearly a painful one for Li Lisan and Liu Shaoqi; even many years later, both men would recall having been reduced to tears by the incident. As Liu Shaoqi observed, the militant tendencies of the Anyuan miners were not easily suppressed: "Some of our workers even wanted to go on strike against the workers' club. . . . I hoped that the workers would not resort to violence [*dongwu*] so readily, and would not take up weapons to kill their own people!"[117]

The outcome of this confrontation was a new modus vivendi between the mining company and the workers' club, brokered by Liu Shaoqi and summed up in a seven-point agreement that pledged a modest wage hike in return for the club's guarantee of a certain daily tonnage of coal production and strict enforcement of worker discipline.[118] Yet the difficulties did not end there. A few months later Xie the Fierce got into another scrap, this time with a local shop owner. When the aggrieved merchant brought his complaint to the workers' club for resolution, Liu Shaoqi had seen enough of Xie Huaide's aggressive behavior. Despite Xie's standing among the workers and his position as deputy head of the club patrols and director of its liaison department, Liu ordered Xie expelled from Anyuan. As a result, Xie Huaide was sent home to his native county of Hengshan in Hunan to focus on peasant mobilization. The following year, when warlord attacks on Hengshan forced Xie to flee for his life, he attempted to seek refuge in Anyuan. But even then Liu Shaoqi refused to relent, and Xie the Fierce had no choice but to hide out in a mountain cave until he could safely return to Hunan.[119]

Liu Shaoqi's frustrations with militant workers were not limited to Xie Huaide. In a report that he submitted on the state of the Anyuan workers' club in 1924, Liu complained about a more general lack of discipline: "Since last year, some of our workers are under the misimpression that 'Now that we are protected by the club, if we create a ruckus the club will shoulder the responsibility'. . . . Some of the workers view the factory regulations as having been drafted by the capitalists and therefore, regardless of whether they are correct or not, purposely refuse to obey them. They also willfully disregard the proper orders of their supervisors at work"[120] Liu's criticism of the workers was even more pointed in a remarkable journal article entitled "Save the Hanyeping Company," which he published in June 1924. Claiming that Anyuan's parent company, the Hanyeping Coal and Iron Company, was the foundation of East Asia's "material civilization," Liu painted a gloomy picture of the future of the company. To rescue the enterprise—the largest industrial conglomerate in China—from the specter of immanent bankruptcy, Liu suggested playing Japanese and American economic interests off against each other so as to retain Chinese ownership. Coming from the "socialist" leader of Little Moscow, Liu's harsh criticism of the workers was particularly striking. He charged that Chinese workers lacked any sense of public morality, citing the folk proverb "People sweep the snow in front of their own doors but neglect the frost on their neighbor's roof." Liu warned that the workers' failure to accept collective responsibility for protecting the source of their livelihood could ultimately seal the fate of the struggling Hanyeping Coal and Iron Company. Add to this the fact that the company itself devoted no attention to workers' education, and the enmity between labor and management was reaching alarming proportions.[121]

Despite the impressive educational effort that the Communists themselves mounted at Anyuan, convincing workers to toe the disciplinary line often proved difficult. In response to Liu's continuing concern that the workers' newfound arrogance (and old vices) were creating a bad impression of the Anyuan workers' club in society at large, the highest representative body of the workers' club issued a notice strictly prohibiting gambling and brawling. Aware that the nightly patrols were inadequate for combating these problems, the general representatives themselves agreed to take on the duty of monitoring workstations to enforce the prohibition and to report back to the club leadership on any infractions. Light infractions were met with fines imposed by the club, which were used to purchase reading materials for the workers' library; more serious cases were handed over to the police bureau for punishment.[122] With gambling such an ingrained part of the local culture, however, it was unrealistic to expect that elected representatives would be able to eliminate it. In the spring of 1924 the Anyuan party branch reported that "gambling is widespread among the workers. Even the general representatives and hundred representatives are not exempt. The union faces many difficulties in prohibiting gambling. . . . When the workers misbehave, they are fined by the club for each infraction. Because of this, the workers are disgruntled."[123] The progressive series of punishments that the workers' club promulgated for repeat offenders suggested that the rank and file and the staff alike remained addicted to gambling . Ordinary workers were fined a single day's wage for the first violation, two days' wages for the second, four days' wages for the third, and eight days wages for the fourth. Upon the fifth infraction, they were expelled from the club. For workers' representatives and club staff, the punishments were steeper still: two days' wages were docked for the first instance, four days' wages for the second, and eight days' wages for the third. Workers lost their representative or staff position for the fourth infraction and were expelled from the club upon the fifth violation.[124]

For some workers, gambling was not the worst of their vices. Despairing that more than a thousand workers were still Red Gang members despite the departure of the local chieftain, the party warned that the union would not protect workers who engaged in armed robbery but would instead turn them over to the government authorities.[125] The arbitration committee of the workers' club reported that fully one-third of the fifty or so disputes that it handled each month involved serious physical assaults.[126] The welfare department found it necessary to stipulate that the compensation provided for industrial accidents would not be forthcoming in cases of injuries incurred in the course of brawls.[127]

### Conflicts with the Local Elite

The problems of the workers' club paled before those of company management. Chagrined by the massive strike that had occurred on his watch and chastened by the economic decline of the colliery and its parent company, Li Shouquan tendered his resignation as director of the Pingxiang Railway and Mining Company as soon as a strike settlement had been negotiated. Although it took the Hanyeping Coal and Iron Company more than a year to acquiesce to Li's request, in November 1923, after decades of service at the Anyuan coal mine, a dispirited Li Shouquan returned home to Jiangsu.[128]

This changing of the administrative guard created complications for Liu Shaoqi and his comrades. Whereas the progressively minded Li Shouquan had been willing to negotiate with the Communists, his successor—a deputy director of the Hanyang ironworks by the name of Huang Xigeng—took a hard-line approach. Pledging to put the workers' club out of business within six months, Huang encouraged the formation of an alternative "employees' assistance society" (zhigong xiejihui) to challenge the club's hegemony. The new association successfully sought support from the energetic rector of the St. James Episcopal Church, the Reverend Long Yongjian, as well as from members of an anarchist party that had been attempting to organize at Anyuan (with lackluster results) since the spring of 1923. Representing what the CCP denounced as a "triangular alliance" of capitalists, Episcopalians, and anarchists, the rival association lobbed criticisms at the workers' club for being under the thumb of Communist intellectuals and sponsored lavish banquets and raucous drinking parties intended to compete with the more aus-

安源路礦工會工人學校戚教員 一九二四，六，一五

Figure 7. Teachers at the Anyuan workers' club schools, June 1924. Many are wearing scholars' robes. Liu Shaoqi stands second from the right in the third row.

tere forms of cultural entertainment promoted by the club. Aiming to isolate the Communist educators from their working-class constituency, the new association called upon the workers to "toss the long gowns out of the union!"[129] (A group photograph of teachers at the workers' club schools, dated June 15, 1924, shows many of the teachers—including Liu Shaoqi—dressed in long Mandarin gowns.)

The workers' club responded vigorously to this multipronged challenge. It first made clear that any worker who joined the anarchists would forfeit all benefits of membership in the workers' club. The result was a quick collapse of the anarchist initiative. The church, however, presented a more formidable opponent. Although the Reverend Long—like many of the local elite—had supported the strike of 1922, his subsequent relations with the Communist leaders were frosty at best.[130] Having once boasted a congregation of several thousand Anyuan residents, the St. James Episcopal Church now found itself in direct competition with the Communist workers' club for converts to fill its pews as well as for students to enroll in its parish schools. An American Episcopal missionary who visited Anyuan in the heyday of Little Moscow remarked on this rivalry. As the Reverend Walworth Tyng wrote of his inspection visit to the coal mine in October 1924:

> Bolshevik propaganda has streamed down from Russia. All the men here and along the railway belong to the Workingmen's Club, with a membership of thirteen thousand, led by young agitators with greater zeal than wisdom. As one enters the club building there faces one a large portrait of Karl Marx. One looks up from talking with a secretary in his office to see a smaller picture of Lenin on that wall. There is a hall to hold 2,000 men, where exhortations are heard against capitalism. We find that men who feel too poor to pay their church pledges have their wages automatically deducted for Club dues regularly, and the Club is a force to be reckoned with—in some respects for good. Much of the Club income goes into maintaining schools for hundreds of children. But in some respects it is a dangerous element. The standard of work goes down.[131]

Having long operated schools for the children of the mining company staff and skilled technicians, St. James Church—with the active encouragement of the company—now opened its classrooms to the sons and daughters of ordinary workers. The mining company had reached the conclusion that Christian education posed less of a threat to control over its workforce than did Communist education. As a result, management offered to bear the entire expense of educating the miners' children in a bid to undercut the popularity of the "red education" being provided by the workers' club.[132]

Aware that the rivalry with the church (in cahoots with the mining company) presented a challenge to the ambitions of the workers' club, Liu Shaoqi responded with a public education campaign designed to expose the evils of capitalists and Christians alike. Didactic lectures and skits with titles such as "Why Oppose Christianity?" and "The Sins of Christianity" drew curious audiences of more than a thousand people a night to the workers' club. Together with widely distributed anti-Christian tracts and handbills, the public performances were instrumental in diluting the influence of the church among the workers.[133]

Of critical important in gaining and retaining its members' allegiance in the face of these various challenges was the fact that the Anyuan workers' club was a full-service agency, offering not only education and entertainment but also many other valuable benefits and commodities that had once been the purview of the local elite. Its consumers' cooperative enabled workers to procure low-interest loans and purchase basic necessities at below-market prices. Its welfare department organized support groups to pay for the funerals of some workers killed in industrial accidents. Its employment agency attempted to match laid-off workers with alternative job opportunities. Its arbitration committee adjudicated all manner of labor disputes. Its security force of more than a thousand worker "pickets," now armed with guns as well as clubs, enforced public order. And its frequent and festive commemoration of revolutionary anniversaries was indicative of the workers' club's new status as the primary center of cultural and ritual power at Anyuan.[134]

Exasperated by his inability to undermine the authority of the Communist-sponsored workers' club, Huang Xigeng abruptly resigned his directorship in September 1924, less a year into his tenure. Deputy Director Shu Xiutai, who had long had his eye on the top management position, was named acting director. Having witnessed the utter failure of Huang's aggressive line of attack, Shu was now amenable to a more accommodating approach. Acceding to the influence and authority of the Communists, Shu resumed Li Shouquan's previous practice of frequent consultations with Liu Shaoqi and other leaders of the workers' club.

The strength of the Anyuan workers' club was demonstrated again in December 1924 when workers struck to recoup back wages. With the Hanyeping Coal and Iron Company deeply in debt to Japanese creditors and close to bankruptcy, the Anyuan mine had fallen into arrears on wage payments. When the company announced that it was planning to renege on a provision of the 1922 strike settlement that promised employees a two-month bonus for the lunar new year, the workers erupted in fury. The protest began as a wildcat strike by several thousand disgruntled workers, but after a couple of weeks of fruitless efforts on the part of the strikers, the workers' club—fearful of violence and aware that the gains of its 1922 strike hung in the balance—decided to intervene on behalf of the protesters. An observer recalled the open air mass meeting that Liu Shaoqi convened on this occasion:

> It was very lively and a huge number of people attended, taking up almost the entire field. There were old people, young people and women. Up on the stage was a portrait of Marx. When people saw it they debated who this bearded fellow was and where he came from. Just at this moment there appeared from within the crowd a man in a long scholar's gown who mounted the stage and said that this bearded fellow was a good guy whose name was Marx and who was concerned about the interests of the workers. He went on to ask why the capitalists didn't issue our wages and why they fed us bug-infested rice. This

was the capitalists' exploitation and oppression of us and we should rise up in unity to struggle resolutely against them. People clapped loudly throughout his speech and the workers were fired up. At the time I wasn't sure who the speaker was but later people told me it was Comrade Liu Shaoqi. Soon afterwards the second Anyuan strike exploded.[135]

Liu Shaoqi did not confine his mobilizing efforts to the restive workers. Following the pattern of the 1922 strike that had originally brought him to the coal mine, Liu again focused on winning over key members of the local elite, especially in the Anyuan chamber of commerce and garrison command. Calling up more than 1,500 armed pickets to enforce public order, the workers' club—with the help of members of the local elite—managed to negotiate a full restitution of pay for the aggrieved workers. By mid-January of 1925 the strikers, savoring their victory, returned triumphantly to work.[136]

## THE REACH OF LITTLE MOSCOW

After three years of intensive mobilization, which included the engineering of two strikes and the education of thousands of workers, the Anyuan experiment was attracting both national and international attention. Even the U.S. government felt compelled to try to find out what was happening at the once obscure coal mining town. An American consul known for his strong anti-Communist views was sent to Anyuan in early 1925 to investigate the local situation. He reported with dismay on the stranglehold that the workers' club exercised over the labor force: "I have just returned from the Pinghsiang [Pingxiang] mines at Anyuan. . . . The technical staff, all of whom are Chinese are very much discouraged. They are completely under the power of the union."[137]

The influence of the workers' club did not go unnoticed by the residents of neighboring towns and villages, to whom the club was happy to extend a helping hand. The Anyuan workers' club offered financial support and the services of trained organizers (as well as educators) to laborers in a wide variety of occupations throughout the western Jiangxi and eastern Hunan region. The costume lectures and other forms of propaganda purveyed by Anyuan activists to surrounding locales often resulted in requests for assistance in establishing branch clubs. Labor unions modeled on the Anyuan prototype cropped up across this area to instigate a series of strikes that were in turn funded by the coffers of the Anyuan workers' club.[138]

Ultimately more significant for the future of the Chinese revolution than these copycat labor unions was the emergence of peasant associations, also inspired by the Anyuan exemplar. With much of Anyuan's labor force still closely connected to their native villages, it was only natural that radicalized workers would share their newfound knowledge with the folks back home. The first place to show the effects of this diffusion was Baiguo in Hunan's Hengshan County, which happened to be the native place of patrolman Xie Huaide as well as of the Hunan governor-general and warlord, Zhao Hengti. Expelled from Anyuan in early 1923 as punishment for his truculent behavior, Xie the Fierce returned home to help organize his fellow villagers into the Beiyue [Hengshan] Peasants and Workers Union (*Beiyue nonggonghui*). Following the Anyuan pattern, every ten rural households elected a "ten representative," every hundred households chose a "hundred representative," and every district in the county selected a general representative. When the union was formally inaugurated on September 16, 1923, more than three thousand households with more than ten thousand people had joined. To mark the occasion, the Anyuan workers club sent not only congratulatory telegrams and banners but also a substantial financial subsidy. Although this particular association was soon forcibly disbanded by warlord Zhao Hengti, it marked the beginning of the famous Hunan peasant association movement, from which Mao Zedong would launch his rural revolution. Like the Anyuan workers club, the peasant associations sponsored literacy classes, consumer cooperatives, and other means of delivering cultural and economic benefits to the rural poor. But, no longer subject to the discipline of Liu Shaoqi and the Anyuan Communist Party, Xie the Fierce led his Hengshan peasant followers on bloodthirsty rampages and violent plundering expeditions against wealthy households of a sort that were anathema to the leaders of the Anyuan workers' club.[139] Xie Huaide's example was followed by other graduates of Anyuan. A coal hauler by the name of Wang Xianzong, from Mao's home county of Xiangtan, who had been educated at an ancillary school of the Anyuan workers' club, founded a peasant association in Xiangtan in May of 1925. He soon led the five thousand members of the peasant association in assaults on the property of local landlords and gentry.[140]

## THE END OF LITTLE MOSCOW

Thanks to the extraordinary achievements and reach of the Anyuan workers' club, as well as the remarkable restraint with which its leaders exercised their newfound advantage, the Communists were able to persevere at Anyuan for three momentous years, but in the end they could not withstand the larger political forces conspiring against them. In April 1925, Liu Shaoqi was transferred out of Anyuan to undertake labor organizing in other locales. Within only a few months of Liu's departure, his beloved workers' club was subject to an attack from which it never fully recovered.

In the fall of 1925, the general manager of the Hanyeping Coal and Iron Company—of which the Pingxiang Railway and Mining Company was a subsidiary—decided to travel from his headquarters in Shanghai to visit his Anyuan holdings. General Manager Sheng Enyi (son of Sheng Xuanhuai, who had founded the Pingxiang colliery thirty years earlier) was accompanied on this journey by Gustavus Leinung, the German engineer who had worked at Anyuan at the invitation of Sheng Enyi's father for twenty years before being expelled during the nationalist fervor of 1919. The men happened to arrive at the mine on the third anniversary of the strike victory in time to witness the gala commemoration organized by the workers' club. Despite advance warnings from the garrison commander to reduce the scale of the festivities in order to avoid angering Sheng Enyi, the club mobilized massive groups of costumed lecturers and singing troupes to celebrate the occasion. With the cautious Liu Shaoqi no longer on hand to enforce restraint, more than ten thousand workers poured out of the coal pits to participate in a boisterous show of strength. Marching behind red banners, they shouted provocative slogans such as "Down with Capitalists!"[141] Shocked by this display of proletarian prowess, Sheng decided to crush the movement. Leinung tried to dissuade him, emphasizing that "capitalists must cooperate with workers. Every country in the world has a labor movement and it cannot be eliminated. To repress it with force is a suicidal policy."[142] But Sheng was not to be deterred; he instructed the garrison to launch a full-scale military assault on the Anyuan workers' club and its schools. Three workers were killed and dozens more were wounded in the attack. Five committed suicide soon thereafter. The workers' club was closed down and its consumers' cooperative and schools were raided; more than seventy teachers and workers' club staff members were placed under military custody. One of the detainees, Huang Jingyuan, a young Communist teacher from Hunan who was serving as school principal and deputy-director of the workers' club, was later executed by firing squad in the exercise ground directly in front of the club. The execution was personally overseen by the Jiangxi garrison commander, Fang Benren, a close friend and longtime patron of General Foreman Wang Hongqing.[143]

The same site where Li Lisan, Liu Shaoqi, and thousands of miners and railway workers had joyously celebrated the victory of their nonviolent strike three years earlier was now the scene of a bloody suppression. Yet the manner in which Anyuan workers, spurred on by Communist cadres, mourned the death of the first officially declared "revolutionary martyr" of the Anyuan labor movement showed how political messages were being combined with religious rituals into an emotionally powerful package that would long outlast the Anyuan experiment. Three days after Huang Jingyuan's execution, his relatives gathered in Liling County to welcome his coffin back to his native province. A mass street demonstration, which newspaper reports characterized as "unprecedented in the history of Hunan Province," converged upon the Liling train station to greet the coffin as it arrived from Anyuan. After chanting, "Huang Jingyuan has not died; long live Huang Jingyuan," the huge crowd proceeded to bow solemnly three times in front of the coffin. Two hours of speeches from Anyuan workers and representatives of Liling civic associations followed, leaving "not a dry eye among the audience." Then, to the deafening sound of firecrackers, the coffin was put back on the train, this time headed to Zhuzhou for a two-hour layover on its way to the provincial capital of Changsha. At Zhuzhou, an altar had been fashioned on the railway platform, where two pigs—ritually slaughtered by local students and workers—were sacrificed as offerings to the spirit of Huang Jingyuan. Following another round of public speeches and wailing mourners, the train carrying Huang's body continued on to Changsha, where it was met at the train station by a crowd of over twenty thousand who shouted three times in unison, "The spirit of Huang Jingyuan has not died!" The coffin was solemnly removed from the train and transported to lie in state at the Changsha Education Association. All along the route, observers chanted, "Down with imperialism; down with militarism; down with capitalism!" "Restore the Anyuan workers' club!" "The spirit of Huang Jingyuan has not died!" When the coffin reached its destination, the throng encircled it three times and bowed three times in a final show of respect. The national newspaper *Shen Bao* reported, "With such intense feelings, it can truly be said that Huang Jingyuan never died."[144]

At Anyuan itself, the grieving for Huang Jingyuan was necessarily muted in light of the overwhelming military force brought to bear against the workers' club. Even so, the mourning rites evidenced the kind of creative cultural positioning that had characterized the Anyuan labor movement since its inception. As one worker recalled, "Soon after the funeral service for Comrade Huang Jingyuan in Changsha, the Anyuan workers convened a memorial service. One evening at twilight, at the spot where Comrade Huang Jingyuan had been executed, a Daoist priest recited prayers, burned incense and paper money, and chanted slogans. . . . Only later did I learn that it was actually a worker and Communist Party member, Chen Chunsheng, who had dressed up as a Daoist priest."[145] Even if the spirit of Anyuan lived on, the military offensive of September 1925 dealt a crippling blow to Little Moscow. After the September Massacre, as it became known in the annals of party history, thousands of Anyuan workers were accused of Communist leanings and dismissed by the railway and mining company. Of the twelve thousand miners who had previously been employed at Anyuan, only eight hundred still held jobs there in the fall of 1926, and only a handful of railway workers remained.[146] Output at the Anyuan mine fell to its lowest level in almost twenty-five years, from 512,300 tons of coal in 1925 to a mere 75,715 tons in 1926.[147]

Among the ten thousand or so dismissed workers, some two thousand workers' club activists from Hunan and Hubei were forcibly returned to their native villages. This repatriation effort, aimed at diluting the radicalism of Little Moscow, had the unintended effect of further spreading the Communist movement from Anyuan to the surrounding countryside. The Hunan peasant associations, soon to be made famous by Mao Zedong, were largely a product of this process, as laid-off workers and their teachers returned home to establish dozens of peasant associations modeled closely on the Anyuan railway and mining workers' club that they had left behind.[148]

The demise of Little Moscow was closely connected to the transformation of the Chinese Communist revolution from a proletarian to a peasant movement. This shift, in what was an overwhelmingly agrarian country, was obviously critical to the ultimate victory of the revolution, but it came at a very high cost. The discipline and restraint that had marked the Anyuan experiment dissolved in the Red Terror of the peasant associations. The escalating violence fed into the militarization of the countryside that gave birth to the Red Army. As the next chapter will detail, former Anyuan workers played a central part in this process, but under circumstances that were vastly different from those that had surrounded their initial mobilization. Meanwhile, Anyuan itself languished both economically and politically. Not for another forty years, thanks to the "new long marches" undertaken by Red Guards during the Cultural

Revolution, would the coal mining town again hold such fascination for radical young intellectuals.

In some respects the Anyuan experiment, known in its day as "China's Little Moscow" and later as the "Anyuan revolutionary spirit," reflects the best of the Chinese Communist revolutionary tradition. Despite its many shortcomings, this was a mobilizing effort that brought education, organization, and self-esteem to tens of thousands of workers, peasants, and their families. The success of the Anyuan workers' club was the product of a remarkable synergy emanating from the cooperative efforts of revolutionaries whose decidedly different leadership styles were brought to bear on a shared objective. Mao's strategic supervision, Li's charismatic creativity, and Liu's disciplined direction—operating in tandem—made for a powerful mode of mass mobilization. As their erstwhile comrade, Zhang Guotao, would later comment of Li and Liu, "Li Lisan and Liu Shaoqi were a good combination in the labor movement. Liu Shaoqi once remarked that Li Lisan had a strong impetus and was an expert in agitation, capable of launching offensives and capturing new beachheads, but the programs he set up were always chaotic, requiring Liu Shaoqi to put in a lot of hard work to sort them out, to get the masses organized, and the programs functioning."[149] At this early moment in the history of the Chinese Communist Revolution, before the brutal leadership conflicts that would eventually divide these men, their common dedication to ameliorating the plight of the working class enabled an impressive outcome. Moreover, the implications of this experiment were felt far beyond the confines of Anyuan itself. Li Lisan credited the experience during and after the Great Strike with providing the basic recipe (night schools, workers' clubs, and nonviolent strikes demanding human dignity) for the party's subsequent success in fomenting Shanghai's historic May Thirtieth Movement.[150]

Anyuan not only provided a template for future labor organizing; it also offered valuable lessons in administrative governance. Although the Communists refrained from calling the reorganized workers' club a "soviet" for fear of alarming the local elite, its operations anticipated the Jiangxi Soviet that would be established only a few years later in the eastern part of the province. In the realm of finance, for example, Mao Zedong's younger brother, Mao Zemin, built upon his experience in managing the Anyuan consumer cooperative to open the first bank of the Jiangxi Soviet, a precursor of the Communist command economy.[151] Liu Shaoqi's experience as director of the first party school in Anyuan paved the way for a recurring pattern of cadre training and rectification that stretched from the Jiangxi Soviet through the Yan'an rectification campaign of the early 1940s to the Socialist Education Movement twenty years later.[152]

The policies of Little Moscow in many respects replicated those of the Soviet Union. Soviet-trained Liu Shaoqi was a confirmed Leninist who believed fervently in Communist Party ideology and discipline. Under his directorship, the Anyuan workers' club adopted an explicitly social-ist platform. After February 1923, the prevailing CCP policy of restraint in the face of warlord aggression obliged Liu to postpone revolutionary ambitions and concentrate his energies on education and organiza-tion rather than violent class struggle. Although born of necessity, the Chinese Communist Party's emphasis on cultural mobilization was also quite consistent with what Lenin himself was proposing for the Soviet Union at that very time. Toward the end of his life, Lenin began to advo-cate what he termed a "cultural revolution." As he wrote in January 1923, "There has been a radical modification in our whole outlook on socialism. The radical modification is this; formerly we placed, and had to place, the main emphasis on the political struggle, on revolution, on winning political power, etc. Now the emphasis is changing and shifting to peace-ful, organizational, 'cultural' work; I should say that emphasis is shifting to educational work . . . that very cultural revolution which nevertheless now confronts us."[153] Of course Lenin's call for a cultural revolution, com-ing well after the October Revolution of 1917, did not in his view obviate the necessity of violent class struggle at some stage of the revolutionary process, but he emphasized that the completion of socialism demanded serious attention to cultural transformation through education.

At the same time that Liu Shaoqi was building the Anyuan workers' club into a hub of grassroots education and cultural activity, the Soviet Union (under Lenin's New Economic Policy) was also establishing net-works of rural reading rooms, cultural clubs, elementary schools, and local party schools as vehicles to eliminate illiteracy and promote revolu-tionary morality. Yet whereas in China these efforts were generally wel-comed by the rural populace as consistent with their own attitudes and aspirations, in the Soviet Union such initiatives seem to have elicited a rather different response among a people who often resented Bolshevism as a violation of prevailing norms.[154]

The "cultural revolution" that Liu Shaoqi and his comrades launched at Anyuan was envisioned as a stepping-stone toward a future socialist revolution. But for the time being, at least, violence was to be averted in favor of "peaceful, organizational, 'cultural' work" (in Lenin's words) that was intended to produce educated workers and peasants who were conscious of their class interests and committed to realizing those interests through collective action. Although this pedagogical effort could be justified ideologically by reference to Lenin, and operationally by reference to national CCP policy, the actual design and content of programs at the Anyuan workers' club drew significantly upon local custom as well. As natives of nearby counties located just across the provincial border in Hunan, Mao Zedong, Li Lisan, and Liu Shaoqi were familiar with homespun habits. All three men, despite their dissimilar personalities and leadership styles, accepted—with varying degrees of enthusiasm and agility—the need to incorporate such conventions in the pursuit of new socialist ends.

The moderation that marked the Anyuan experiment throughout the existence of Little Moscow was in full compliance with Chinese Communist Party directives at the time. Mao Zedong's circumspect advice to Li Lisan—that "the bent bow must await release"—summed up the party's judicious response to the inhospitable circumstances of the period. To avoid triggering another devastating warlord assault of the sort that had occurred on February 7 along the Jing-Han Railway, the Communist Party was committed for the time being to a defensive stance.

Decades later, during the tumultuous Great Proletarian Cultural Revolution, the interpretation of both "cultural revolution" and the "Anyuan revolutionary tradition" would be dramatically altered in favor of a violent class struggle attributed to Chairman Mao. But in the early 1920s, Liu Shaoqi's restrained approach was, in fact, aligned with the official party line articulated by his immediate superior within the Hunan Labor Secretariat, Mao Zedong. Liu's own cautious instincts, although contributing to serious tensions with some of the more militant members of the workers' club, nevertheless rendered him an ideal person to implement temperate tactics during trying times. To his credit, however, Liu did much more as director of the Anyuan workers' club than simply dampen radical impulses among the workforce. Building upon the firm foundation laid by Li Lisan, Liu helped to consolidate at Little Moscow a grassroots organization that provided a remarkable array of valued services—educational, cultural, political, and economic—to its working-class constituency.

Under Liu Shaoqi's watchful eye, the Anyuan workers' club and its ancillary organizations flourished as a socialist experiment that emphasized the *wen* of education over the *wu* of warfare. While Kam Louie and

Louise Edwards apply the *wen-wu* dualism to Chinese conceptions of masculinity, it can also be understood more broadly as pointing to complementary yet competing bases of cultural and political authority.[155] The distinction was explicitly recognized in imperial Chinese political administration in the simultaneous reliance upon, yet important distinction between, civil officials *(wenguan)* and military officials *(wuguan)*.[156] But this was not simply a bureaucratic division of labor; it also reflected quite different, yet mutually supportive, forms of cultural power, one derived from proficiency in the literary arts *(wenyi)* and the other from skill in the military arts *(wushu)*. The Communists' success at Little Moscow reflected a shift in the balance of power in this region where secret-society chieftains and martial arts adepts had long wielded the upper hand. The result was a remarkable interlude in which education and entertainment overshadowed intimidation as the primary instrument of rule.

In April 1925, as Liu Shaoqi prepared to leave Anyuan after nearly three years of service at the coal mine, he summed up—with understandable pride—what he considered to be the major accomplishments of his tenure:

> Today, after work Anyuan workers can read a book or see a play or listen to a lecture. They can also engage in all kinds of recreational activities. Their children can study free of charge. Order is maintained by their own patrols and they are not disturbed by the rampages of soldiers or police. Crimes are adjudicated by their own arbitration committee and they do not suffer maltreatment at the hands of corrupt courts. Young workers enjoy the recreation and education offered by the union and will not lose their jobs when they grow old. They have their own cooperative to buy things and are no longer exploited by merchants.[157]

Despite these substantial achievements, 1920s Anyuan, as we have seen, was no proletarian paradise. In this rough coal mining town, even in the heyday of Little Moscow, conflicts frequently erupted among the workers, and on occasion between workers and their Communist leaders. Nevertheless, it seems clear from numerous firsthand accounts that life in Anyuan after the Great Strike and before the Northern Expedition was experienced by thousands of downtrodden coal miners as a kind of liberation. Although the meaning of Anyuan's revolutionary tradition would be obscured and altered over the years by political posturing and cults of personality, its memory was cherished by many of those who lived through it as an effort propelled by the quest for human dignity through education and grassroots organization.

Today, appalled by later events, we are hard-pressed to look charitably upon any part of Chinese revolutionary history. It is easy to see why a book like Jung Chang and Jon Halliday's *Mao: The Unknown Story*, which depicts the revolution as a cynical and sadistic enterprise from start to finish, would strike a chord among contemporary readers.[158] But eyewitness observers at the time, including many who were predisposed to be hostile, credited the Communist experiment at Anyuan with impressive achievements, especially in the realm of mass education and organization.

The most telling testimony to the Communists' success at Anyuan can be found in the archives of their bitterest foes. In September 1928, at the height of the Nationalists' White Terror against the Communists, the Nationalist military command prepared a top-secret memorandum on the progress of its rural pacification campaign in central China. Noting that its mop-up effort was encountering exceptionally stiff resistance at Anyuan, the Nationalists offered the following grudging endorsement of their enemies' achievement:

> The reason the Communist Party has such a deeply rooted and firm foundation at Anyuan is because in the past the Communists carried out comprehensive "red education" at Anyuan. Six or seven years ago the Anyuan workers were all country bumpkins. . . . Not one of them could stand up at a meeting and say a word, let alone deliver a speech. Still less had any of them ever heard of organizing anything. It was only after the Communist bandit Li Lisan went to Anyuan and established a workers' club . . . that the knowledge of how to organize became widespread. Now workers were speaking up at public meetings and even giving lectures!
>
> The Communists at Anyuan greatly valued education but they did not mechanically evangelize Communism like a missionary cramming a religious belief into a worker's head. At first they focused on literacy and basic knowledge. Every week they convened easy-to-understand lectures and costumed lectures as well as workers' debate societies and study groups. It was through these media that Communist ideas infiltrated the worker masses. Their educational style at Anyuan was extremely stimulating, using flashy magical methods to attract ordinary workers. . . .
>
> The sophisticated teaching methods of the Communists at Anyuan captivated the ordinary workers, allowing Anyuan to become the Communist Party's "Little Moscow." Now all the important elements in the peasant associations in all the counties of Hunan are workers from Anyuan. . . .
>
> Looked at from this perspective, some of the Communists' past educational work at Anyuan actually was correct. We can't oppose

it wholesale. Stressing workers' literacy and raising workers' basic knowledge is the most important kind of education to the workers. Today when one speaks with an Anyuan worker, everything he says is crystal clear. No longer is he a country bumpkin. This is also the result of having received that education in the past.[159]

The Nationalists' White Terror ensured that Anyuan would never return to its former glory days as Little Moscow. But the thousands of Anyuan workers and their children who had been awakened through education would also never revert to being "country bumpkins."[160] Energized by the pedagogical efforts of their workers' club, these graduates of Little Moscow were poised to make a major contribution to the development of the Chinese revolution. For better *and* for worse, politicized former miners would play a central role in the transformation of the revolution from a proletarian to a peasant movement. It was in the course of this crucial transformation that moderation gave way to militarization.

# 4    From Mobilization to Militarization

The demise of Little Moscow signaled a critical juncture not only in the development of the Anyuan labor movement but in the history of the Chinese revolution more broadly. The disintegration of the Anyuan experiment in the fall of 1925 was followed by a new phase of ruthless reprisals and mounting militarization in which the CCP's previous stress on workers' education and organization was superseded by a call for armed class struggle. The murderous zeal with which many former Anyuan workers and their peasant allies would answer this call suggested something more than a dutiful response on the part of obedient operatives to altered party directives, however. It also marked the recrudescence of an older, less controlled pattern of rural violence that had long predated the Communists. The militancy of secret-society martial artists and gangsters, checked for a time by the firm hands of Li Lisan and Liu Shaoqi, was breaking loose. And Mao Zedong, who had once cautioned against precisely this danger, now actively championed it. Increasingly indiscriminate violence on the part of warlords, Nationalists, and Communists alike generated a vicious cycle of armed attacks and counterattacks.

## DISCREDITING THE ANYUAN MODEL

Just prior to the September Massacre of 1925, the Anyuan workers' club had augmented its regular patrols from two hundred to five hundred pickets in order to defend against a suspected offensive by the Hanyeping Coal and Iron Company. Even so, the Communists were caught quite unprepared for the crushing repression that Sheng Enyi brought to bear against them (see chapter 3). Concluding that Communist-controlled

Anyuan had become more of a burden than a benefit to his economic empire, Sheng was willing to unleash overwhelming military force. Fifteen hundred soldiers armed with machine guns proved more than either the workers' organizations or the mining operations could withstand.[1]

The economic devastation was sudden and substantial. The closing down of the workers' club and consumers' cooperative rendered valueless the co-op-issued vouchers that had previously served as legal tender for low-priced goods and low-interest loans. Several workers, unable to make ends meet, committed suicide. Miners were not the only victims of this change in currency. Shopkeepers in the town of Anyuan who had accumulated sizable stockpiles of the now worthless vouchers were plunged into bankruptcy. Farmers and craftsmen in the surrounding villages also suffered severe losses from the collapse of the local economy. The widespread economic distress prompted the opening of two soup kitchens in Anyuan financed by private donations. Soon some eleven thousand desperate people a day (out of a total Anyuan population of less than eighty thousand) were regularly availing themselves of this grim institution.[2]

More significant for the future of the Communist revolution than the precipitous economic downturn was the equally sharp political turnabout that followed in the wake of Little Moscow's collapse. The execution of school principal Huang Jingyuan, together with the detention and repatriation of thousands of other activists associated with the Anyuan workers' club, decimated the Communist presence at Anyuan. It also had a profound impact on the strategic outlook of the Chinese Communist Party. The month after the September Massacre a meeting of the Central Communist Committee in Beijing rendered a decidedly negative verdict on the Anyuan experience:

> The work of the Hunan District has exhibited some very serious
> and dangerous political shortcomings; namely, in the course of
> various movements and work it has avoided struggle and leaned
> toward peaceful development. . . . Under our direction, the more
> than ten thousand railway workers and miners of Anyuan engaged
> in three years of economic conflicts but never undertook political
> work. . . . Although their union had been established for three years,
> it remained in a precarious position and never prepared a secret orga-
> nization. So when intense pressure was brought to bear, it completely
> collapsed. . . . In future the Hunan District must correct this tendency
> in order to construct a successful Bolshevik mass party.[3]

The commitment to nonviolence and transparency of operations that had characterized the Anyuan workers' club under Liu Shaoqi at Mao

Zedong's urging was repudiated in favor of a more militant and secretive mode of mobilization. A follow-up resolution by the Hunan District party committee reiterated this conclusion:

> After the victory of the first Anyuan strike, the labor movement embarked upon a peaceful path. It focused solely on expanding education and improving economic livelihood and neglected political struggle. . . . Our party must take full responsibility for this mistake. The organization of the Anyuan workers' club, from top to bottom, was completely open. Even the names of everyone who held any position in the club, whether small or large, were made public. In this reactionary climate, that was an entirely inappropriate organization for the demands of struggle. And thus when the suppression came, the workers' club was powerless to counter attack.[4]

Although Liu Shaoqi had left Anyuan five months before the debacle, retrospective accounts by other party principals pinned much of the blame on his legalistic approach. Li Weihan, who served as party secretary of the Hunan District during the rise and fall of Little Moscow, recalled in his 1986 memoir,

> After the victory of the Anyuan Great Strike, the workers' club attained a legal political position and also gained certain economic privileges. As a result, we developed a mentality of peaceful paralysis and were not sufficiently alert to possible reversals. . . . In September 1923 when I went to Anyuan to participate in the first anniversary of the victory of the strike, many cadres . . . emphasized to me that the Anyuan workers' club paid attention only to open, legal activities and sought the company's permission for everything it did. It ignored illegal, secretive work. I shared these concerns with Liu Shaoqi. In the spring of 1924 when Shaoqi passed through Changsha on his way to Guangzhou, I again raised this with him. Shaoqi disagreed and we got into an argument. He left before any agreement was reached.[5]

Liu Shaoqi's penchant for legalism, although cited during the Cultural Revolution as early evidence for "rightist" tendencies that placed him in opposition to Mao Zedong's "revolutionary line," at the time was in close accord with Mao's own stated position. Moreover, Mao clung to this moderate stance throughout the duration of Little Moscow. Several months after Liu Shaoqi had left Anyuan, in July 1925 Mao made another trip to the colliery to meet with party leaders at the workers' club. On this occasion, just two months before the September Massacre, Mao still railed against the dangers of "leftism" and stressed the importance of taking full advantage of the union's legal status to carry out open activities.[6]

Whether or not the "legalistic" approach of the Anyuan workers' club's paved the way for its premature downfall, in the aftermath of the repression top party leaders would no longer tolerate the kind of openness that had characterized Little Moscow on Liu Shaoqi's watch. With this sharp shift in central policy, a new and bloodier chapter of the Chinese revolution was about to be written. Soon Liu himself, taking a page from Lenin's earlier playbook, would gain a reputation as the quintessential underground apparatchik, renowned for his organization of clandestine party cells in the face of enemy hostilities.[7]

The Chinese Communist Party's turn from transparency to secrecy was accompanied by an increased emphasis on class struggle. In an October 10, 1925, proclamation to the workers of China, the CCP signaled its new militant stance: "In this dark and frightful society, the interests of capitalists and workers are diametrically opposed and there is no room for compromise. . . . The workers of Anyuan, having suffered this senseless cruelty, are united in fury. . . . Their bloodshed today has sowed the seeds of tomorrow's victory for the proletariat of the whole country. . . . Workers, time is of the essence. . . . Rise up to help our fortress: the Anyuan railway and mining workers' club."[8] Gone was the moderate plea for human dignity that had marked the early years of the Chinese Communist labor movement. In its place was a strident call for class warfare that denied the possibility or desirability of cooperation with the local elite. As Communists and Nationalists joined forces in armed struggle against the warlords, the entire rural social order came under violent attack.

## BUILDING A PEASANT MOVEMENT

Two months after the 1925 September Massacre, the Hunan District party committee assigned to a former leader of the Anyuan Communist Youth League the task of making contact with the remnants of the Anyuan workers' club in order to reconstitute the Youth League organization. In addition to mobilizing more than eighty league members, he established a secret communications channel along the Zhuping railway to transmit important documents and letters between Anyuan and other sites of Communist activities. The following month the Anyuan Communist Party organization was also reestablished. A former coal miner by the name of Liu Changyan, who had joined the Anyuan CCP in 1923 and, as reward for his activism, had spent the next year studying in the Soviet Union, was now sent back to serve as party secretary of the revived branch. Liu not only set about contacting other former party members in the vicinity of the coal mining town, but he also focused on organizing the peasantry in villages along the Zhuping railway. In the summer of 1926 the first village party cell was established in Pingxiang County. It soon secretly organized a peasants' association that was poised for attacks on landlord holdings.[9]

The situation in Pingxiang was replicated in counties across western Jiangsu and Hunan, as graduates of Little Moscow returned to their native villages determined to translate their Anyuan (and, in some cases, Soviet) experience into a rural context. Although the difficult political conditions made it impossible for the Communist Party to exert tight control over this process, the Hunan and Anyuan League and Party organizations did provide intermittent logistical support to the returned activists. In addition, the party assigned a few former Anyuan cadres to locations other than their native places in a determined effort to spread the revolutionary movement more widely. At this time, for example, Xie Huaide—the martial arts adept and founder of the first Hunan peasant association who had been expelled from Anyuan for his belligerent behavior—was transferred from his home in Hengshan to southern Hunan in order to energize the nascent peasant movement in that part of the province. The combination of bottom-up and top-down efforts yielded results. At the third national labor congress in May 1926, Zhu Shaolian, the former railway engineer from Liling who had collaborated closely with Li Lisan and Liu Shaoqi at Anyuan and was then serving as Hunan's chief representative to the congress, reported on the situation in his home province: "The main organizers of the recent peasant movement in every Hunan county are Anyuan miners and railway workers. In the past two months, the Hunan peasant movement has developed extremely rapidly (it includes twenty-nine county organizations with more than two hundred thousand members)."[10]

A year later a summary report of the Hunan Youth League stressed the continuing contributions of Anyuan workers to the peasant movement: "Anyuan workers are extremely important in Hunan's revolutionary struggle, not only within the working class itself. The peasant movement in many places was also instigated by Anyuan workers. From the Yuebei [Hengshan] peasant uprising to the recent village struggles, from developed Liling to nearby Pingxiang, all have been greatly influenced by the efforts of many Anyuan workers."[11] Thanks to the literacy and political training that they had acquired at schools operated by the Anyuan workers' club (which enrolled over 1,300 workers and 2,300 children at the time of the September Massacre in 1925), these graduates of Little Moscow were equipped to play a central role in the unfolding revolutionary drama.[12]

When Anyuan workers first fanned out into the Hunan countryside to establish the peasant associations that would later be made famous by Mao Zedong, they adhered to the basic recipe of education and grassroots organization that they had learned as denizens of Little Moscow. It was not long, however, before the peasant associations embarked upon a much more violent path that distanced them from the legalism and pacifism of the Anyuan workers' club. Following in the footsteps of Xie the Fierce, founder of the first peasant association in Hengshan, the Hunan and Jiangxi peasant associations soon became better known for their militancy than for their educational achievements. The new direction was in line with changing party policy, but it also drew strength from the long tradition of bloody uprisings for which this area was well known.

## THE VIOLENCE OF THE NORTHERN EXPEDITION

This critical transformation in the character of grassroots revolutionary organizations (from *wen* to *wu*) occurred during the course of the Northern Expedition, the joint Nationalist-Communist military campaign to rid China of warlords and unify the country. Like previous large-scale armed confrontations in this area, most recently the Taiping Rebellion of the mid-nineteenth century and the Ping-Liu-Li Uprising of the early twentieth century, the Northern Expedition occasioned an explosion of mass violence. Justified in the name of revolution, the vengeful bloodletting was often an opportunity to settle old scores.

Important for this new phase of the revolution was a returning cadre of former Anyuan workers who, after the demise of Little Moscow, had headed south to Guangzhou to study at the Peasant Movement Training Institute (with Mao Zedong) and the Whampoa Military Academy (with Zhou Enlai). Established in 1924 under joint Communist-Nationalist auspices, these two institutional expressions of the United Front served as recruitment and training centers for the new National Revolutionary Army (NRA), which would soon sally forth on its Northern Expedition against the warlords. The political and military instruction that former Anyuan activists received at one or another of these institutions in Guangzhou was instrumental in converting more than a few of them from labor organizers into revolutionary soldiers. For example, Zhou Huaide—the miner, martial arts adept, and Red Gang member who had served as director of the armed pickets during the strike of 1922—returned to his native Hunan in 1926 as the head of a propaganda unit in the NRA after undergoing a stint of military training in Guangzhou.[13] Former Anyuan workers comprised nearly two-thirds of the soldiers of the most important division of the NRA, Ye Ting's Fourth Army, known popularly as Ironsides for its firm resolve and fighting spirit. Many of these soldiers had enlisted while in Guangzhou following a period of study at Whampoa Military Academy or the Peasant Movement Training Institute.[14]

In recognition of Anyuan workers' contributions to the Northern Expedition, Chiang Kai-shek, commander of the NRA, paid a visit to the colliery in September 1926. Chiang was welcomed by a crowd of over fourteen thousand people, including representatives of a dozen local civic associations. Standing in the same open field in front of the workers' club where Li Lisan had presided over the celebration of the victory of the 1922 strike and where Huang Jingyuan had been executed by firing squad three years later, Chiang praised the revolutionary spirit of the Anyuan workers and called for them to attack the capitalists and seize direct control of the coal mine—a more radical proposal than the Communists had ever made.[15] Coming at a time when the mine was virtually bankrupt and the few workers who remained on site were destitute and dispirited, Chiang's incendiary words fell on deaf ears. His unfamiliar Zhejiang accent further muted his message. As one worker recalled, "When Chiang Kai-shek visited Anyuan, the Anyuan branch of the Guomindang convened a mass gathering to welcome him. We couldn't understand a thing he said. But he was surrounded on stage by security guards armed with assault rifles; it was very imposing."[16] Chiang's failure to incite a workers' insurrection did not, however, spell an end to his support for class conflict between Anyuan workers and managers.

A few days later Chiang Kai-shek personally approved the execution of the much hated general foreman of the Anyuan coal mine, Wang Hongqing (see chapters 1–3) at the hands of former miners who were now serving as soldiers in the National Revolutionary Army.[17] Bearded Wang the Third, as he was known, had been apprehended in Xinyu County by former members of the Anyuan workers' club patrols who recognized their former boss (despite his effort to disguise himself by having shaved off his telltale beard) as he was attempting to flee for his life. More than a hundred former Anyuan workers in the NRA petitioned Chiang Kai-shek for permission to return Wang to Anyuan for execution there. Deciding that there was no time for extradition, Chiang ordered a public execution on the spot. After the execution by firing squad, Chiang Kai-shek sent an explanatory telegram addressed to various civic groups in Anyuan, characterizing Wang as guilty of "inescapable crimes, from conniving with warlords to crushing the workers."[18]

Whether Chiang Kai-shek's radical pronouncements reflected genuine revolutionary sympathies or mere pragmatism is open to debate. The Communist Party secretary of Hunan, Li Weihan, submitted a report to Party Central the following month in which he attributed Chiang's support for the Anyuan workers to purely political calculations:

> After Chiang Kai-shek left Hubei for Jiangxi, realizing his own military weakness, he very much wanted to improve his political standing. When he went to Anyuan, he greatly praised the Anyuan workers at a mass meeting saying that he wanted to hand the Pingxiang mine over to the workers to operate. When he went to Yuanzhou he executed the scab who destroyed the workers' club last year, Wang somebody. He then issued an open letter to all the people of the country. Seventy percent of the above activities were copied from proposals in our Central and Hunan district bureaus. This makes clear that he really wanted to use politics to gain position.[19]

Regardless of what Chiang Kai-shek's actual motives may have been, the generalissimo was certainly not alone in converting the Anyuan connection into a bloodthirsty game of hardball politics.

The Northern Expedition spread in its wake what Hans van de Ven has characterized as "nasty cultures of violence."[20] In the process, the peasant associations founded by Anyuan activists turned into the terrorist tribunals that caught Mao Zedong's eye in early 1927, prompting him to write what are perhaps his most memorable and most frequently quoted lines:

> A revolution is not a dinner party, or writing an essay, or painting a picture, or doing embroidery; it cannot be so refined, so leisurely and gentle, so temperate, kind, courteous, restrained and magnanimous. A revolution is an insurrection, an act of violence by which one class overthrows another. . . . To put it bluntly, it is necessary to create terror for a while in every rural area, or otherwise it would be impossible to suppress the activities of the counter-revolutionaries in the countryside or overthrow the authority of the gentry.[21]

The five counties on which Mao based his influential "Report on an Investigation of the Peasant Movement in Hunan" (his native Xiangtan, as well as Hengshan, Lilin, Xiangxiang, and Changsha) all boasted truculent peasant associations established by former workers from Anyuan. Mao's report expressed gleeful enthusiasm for the violence taking place in these counties, including peasant attacks against local religious practices and institutions. Nevertheless, Mao did not recommend that party cadres themselves initiate such attacks. As he chided the more zealous iconoclasts among his revolutionary comrades, "It is the peasants who made the idols, and when the time comes they will cast the idols aside with their own hands; there is no need for anyone else to do it for them prematurely." Then, quoting a line from Mencius, Mao continued, "The Communist Party's propaganda policy in such matters should be, 'Draw the bow without shooting.'"[22]

Mao's praise for the Red Terror notwithstanding, recently released internal party documents from that time reveal that the Central Committee of the Chinese Communist Party issued a string of directives in 1927 ordering its organizations at all levels to put a stop to the violence.[23] And even Mao's own enthusiasm for the excesses of the peasant associations soon waned. Historian Stephen Averill in his carefully researched study of the Jinggangshan base area points out that by January 1928 Mao was already questioning the wisdom and effectiveness of the Red Terror in favor of returning to a more moderate approach aimed at preserving the rural economy.[24] Yet once the bloody cycle began, it was not easily restrained by party proclamations; local residents had their own habits of revenge.

## RED TERROR

In light of the many modifications and reversals in party policy over the subsequent course of the Chinese revolution, it would clearly be a historical oversimplification to insist that the Northern Expedition constituted a path of no return after which the revolution was doomed to an irreversible fate of escalating violence. Yet it is equally clear that the Red Terror of the Hunan and Jiangxi peasant associations, so celebrated in Mao's investigative report, did mark a turning point after which brutality became a major theme in Communist (and Nationalist) revolutionary practice. That this vicious turn resonated with longstanding local patterns of secret-society militancy and class vengeance rendered it especially difficult to moderate once set into motion.

In September 1926, only a few days after warlord Fang Benren and his Beiyang forces retreated in the face of the Northern Expedition, more than a thousand remnant workers at Anyuan stormed into the general office of the mining company and beat to death three of the mine police.[25] Seeing an opportunity, the underground Communist Party directed a number of party and league members to infiltrate and assume control of the weakened police force. As one of those involved recalled,

In September 1926 the Anyuan Youth League mobilized some young workers to enroll in the mine police. The mine police were the armed security force of the mine, established to protect mine property. Originally most of the members of the mine police had been northerners . . . but when the National Revolutionary Army of the Northern Expedition arrived, these northern soldiers all fled. Our party took advantage of this situation to mobilize some workers to serve as soldiers in the mine police so that the party controlled an armed force.[26]

The practice of infiltrating rival paramilitary forces was part of a broader Communist strategy during this period (also promoted in Shanghai by Zhou Enlai, among others) that prepared the way for the CCP's fateful turn toward "red terrorism."[27] At Anyuan, the Communist-controlled mine police soon set about their new revolutionary mission with exceptional gusto, avenging "local bullies and evil gentry," suppressing "counterrevolutionaries," and attacking landlord militias. More than fifty labor contractors were sent packing at this time.[28]

Once control of the mining area had been secured, the Anyuan party committee set its sights on Pingxiang County more broadly. In October 1926 it encouraged a series of armed conflicts directed against leading members and institutions of the Pingxiang elite. The countywide campaign had three principal targets: Liu Zenghua, one of the largest landlords in Pingxiang; the Six Halls, the county's traditional conduit of private charity and Confucian education; and Ye Ziping, one of Pingxiang's most notorious local power holders.

Landlord Liu Zenghua, who in addition to his extensive landholdings owned a number of silk and cloth shops in the towns of both Pingxiang and Anyuan, had forged close relations with the Beiyang garrison commander, Fang Benren. Thanks to these links, Liu served for a time concurrently as magistrate of Nanchang county and head of the Jiangxi mint. Although he attempted to flee the area a few days before the arrival of the Northern Expedition, Liu was soon apprehended and his property liquidated by the revolutionary forces. Several of his retail stores were converted into consumer cooperatives for workers. Soon after the attack on Liu, the substantial property of the lineage-controlled benevolent associations, the Six Halls, was targeted. Their holdings were transferred to a newly established Pingxiang Public Property Commission, which redirected the lion's share of the income toward the support of dozens of new night schools for workers and farmers.[29]

The most dramatic in this series of party-led attacks was the public execution of Ye Ziping, a "local hegemon" whose close connections to the Beiyang warlords had provided cover for a litany of misdeeds. On December 22, 1926, tens of thousands of people braved a snowstorm to attend the mass trial of Ye Ziping, presided over by Liu Changyan, a former Hunanese miner recently returned from the Soviet Union who was now serving as party secretary of the Anyuan party committee. Order was maintained by workers' pickets and peasant self-defense forces armed with spears and swords. After Liu read out a long list of Ye's alleged crimes, selected victims were invited to step forward to relate their personal stories of suffering at the hands of the tyrant. Moved by these emotional testimonials, the assembled crowd, many of whom wore red kerchiefs around their necks and waved small triangular flags, clamored for his death. Ye was executed on the spot with a bullet to the head.[30]

The execution of Ye Ziping unleashed a torrent of violence across the county. As one of the participants later described the situation, "The Pingxiang peasant movement did everything that Chairman Mao Zedong mentioned in his *Report on an Investigation of the Peasant Movement in Hunan* . . . arresting and parading around landlords, imposing fines and punishments, confiscating property, reducing rents and interest, opposing miscellaneous fees and taxes, liquidating bandits, attacking hegemons, and so on."[31] In April 1927 the Pingxiang People's Special Court for Local Bullies and Evil Gentry was established to deal expeditiously—and mercilessly—with more than forty "counterrevolutionaries" who were rounded up across the county. As the struggle fever spread, various symbols of Confucian authority—lineage halls, ancestral tablets, local temples, placards marking success in the imperial examinations, stelae commemorating female chastity, and so on—were smashed to bits by the rampaging peasant associations.[32] Granaries were seized and their contents opened to the public, while rent and loan contracts were tossed onto open bonfires.[33]

Women's liberation was an important concern in the revolutionary upsurge.[34] The Pingxiang Women's Federation, led by the daughter of an Anyuan coal miner who had studied at a workers' club school and starred in one of its costume lecture troupes, convened mass meetings in every district of the county.[35] At these emotional gatherings women were ordered to free themselves from the "shackles of feudalism" by unbinding their feet and cropping their hair. Small groups of activists, often including students from the local girls' school, went door-to-door to enforce the injunction.[36]

Anyuan was widely acknowledged as a pacesetter in the revolutionary turmoil of the day. For the better part of a year, the radicalized union at Anyuan, following Chiang Kai-shek's earlier admonition, even gained control of the general operations of the mine in what was hailed as China's first experiment in workers' enterprise management. Under this makeshift (and short-lived) arrangement, all major budgetary decisions, purchasing and sales agreements, construction plans, and personnel matters were subject to union authorization.[37]

At the height of the Red Terror, the left-leaning *Hankou Republican Daily* reported approvingly:

> The Anyuan party and peasant movements are extremely active and are generally considered to be the most active in all of Jiangxi. Since last year their contributions in assisting the revolutionary troops of the Northern Expedition, consolidating local public property, liquidating bandits . . . and striking down evil gentry have been of real benefit to the revolutionary masses. Their internal work such as establishing workers' consumer cooperatives, organizing workers' pickets and peasant self-defense forces, establishing rural banks and consumer cooperatives, operating party training programs and peasant movement training programs, etc., are equally noteworthy.[38]

Across the border in Hunan, as Mao Zedong detailed in his dramatic investigative report, the situation was similarly tumultuous. According to the account of CCP leader Zhang Guotao, Li Lisan's own father was branded a "local bully, evil gentry" at just this time. As a result, the "kind" and "gentle" elder Li, whose connections at Anyuan had facilitated his son's successful mobilization effort there (see chapter 2), was summarily executed by his local peasant association. Zhang Guotao explains that a letter from Li Lisan guaranteeing his father's cooperation with the revolution, which had been forwarded to the peasant association of Liling County through the Hunan District party committee, had no effect in moderating the "state of madness" that prevailed. Zhang describes Li Lisan as "very crestfallen for a time; but he gritted his teeth and never mentioned the incident again. . . . I myself was depressed over the incident for a long time."[39]

## WHITE TERROR

Shocking as it was, the high tide of Red Terror subsided with Chiang Kai-shek's coup in Shanghai on April 12, 1927, which shattered the United Front between the Nationalists and Communists and generated an equally frightful backlash of White Terror.[40] Landlords and lineage elders who had been attacked in the Red Terror now struck back with a vengeance. In June 1927 a combined force of landlord-led vigilantes and militias from across Pingxiang attacked the Anyuan party, workers' union, and peasant association headquarters, killing more than forty Communist activists and arresting an additional one hundred. Long-time Communist leaders Liu Changyan and Zhou Huaide, both of whom hailed from Hunan, lost their lives in the confrontation. For more than ten days Anyuan was subject to a blockade intended to starve its residents into submission. Giving voice to regional rivalries between Pingxiang locals and Hunanese transplants that dated back to the founding of the modern coal mine in 1898, landlords directed their militias in an armed assault on Anyuan fueled by nativist slogans such as "The coal of Pingxiang should be mined by the people of Pingxiang!" and "Drive out the Hunanese!" The anti-Hunanese initiative was not merely an indication of economic protectionism on the part of the Jiangxi local elite; with the Anyuan labor movement having been organized by the Hunan Communist Party, the backlash was also an expression of anti-Communism, a sentiment heightened by the recent attacks on the Pingxiang elite led by Communists from Hunan.[41] Eventually, however, the combined forces of workers' pickets and mine police (armed with grenades and other weaponry produced in the colliery machine shops) succeeded in breaking the encirclement and rescuing the Anyuan Communists from extinction.

At the same time that Anyuan was under siege from hostile landlord militias, peasant associations all across Jiangxi and Hunan were facing similar retaliation in which institutions and individuals connected to the Communist movement were subject to severe reprisals. Women with bobbed hair and unbound feet, as visible symbols of the Red Terror, were a particular target of this reactionary upsurge. When Anyuan proved able to break the enemy blockade, it became a refuge for vulnerable members of the peasant associations. Battered peasant fighters from five surrounding counties (commanded by former Anyuan workers) retreated to the mining town to join forces with the pickets and police. This constellation of some fourteen hundred fighters, armed with more than a thousand rifles, formed the core force of the next major milestone in the Chinese revolution, the Autumn Harvest Uprising of September 1927.[42]

## AUTUMN HARVEST UPRISING

The Autumn Harvest Uprising, which was planned and executed from the site of the first party school in Anyuan, is often seen as the opening act in the Maoist pageant of peasant revolution. Centered in the same three counties as the Ping-Liu-Li Uprising that helped prepare the ground for the Revolution of 1911, the Autumn Harvest Uprising put in motion an even more momentous revolutionary dynamic. As Roy Hofheinz notes, although Mao himself deserves only partial credit for the dramatic shift in party policy, this "was the first time Chinese Communists sought to transform their rural influence into political power, to deploy peasant-based armies against the ruling elites, and to build independent areas in the countryside insulated from government influence."[43] The Communists now dispensed with the Nationalist flag in favor of their own hammer and sickle banner and openly declared their intention to conduct a thorough redistribution of landholdings and replace county governments with rural soviets.

Despite the new emphasis on the peasantry as the main revolutionary force, by all accounts the most reliable troops in the Autumn Harvest Uprising were former workers from Anyuan. As the Hunan party committee reported to Party Central in October 1927, "During the course of the Autumn Harvest Uprising, the Anyuan miners and railroad workers demonstrated an exceptionally firm and courageous fighting spirit; truly they were the revolutionary vanguard."[44] Two months later, Party Central confirmed this assessment: "The reality of the Autumn Uprising has taught us that the leaders and vanguard of the bloody battles in Pingxiang, Liling, and Liuyang were the previously trained workers of Anyuan. It can be said that the fame of the Autumn Uprising is really due to the Anyuan workers."[45] Over a thousand Anyuan workers participated in grenade brigades, saber brigades, bodyguard squads, propaganda teams, and other combat and support units.[46]

The acknowledged contribution of the Anyuan workers notwithstanding, the Autumn Harvest Uprising was quickly crushed by combined Nationalist and landlord forces. In hindsight, it was clear that the Chinese Communists were not yet up to the military mission of staging successful attacks on county seats. The abysmal failure of the Autumn Harvest Uprising sent Mao Zedong in retreat to the secluded Jiangxi mountaintop of Jinggangshan to build a Red Army that would eventually prove capable of seizing political power.[47] The proportion and prominence of Anyuan workers in Mao's revolution would naturally diminish as the ranks of the Red Army expanded exponentially to include more than half a million soldiers by the end of World War II, but many former Anyuan miners continued to play important military roles throughout the wartime era and after.

Meanwhile conditions at Anyuan itself reflected the troubled economic and political circumstances of the day. Although the labor force at the mine had grown to more than seven thousand by the eve of the

Autumn Harvest Uprising, nearly two thousand employees were laid off as a result of the economic downturn that followed in the wake of the uprising.[48] For the next decade, annual coal tonnage reached only one-fourth to one-fifth the level of what it had been during World War I.[49] With only a thousand or so alumni of Little Moscow still working at the coal mine, the Communist Party's former dominance over the labor force had eroded. A confidential party report on conditions at Anyuan in October 1927 observed that "the workers have little understanding of us. Due to reactionary propaganda, the majority of the workers have become anti-Communist."[50] An attempt by CCP operatives to convert a wildcat strike at the mine into a protest against the Nationalists' Rural Pacification Office was an utter failure.[51]

The Communists were not the only ones unable to control the Anyuan workers in the difficult days that followed the Autumn Harvest Uprising. Rampant unemployment brought severe social discontent and disorder that the local elite was hard-pressed to contain. The decline of the workers' club encouraged its erstwhile rival, the St. James Episcopal Church, to resume a more active role. The rector, the Reverend Long Yongjian, worked closely with the new director of the mining company, Ling Zizhen, who was also a member of his congregation, to try to calm the unrest. The American Episcopal journal *The Spirit of Missions* reported, "Anyuen [Anyuan] is a dangerous center with a labor union and a prostrate and bankrupt mining industry. We have a good man there. . . . Our priest at Anyuen is in great demand now as a mediator."[52] Mediation, however, proved ineffective in stemming the rising tide of restlessness that accompanied the economic deterioration of the coal mine.

In November 1927 the skeleton crew of poorly paid workers at the mine—instigated by a newly arrived CCP cadre from Hunan—went on strike to protest the withholding of wages and to demand a year-end bonus. In sharp contrast to previous Communist-led strikes at Anyuan, this confrontation was not framed as a defensive cry for basic subsistence and human dignity intended to elicit the widest possible public support. The politicization and radicalization that had occurred in recent years was visible in the aggressive strike slogans of the day: "Down with the new warlords!" "Turn the battle against new warlords into a revolutionary battle!" "Kill every last reactionary and scab that interferes with the strike!"[53] The work stoppage lasted for six days but did not result in a major victory for the strikers. Although the strike settlement provided for a modest wage increase, neither the economic demands of striking workers nor the political ambitions of CCP organizers, who hoped that the strike might turn into an armed uprising, were realized.[54] Follow-up efforts to ignite armed struggles in and around the mining town ended even more disastrously.[55] Henceforth the Communists' attention in Pingxiang would be devoted primarily to organizing peasant guerrillas under the command of former Anyuan workers for sporadic attacks on the persons and property of landlords.

## TURNING THE TABLES

One year after the Autumn Harvest Uprising, the Nationalist military spearheaded a major pacification campaign in Hunan and western Jiangxi intended to root out lingering Communist influence in the region. According to internal KMT records, a total of 937 "Communist bandits"—many of whom had ties to Anyuan—were executed in conjunction with this campaign.[56] In both terminology and tactics, the Nationalist offensive mirrored techniques of mass mobilization previously adopted by the Communists.[57] Having cooperated as fraternal revolutionary parties during the course of the Northern Expedition, the now bitter rivals redirected their military offensive from the warlords to each another.

In September 1928 a Nationalist "propaganda brigade" (*xuanchuan dadui*) with the mission "to awaken the workers from their false illusions" arrived at Anyuan. After plastering political posters and slogans around the mine and adjoining town, the brigade members divided into small groups to carry out on-the-spot investigations of working and living conditions at each marketplace and work site. Representatives of various civic associations active in Pingxiang and Anyuan were invited to attend an assembly at which the Anyuan Anti-Communism Commission was formed. As the social pressure mounted, more than six hundred workers stepped forward to confess their former Communist connections. The Nationalists converted the Anyuan workers' club building, originally designed by Liu Shaoqi as the symbol of Little Moscow, into a platform for their own propaganda, staging performances of a new drama aimed at discrediting Communism. The performances were followed by anti-Communist lectures that reportedly drew audiences of more than three thousand representatives of government agencies as well as nongovernment associations. Although the propaganda brigade departed after five days, several Nationalist operatives remained at Anyuan to oversee the investigation and exoneration of the hundreds of workers who had renounced their Communist ties. All of the turncoats were duly registered and issued official "confession certificates" by the general headquarters of the pacification command.[58] In another move reminiscent of their enemies, the Nationalist cadres proceeded to organize the rehabilitated workers into "groups of ten" for the purposes of mobilization and mutual surveillance.[59]

Institutions that had once been central to the mission of Little Moscow were now—at least superficially—made to serve new purposes. The Anyuan schools, having suffered considerable damage when the Northern Expedition forces stationed troops there in the fall of 1926, reopened in 1928. Operating under the joint supervision of the mining company director, Ling Zizhen, and the pastor of St. James Episcopal Church, Long Yongjian, the revamped schools offered an anti-Communist curriculum that included instruction in the creed of the Nationalist Party, the Three Principles of the People. The mine police, despite having been relieved by the Communists of nearly all their weaponry during the Autumn Harvest Uprising, were also reconstituted and rearmed.[60]

## BUILDING A RED ARMY

Although the White Terror dealt a crippling blow to the Anyuan labor movement, a handful of loyal workers at the mine continued to provide crucial assistance to the Communist cause. Thanks to its strategic location midway between Changsha and Jinggangshan, Anyuan served from 1928 to 1930 as a critical conduit linking Mao's mountain redoubt to the rest of the Chinese communist movement. Letters, supplies, and personnel moved back and forth between Jinggangshan and other party cells via Anyuan. Moreover, with the coal mine edging ever closer to bankruptcy, destitute Anyuan workers provided a steady source of recruits for Mao's growing Red Army. A member of the Anyuan party committee recalled of this period,

> Documents from Shanghai Central were sent to Jinggangshan via Anyuan and documents from Jinggangshan also were sent to Shanghai Central via Anyuan. The liaison for the Anyuan committee was a twentysomething young man named Wang Meisheng, from Changsha, who worked at Anyuan. He specialized in transmitting documents. Sometimes he received Central documents in a gramophone carrier, and sometimes in a wine bottle. After someone at Anyuan had transcribed the documents, he put them in the bamboo handle of an umbrella and transported them to Jinggangshan.
>
> Chairman Mao wanted the Anyuan party committee to send workers to Jinggangshan to become lower-level cadres in the Red Army. When I was at Anyuan, the party committee sent a number of people.[61]

For a Red Army struggling to graduate beyond its initial bandit base, this infusion of trained and committed workers was seen by party leaders as something of a godsend. In a June 4, 1928, letter to Mao Zedong and Zhu De on Jinggangshan, Party Central noted that, after consulting with the Hunan underground party, it was recommending a number of Anyuan workers to serve as key military recruits: "Anyuan is the great fortress of the proletariat. Many worker comrades possess considerable struggle experience and party training. You should discuss with the Hunan party committee how best to dispatch these activists to every army unit to undertake political and party work."[62] Five months later Mao Zedong reported back to Party Central, "The Hunan party committee has agreed to send Anyuan workers here. We are very much looking forward to that."[63] Over the next two years hundreds of former Anyuan workers—many of whom were now seasoned Communist party operatives—assumed Red Army roles as political instructors, political commissars, and the like.

In 1930 Mao Zedong, Zhu De, Peng Dehuai, and other Red Army commanders led a series of four expeditions to Anyuan for the purpose of repairing and replenishing their weaponry as well as enlisting new recruits from among the unemployed laborers. In the course of these expeditions, the machine shop at the coal mine was converted into an arsenal for the Red Army. More than three thousand former workers, on top of the hundreds who had already enlisted, were added to the ranks at this time.[64] One of those who enrolled remembered,

> At the mass meeting I listened to Mao's speech and call to arms.
> Along with over a thousand worker brethren I joined the Red Army.
> At that time the spectacle of workers registering for the army was
> exciting and moving. After Mao mobilized people, all the Red Army
> divisions set up registration points in the open field in front of the
> workers' club. Every point was flooded with miners and peasants
> from nearby villages rushing to sign up to join the army. There were
> pairs of fathers and sons and brothers who enlisted together. There
> were barefoot boys pleading with the Red Army cadres to be allowed
> to enlist, and little girls crying by the sidelines because they had been
> refused permission. . . . In the midst of this hot tide, I enrolled in the
> third division of the Red Army.[65]

Not everyone at Anyuan experienced Mao's arrival so positively, however. After the first visit of the Red Army in May 1930, the rector of the St. James Episcopal Church, Long Yongjian, who had for years played a major role as a local educator and mediator, fled Anyuan for the relative safety of Changsha. A Chinese Episcopal minister from Hankou who visited Anyuan a few months later bemoaned the heavy toll that the repeated Red Army forays were exacting on both the mining company and the church. The windows, doors, and floors of the St. James church and rectory had all been stolen, while the school building (jointly operated by the mine and church) lay in ruins. As he reported in the Chinese Episcopal Church newspaper in December 1930,

> The Red Army came to Anyuan four times this year. The first time was on the early morning of May 16; they departed that same night. About three thousand came on this occasion. Anyone who was on the mine staff was robbed. About twenty people were killed, including the head of the mine police and subordinate officers. The second time was from June 27 to 29. Again about three thousand came on this occasion. This time they robbed all the merchants. The third time was July 9. Calling themselves the Red Guards, they killed one or two hundred people. Then the regular troops arrived, staying only for an hour before they withdrew. The fourth time was from September 17 to 27. During these ten days there were about ten thousand people stationed at Anyuan and almost another one hundred thousand (saber brigades, etc.) that passed through Anyuan. The Episcopal church was ransacked at 10 A.M. on September 21. This was the work of the Fifth Division of the Red Army, commanded by Peng Dehuai. The one hundred thousand soldiers were under the combined command of Zhu [De], Mao [Zedong], Peng [Dehuai], and Huang [Gonglue]. I heard that on the day that they came to the church, they carried kerosene in preparation for setting fire to the church and rectory. But unexpectedly they encountered loud cries of protest: "Rector Long helped us so many times in the past. No way can you set fire to this church." As a result, they did not proceed with their original plan. But they could not be prevented from plundering. Although parishioners watched from the sidelines, they dared not say much. . . .
>
> Most fortunately, although the Red Army invaded Anyuan on four occasions, except for the director of the mine, Ling Zizhen, no members of our congregation were themselves robbed, let alone killed. They did not suffer directly, although of course they were indirectly afflicted. Currently the greatest hardship for this place is that the mine is no longer able to operate. The difficulties of the workers are extreme.[66]

Due to the collapse of mining operations, combined with the Communists' successive recruitment drives, by the end of 1930 many more former Anyuan workers could be counted among the ranks of the Red Army than remained at Anyuan itself.

The transition from miner to soldier was not always an easy or seamless one. Even some who later would rise to become decorated officers in the People's Liberation Army, like Lieutenant General Wang Yaonan, did not initially find military life to their liking. Wang, who began to work in the Anyuan coal pits at the age of eight as an explosives operator and joined the Autumn Harvest Uprising at age fifteen, decades later still remembered the pain and uncertainty that he had experienced as a homesick young soldier:

> My father, Wang Shushan, was the party branch secretary inside the coal pit, but he never told me he was a party member. In 1930 in the second battle of Changsha I was injured. When my father saw me I was just hoping he would say, "Child, go home; you're too young for this and there will be plenty of time in the future for you to join the revolution," but when he asked "What's wrong?" and I replied "I've been wounded in battle" (thinking he would tell me to go home), he said, "No matter. What kind of revolution would it be if you didn't shed blood, didn't sacrifice? A revolution means blood and martyrdom." He even said I should not go home: "You're a foolish one. What would you do if you returned? Haven't you had enough of starvation and leather whips? The only way out is to follow Mao and the Chinese Communist Party until the time of Communism." I didn't understand why my father spoke this way, and I shed tears when I said goodbye to him. . . . Only later was I told that he was the party secretary. That time that my father didn't permit me to go home was the last time I ever saw him.[67]

Difficult as their personal sacrifice often was, Anyuan workers-turned-soldiers made a notable contribution to the Communist cause. Familiar with the use of dynamite from their experience in the mine pits, they performed crucial demolition and construction services for the Red Army. They also put to use the political lessons taught by the Anyuan workers' club. A miner who enrolled in the Red Army in 1930 and forty years later held the position of vice-commander of the Anhui military region reflected on the role of his fellow workers in the development of the Red Army:

> Anyuan workers were a source of fresh blood for the Red Army. The political standing of these workers in the military ranks was quite high, as they performed a backbone function. At that time, Chairman Mao regarded the Anyuan workers very highly. Not long after Anyuan workers joined the army, many were absorbed into the party organization, strengthening the party's leadership over the army. In a very short period of time they were promoted to cadre positions such

as squad leader, platoon leader, and even company commander—performing major functions. The Anyuan workers made enormous contributions in battle, with many comrades sacrificing their own lives.
The several thousand workers from Anyuan, having gone through
decades of battles, are now few in number. When the Anyuan workers joined the army, they added a new kind of military unit, namely
the demolition team. . . . When attacking a city, the Anyuan workers
first dug trenches and then, using sticks of dynamite packed inside
coffins, blasted their way in. This was the forerunner of the engineering units of the People's Liberation Army. . . . The Anyuan workers
shouldered a relatively heavy burden inside the army and the party
in terms of political work. Especially during the counterrevolutionary campaign in the winter of 1930, the majority of Anyuan workers
participated in the committee that oversaw the counterrevolutionary
work.[68]

In short, Anyuan workers made crucial contributions in both military
and political terms.


ANYUAN UNDERMINED

Important as Anyuan workers were to the development of the Red Army,
their massive enlistment signaled difficulties at the mining town itself.
The thousands of workers who marched off as soldiers with the Red
Army left behind a depleted and dispirited community. The vacuum was
quickly filled by a resurgence of Red Gang activity. From 1933 until after
the establishment of a Communist state in 1949, secret societies were
once again the primary power holders in the region.[69] An investigation
conducted in 1935 by the Jiangxi provincial government painted a bleak
picture of life at Anyuan. Years of bloody battles between Communist
and Nationalist troops had generated severe losses in both population
and morale. Due to lingering suspicions of Communist sympathies
among the locals, Anyuan residents were subject to tight surveillance
and severe mobility restrictions. The mine workers, who now numbered
fewer than three thousand, suffered from unpaid wages. Cases of suicide
and the selling of wives and children were rampant.[70]

Three years later, the exigencies of the war against Japan convinced
government authorities of the advisability of ramping up coal mining
operations at Anyuan. As with a number of other key industrial enterprises, the wartime effort triggered a government takeover.[71] In January
1938 the National Resources Commission (NRC) of the Nationalist Government seized control of the Anyuan mine and established its own man-

agement bureau there.[72] The next month the NRC named as new director of the Anyuan mine Wang Yebai, an American-educated engineer bent on improving efficiency. Arriving at the mine with a large contingent of workers freshly recruited from Hubei, Wang immediately announced a raft of layoffs and a harsh regimen of wage cuts and administrative controls to be imposed upon the remaining labor force. Particularly galling to the workers was a requirement that they wear metal identification tags around their necks (to be matched with photo IDs at the mine entrances) in order to be allowed down into the pits each day. The new policy evoked particularly intense opposition from the veteran miners who had experienced life at Anyuan during the Great Strike, for whom the dog tags stirred unpleasant memories of their pre-1922 status as "beasts of burden."[73]

Under the leadership of a few remnant underground Communist party members, some of these older workers launched a strike to protest the unpopular regulations. When the walkout proved partially successful at rolling back Wang's proposed new order, the party members were emboldened to take further steps. They sent an emissary to the Communist capital of Yan'an to seek help. In June 1938 Party Central, acting on the advice of Liu Shaoqi, dispatched a party member and former Anyuan worker, Yuan Xuezhi, as a special envoy to resume party organizing at Anyuan. Yuan, whose father and older brother had also previously worked at Anyuan, still had extensive contacts at the mine that Liu believed would prove beneficial in sorting out the complicated politics there.[74] Once back at Anyuan, Yuan proceeded to carry out an investigation on the basis of which he concluded that a number of former Communist party members who had made confessions under the duress of the White Terror were still basically sympathetic to the revolutionary cause and should be welcomed back into the party. Thanks to this magnanimous policy, Yuan was able to reestablish at Anyuan a general party branch with more than a hundred members.[75]

As promising as this development may have appeared to Communists at the time, it could not be sustained. Fear of a possible Japanese takeover led to the suspension of all mining operations at Anyuan in April 1939. Nationalist soldiers removed the electrical generator and sealed up both the eastern and western entrances to the pits.[76]

With the mine closed, the Communist underground arranged for unemployed workers to enlist as soldiers in the New Fourth Army, the direct descendant of the Ironsides army of Northern Expedition fame, in which Anyuan workers had played such a prominent role.[77] Soon the

Pingjiang Incident—in which Nationalist forces attacked a Communist stronghold on the Hunan-Jiangxi border on June 12, 1939, and killed some 140 party operatives in the region—put a halt to all Communist activities at Anyuan.[78] The glory days of the Anyuan labor movement were over.

## CIVIL WAR

In January 1946, after a nearly seven-year hiatus, coal mining resumed at Anyuan. Although encouraged and supervised by the Nationalist government to fuel its war effort against the Communists, the reopened Anyuan colliery was a sorry reminder of a once impressive enterprise. The years of neglect had wreaked havoc on the main coal pits, which were completely blocked by water and mud. Primitive mining in small pits scattered around the area, not unlike the situation that had prevailed for centuries before the opening of the modern mine in 1898, was again the norm.[79] Red Gang rule enforced by labor contractors had returned with a vengeance, exerting a stranglehold over the miners reminiscent of the days before the strike of 1922.

Under these challenging circumstances, Wang Yebai of the National Resources Commission resumed his post, now with expanded responsibilities for the amalgamated Western Jiangxi Coal Mining Bureau.[80] Just as the NRC had spearheaded the Nationalists' wartime economy during the hostilities with Japan, so now it oversaw industrial support for the civil war effort. As the internecine battle between the two parties moved southward, Anyuan's coal reserves—the only extensive seams located south of the Yangzi River—were viewed as a critical source for military-related production. In June 1948, deciding that Wang Yebai had outlived his usefulness, the NRC appointed a new director of the Western Jiangxi Coal Mining Bureau, Guo Xiangyu, to safeguard Nationalist economic interests in the region.[81]

At the same time that the Nationalist leadership changed hands, two Communist operatives arrived at Anyuan to organize secretly among the workforce. Following in the footsteps of their forerunners nearly thirty years earlier, the cadres began by focusing on workers' education. Study groups, initially targeted at skilled workers, were convened to discuss the meaning of exploitation and class struggle. When news of the Communists' stunning defeat of the Nationalists in the Battle of Huaihai reached Anyuan at the end of the year, anticipation of an impending Communist victory in the ongoing civil war led to increased worker interest in this underground mobilization effort. In response, the Hunan provincial Communist Party dispatched an experienced cadre to oversee the growing movement. His charge was to protect the productive capacity of mining operations so as to facilitate a smooth Communist takeover while educating the workers and developing a reliable party base. In May 1949 an underground party work committee was established for the mining district. A major recruitment drive was launched to persuade workers, especially those with a history of involvement in revolutionary activity, to join the Communist Party.[82]

Under government orders to keep the mine operating to fuel the Nationalist military effort, Guo Xiangyu organized an officially approved "preservation committee" *(weichi weiyuanhui)* to maintain order. Drawing on earlier experience with enemy paramilitary forces, the Communists immediately targeted the committee for infiltration. Although Guo chaired the preservation committee himself, unbeknownst to him most of the other committee members were actually underground Communists. Thanks to its official status, the committee was able to requisition a cache of rifles from the mine police. Thus armed, this committee became the Communists' primary vehicle for protecting and later occupying the Anyuan coal mine.[83]

Emboldened by the rapid advance of the New Fourth Army, CCP operatives at Anyuan persuaded a group of miners to struggle against a despised engineer. The workers tied up the engineer in question and delivered him to company headquarters with the demand that he be subject to disciplinary punishment. When alarmed mine policemen proposed suppressing the protest by opening fire on the workers, a Communist sympathizer who served as an officer in the police force intervened to turn the tide in the workers' favor. As a consequence, the workers made off with a sizable cache of guns from the mine police arsenal. Fearful of the now well-armed workers, management offered the protesters gifts of liquor and an apology in exchange for returning the guns. This settlement temporarily calmed the storm, but it did little to diminish workers' growing confidence in their own power.[84]

As the People's Liberation Army (PLA) continued its southern advance, a stack of handbills publicizing the PLA's signature "three rules of discipline" and "eight points of attention" along with its policies for occupying cities was delivered to the Western Jiangxi Coal Mining Bureau with instructions to distribute them among the local populace. The bureau was admonished to protect the mining district, with a promise to Guo Xiangyu and his staff of leniency and the retention of their administrative positions and salaries if they handed over the Anyuan coal mine undamaged.[85] Reading the handwriting on the wall, Guo agreed to comply with all PLA demands and paid the Nationalist troops 1,200 silver dollars to vacate the area.

On July 25, 1949, Communist soldiers marched unopposed into Anyuan, greeted by Yang'ge folk dancers, a sea of red flags, and a deafening explosion of firecrackers. Despite the drenching rain that accompanied the arrival of the PLA troops, local residents poured into the streets to welcome their "liberators" with shouts of "Long live the Chinese Communist Party!" "Long live Chairman Mao!" "Long live the Chinese People's Liberation Army!"[86] Not since its days as China's Little Moscow had the mining town experienced such public jubilation.

Much had changed in the intervening twenty-five years, however. Mao Zedong and his fellow "red literati" had shed their scholars' gowns for military uniforms. The Communists were no longer naive young intellectuals but battle-hardened soldiers who had survived the Autumn Harvest Uprising, the Long March, the war with Japan, and the civil war against the Nationalists. In the course of these deadly struggles, Mao Zedong had emerged as the paramount leader of the Chinese Communist Party, with Liu Shaoqi (first vice-chairman of the CCP) as his top lieutenant. Mao was revered for his strategic brilliance, which had enabled the waging of a successful rural revolution and national liberation, while Liu had gained a solid reputation, traceable back to his Anyuan days, for institution building and party discipline.[87] If Mao was now the undisputed leader of the Chinese peasantry, Liu was widely viewed as a labor organizer par excellence. By contrast, Li Lisan—once hailed as the premier leader of the Chinese proletariat and who in 1928 ranked above both Mao and Liu in the party hierarchy—had been banished to the Soviet Union in 1931 as punishment for continuing to advocate workers' uprisings well after the party had already lost its urban foothold.[88] Li would spend the next fifteen years in forced political exile in the USSR, permitted to return to China only in 1946 when the CCP, preparing its return to the cities, faced a severe shortage of experienced labor cadres.

Li Lisan's political disgrace and prolonged absence encouraged his former comrades to cast aspersions on his part in their earlier collaboration. Mao, looking back on his first encounter with Li Lisan, remarked in a conversation with American journalist Edgar Snow in 1936, "Li listened to all I had to say, and then went away without making any definite proposals himself, and our friendship never blossomed."[89] Li Lisan's behavior at Anyuan also came in for belated criticism. In a lecture entitled "Strategy and Tactics" at the East China Party School in 1941, Liu Shaoqi contrasted his own assiduous style of leadership with that of his ostentatious colleague: "Leaders come from the masses. At Anyuan, the flashy one was Li Lisan, the hidden one who did the hard work was myself."[90] This seemingly offhand remark foreshadowed a self-conscious rewriting of Anyuan history that would soon take place under the authoritative auspices of the Communist party-state. The cultural patronage of the People's Republic of China, although in some respects an extension of the cultural positioning that had previously animated the Anyuan experiment, was, by virtue of its connection to the powerful state propaganda system, a far more muscular phenomenon.

The appalling violence of the late 1920s may have been neither inevitable nor irreversible, but it marked a critical juncture in the trajectory of the Chinese revolution nonetheless. The establishment in 1925 of the National Revolutionary Army, jointly commanded by the Nationalist and Communist parties, followed two years later by the founding of the Red Army under Communist control, signaled a fundamental reorientation in revolutionary objectives and operations. The *wen-wu* pendulum had swung decisively away from nonviolent cultural mobilization toward armed combat. From this time forward, military squadrons (composed predominantly of peasant-soldiers) replaced schools and labor unions (composed of worker-students) as the primary focus of organizational efforts. As revolutionary parties turned their guns from warlords to each other, armies became the key loci of revolutionary activity.

Decisive as this militant transformation was for the future direction of the Chinese Communist revolution, its impact on the mentality of Anyuan workers is less clear. When the American journalist Anna Louise Strong interviewed an Anyuan miner in 1927, during that radical moment when the management of the mine had fallen under workers' control, she was surprised by her informant's decidedly unrevolutionary expectations. A veteran of the 1922 Great Strike who had enlisted in the National Revolutionary Army in Guangzhou and then returned to Anyuan after fighting warlords in the Northern Expedition, interviewee Tang Shouyi seemed remarkably unaffected by his experience. According to Strong's account, Tang's participation in the takeover of mining operations in 1927 was prompted more by simple hunger than by revolutionary ambition: "From a backward peasant family, illiterate, working long years underground, he reckons time still in terms of the Ching [Qing] Dynasty. Ideas of socialism or syndicalism seem never to have entered his head. Nevertheless he was also part of the Chinese Revolution. He and his fellow workers, moved by hunger, had taken control of the empty mine and opened it under their own management, even while they were begging the capitalists to return!"[91] Incredulous that so conservative an outlook could accompany such ostensibly radical behavior, Strong asked Tang whether the Anyuan miners had seized the mine for themselves:

> He looked shocked. "Oh, no," he said, "the mine belongs to the Han Yeh Ping [Hanyeping] Company. Only they do not work it, for they are afraid of the soldiers. So we ourselves work it since we are unemployed. We hope the Nationalist Government will make an end of these disorderly militarists and restore order so that the Han Yeh Ping Company will come back and open all the mine with much capital. For we ourselves are not strong enough to run more than a little part." . . . So mild and unrevolutionary were the demands of Tang Shou I [Tang Shouyi], who had spent all his life in the mines from the days of the Emperor Kwangsu [Guangxu], and into whose mind ideas of socialism or syndicalism had hardly entered. . . . All that he asked of life was peace and steady employment at a very modest wage, and the right to organize a union. Yet under the conditions existing in China, those modest demands made him part of the revolution. . . . In pursuit of his desire for food he and his fellow miners had taken control of the mines and opened them. . . . They had armed themselves and fought as soldiers.[92]

It is of course difficult, if not impossible, to probe deeply into the psyche of ordinary Anyuan workers. But to the extent that Tang Shouyi's perspective was typical, the workers of Anyuan seem to have remained more attuned to the Communists' initial agenda at Little Moscow—namely, "peace and steady employment at a very modest wage, and the right to organize a union"—than to the subsequent militarization and radicalization of the movement.

As Strong points out, however, the exigencies of the time made revolutionary (if often reluctant) soldiers out of ordinary workers. From the Northern Expedition (1926–27) through the War of Resistance against Japan (1937–45) and the civil war with the Nationalists (1946–49), thousands of former Anyuan workers played a crucial role in the development of the Communist Red Army. The American journalist Nym Wales, who interviewed a number of former Anyuan miners at the Communists' revolutionary capital of Yan'an, found that most of them had joined the Nationalist Revolutionary Army more than a decade earlier. Concentrated in the "Ironsides" Fourth Army commanded by Ye Ting, they had been regarded as the crack troops in the Northern Expedition. In 1938, when Ye Ting organized the Communists' New Fourth Army (named for the original Fourth Army) to wage guerrilla warfare against the Japanese military in central China, a sizable number of Anyuan veterans could still be counted among the ranks.[93] The involvement of Anyuan soldiers did not end with the military defeat of the Nationalists in 1949. Twelve of the generals who commanded the People's Liberation Army in the first decade after the establishment of the new Communist regime were former Anyuan workers who had been recruited to the Red Army during the Autumn Harvest Uprising and its aftermath.[94]

Anyuan's lasting contribution to the Communist revolution extended beyond the supply of officers and soldiers. Many of the former workers who enlisted in the Red Army assumed important political roles as commissars and propagandists, bringing to their assignment a facility with cultural mobilization acquired during their years as members of the Anyuan workers' club. Although the educational effort so central to the success of Little Moscow had long since been eclipsed by military considerations, key elements of the earlier Anyuan experiment lived on in later CCP policies and practices.

Cultural propaganda was a critical weapon in the arsenal of the Red Army and its successor, the People's Liberation Army. As Chang-tai Hung points out in his study of the decisive wartime period, the Chinese Communist leaders, in contrast to their Nationalist rivals, "were superb craftsmen in utilizing a rich array of popular culture forms to wage war against Japan, to win public support, and, most important, to spread revolutionary ideas and socialist reforms."[95] Hung offers no answer to the intriguing question of why the Communists proved so much more adept at the task of cultural mobilization than their competitors. One likely explanation for the disparity was the fact that Communist leaders came from backgrounds that were, on average, significantly more rural than those of their Nationalist counterparts.[96] Thanks to these origins, the Communists enjoyed a firmer grip on the pulse of the rural populace, an advantage that they pressed at Anyuan and after. The result was a more effective mode of cultural mobilization, deeply influenced by the folk traditions of the Hunan-Jiangxi region, than their urbanized enemies could muster.[97] The long-term implications of this early experience were profound. The CCP's renowned "red theater," which was similar to the costume lectures developed at Anyuan, became a staple ingredient in Communist Party propaganda from the Jiangxi Soviet through at least the Cultural Revolution.[98] The "workers' cultural palaces" established under the PRC also bore more than a passing resemblance to the Anyuan workers' club.[99] The shift from mass mobilization to militarization that occurred after the September Massacre of 1925 was transformative, to be sure, but it did not erase the influence of earlier practices.

This is not to suggest that Chinese Communist cultural strategies remained stable or static from the early years of the revolution through the Maoist era. Nor is it to argue that all Chinese Communists' attempts at cultural positioning and patronage, at Anyuan or afterward, proved equally compelling to their target audience. More than a few CCP cadres were evidently just as clumsy at this challenge as their KMT rivals. Early CCP leader Qu Qiubai berated his comrades for a tendency to dismiss the power of Chinese folk culture in favor of what Qu criticized as a "European type of bourgeois culture" unsuited to the Chinese context.[100] Mao Zedong's own pronouncements on this issue—as on so many issues—were inconsistent, but he repeatedly stressed the importance of respecting "local characteristics" in the process of popular mobilization.[101] Even at the height of the Red Terror, as we have seen, Mao cautioned zealous party cadres against a frontal attack on folk religion. During both the Jiangxi Soviet and the Yan'an periods, he chastised certain of his colleagues—especially those trained in the Soviet Union—for esteeming foreign ideas over native ways.[102]

Well before the establishment of the People's Republic of China, Mao was recommending a "creative re-fashioning of Chinese 'old forms' as the basis for China's future national culture."[103] And ordinary people responded to this invitation in ways that prefigured later developments. When a drought gripped the Yan'an revolutionary base area in the early 1940s, for example, overeager local officials, hoping to turn the villagers against folk religion, "tore the idols from their foundations and broke their heads off." But once the famine passed, "not a few peasant families put little pictures of Mao in the tiny household shrines where they had formerly kept clay images."[104] A ritual that would become commonplace with the state-sponsored Mao cult of later years was already anticipated in this spontaneous "re-fashioning of Chinese 'old forms.'" As Mao and many of his colleagues had come to appreciate, religious beliefs and practices presented opportunities, as well as obstacles, to their own political ambitions.

# 5 Constructing a Revolutionary Tradition

Like any state born from revolutionary struggle, the newly established People's Republic of China was faced with the tricky problem of how to legitimate its origins without at the same time introducing incendiary ideas into the heads of restive citizens. This challenge of constructing a sanctified yet sanitized revolutionary tradition that would serve to reinforce the ruling authority of the new party-state was further complicated in the Chinese case by the unusually protracted and protean nature of the Communist revolution. Former revolutionary sites existed in abundance, but many of these places were compromised by their close association with particular periods, policies, and personalities. In light of these considerations, Anyuan emerged as an unusually appealing subject for historical attention.

Unlike most other revolutionary centers, Anyuan could take credit as a cradle of both the proletarian and the peasant movements. Its importance to the development of the revolution was also comparatively long-lived, spanning a decade from the founding of the Chinese Communist Party through the formation of the Red Army. Despite this rich historical record, Anyuan offered a seemingly safe model for postrevolutionary celebration and emulation. The fiery socialist rhetoric that had inspired the Anyuan experiment notwithstanding, China's Little Moscow was noteworthy for its nonviolent, legalistic methods. It was a place where the education and culture (wen) of the workers' club had for a time triumphed over the militancy (wu) of secret-society criminal elements. While the Great Strike of 1922 could be presented as a heroic proletarian victory, Anyuan's established reputation as a center of grassroots education and cultural mobilization connoted priorities consistent with the current objective of regime consolidation. Moreover, Anyuan enjoyed the special advantage of having at one time or another attracted the services of a disproportionately large number of now prominent CCP leaders—among them, most notably, both the chairman and the vice-chairman of the party, Mao Zedong and Liu Shaoqi.

Although Anyuan's special attractiveness as an object of revolutionary reconstruction was due in good measure to its historical links to individuals who were now top party officials, those very connections also constrained and complicated the task of interpreting the past to a contemporary audience. The three veteran leaders of the Anyuan labor movement—Mao Zedong, Liu Shaoqi, and Li Lisan—stood shoulder to shoulder atop Tiananmen at the founding of the People's Republic of China on October 1, 1949, but this display of solidarity was short-lived. The years ahead would witness sharp splits over competing claims to proletarian leadership in which contrary interpretations of Anyuan history played an important role.

The value of Anyuan's "glorious revolutionary tradition" was recognized from the beginning of the new regime. When a labor union was reestablished in the Pingxiang mining district a few months after the Communist takeover, Li Lisan—who had returned from his fifteen-year exile in the Soviet Union to become the first minister of labor and de facto head of the All-China Federation of Trade Unions in the new Communist government—sent a congratulatory message calling upon the workers of Anyuan to "carry on the spirit of the revolutionary tradition."[1] Li Lisan's encouraging message may have seemed, on the face of it, straightforward enough. As the next several decades would show, however, carrying on Anyuan's revolutionary tradition was far from simple.

## CULTURAL PATRONAGE

The criteria for reconstructing the revolutionary tradition had less to do with either historical accuracy or popular memory than with contemporary politics. As the new Communist order took shape, central and provincial government officials sponsored rival interpretations inspired by ulterior motives that were not always fully apparent even to those who executed them. But cultural patronage was not only a top-down process. Local authorities and ordinary residents also aggressively pursued such projects in hopes of securing higher-level attention and resources.

The practices of the new Communist regime extended and elaborated patterns of cultural mobilization that had been operating in embryonic form since the Anyuan workers' club of Little Moscow fame. There were, however, important differences. Rather than aiming to awaken the collective consciousness of a protorevolutionary proletariat, as had once been the goal of the Anyuan workers' club, cultural initiatives were redirected toward advancing the interests of ruling agencies and actors. The outcome was a shift in the interpretation of the Anyuan revolutionary tradition, from seeing it as a cry for human dignity to regarding it as a claim for elite legitimation.

In the first decade of the PRC, the Communist Party reorganized the cultural arena so that henceforth the party-state itself would serve as the primary patron of the arts. The result of this restructuring was a cultural system dominated by the propaganda apparatus, which was especially privileged because of its role in spearheading mass campaigns.[2] The PRC propaganda system was patterned both institutionally and operationally on that of the Soviet Union. In contrast to the Bolsheviks, however, Mao and his comrades enjoyed the advantage of having tinkered with this system for nearly three decades prior to the establishment of a Communist party-state. The result, Chang-tai Hung observes, was that in China, "Soviet models were never blindly followed, and, on many occasions, they were either rejected by Chinese officials or appropriated for their own use."[3] The PRC, moreover, had a rich domestic history of censorship and cultural control on which to draw. As Julian Chang concludes from his comparative study of the Chinese and Soviet state propaganda systems, "The Chinese Communist Party put a nationwide propaganda system into place by adapting a Soviet model to the Chinese context but, more importantly, by building on traditions of public communication found in the imperial, Guomindang, and Yan'an experiences."[4] Those constructing the Anyuan revolutionary tradition would take many a tip from the Soviets, yet they added a distinctive Chinese twist.

Among the more problematic Soviet precedents to be adopted by Chinese practitioners of cultural patronage, albeit in altered form, was the cult of personality intended to buttress the authority of paramount political leaders. As is well recognized, Mao's cult of personality was an extreme expression of a Soviet political ritual that found earlier articulation in the state-sponsored hero worship surrounding Stalin (and, to a lesser degree, Lenin). Although a foreshadowing can be traced back to the 1930s, the Mao cult reached its apogee during the Cultural Revolution, when China—renouncing its former subservience to the Soviet Union—promoted adulatory practices that drew inspiration from indigenous traditions of ancestor and emperor worship. Less well recognized, however, is that Mao's cult of personality was not the only one to be constructed by the PRC propaganda system. More than a decade prior to the Cultural Revolution, a personality cult was advanced on behalf of Vice-Chairman Liu Shaoqi to strengthen his claim as the rightful successor to Chairman Mao. The history of Anyuan would figure centrally in Liu's ill-fated effort at cultural patronage.

## CONSOLIDATING A NEW ORDER AT ANYUAN

The Communist takeover at Anyuan, like that of other industrial units around the country, was trumpeted in party propaganda as the sudden dawning of a new age. The transition to an alternative socialist order did not occur overnight, however. The initial concern, as under the Nationalists, remained the conservative goal of safeguarding economic production. Reassured by the smooth transfer of power that had allowed the People's Liberation Army to march into Pingxiang unopposed, the new military authorities made good on their wartime promise to retain the previous administrative staff. For the next three years, Guo Xiangyu, formerly of the National Resources Commission, would occupy a leadership role in reorienting the Anyuan coal mine to serve the Communist regime.[5]

This is not to say that industrial relations remained unchanged. The longstanding labor contract system *(baogongzhi)*, denounced by the Communists since before the Great Strike of 1922 as a form of "feudal exploitation," was officially abolished a few months after the takeover of the Anyuan mining district. In its place a piecework system *(jiangongzhi)* was implemented by which the workers were paid according to how much they produced, with no cut taken out for middlemen. The reform was not universally popular, however, since it subjected workers to the relentless pressure of having to produce more in order to see an increase in their wages. Moreover, a number of former labor contractors continued to work in the mines as supervisors, and, thanks to their ties to remnant secret societies and other armed organizations, they still exercised a certain influence over ordinary workers.[6]

To undermine the residual authority of such groups, the newly established public security apparatus took aim against militarized units operating in the Pingxiang area. By the end of 1950 twelve bandit outfits and landlord militias had been liquidated, with some 1,900 of their members taken prisoner and another 262 surrendering voluntarily.[7] Having rid the county of major armed competitors, the Communists turned their attention to the coal mine itself. From December 1950 until well into the following year, Anyuan (like other Chinese enterprises at the time) saw the unfolding of a concerted movement to suppress "counterrevolutionaries."[8]

Although more premeditated and centrally coordinated, the Campaign to Suppress Counterrevolutionaries recalled the mass trials that had occurred during the Red Terror twenty-five years before. At Anyuan, a work team of more than twenty cadres was assembled to initiate the campaign. The team's assignment was to visit every workplace to educate workers in the meaning and aims of the struggle and to identify "activists" and "backbones" among the labor force who would take the lead in attacking designated struggle targets. A series of three highly emotional mass struggle meetings, each attended by more than three thousand people, soon followed. At these heated sessions, workers and their relatives leveled accusations of terrible mistreatment at the hands of abusive labor contractors. Prompted by the well-rehearsed denunciations of the activists and backbones, the agitated participants poured forth a barrage of hair-raising tales of beatings, torture, and rape. Immediately afterward seven contractors were executed by firing squad, thirteen Red Gang chieftains were sentenced to life imprisonment, and nine petty gangsters were assigned to hard labor.[9]

With the advantage of hindsight, the calculated ferocity of the Campaign to Suppress Counterrevolutionaries—which came so soon after the joyous celebration of Liberation—strikes an observer as excessively brutal on the part of a regime that had already secured its military victory. The atmosphere was kept tense by seemingly paranoid warnings about the possibility of a political reversal due to the connivances of "hidden counterrevolutionaries" and "secret agents."[10] Yet it is worth noting that events on the ground at the time did lend some credence to these dire admonitions. In the early years of the PRC, the Communist Party's hold on power appeared more tenuous than is sometimes remembered. Countless conflicts and confrontations erupted across the country, putting local authorities on the defensive.[11] This contestation, moreover, offered ample evidence that China's revolutionary tradition was amenable to alternative interpretations.

In August 1950, in the midst of a serious drought in the Hunan-Jiangxi border region, the Pingxiang Public Security Bureau caught wind of an uprising planned by a group calling itself the Central China Anti-Communist Revolutionary National Salvation Army. According to informants, members of this self-declared "revolutionary" group were spreading frightening rumors that "World War Three has begun; the U.S. has already used an atom bomb to defeat North Korea and has occupied

Manchuria," that "the U.S., France and Japan are invading China and soon the Nationalists will return," and—more accurately—that "soon there will be a land reform in which all those who served in the former government and military as well as petty gangsters will be arrested." Leaders of the incipient insurgency, several of whom were local Red Gang chieftains, had prepared for the uprising by swearing a Triad-style secret oath of brotherhood, which was sealed with a canonical ritual of wine and rooster blood.[12]

It turned out that one of these Red Gang leaders, an Anyuan coal miner by the name of Zhang Guangxin, had joined the Communist underground a few months before the Communist takeover and soon thereafter had completed a forty-three-day political training course for workers. But when he failed to be assigned a cadre position at the mine, Zhang was open to other suggestions. According to his subsequent confession to the police, Zhang Guangxin was recruited to the brewing insurgency by a former petty official under the Nationalists who visited his home with a persuasive message: "We have a powerful organization with a radio and the chance to import guns from Taiwan. Now is the time for heroes. In the past you gave your all for the revolution and now you're unemployed. In the future you'll be destitute unless you join this organization."[13]

Conveniently, Zhang Guangxin's elder brother, Zhang Fusheng, served as the captain of the workers' militia at the coal mine. The insurgents' plot called for Zhang Fusheng to turn over the militia's guns to the rebels, after which they would incite some sympathetic miners to seize the weapons of the mine police and take control of the major coal pits in the area before marching en masse on the Pingxiang county seat. Zhang Fusheng went along with the idea, gathering a sizable number of militiamen and guns in the dead of night to await further instructions. The anticipated signals never materialized, however. In the meantime, public security agents had learned of the plot, and the Zhang brothers along with thirty coconspirators at the Anyuan coal mine were detained before they could take action.[14] In all, more than fifty leaders of the planned uprising were arrested in a combined military and public security roundup; eighteen of them were subsequently executed.[15]

Although the revolt of the Central China Anti-Communist Revolutionary National Salvation Army was foiled before it even began, the incident unnerved the local authorities. Follow-up interrogations revealed that among the more than nine hundred people who had a hand in the conspiracy were a number of government officials as well as ordinary workers. Those involved included an employee of the Pingxiang Public Security Bureau who later confessed that he had been persuaded to participate by rumors that all the miners had already been organized to join the uprising and that anyone who assisted in the attack on Pingxiang would be rewarded with a handsome monthly stipend of twenty silver dollars and ample food and clothing.[16]

Further investigation revealed that the plotters had indeed carried out extensive mobilizing efforts among the local miners, aided by widespread resentment of the recently imposed piecework system of compensation. Capitalizing on this discontent, the insurgents criticized the new payment system as being even more exploitative than the previous labor contract system. Especially galling to the authorities was the rebels' creative use of the Anyuan revolutionary tradition. The protest grievances were presented as a plea for human dignity, harkening back to Li Lisan's slogan for the 1922 strike, "Once beasts of burden, now we will be men." Employing the arcane art of glyphomancy (analyzing the component parts of Chinese characters to discover hidden meanings), the would-be rebels stoked mounting dissatisfaction with the piecework system among the miners by pointing out that the character for "piece" (*jian*) contained within it the character for "cattle" (*niu*), indicating that under the new regime the workers were no better off than "beasts of burden" (*niuma*). By contrast, the old contract labor system was said to be more humane because the character for "contract" (*bao*) contained within it the character for "self" or "person" (*ji*). In protest manifestos the insurgents called for a "second liberation" that would free workers from the tyranny of the piecework system.[17]

Inventive and appealing as the rebels' cultural positioning was, it was obviously not a use of the Anyuan revolutionary legacy that the state wanted to encourage. The Campaign to Suppress Counterrevolutionaries, which began only a few months after the demise of the Central China Anti-Communist Revolutionary National Salvation Army, was intended to ensure that such challenges to the new order did not recur. At Anyuan the attack on labor contractors and secret-society chiefs was quickly followed by an intensive two-month campaign to eradicate drug trafficking and addiction, so as to eliminate one of the chief economic pillars of the Red Gang. By the fall of 1952, dozens of drug peddlers and addicts had been registered with the Pingxiang Public Security Bureau, and a large amount of opium, heroin, morphine, and other drugs had been confiscated.[18] In addition to ridding the area of potential challengers to state authority, mass campaigns were designed to provide a means of identifying and encouraging a cohort of young activists who could be counted upon to offer enthusiastic support for the party's policies. At the Anyuan coal mine, four new party members and 323 Youth League members were recruited during the course of the campaign.[19]

In light of the region's long history as a center of rebellious secret societies and violent criminal activity, it is hardly surprising that the new government's efforts to eradicate old habits elicited a certain degree of resistance. Indeed, reports from the Pingxiang Public Security Bureau indicate that drugs, gambling, theft, prostitution, "superstition," and other familiar vices continued to create headaches for local authorities for years to come.[20] But the immediate threat of large-scale rebellion against the newly established Communist state was successfully eradicated by the Campaign to Suppress Counterrevolutionaries.[21] Once public order was guaranteed, the state set about reconstructing its own version of the Anyuan revolutionary tradition.

## RESTORING REVOLUTIONARY REMINDERS

Although decades of warfare and neglect had taken a severe economic toll, the political significance of the Anyuan coal mine was still widely appreciated. As a result, local and national governments shared an interest in restoring the colliery to some facsimile of its former glory. In October 1954 a central party directive authorized reopening the adits and shafts that had been in use during the revolutionary era. After nearly fifteen years of closure, the heavily damaged passageways required months of backbreaking labor to be rendered usable. A large cadre of skilled technicians recruited from around the country was dispatched to Anyuan to supervise the difficult and dangerous work. In November 1955 the central pit where Mao Zedong and other leaders of the Communist Party had descended to mobilize among the workers more than thirty years earlier was reactivated. In early 1956, following a year of restoration work that had to be carried out almost entirely by hand due to the fragile condition of the pits, the old eastern pit of the Anyuan coal mine reopened. In February 1957 the western pit also resumed operations.[22]

As former coal pits were restored and new ones brought into operation, production at the Pingxiang Mining Company (which now included six other coal mines in addition to Anyuan) steadily increased so that by 1957 it boasted an annual output of 1.8 million tons, double what it had ever produced annually in the pre-1949 period.[23] The size of the workforce rose in tandem with the growth in production, reaching a total of

12,870 employees by the end of 1957—roughly equal to what it had been at the time of the Great Strike.[24] As had been the case before its closure in 1925, the Pingxiang colliery was once again the largest coal mine—in terms of both output and labor force—south of the Yangzi River. But, due to much greater state investment (and Soviet assistance) aimed at coal mines located in China's northern and northeastern provinces, the Anyuan coal mine occupied a less prominent place in the national economy than it had in its glory days.[25]

At least as relevant to the revival of the Anyuan revolutionary tradition as the resumption of production at the original coal mine was the reopening of the Anyuan workers' club. Having served as the springboard for Li Lisan's pioneering organizational efforts in preparation for the Great Strike of 1922, and then, under Liu Shaoqi, as the political and cultural hub of Little Moscow until the September Massacre of 1925, the workers' club was the core physical symbol of the Anyuan revolutionary tradition.

Hopeful that Liu Shaoqi might still have a soft spot for his old bailiwick, the labor union of Anyuan township wrote directly to him in the spring of 1952 to seek approval for, among other things, a plan to honor past revolutionaries by restoring the now dilapidated workers' club to its former grandeur according to the exact architectural design of Liu's 1924 renovation. Three months later they received an encouraging reply that affirmed the vice-chairman's personal connection to the revolutionary history of the locale:

Comrades:

I have received your letter to me of April 8. Thank you! Your requests to add two full-time cadres to the labor union and to repair the light rail have already been passed along to the Jiangxi General Trade Union and the Ministry of Railroads, which will determine how to implement them. In the past I worked at Anyuan for three years and even today I still remember many things about Anyuan very clearly. I personally handled the renovation of the worker's club meeting hall. I very clearly remember many past revolutionary comrades. . . . There should be a memorial plaque erected to them in Anyuan and a memorial service to remember all the deceased martyrs of Anyuan. I hope that you will take care of this in consultation with the Pingxiang county government.

Regards
Liu Shaoqi
July 8 [26]

Liu Shaoqi's acknowledgment of his Anyuan past had concrete results. As one appreciative elderly worker recalled thirty years later, "We all know about Comrade Liu Shaoqi's letter to the Anyuan township union. He cared about the older workers. We all picked up money at the Bureau of Civil Affairs."[27]

Heartened by this attention from the number two power holder in the country, local officials persisted in the quest to restore Anyuan's revolutionary heritage. A major obstacle during this time of economic austerity, however, was the scarcity of funds. With both the county and province hard-pressed to provide additional assistance, higher sources of aid were sought. In 1954 Guo Qingsi, a Stakhanovite-style labor model from the Pingxiang mine who held the national record for coal tonnage mined by hand with a pickax, took advantage of his attendance as a delegate to the first session of the National People's Congress to explore the possibility of securing central assistance. Shortly before heading to Beijing for the congress, Guo met with members of the Pingxiang Mining Company party committee, who suggested that he raise several requests directly with Vice-Chairman Liu Shaoqi. Guo, who had only just completed a basic literacy course for workers, asked the party secretary to jot down several simple talking points for him to take along on his trip to Beijing. The secretary wrote down the requests, which, in addition to seeking support for restoring the Anyuan workers' club, included designating September 13, the anniversary of the Anyuan Great Strike, as a national holiday to honor miners and inviting Liu Shaoqi to contribute his own calligraphy to the masthead of the local daily newspaper, *Pingxiang Miners' Journal*, as well as to the nameplate of the restored workers' club.[28]

After arriving at the National People's Congress, Guo grew reluctant to make the request for financial assistance once he heard Zhou Enlai's opening speech outlining the dire national economic situation. However, he was subsequently encouraged during a face-to-face meeting with Liu Shaoqi (a meeting that also included the Jiangxi provincial party secretary) in which the vice-chairman indicated that such a proposal would be beneficial for Jiangxi and would be favorably received by the State Council. The result, after the proposal won State Council approval, was a disbursement in January 1955 by the Ministry of Internal Affairs of thirty thousand yuan earmarked for the restoration project. One year later the renovated Anyuan workers' club reopened. A souvenir pamphlet, which prominently featured Liu's 1952 letter to the Anyuan labor union, was published and widely distributed to mark the occasion. The restored rail line from Pingxiang to Anyuan, which had been authorized in Liu's letter, was also completed at this time. Thousands of local residents lined the tracks all the way from the county seat to the mining town, where a gala celebration was held. National and provincial representatives were on hand to lend political weight to the occasion.[29]

The participation of these officials in the ceremony to reopen the workers' club indicated the pivotal position of Anyuan in Jiangxi's bid to attract higher-level attention and assistance. Claims to special consideration based upon Anyuan's revolutionary credentials were a key element in the province's overall political and economic strategy during this period. Feng Chongyi explains,

> Throughout the 1950s and 1960s, the [Jiangxi] leadership maintained a close political association and personal ties with top leaders in Beijing and worked closely with the central government to secure preferential treatment and resources for their province. The position of Jiangxi as "the cradle of the Chinese Revolution" served as their justification when, for example, Yang Shangkui, the first secretary of the CCP Jiangxi Provincial Committee, argued in 1956 in his report at the Eighth Party Congress that Jiangxi deserved special attention and more resource allocation, because its economic backwardness had much to do with the cost of the revolution to the province. Jiangxi clearly fared well in economic development during the Mao Era.[30]

For much of the Mao period, Jiangxi successfully parlayed its revolutionary pedigree into central government patronage. Underlying its request for revolutionary reparations were the historical connections that linked the province to leading officials in Beijing. Although the Anyuan labor movement of the 1920s had actually operated under the auspices of the Hunan Communist Party, thanks to Anyuan's closer cultural and economic affinity to Hunan than to Jiangxi, the bureaucratic logic of the new party-state elevated and empowered formal administrative jurisdictions over other preexisting connections. To take maximum advantage of its political position, Jiangxi Province—through its Department of Propaganda—sponsored a systematic effort to publicize and popularize the role of top party leaders in its revolutionary history.[31]

This initiative, which gained momentum over the course of the Mao era, began soon after the establishment of the PRC. On the eve of the CCP's thirtieth anniversary in the summer of 1951, a local historian by the name of Peng Jiangliu was transferred from the Pingxiang Propaganda Department to the *Jiangxi Daily* editorial department in Nanchang with the assignment of preparing a simplified version of Anyuan history that would highlight the "glorious, correct relationship between leaders and masses." For the next several years Peng conducted extensive interviews among elderly workers from Anyuan as part of an explicitly political mission intended to illuminate the heroic contributions of Mao Zedong and Liu Shaoqi to the Anyuan labor movement.[32] This special attention from Nanchang helped inform veteran workers and residents at Anyuan about their own political worth as living witnesses to the past achievements of central leaders.

When the doors of the restored Anyuan workers' club opened to the sound of thunderous firecrackers and stirring martial music on January 1, 1956, a flurry of red flags fluttered over a procession of elderly workers holding aloft various objects that they claimed had been used by Liu Shaoqi and Mao Zedong during their Anyuan days.[33] The climax of the ceremony was an impassioned speech by an old woman whose son-in-law, a former club and party member named Yang Shijie, had lost his life in the White Terror of 1928.[34] Waving a bloodstained shirt that "Granny Tan" said she had saved for decades as a reminder of her son-in-law's ultimate sacrifice, she exclaimed,

> I'm an old woman of seventy-five years with clouded vision and a lame leg. The reactionaries called me "bandit granny." This "bandit granny" knows and appreciates this "bandit nest," our club, more than anyone else around. My son-in-law, Yang Shijie, sacrificed his life for the labor movement.
>
> This club contains the blood of my relative. In the past, whenever I would pass by the club my heart ached and my eyes filled with tears. The club is the workers' home, but it was occupied by the enemy. I longed for the Communist Party to come back and reclaim the club. Today my wish has come true. Even though I can't see clearly, I can sense that the club is even better than before. In the future when I pass by here I will no longer shed tears. . . . I recall Chairman Mao's words when he was about to depart from here: "The Communist Party will return. Raise your children well so that they can carry on the mission of the martyrs." Today I want to say to Chairman Mao, "I remained steadfast. My children have grown up. . . . The martyrs did not die in vain. As they look out on this day from the netherworld, they must be smiling."[35]

Stirred by the old woman's emotional testimonial, a number of young people in the audience leapt up to pledge their own commitment to follow in the footsteps of the martyrs, obey the Communist Party, and contribute their all to the socialist construction of the nation.[36] The restored Anyuan workers' club faithfully duplicated Liu Shaoqi's 1924 architectural blueprint (which, according to Liu, had been modeled on

Figure 8. Young pioneers pledge loyalty to the Communist Party in front of a plaque marking the spot where Huang Jingyuan was executed in 1925. Note the Anyuan workers' club in the background.

the Bolshoi Theater in Moscow), but the function of the new building differed significantly from its former one. Whereas the workers' club of Little Moscow had been the heart of a vibrant labor union that promoted workers' economic interests and pioneered an innovative effort in workers' education, organization, and cultural mobilization, the contemporary club was intended as a memorial to the revolutionary activities of renowned Communist leaders.

As a consequence of its new role, the reopening of the workers' club attracted attention well beyond the provincial borders of Jiangxi. A report on a trip to Anyuan was featured in a 1956 national travel magazine, which recommended the excursion to prospective tourists around the country as a means of seeing firsthand where "Mao Zedong, Liu Shaoqi, and other comrades planted the seeds of revolution." The article included photographs of the recently reopened coal mine and workers' club and an interview with an elderly worker who recalled details of the 1922 Great Strike.[37] A few months later a New China News Agency broadcast, translated into multiple foreign languages and transmitted around the globe on shortwave radio, announced the reopening of the Anyuan workers' club as a fitting testimony to Liu Shaoqi's revolutionary achievements.[38]

Having thus reestablished the central symbols of Anyuan's former glory in the annals of Communist Party history, local union and government authorities proceeded to capitalize on their investment. On the second and third floors of the renovated workers' club they installed a make-shift display of revolutionary artifacts, which soon drew as many as three to four thousand visitors a month. On May 1, 1957, festivities to mark the thirty-fifth anniversary of the founding of the Anyuan workers' club featured a much more carefully crafted exhibit on the history of the Anyuan labor movement, which attracted a stream of foreign as well as domestic tourists. As part of the expanded exhibit, a number of "revolutionary" locations in the area—including places where Mao and Liu had stayed while visiting or working at Anyuan—were designated as protected heritage sites by the governor of Jiangxi Province, Fang Zhichun. The effort to convert the Anyuan workers' club into an international sightseeing spot was successful, at least among fraternal Communist countries. Soon a steady stream of delegates from the Soviet Union and North Vietnam could be observed at the coal mine, plopping themselves down in chairs where Chairman Mao had supposedly once sat and delighting their hosts with assurances that the revolutionary achievements of the Anyuan workers were famous in their own countries as well.[39]

## POLITICAL COMPLICATIONS

Even at this early stage in the construction of Anyuan's revolutionary tradition, however, political complications clouded the process. Although Liu Shaoqi had authorized the erection of a monument to the martyrs of Anyuan in his letter of 1952, it would be another thirty-six years before the project was finally brought to fruition.[40] With so many of those who died in the White Terror having also been associated with the Nationalists, decades of investigation and rancorous debate—the terms of which changed with the shifting political winds—were required to reach agreement on exactly which names deserved to be carved in stone. More complicated still, the political controversies were not limited to the deceased. Li Lisan, who deserved primary credit for the strike of 1922 and who retained a legendary reputation among the Anyuan miners, had again fallen out of political favor on the grounds of having encouraged working-class autonomy at the expense of party authority.

From the moment of his return to China after a fifteen-year hiatus in the Soviet Union, Li Lisan resumed his tireless advocacy of proletarian power. During the September 1949 meeting of the People's Political

Consultative Congress in Beijing, at which Chairman Mao famously proclaimed that the Chinese people, one-quarter of humanity, had finally "stood up," Li's own remarks underscored the special role that he expected the proletariat to play in the new national order: "Our working class, as the most conscious masters of the country, will carry forward the revolutionary spirit of heroic struggle, shouldering the arduous burden of constructing a new nation and a new society."[41] The unwavering faith that Li Lisan continued to place in the Chinese proletariat contrasted sharply with doubts expressed by Liu Shaoqi just a few months earlier: "The workers must be reliable. But are the workers reliable? Marxism holds that the working class is the most reliable. And this is true in general. But speaking concretely, there are problems. Therefore we must strive to make the working class reliable. If we neglect this work and just rely on them, they will be unreliable."[42] Differences that had characterized the two men's approaches to labor organizing back at Anyuan continued to separate them. To Li Lisan, the challenge for the Communist Party was not to discipline unruly workers but to reward their loyalty and sacrifice by raising their political status and improving their livelihood. As first minister of labor under the new Communist government, Li Lisan quickly set about drafting a remarkable labor insurance law that provided a generous package of welfare benefits—medical coverage, job security, a housing subsidy, decent wages, and pensions—to employees of state enterprises.[43]

As de facto director of the national trade union, however, Li Lisan was also caught in the middle of a massive wave of labor unrest that swept over China's industrial centers within months of the establishment of a new Communist state.[44] Famous for his leadership of the Anyuan Great Strike and the Shanghai May Thirtieth Movement, Li now found himself in the uncomfortable position of having to navigate a fine line between advocating workers' rights and yet admonishing workers against the exercise of those very rights: "Are strikes prohibited? That would be impossible and improper. Strikes are the workers' right, but today the workers don't need this method. In the past they had no choice but to strike; today, however, they can use rational methods to settle things. If negotiations fail, they can go to the Labor Bureau. . . . The old method is not only not beneficial but harmful. This is a new form of class struggle. To deny class struggle would be fallacious, but class struggle takes many forms."[45] The question of strikes was part of an emerging controversy over the role of the trade union, and indeed of the proletariat, in the new political order.

The debate came to a head in December 1951 when Li Lisan was criticized for "representing backward workers" and "promoting syndicalism" by treating the union as though it were above party supervision.[46] Several local union constitutions promulgated with Li Lisan's blessing between 1950 and 1951 had in fact failed to mention that the trade unions operated under party leadership.[47] His former fellow labor organizer, Liu Shaoqi, who in orthodox Leninist fashion had long advocated strict party control and was perturbed by the prominent role of the trade union in instigating the current strike wave, put the argument for party supremacy bluntly: "The union is not the vanguard of the working class."[48] In December 1951 a meeting of the party committee of the All-China Federation of Trade Unions decided to relieve Li of his leadership of the national trade union on the grounds that he had encouraged worker autonomy at the expense of party control. Three years later, at the same National People's Congress that approved financial support for the renovation of the Anyuan workers' club, Li Lisan learned that he had been dismissed as minister of labor as well.

Despondent over being sidelined politically yet again, Li Lisan returned to his family home in Hunan for the first time in more than thirty years. Although Li's home in Liling County was separated from Anyuan by only a few miles, he decided against visiting his old stomping grounds to avoid further provoking the ire of other high-ranking political leaders with a claim to Anyuan revolutionary credentials. Instead, Li settled for inviting a few elderly workers from the coal mine to his home to reminisce about the past.[49]

Despite being officially reprimanded for the errors of "economism" and "syndicalism," Li Lisan remained an immensely popular figure within union circles and among the workers in general. When the next national strike wave rolled across industrial China in the spring of 1957, among the demands put forward was a call to reverse what many unionists perceived as an unfair party verdict on Li Lisan.[50] With the reassertion of party authority over the trade union during the Anti-Rightist Campaign that summer, however, any hopes of reinstating Li Lisan at the head of the union were dashed. On August 17, 1957, the All-China Federation of Trade Unions issued an official explanation for the previous decision to dismiss Li, charging that the former deputy director had focused his attention on labor insurance at the expense of production and had ignored the political leadership of the Communist Party. In short, the December 1951 decision to purge Li Lisan on grounds of "economism" and "syndicalism" was deemed correct.[51] Party authority, not workers' welfare, was of paramount concern to the national trade union.

## POLITICAL CONNECTIONS

Although Li Lisan was asked to contribute his congratulatory calligraphy to the thirty-fifth anniversary celebrations of the Anyuan Great Strike in 1957, the exhibit that took shape at the workers' club that spring showcased the activities of the two other former Anyuan revolutionaries who now occupied the top leadership posts in the land: Chairman Mao Zedong and Vice-Chairman Liu Shaoqi.[52] Doctoring the historical record, it seemed, was a small price to pay for the chance to curry favor with those in power.

The central role of Liu Shaoqi in reconstructions of the Anyuan revolutionary tradition was especially striking. Visitors to the renovated Anyuan workers' club were greeted at the entrance by a large oil painting of the young Liu Shaoqi garbed in a Mandarin scholar's gown. Quotations from the vice-chairman's writings and speeches adorned the surrounding walls. Once inside the club, tourists were directed to rooms marked as Liu's former offices and bedroom, which included furniture, books, bedding, and other items supposedly used by Liu Shaoqi during his days at Anyuan. Photographs of the young Liu and copies of some of his early essays, written while at Anyuan, were also featured in the display.[53]

The trend toward presenting Liu Shaoqi as the paramount leader of the Anyuan labor movement and, by extension, of the Chinese proletariat was not limited to the workers' club display. Around the same time as the exhibit opened at Anyuan, a children's story entitled "Liu Shaoqi, Brave from Head to Toe" (*Liu Shaoqi yishen shi dan*) was introduced as required reading in elementary school textbooks across China. In melodramatic terms, the story recounts Liu Shaoqi's courageous confrontation with the capitalists to negotiate the victory of the Anyuan strike of 1922. Although according to historical sources it was actually Li Lisan who served as the chief representative of the Anyuan workers throughout the strike, Li does not appear in the text. Instead, in this tale all the praise and affection that the workers once lavished upon Li Lisan is redirected toward Liu Shaoqi. When workers marvel at Liu's bravery and ask whether it derives from a twelve-karat (or, in some versions, thirteen-karat) golden suit of protective armor, the fictionalized Liu Shaoqi—unlike the real Li Lisan, who encouraged rumors of his invulnerability as part of his charismatic persona—modestly insists that his only protection is the unity of the working class.[54]

Other cultural media under party direction offered a similarly one-sided account of the history of the Anyuan labor movement. A few years after the establishment of the PRC, the Ministry of Culture had conducted a national survey of local operas that bestowed official recognition on Pingxiang's traditional "tea-picking opera" *(caichaxi)*. Encouraged by this accreditation, the Jiangxi Propaganda Department in June 1956 produced a tea-picking opera entitled *The Anyuan Great Strike*.[55] Remarkably, the opera made no mention of either Li Lisan or Mao Zedong. Complete credit for organizing and leading the strike was assigned to Comrade Liu Shaoqi. Liu, not Li, was praised as the teacher at the workers' club who exerted a magnetic attraction on the workers. And Liu alone was singled out for negotiating a victorious strike settlement that guaranteed workers' rights. The opera concludes with a paean to Liu Shaoqi's courage in which the chorus sings of Liu's reputed twelve-karat-gold protective vest, to which Liu responds, "Your power is my courage; your resolve is my protective vest. You must unite to strive for a more beautiful tomorrow!" The chorus then chirps, "The revolutionary victory has already been achieved, the glorious tradition must flourish. Long, long live the workers' victory."[56]

The portrait that emerged of Liu Shaoqi as the sole leader of the Anyuan Great Strike was a blatant contradiction of the historical facts. Although workers' folk songs from the 1920s could perhaps be suspected of having embroidered the role of the immensely popular Li Lisan, even unsympathetic sources—from contemporary newspaper articles to the diary of the director of the Anyuan mining company—make clear that credit for the workers' victory belonged primarily to Li Lisan rather than to Liu Shaoqi. Director Li Shouquan's daily log during the course of the strike indicated that Liu Shaoqi's singular contribution was to concede and communicate to the workers the three basic demands of management: to protect the boiler and ventilation rooms, to keep the electricity running, and to preserve public order. It was Li Lisan who initiated and concluded the ultimately successful negotiations, and it was his tenacity that convinced the company to accept the strikers' demands. As director Li Shouquan recorded in his diary entries at the time of the strike, "According to Li Longzhi [i.e., Li Lisan], there could be no further concessions on the conditions. If we agreed, they would resume work. If we refused, he would leave Anyuan and allow the workers to have their own way with a violent uprising. . . . With things in this critical state, if there were a violent uprising production could not be guaranteed, and how would I explain to company headquarters? . . . We sent representatives to sign with Li Longzhi. . . . The next day work resumed."[57]

In January 1959, after viewing a performance of *The Anyuan Great Strike* that purported to tell the story of the Anyuan strike by referring exclusively to Liu Shaoqi, Li Lisan curtly remarked, "It wasn't true to life."[58] Even Liu Shaoqi's own verdict on a performance later that year by the Beijing Number Three Drama Troupe was guarded: "Historical circumstances at the time weren't quite like that."[59]

Although the melodramatic reconstructions of the Anyuan strike varied in detail, a consistent element in these 1950s renditions was the depiction of Liu Shaoqi as the daring defender of the proletariat against capitalist oppression and exploitation. Liu's unwavering courage was highlighted as the decisive factor in thwarting the nefarious machinations of Shu Xiutai, deputy director of the Anyuan coal mine, who is presented in these accounts as the personification of capitalist cruelty. Such Manichaean portraits of the Anyuan dynamics were not only historically inaccurate; they also, as Liu Shaoqi was well aware, contradicted contemporary complexities. On May 1, 1956, Shu Xiutai, now living in difficult financial straits in Shanghai, wrote a personal letter to Liu Shaoqi recalling that during their years together at Anyuan he had often turned to Liu for help in resolving problems. Praising Mao and Liu's leadership of the Chinese Communist Party, and noting that he had recently come to accept the truth of Marxism-Leninism, Shu explained that he had lost touch with his overseas relatives who had been sending remittances and as a result was no longer able to feed his family of ten. He asked for Liu's assistance in arranging a position with the Shanghai Culture and History Institute *(Wenshiguan)* so that he might receive a regular monthly salary and thereby avoid his family's starvation. A few weeks later Liu approved Shu's request and instructed the Shanghai Party Committee to make appropriate arrangements. In his May 26 note of approval, Liu pointed out that Shu had already left Anyuan for Shanghai by the time of the September Massacre in 1925, and therefore he was not implicated in the killing of Anyuan martyr Huang Jingyuan. Thanks to Liu Shaoqi's personal intervention and exoneration, former "capitalist" Shu Xiutai was soon employed by the Shanghai Culture and History Institute for a comfortable salary of more than seventy yuan per month.[60]

## CULTURAL PATRONAGE

That the Communists' legendary successes at Anyuan had actually hinged more upon the cooperation of members of the local elite than upon Liu Shaoqi's superhuman courage in opposing the capitalists did not soften the class conflict story line that had become the orthodox interpretation of the Anyuan Great Strike. Such simplification was not only the reflection of official party historiography emanating from Beijing; it also represented a calculated effort on the part of local authorities to gain favor with the vice-chairman of the Chinese Communist Party. Cheered by Liu Shaoqi's early support for the restoration of the Anyuan workers' club, Jiangxi officials saw the historic connection to Liu as an opportunity to leverage additional resources for their struggling province.

For much of the period preceding the Cultural Revolution, the deputy director of the Jiangxi Propaganda Department, Li Dingkun, oversaw a multifaceted initiative to publicize Liu Shaoqi's past activities in the province.[61] Li Dingkun was a seasoned journalist, novelist, and playwright who brought to this task of cultural patronage considerable experience and energy. Li enlisted the assistance of local labor activists, elderly workers, and party historians at the Anyuan coal mine, whose combined efforts resulted in an impressive outpouring of both visual and literary cultural products—museum displays, children's stories, operatic performances, poetry, paintings, and film—that featured the vice-chairman's revolutionary contributions at Little Moscow.

During this period Liu Shaoqi himself intermittently intervened to underscore his personal connection to the Anyuan revolutionary tradition. In response to labor model Guo Qingsi's request that Liu contribute his calligraphy to serve as a new masthead for the Anyuan daily newspaper, for example, Liu allotted time during the final evening of the 1954 National People's Congress to take up his ink brush and produce multiple versions, in both vertical and horizontal arrangements, of the five characters that constituted the name of the *Pingxiang Miners' Journal* (*Pingkuang gongren bao*). The new masthead was formally unveiled as part of the celebrations for National Day on October 1, 1955.[62] Until its closure during the Cultural Revolution a decade later, the newspaper—the only one in the country that carried Liu's calligraphy on its front page—published a steady stream of "quotations," stories, and photographs highlighting the vice-chairman's longstanding connection to the Anyuan labor movement.[63] This ambitious effort at historical reconstruction, it became apparent, was directed both toward burnishing Liu Shaoqi's leadership credentials as a champion of the proletariat and toward raising the political and economic profile of Anyuan and, by extension, of Jiangxi Province.

Higher-level patronage inspired Anyuan's own residents to try to take advantage of their past history for present needs. Heartened by Guo Qingsi's successful quest for central funds at the 1954 National People's Congress, a group of forty-four representatives of elderly Anyuan workers journeyed to Beijing the following year to lodge a petition calling upon Liu Shaoqi to resolve the economic difficulties of retired miners.[64] When this confrontational approach did not bear fruit, a more conciliatory strategy was adopted. Upon learning that the daughter of Liu Shaoqi's closest former colleague in the Anyuan labor movement was about to head to Beijing for advanced studies, the veteran workers encouraged her to seek an audience with the vice-chairman on their behalf. Zhu Zijin, daughter of railway engineer Zhu Shaolian (who was among Li Lisan's first recruits to the night school and who served at Liu Shaoqi's side throughout the Little Moscow period), later recalled her role in Anyuan's effort to convert historical connections into contemporary assistance:

> When I was about to depart from Anyuan to study at the Beijing School of Coal Industry, some elderly workers came to my home to urge, "When you reach Beijing, you should represent us by paying a visit to Comrade Shaoqi. Although he has been gone from us for over thirty years, we still miss him." . . .
>
> On November 13, right in the middle of classes, I suddenly received a phone call. The voice on the other end was that of a comrade with a Hunan accent who asked, "Is this Comrade Zhu Zijin? Comrade Liu Shaoqi asked me to see if this evening you might have time to come over to Huairen Hall to chat." This unexpected news made me incredibly excited.
>
> That afternoon, as soon as classes let out, I rushed out the school gate and hopped on a bus for the city center. The other passengers chatted and laughed, but I was deep in thoughts about the past. My grandmother and the elderly workers had told me stories of how Comrade Shaoqi led the workers at Anyuan to launch a strike. It was just like a movie that played out, scene after scene, in my head. . . . The strike ended in victory and the workers had enormous admiration for Comrade Shaoqi's courage during the course of the struggle. Even today some older workers who participated in the strike recall, "Comrade Shaoqi was brave from head to toe; he truly is a good leader of us workers."
>
> In Huairen Hall . . . Comrade Shaoqi drew me under a light and examined me carefully and then declared, "Very good. You look just like your mom." . . . Comrade Shaoqi showed great concern about the situation in Anyuan. He asked me whether the coal pits were operating, how much coal the whole mine could produce in a day, whether there was still a coking factory. I told him that the main adit where . . . all the workers had rushed out during the Great Strike now served as the entrance to the pits. In addition, a new shaft had been opened. Comrade Shaoqi listened and then said, "I've been down in all the Anyuan coal pits."

However, Zhu Zijin's attempt to parlay Liu Shaoqi's familiarity with Anyuan into a means of securing additional central subsidies for the workers of her native place did not turn out quite as she had anticipated. Local problems, the vice-chairman emphasized, required local solutions:

> Then Comrade Shaoqi inquired about the living conditions of the elderly workers and asked whether or not the mine took care of them. I answered that they received some assistance, but it was not enough. Comrade Shaoqi shot back, "Why isn't this being well handled?" I replied that it was because the mine lacked sufficient funding and, although it had made numerous requests to higher levels, had not received approval. When Comrade Shaoqi heard this, his attitude grew stern: " . . . The mine can write a letter to the local government to help out. This is something you should do. . . . If this doesn't work, then you can rely on the masses. The working masses have a high degree of class affection and spirit of mutual aid. If you have difficulties, you can turn the problem over to the worker comrades for discussion and study and they will figure out a way to resolve the matter. For example, they might mobilize the workers to help out by providing a day of free labor or by contributing a day's or half a day's wage—wouldn't that take care of the problem? This would be a glorious thing and could improve relations between old and new workers. I think everyone would be happy. Anyuan has so many workers. Just trust in the masses and ask the workers' opinions and there will be many solutions. Isn't that right?"[65]

Although the residents of Anyuan had hoped to leverage their history of revolutionary sacrifice into material compensation from the central authorities, their potential benefactor saw the situation differently. The vice-chairman patted his young guest on the shoulder and offered his avuncular advice: "You should take the lead in telling the young workers that someday you too will be old. Wasn't the main lecture hall of the Anyuan workers' club built with the contributions of the workers' own wages? This method can help the elderly workers without increasing the burden on the state."[66] To ensure that his insistence on self-reliance was not misunderstood, Liu reached for Zhu Zijin's notebook and wrote down his instructions: "The union should call upon every employed worker to contribute one or one-half of a day's wage to the union to manage so as to relieve and resolve the issue of the elderly workers' hardships."[67] He directed Zhu to share his words with the Anyuan workers.

Although the vice-chairman had earlier been instrumental in releasing central funds for the restoration of the Anyuan workers' club, with which his own revolutionary reputation was so closely entwined, he drew the line when it came to state assistance for elderly workers. For that purpose, he proposed, the masses themselves could sacrifice. Liu Shaoqi's lukewarm response indicated the limits of cultural patronage as a channel for economic gain on the part of the workers. But this did not end local efforts at securing central assistance. Nor did it diminish central attention to local connections.

Liu Shaoqi's refusal to commit funds to provide for the welfare of his old revolutionary comrades did not bespeak a waning interest in Anyuan's revolutionary past. Indeed, when his conversation with Zhu Zijin shifted from the topic of state assistance to the Great Strike of 1922, the vice-chairman grew quite animated. He even went to some lengths to embellish his own record at the expense of others: "I went [to Anyuan] a few days before the strike; as soon as I arrived there I actively advocated a strike. Li Lisan was rather hesitant and indecisive. After the strike began Li Lisan went into hiding, so I served as the general representative for all the workers. . . . When I went to negotiate, there were many enemy soldiers . . . but I was not afraid."[68] The vice-chairman had given his personal stamp of approval to the exaggerated portrait of his Anyuan accomplishments being manufactured by the Jiangxi propaganda system.

## WORKERS' RESPONSES

Meanwhile, at Anyuan itself the restored workers' club served as the local hub for a succession of centrally initiated campaigns.[69] Ironically, it was here that an outpouring of criticisms of the inadequate welfare provisions for elderly workers—along with a host of other complaints ranging from imperious cadre leadership style to inhumane labor conditions—accumulated during the Hundred Flowers Movement of 1956–57.[70] A gigantic bulletin board some 240 meters in length was erected just outside the workers' club to display the seemingly endless stream of big-character posters generated as part of the campaign. To enable its many illiterate workers to participate in the criticism campaign, the mine assigned nine teachers to work full-time at four "scribe stations" where workers with grievances could go to have their oral complaints written up as posters. As a result of this facilitation, more than three thousand posters were produced in just a few days of "blooming and contending." When the Anti-Rightist Campaign swept across China in the summer of 1957, however, the contents of some of these posters became the basis for criticisms of the authors themselves. Complaints that had been raised about the welfare system were now denounced for failing to show proper gratitude to the party leadership. As one politically correct elderly worker framed the issue at a mass struggle session against alleged rightists, "In the past, under the leadership of Comrade Liu Shaoqi himself, we shed blood and struggled against the bureaucratic capitalists. To safeguard the fruits of victory, we must struggle with rightists to the end. We old workers can now retire and live off of labor insurance. Isn't this because of Communist Party leadership?"[71]

In fact, such state-sponsored beneficence as the retired workers enjoyed was due above all to the labor insurance law drafted by the now disgraced Li Lisan. Liu Shaoqi's own contribution to their material welfare had been largely limited to his advocacy of local charity. After Zhu Zijin returned to Anyuan to communicate Liu Shaoqi's stern admonition for younger workers to underwrite the costs of eldercare, the workers of Anyuan themselves gave more than thirty thousand yuan in forgone wages to this cause. Even so, the credit for their achievement went to others. When a retirement home for veterans of the 1922 strike was opened with monies deducted from the paychecks of younger workers, a retiree who moved into the facility clasped Zhu Zijin's hand and appreciatively exclaimed, "Chairman Mao and Chairman Liu are benevolent officials. We will remember their kindness for generations."[72]

The tendency to credit central leaders with local accomplishments was a natural byproduct of the patronage politics of the Communist party-state. Any indication of higher-level attention—most notably Liu Shaoqi's meetings with labor model Guo Qingsi and revolutionary martyr's daughter Zhu Zijin—was hailed back at Anyuan as auguring an incipient infusion of outside resources for the impoverished coal mining town. In hopes of facilitating this objective, those who could claim a credible connection to the central authorities were promoted to positions of local prominence.

The person appointed to take charge of the new retirement home for veterans of the Great Strike (established with contributions from Anyuan workers themselves) was Yuan Pin'gao, Liu Shaoqi's bodyguard during his days at Little Moscow. Although Yuan, like a number of former Anyuan revolutionaries, had allegedly sold out to the Nationalists during the height of the White Terror in 1928, he was still remembered fondly by his erstwhile employer. When Liu learned in his meeting with Zhu Zijin that his former retainer was living back home in nearby Liling County (also the native place of Li Lisan, who had initially recruited Yuan to the Communist cause), he proposed that Yuan be transferred to Anyuan to work alongside Zhu at the reopened workers' club. After Yuan Pin'gao's return to Anyuan in early 1958, he was named deputy director of the club (where Zhu was now the director) as well as head of the home for elderly workers. Although the former martial arts adept was resented by some local residents for a tendency to lord his new authority over other veteran workers, Yuan served as a loyal—and loquacious—advocate for the revolutionary credentials of his Beijing benefactor.[73]

After returning to Anyuan, Yuan Pin'gao, known familiarly as Uncle Yuan, became the chief raconteur of local revolutionary lore. An Anyuan resident who was a child at the time remembered, "Uncle Yuan of the [workers'] club led classes for the Young Pioneers. Most of his stories were about 'Representative Liu [Shaoqi]' at Anyuan. At that time there were two large gum trees in the club courtyard under which was erected a plaque that read 'planted by Comrade Shaoqi.' Most of Uncle Yuan's stories started with this."[74] The highpoint of a sightseeing trip to Anyuan was the chance to sit under the shade of the beautiful gum trees that graced the entrance to the workers' club and hear firsthand from Yuan Pin'gao about how Liu Shaoqi, "brave from head to toe," had steadfastly defended the interests of the workers against the oppressive capitalists.[75]

Carrying on the Anyuan revolutionary tradition was becoming synonymous with celebrating the past contributions—and responding to the contemporary signals—of top leaders of the Chinese Communist Party. At the second session of the Eighth Party Congress in May 1958, Liu Shaoqi declared that "in order to meet the needs of technical revolution, we must also launch a cultural revolution."[76] The response at Anyuan (as elsewhere) to Liu's call for a cultural revolution was a frenetic campaign against illiteracy. Noting the indignity and inconvenience that illiterate workers suffered in having to rely upon scribes in the prevailing "long live big-character posters" climate, the Anyuan mine established the Committee to Eliminate Illiteracy, which was led directly by the Communist party branch. Unlike the night schools operated by Li Lisan and Liu Shaoqi thirty years earlier, however, this latter-day effort to stamp out illiteracy among the Anyuan workforce through a Leninist-style cultural revolution was supposed to be accomplished almost overnight. More than two thousand employees, of whom 726 were completely illiterate, registered for intensive formal classes. In addition, party secretaries and other cadres participated in informal round-the-clock efforts to teach character recognition, with blackboards erected throughout the mining area to form makeshift classrooms. After six weeks of frenzied activity, the party, in what was surely an exaggeration typical of the times, proclaimed Anyuan a "cultured mine" where illiteracy had been totally eradicated.[77]

Although it strains credulity to imagine that the level of literacy acquired in the course of this crash campaign actually equipped workers with the necessary tools for composing their own big-character posters, the number of posters created continued to increase exponentially. In the single month of March 1958, an astounding total of more than one hundred thousand posters reportedly went up at the mine; in one workshop each worker was credited with contributing an average of 153 posters that month. Amazing (and perhaps apocryphal) as this outpouring was, the scope of suggestions presented in the posters was actually quite limited. The experience of the Anti-Rightist Campaign the year before had put a damper on public criticism of party policies, and this new wave of big-character posters focused instead on how to streamline production and reduce waste. The "imperialist" powers of Britain and the United States now replaced party cadres as the only safe targets of political attack.[78]

Even as workers learned to frame their concerns in terms acceptable to the political authorities, however, they did not lose interest in ameliorating their own plight. After hearing in the summer of 1958 that Shanghai workers had received official endorsement for the Great Leap Forward slogan "Put politics, not money, in command," workers at Anyuan saw an opening for advancing their own agenda. Citing the Shanghai slogan as justification, they began to agitate for an end to the unpopular piecework method of compensation. In response, that November Anyuan's main coal pit introduced an experiment by which workers were paid according to the hours worked rather than their output. When initial reports suggested that workers, pleased with the new arrangement, had actually increased their productivity, the system of hourly pay spread quickly to the entire mine.[79]

Dispensing with piecework pay was one of a number of transformations that the Great Leap Forward brought to Anyuan. The nationwide push for steel production generated an almost insatiable appetite for coal that led to a major expansion in the Anyuan labor force. In 1957 the total number of employees at the Anyuan coal mine stood at just under thirteen thousand, approximately what it had been thirty-five years earlier at the time of the Great Strike. In 1958 alone, however, an additional 9,968 workers were recruited. By 1960 the total workforce had more than doubled to 27,526.[80] The rapid expansion brought a significant change in gender composition. Many of the new positions were filled by women, some of whom even labored belowground in the pits at backbreaking jobs that had previously been performed only by men. The crash program to increase coal production was not sustainable, however; annual tonnage declined precipitously, with the mine suffering its worst losses in 1962.[81] The downturn was reflected in employment figures. The main pit at Anyuan had employed 4,818 miners in 1961; in 1962 the number dropped to 3,130; and by 1965 it was down to 2,219.[82] Although Anyuan workers, like most industrial employees, were more fortunate than many of their rural relatives during the terrible famine that gripped the Chinese countryside in the aftermath of the Great Leap Forward, the economic toll on the coal mining town was severe nonetheless.

## REWRITING REVOLUTIONARY HISTORY

The demands of workers during this period of national crisis focused, naturally enough, on the pressing matter of improving living conditions for themselves and their families. But outside parties, mindful of the symbolic significance of Anyuan miners in the annals of the revolution, were anxious to impute more ideological motives. As China pulled away from the Soviet orbit in favor of its own development trajectory, indigenous revolutionary history was seen as a valuable political asset. That year several major oral history projects were launched to preserve and publicize the revolutionary contributions of the Anyuan labor movement.

The projects were part of a national program to compile "factory histories" *(changshi)* and "revolutionary histories" *(gemingshi)* intended to legitimate the rise of the Chinese Communist Party and inspire the application of revolutionary mass enthusiasm to contemporary goals. Unlike "party history" *(dangshi)*, which concentrated on the policies and sacrifices of party leaders and members, these other compilations belonged to the new genre of "revolutionary struggle history" *(geming douzhengshi)*, which highlighted the "insistent demands" and "heroic actions" of the masses. Teams of researchers descended upon targeted enterprises to interview elderly workers about their past experiences and to elicit favorable testimonials about the benefits bestowed by "Liberation." The goal was to compose easily accessible narratives of longstanding traditions of popular insurrection that demonstrated the inevitability of Communism as well as the potential for building upon China's unique revolutionary past to promote rapid socialist development in future.[83] In the spring of 1958, the central officials responsible for propaganda and culture, Lu Dingyi and Zhou Yang, put forward a joint call to "remember revolutionary history, praise the Great Leap Forward." The deputy director of the Jiangxi Propaganda Department, who for some years had been actively encouraging the publication of local revolutionary history as a means of promoting the province's national standing, was among the first to respond to the central appeal. Li Dingkun immediately convened a meeting of Jiangxi local historians and writers at which he urged representatives from the Pingxiang mining company to speed up their work on heroic accounts of the Anyuan strike.[84]

In concert with China's effort at this time to blaze its own revolutionary trail, separate from that of the Soviet Union, the Great Leap Forward fostered an interest in recovering and reconfiguring distinctively Chinese aesthetic standards and practices. In art and literature, the previous Soviet-inspired emphasis on "socialist realism" was superseded by Mao's call to combine "revolutionary realism and revolutionary romanticism."[85] The objective was to draw upon China's rich history of popular protest to create readily intelligible cultural products that would help to mobilize the masses for the current task of economic development. Officially sponsored projects to unearth local revolutionary histories and legends were widely promoted.

The Great Leap Forward's attention to the revolutionary past encouraged an outpouring of interest in Anyuan. Teams of researchers descended upon the coal mining town in search of material. For example, a group of scholars from the History Department of Beijing University spent several months at Anyuan in 1958–59, conducting interviews with more than twenty elderly workers who had participated in the strike of 1922 in order to gather material for a lengthy history of the Anyuan labor movement.[86] Another team of teachers and students from Hunan Normal College also carried out fieldwork at Anyuan in 1958, resulting in a 224-page draft history of the mine.[87]

By far the most influential product of this Great Leap attention to Anyuan revolutionary history was a popular book sponsored directly by the Jiangxi Propaganda Department entitled *Red Anyuan*. *Red Anyuan* is an interview-based narrative of "revolutionary struggle" at the coal mine that first appeared in 1959 as a 630-page edition in traditional characters published by Jiangxi People's Press. It was republished as an abbreviated 401-page edition in simplified characters in 1960, and then issued again in 1961 by the prestigious Writers' Press in Beijing. Edited by the Propaganda Department of the Chinese Communist Party Committee of the Pingxiang Mining Company, with direct sponsorship by Li Dingkun and the Jiangxi Party Committee, *Red Anyuan* presents a series of folksy vignettes (ninety-five in the original version and fifty-three in the second and third editions) that chronicle a pageant of worker militancy spanning more than half a century, from the Ping-Liu-Li Uprising to the start of the Great Leap Forward. The book was compiled by a four-person writing group headed by a former coal miner and current deputy party secretary of the Anyuan coal mine, Peng Yonghui. The other members of the group were Zhang Zhenchu, editor in chief of the local newspaper, *Pingxiang Miners' Journal* (which carried Liu Shaoqi's calligraphy on its masthead); Zhu Zijin, daughter of the worker-revolutionary Zhu Shaolian and director of the Anyuan Railway and Mine Workers' Labor Movement Memorial Hall; and Huang Zhenhui, deputy director of the Anyuan coal mine. Although all of these individuals had been active as local boosters of Anyuan's revolutionary reputation for some time, in 1958 they were commissioned by the Jiangxi and Pingxiang party committees to work together to produce the official factory history.[88] First serialized in the literary section of the *Pingxiang Miners' Journal* over a six-month period, the book was reviewed prior to publication in draft form by both Li Lisan and Liu Shaoqi.[89]

*Red Anyuan* opens with a photocopy of Liu Shaoqi's 1952 letter to the Anyuan labor union encouraging the establishment of memorials to its revolutionary heritage. Although Mao Zedong and Li Lisan as well as other early Communist leaders all receive some attention in the factory history, by far the greatest space is devoted to laudatory stories about Liu Shaoqi. First published in October 1959, on the occasion of the tenth anniversary of the founding of the People's Republic of China, the book describes its purpose as educating younger workers about the "revolutionary spirit" of the previous generation so that they might "advance the glorious tradition" and "with their own labor enthusiasm . . . create miracles in production."[90] But the book also had another obvious aim: to highlight the leadership credentials of Liu Shaoqi, who was emerging at the time as Mao's putative successor. The instant fame of *Red Anyuan* propelled its lead author, Peng Yonghui, into the ranks of national celebrity. In 1959 Peng was admitted into the Chinese Writers' Association and honored as a "national mass hero."[91] The following year he toured the Soviet Union and Eastern Europe as part of a privileged delegation of revolutionary writers.[92]

Written in a colloquial style that purports to replicate the words of the elderly miners themselves, *Red Anyuan* presents the history of the Anyuan labor movement as a vital resource for constructing Chinese socialism. Typical of the book's chapters is one entitled "An Old Miner

Returns," which describes a recent visit to the coal mine by Yuan Xuezhi, an Anyuan native and former miner closely associated with Liu Shaoqi. Yuan had left the area to join the Red Army in 1930 and on Liu's recommendation returned briefly in 1938 on a mission from Yan'an to reestablish a party branch (see chapter 4). Twenty years later, while serving as the deputy director of the Hunan provincial trade union, Yuan made a much-heralded return to Anyuan with his two sons to offer lunar new year's greetings to the elderly workers and to educate his own offspring in the revolutionary history of the coal mine. In the *Red Anyuan* rendition of Yuan's 1958 visit, the returning cadre instructs his children to remove their caps and bow reverently in front of the workers' club to pay their respects to the revolutionary martyrs. He explains,

> This was the headquarters where in the past Chairman Mao and Comrade Liu Shaoqi personally led the workers to struggle against the capitalists. At that time I was only as big as you are now, and I saw Comrade Liu Shaoqi himself standing right on this platform to address the workers. At that time the workers' lives were very difficult, with no food to eat and no clothing to wear. And they were beaten. This back of mine felt the whip of the labor contractors. Many comrades sacrificed themselves so that everyone could have a good life. Now Chairman Mao has led us to "turn over" and to enjoy happy days, but we must not forget these martyrs.[93]

Although this tale of Yuan Xuezhi's visit is included in all the editions of *Red Anyuan*, a number of other stories can be found only in the original 1959 version. Presumably many of the stories were eliminated simply to create a shorter, more readable book that would enjoy wider circulation. Some of the omissions, however, seem to be the result of deliberate political considerations.

A vignette entitled "Not a Myth" was among those dropped from the second edition of *Red Anyuan*, probably because of its laudatory treatment of both Li Lisan and the Soviet Union. In this story, which takes place at the beginning of the Great Leap Forward, a woman known as Granny Tan—the same elderly woman who had displayed her son-in-law's bloodstained shirt at the reopening of the workers' club the year before—is awakened one morning by her excited grandson, who runs to bring her the news that rice and vegetables will now be available free of charge thanks to the establishment of people's communes. After her grandson reads her a newspaper report that verifies his seemingly fanciful claim, Granny Tan's thoughts return to the time of the Great Strike, when Li Lisan, who then had a six-hundred-dollar bounty on his head, took refuge at her house to evade assassination. She recollects Li having told her that he was working to bring about a wonderful world where everyone would be equal and enjoy decent food, clothing, housing, and education. At the time, Granny Tan ridiculed the young Communist cadre for being a naive dreamer with a vision that could never be realized on this earth, but Li Lisan explained that there was, in fact, a country where his vision had already been realized: Soviet Russia. After hearing Li's revelation, the old lady recalls, she prayed to the bodhisattva every day to protect Li and his comrades from harm so that they could achieve their sacred mission. Shortly before Li Lisan left Anyuan, he promised Granny Tan that a better world was indeed on the way, as she would soon see. By her account, the Great Leap Forward was the vindication of Li Lisan's prophetic words: "What he said all came true under the leadership of the Communist Party and Chairman Mao. Now everyone is equal, everyone has a job, food to eat, clothing to wear, books to read. Today rice and vegetables are free and we can just concentrate on working hard. Looking ahead, our country is about to enter a communist society!"[94]

By 1960, when the revised edition of *Red Anyuan* was published, the devastating effects of the Great Leap Forward were becoming tragically evident. Millenarian hopes were dashed by the terrible reality of the famine. Li Lisan and the Soviet Union, neither of which bore blame for the debacle, were no longer regarded as suitable objects of popular reverence. Instead, state propagandists were hard at work creating cults of personality to be conferred on none other than the principal architects of the Great Leap Forward disaster.

## BURNISHING LIU SHAOQI'S PROLETARIAN IMAGE

While the workers of Anyuan expressed appreciation to the Chinese Communist Party, the chief beneficiaries of their gratitude—Chairman Mao Zedong and Vice-Chairman Liu Shaoqi—were actively promoting the ill-advised policies that would soon result in tens of millions of deaths by starvation in the worst famine in recorded history.[95] The disjuncture between the modest aspirations of the workers and the megalomaniacal ambitions of the top leadership was reflected in a rewriting of Anyuan revolutionary history that began in the mid-1950s and continues to the present day. Although some of the responsibility for this revisionism must be attributed to locals' attempts to ingratiate themselves with central authorities in order to secure high-level patronage for their struggling community, top leaders were far from immune to the temptation to rewrite the past in ways that presented themselves in the most politically favorable light.

When Liu Shaoqi learned, for example, that the three essays he had written in 1923 on the occasion of the anniversary of Anyuan's Great Strike were slated to be republished in a journal of Hunan historical materials, the vice-chairman himself went over the drafts carefully and made a number of deletions and revisions. In a November 1957 letter, Liu congratulated the journal editors on having managed to locate copies of his now-rare articles and offered his personal endorsement to reprint the pieces in a form that he claimed differed from the originals only in the deletion of certain "unimportant" details.[96]

A close comparison of the 1958 reprints with the original essays, however, reveals that the revisions were hardly trivial. An editorial note introducing the series of reprints exaggerated Liu's contribution to the Anyuan revolutionary experiment. Although in fact Liu Shaoqi had no involvement with the impressive Communist educational program at Anyuan until mid-September 1922, just a few days before the strike of thirteen thousand workers was declared (see chapter 2), the editorial note states that "in the winter of 1921 the Chinese Communist Party of Hunan organized comrades Mao Zedong, Liu Shaoqi, and Li Lisan to go to Anyuan to mobilize and lead the labor movement, to establish a workers' night school, to carry out education among the workers. The next September they led the Great Strike by nearly twenty thousand railway and mine workers."[97] In this rewriting of the historical record, credit for Li Lisan's nine months of energetic and imaginative mobilizing efforts (with Mao's intermittent supervision) in preparing the groundwork for the historic Anyuan strike is inaccurately shared with Liu Shaoqi.

Even more telling than such editorial embellishment was the deletion of certain key sections of Liu Shaoqi's original articles. In the 1958 version of the piece entitled "Past Criticisms and Future Plans of the Club," the frank assessments of individual leaders of the Anyuan workers' club that had appeared in Liu's original version were missing. In the 1923 edition, Liu had praised Li Lisan's record at Anyuan for an "outstanding ability to accomplish things" and a high degree of "adaptability" while gently chiding his predecessor for a lack of attention to detail and procedure. Liu had been much tougher on himself, offering no self-congratulations and candidly admitting to an "unenergetic and overly cautious work style," a "reluctance to interact with the workers," and a "failure to fulfill responsibilities to the worker's club" that had generated "misunderstandings among the workers."[98] Such admissions, which obviously did little to enhance Liu Shaoqi's image as a charismatic proletarian leader, were not included in the 1958 edition. Also missing from the later edition was a provision in the original regulations of the Anyuan workers' club, promulgated under Liu's supervision, which permitted the participation of labor contractors. An even more glaring omission from the 1958 reprints was a substantial discussion about the superiority of the Soviet Union that had been contained in Liu's original article entitled "The Organizational Condition of the Club." Acknowledging that the Anyuan workers' club had fallen short of its goal of fully replicating the Soviet exemplar, the 1923 article had concluded with a pledge that "in the year ahead, we will urge the club to approach more closely its organizational mother, Soviet Russia."[99] Thirty-five years later, as China headed down its own path to socialism under the autarkic banner of the Great Leap Forward, it was unacceptable for the vice-chairman of the CCP to be openly touting the Soviet Union as the proper model for emulation.

When Liu Shaoqi was named head of state in the spring of 1959, following Mao's pledge to withdraw from day-to-day economic decision making once the adverse effects of the Great Leap became apparent, the effort to build up the image of Liu as revolutionary leader gained greater momentum. Despite the growing rift with the Soviet Union, Liu was not averse to invoking Soviet precedent behind closed doors. He was in fact quite explicit about the benefits of a Stalinist cult of personality. At an expanded meeting of the Central Military Affairs Commission in September 1959, he expounded on the need for leadership cults in China:

> After the Twentieth Party Congress of the Soviet Union in 1956, which opposed the personality cult of Stalin, some people in China also opposed a personality cult. . . . As for me, I have always enthusiastically advocated a cult of personality. . . . For a long time, I have pushed this. . . . Even before the Seventh Party Congress I promoted Chairman Mao. . . . Now I'm still doing this, even advocating cults of personality for Comrade Lin Biao and Comrade [Deng] Xiaoping. Even if you don't approve, I'm going to do this. I don't need people to agree. I'm simply going to do this. In the future, will I advocate cults of personality for other comrades? Probably so. This isn't for the sake of any particular person, let alone for me personally. . . . Unless we raise the prestige of the proletariat and its leader(s), the proletariat will not prevail. . . . Our party is led by the Central Committee, with a chairman and a vice-chairman. . . . Because of this, without the prestige of an individual, without the prestige of several individuals, the prestige of the party and the proletariat cannot be established. . . . Stalin's individual prestige was extremely high and included a small

number of things that were not so healthy . . . but Chairman Mao and the Party Central already denounced those things a long time ago.[100]

It soon became clear that the "leader of the proletariat" whose cult of personality would supposedly augment the prestige of the proletariat was Liu Shaoqi himself, and a revised history of the Anyuan labor movement provided much of the material for this exercise in aggrandizement.

The four-person writing group at the Anyuan coal mine that had produced *Red Anyuan* now put their pens to work editing the long narrative folk song about the 1922 strike, which dated back to the days of Little Moscow (see chapter 2). Although the three extant original versions of the song (written down by three different people in 1925) had all presented Li Lisan as the main protagonist, with Liu Shaoqi and Zhu Shaolian playing minor supporting roles, Peng Yonghui and his writing group substantially revised the lyrics to make Liu Shaoqi the hero of the movement.[101] A lengthy recapitulation of the elementary textbook story "Liu Shaoqi, Brave from Head to Toe" became the centerpiece of the folk song. Although he had made no appearance in the original renditions of the song, Liu's former bodyguard, Yuan Pin'gao, now director of the Anyuan old folks' home and chief raconteur of Liu's revolutionary deeds at the coal mine, was introduced into the updated version as a "courageous and clever strategist" of the strike.[102]

All this attention to Liu Shaoqi's heroic role at Anyuan apparently sparked some desire on the part of the head of state himself to revisit the scene of his youthful exploits. On May 20, 1960, the Pingxiang party committee received an electrifying piece of news: Liu Shaoqi, currently in Hunan conducting a nationwide investigation of the economic consequences of the Great Leap Forward, intended to proceed at once to Anyuan. The thrilled local authorities sprang into action, making the necessary arrangements so that Liu's special train could travel unimpeded from Changsha through Pingxiang and on to Anyuan. As word of Liu's impending visit spread, excitement in the coal mining town reached fever pitch, with children and elderly workers mobilized to provide a hero's welcome at the Anyuan train station. But, after waiting all day with no sign of Liu's special train, the deeply disappointed throng was finally told to go home at dusk. Soon after returning home himself, the Pingxiang party secretary, Li Shujia, received a phone call explaining that Liu Shaoqi had been called back to Changsha on urgent business. Dejected by this unhappy turn of events, the party secretary retired for the night. A few hours later, however, Li was awakened with news that the head of state's train was just then pulling into Pingxiang. Grabbing a few other top municipal officials, Li Shujia rushed to the municipal railway station. The first to disembark was Liu Shaoqi's wife, Wang Guangmei, who curtly informed the local officials that her husband was on his way to a Politburo meeting in Hangzhou the next day and didn't have time to spend the night in Pingxiang, let alone visit Anyuan. Perhaps sensing that this was a rather shabby way to treat his political boosters, Liu Shaoqi himself soon emerged to greet his disappointed would-be hosts. When Liu learned that one of the welcoming officials was the party secretary of the Pingxiang mine, Liu shook the cadre's hand and asked him to convey his regards to the workers of Anyuan. After a few cursory questions about local economic conditions, Liu concluded the meeting with an instruction to the Pingxiang party secretary to "carry on the Anyuan revolutionary tradition." Noting that the veteran workers of Anyuan had sacrificed much for the sake of the revolution, he urged local authorities to provide properly for their retirement. Within half an hour, Liu Shaoqi's special train had departed.[103]

Considering the lengths to which local officials, scholars, and ordinary residents had gone to promote the image of Liu Shaoqi as the hero of Anyuan, it was understandably a letdown when the head of state passed through without so much as a visit to the coal mine. But this did not deter the locals from continuing to produce flattering, and historically problematic, accounts of Liu Shaoqi's historic accomplishments. An official "revolutionary struggle history," compiled by the Pingxiang municipal party committee in 1962, offered a notably overblown portrait of Liu Shaoqi's role in the 1922 strike. Among other egregious errors, full credit for Li Lisan's stirring strike slogan—"Once beasts of burden, now we will be men!"—was accorded to Liu Shaoqi.[104]

The project to embellish Liu Shaoqi's Anyuan experience was not confined to revising the *written* record; visual arts played a role that was at least as important. In 1961 the artist Hou Yimin—deputy dean of the Central Academy of Fine Arts in Beijing—produced a large oil painting entitled *Liu Shaoqi and the Anyuan Miners* for display in the newly opened Museum of Revolutionary History in Tiananmen Square. Hou's monumental painting was the product of considerable calculation and alteration that spanned nearly a decade.[105] Art historian Ellen Laing has written of the "special attention" that the painting received when it was unveiled at the inauguration of the national museum. The interest aroused by Hou's painting was due not only to its size but also to the arresting manner in which Liu Shaoqi's revolutionary leadership was presented:

Figure 9. *Liu Shaoqi and the Anyuan Miners,* oil painting by Hou Yimin, 1961. Photo courtesy of Eugene Wang.

> In one report, Hou Yimin, the man who made the painting, described some of the problems encountered in history painting: such as . . . the problem of how to depict the ideologically correct relationship between the leader and the masses. A preliminary version of the painting had Liu in profile at one side of the painting, leading a file of workers to a negotiation meeting to resolve the miners' strikes in 1922. In the second version, the artist gave greater visual prominence to Liu by now placing him as seen from the front, in the center of the painting, and surrounding him on three sides with youthful miners as they make their way to the negotiations.[106]

Historically inaccurate though the image was—there is no evidence that Liu Shaoqi led the miners out of the coal pits, as the painting indicates—it was prominently exhibited on a wall of the Museum of Revolutionary History when it formally opened its doors to the public on June 29, 1961. According to a Red Guard account six years later, it was Deng Xiaoping who insisted that this outsized image of Liu Shaoqi's revolutionary contributions be centrally displayed in the museum's inaugural exhibition.[107] Whether or not Deng actively intervened in planning the exhibition, art historian Julia Andrews concludes that "there is every reason to believe that the painting's prominence in 1961 derived from a broad view of party history that corresponded more closely to the Liu-Deng view than to that of the Maoists."[108]

Hou Yimin's painting of Liu Shaoqi striding out of the Anyuan coal mine amid a crowd of miners was eerily reminiscent of a key visual pillar in the cult of Joseph Stalin, a famous 1931 poster by Gustav Klutsis that depicts Stalin marching alongside a procession of coal miners. Sociologist Victoria Bonnell explains that the iconic Soviet poster "marked a major point along the path toward a new sacred center. The appearance of Stalin alongside coal miners signaled the beginning of a process whereby the heroic proletariat was gradually displaced by Stalin."[109] The veneration of Stalin in the Soviet Union, Bonnell observes, acquired religious connotations akin to the worship of Christ.[110]

That the painting *Liu Shaoqi and the Anyuan Miners* was part of a proto–cult of personality developing around Liu Shaoqi at the time is revealed in the artist's own discussion of its genesis and contemporary import. Hou Yimin wrote of his creative process:

> After repeatedly studying historical materials and even going to Anyuan to live for a week, I began to explore the main theme and human subject. The image of the leader as a young revolutionary . . . moving heaven and earth kept reappearing before my eyes and making it impossible for me to calm down. . . . The image should not be based simply on the actual mundane conditions of that period but should also match the idealized image in the mind of the masses today of Comrade Shaoqi's many years of revolutionary activities. . . .
>
> The twenty-three-year-old young revolutionary, filled with class devotion, armed with scientific communist thought, knowing the enemy and knowing himself, in full command of the strategy and tactics of struggle, naturally stood out from the workers in his unusual forthrightness, calm, and seriousness. Seen in this light, the leader is different from the masses.[111]

Hou Yimin also devoted a good deal of thought to the question of how to portray the miners, even modeling several of the workers in his painting on actual individuals who had been close to Liu during his years at Anyuan, but it is clear from the final composition of the work that the miners constitute a backdrop for the central focus of the canvas, Comrade Shaoqi.

Forty years earlier, Liu Shaoqi had taken pains to try to reduce the obvious distance that separated him, a cosmopolitan young intellectual, from the workers of Anyuan. But now the head of state, anxious to establish his credentials as Mao's successor in the wake of the Great Leap disaster, was inclined to assume a more imposing air. The heroic portrait of Liu as leader of the proletariat, prominently featured in the Museum of Revolutionary History, was a useful stepping-stone in the process. Between 1962 and 1965, during the height of Liu's political ascendance, the People's Art Press published an impressive number of copies—

172,077, according to one count—of *Liu Shaoqi and the Anyuan Miners* in various formats.[112]

As widely recognized and appreciated as Hou Yimin's iconic painting came to be, its popularity paled before that of another visual image of Liu Shaoqi at Anyuan. In 1962 the movie *Prairie Fire (Liaoyuan)* opened to packed theaters across the country. The movie depicted Liu Shaoqi, thinly disguised as the lead character, Lei Huanjue, as the lone protagonist of the Anyuan labor movement. Produced by Shanghai's Tianma studio for national distribution, the picture was written by the same man who had led the *Red Anyuan* writing group at the Pingxiang coal mine, Peng Yonghui, and was filmed on location in Anyuan. It featured performances by the Anyuan workers' song and dance troupe as well as the Jiangxi drama troupe.[113]

A key local informant for the Shanghai film crew was Liu Shaoqi's former bodyguard, Yuan Pin'gao, who of course gave his benefactor complete credit for the victory of the 1922 strike, attributing to Liu Shaoqi the slogans and stratagems that had actually been developed by Mao Zedong and Li Lisan. As a member of the movie crew remembered,

> The old miner, Yuan, was especially important. His experience was reputed to be unusually colorful. He had always been by Comrade Shaoqi's side during his time at Anyuan, protecting Comrade Shaoqi's safety. He was thin and short, with a dark complexion. He led us to every nook and cranny around Anyuan to see where the older generation of revolutionaries had planted the seeds of revolutionary fire. He told us how Comrade Shaoqi had shed his long scholar's gown as soon as he arrived at Anyuan . . . to gain a detailed understanding of the situation and carefully craft the struggle strategy. He spoke of how on the eve of the strike Comrade Shaoqi calmly destroyed the nefarious plots of the labor contractors and supervisors and maintained an inspiring tone. Naturally this old Yuan spoke most emotionally and proudly of Comrade Shaoqi's steadfast courage in representing the ten thousand miners during the negotiations at the Anyuan mine headquarters. In his thick local dialect he pronounced the popular saying "Brave from head to toe." Back in that day the mining district had seethed with grievances and the miners were itching to rise up. It was an extremely volatile situation. Comrade Shaoqi adapted his leadership to the circumstances, coining slogans that could gain the broadest social sympathy and support, such as "Move the people through righteous indignation" and "Once beasts of burden, now we will be men!" thereby guiding the miners to carry out a reasonable, rewarding, and restrained struggle against the capitalists.[114]

The movie faithfully reflected Yuan Pin'gao's one-sided interpretation of the Anyuan strike. The opening scene features the handsome young stand-in for Liu Shaoqi, Lei Huanjue, on his maiden visit (by train) to Anyuan. When Lei first appears on screen amid the stunning scenery of the Wugong Mountains, dressed in a long Mandarin gown and holding a Hunan oiled-paper umbrella, rays of sunlight stream from above his head. The messianic aura ascribed to Liu Shaoqi was but one of many fictional elements in the film. Some of the historical inaccuracies (e.g., misidentifying the heartless owners of the coal mine as Japanese rather than Chinese capitalists) could perhaps be overlooked as latter-day literary license. Other alterations of the historical facts, however, were so blatant as to grab the attention of anyone familiar with the Anyuan story. Most noteworthy of all, the film afforded neither Li Lisan nor Mao Zedong a role. Although the title of the film, *Prairie Fire*, derived from a letter written by Mao in January 1930 in which he invoked the old Chinese saying "A single spark can light a prairie fire" to predict an imminent "high tide of revolution," no attribution to Mao was made. Every achievement—from the establishment of a school for workers and the inauguration of the Anyuan workers' club to the victory of the Great Strike—was credited solely to one individual.[115] Liu Shaoqi was presented as the lone seer and savior of the Chinese proletariat.

Much of the movie's plot revolves around the patient efforts of Teacher Lei Huanjue (a stand-in for Liu Shaoqi) to recruit and cultivate a hotheaded young miner known for his martial arts prowess. After convincing the young firebrand to attend his night school classes for workers, the refined Teacher Lei persuades the rough miner to abandon his belligerent militancy in favor of joining the workers' club and participating in its nonviolent strike. Given the fictional name of Yi Mengzi (Yi the Fierce) in the movie, the character of the martial arts adept was widely recognized as a stand-in for Yuan Pin'gao, who was now deputy director of the Anyuan memorial hall and official interpreter of Liu Shaoqi's Anyuan experiences. Just as the character of Liu Shaoqi takes credit in the movie for what was actually Li Lisan's pioneering educational work, so Liu's sidekick Yuan Pin'gao appropriates the reputation for fearless truculence that in historical fact had belonged to Liu Shaoqi's nemesis, deputy director of the Anyuan workers' pickets and founder of the Hengshan peasant association, Xie Huaide (Xie the Fierce). If anyone missed the resemblance between Lei and Liu or Yi and Yuan, the director of the memorial hall, Peng's erstwhile coauthor Zhu Zijin (who, at Liu Shaoqi's

suggestion, had arranged for Yuan's return to Anyuan a few years earlier)
published several essays and undertook an extended lecture tour to hammer home the political implications of the film.[116]

The script for *Prairie Fire* was not simply a product of Yuan Pin'gao's
self-serving storytelling. It had taken more than four years and seven
rewrites, personally overseen by the vice-minister of culture, Xia Yan,
before the script finally saw the light of day. Whereas the original
draft had included twenty-one references to the leadership role of Mao
Zedong, by the final version all references to Mao had been removed.[117]
As in the case of Stalin's personality cult, this was not just an exercise in self-aggrandizement but a broader political project intended to
heighten popular loyalty to the party and the state by raising the image
of the proletarian leader. Historian David Brandenberger notes that the
Stalin cult "was designed to serve as a mechanism for political mobilization by advancing a larger-than-life hero capable of embodying the
power, legitimacy and appeal of the Soviet 'experiment.'"[118] According to
Brandenberger, party ideologists in the Soviet Union turned to the cult
of personality after 1929 as a new means of bolstering state authority
when more conventional modes failed to sustain popular enthusiasm.[119]
Thirty years later, as China broke from the Soviet orbit to pursue its own
disastrous path, the need to rally popular support inclined Chinese propagandists, ironically enough, to steal a page from the Stalinist playbook.

The climax of the movie *Prairie Fire*, which marked an escalation
of this propaganda effort, centered on Liu Shaoqi's negotiations to end
the Anyuan Great Strike. Like the familiar elementary school textbook lesson, "Liu Shaoqi, Brave from Head to Toe," the movie depicts
an unflinching Liu Shaoqi who refuses to compromise on the workers'
demands despite the overwhelming military might that the capitalists
have brought to bear against him. Liu wins a complete victory for the
strikers after declaring defiantly, "I cannot be frightened by guns." The
final words of the movie are also his: "We will be the masters of China,
the masters of the world."

Years later, when the film came under withering attack for its lion-
ization of Liu Shaoqi, the screenwriter Peng Yonghui would claim that
the lead character of Lei Huanjue was actually intended to represent a
composite of Liu Shaoqi, Mao Zedong, and Li Lisan, distilled into a single
character for dramatic effect. However, when the movie was released at
the end of 1962, at precisely the same time that a revised edition of Liu
Shaoqi's most famous essay, "On the Cultivation of Communist Party
Members," was issued with great fanfare, few viewers doubted that Lei

was meant to be Liu. Before reaching the movie theaters, the film premiered for seven nights in the open field in front of the Anyuan workers' club to overflow audiences who remarked on the close physical resemblance of the lead actor, Wang Shangxin, to the young Liu Shaoqi, who could be seen dressed in a long scholar's gown in a picture that was prominently displayed just inside the entrance to the club.[120] And it was not only at Anyuan that this connection was drawn. The renowned historian Gu Jiegang recorded in his diary entry for October 3, 1964, when he was convalescing at a sanitarium in Qingdao, "Saw the movie *Prairie Fire* . . . the story of the conflict between workers and capitalists at the Anyuan coal mine in Jiangxi. The leader was the director of the workers' club, Mr. Liu [sic]. This referred to Chairman Liu, whose courage and resourcefulness were put on full display."[121]

Not long after the premier of *Prairie Fire*, a critical review of the film by no less an Anyuan authority than Li Lisan appeared in the pages of the *People's Daily*. Li framed his critique as a defense of the importance of Mao Zedong Thought. As Li pointed out, the title of the movie came from Mao's famous revolutionary adage, "A single spark can light a prairie fire." The events at Anyuan, "led by the Communist Party under the direction of Great Leader Comrade Mao Zedong," were according to Li but one illustration of this general principle of the Chinese revolution. Li Lisan then proceeded to tell his side of the Anyuan story, stressing that Mao had sent him to the coal mine with very clear instructions to use legal methods to open a workers' school and then a party branch. Mao had determined the timing of the strike, and a letter from Mao, Li noted, inspired the slogan that Li himself had coined, "Once beasts of burden, now we will be men!" Li acknowledged that Mao had sent Liu Shaoqi to Anyuan shortly before the strike began in order to strengthen the leadership, and that Liu had indeed provided important supervision. Li even endorsed the climactic scene in the movie, in which the character of Lei/Liu braves enemy military fortifications to negotiate a victorious strike settlement, as accurately representing Liu Shaoqi's courage. But Li stressed that the movie fell short by failing to emphasize the overriding importance of Mao Zedong Thought in sparking the Anyuan "prairie fire," thereby confusing the movie audience about why the actions of "a certain character" (i.e., Liu Shaoqi) could be effective. Li emphasized that the Anyuan experience established the pattern for Shanghai's historic May Thirtieth Movement, during which Li Lisan again validated the wisdom of Mao's strategic advice by establishing workers' schools as a prelude to a general strike with wide public support. As had been the case at Anyuan, Li pointedly observed, Liu Shaoqi appeared on the Shanghai scene only after the May Thirtieth Movement had exploded, in order to take charge of the labor union and direct the strike.[122] Reading between the lines, Li Lisan was accusing Liu Shaoqi of being a Johnny-come-lately to the labor movement, whose achievements were attributable to the prior foundation laid by Mao's ideological inspiration and Li's own on-the-ground implementation.

Perhaps in answer to Li Lisan's thinly veiled criticism, Liu Shaoqi soon launched his own public relations campaign. When Liu's protégé at Anyuan, Yuan Pin'gao, went to Beijing to attend Labor Day festivities in the spring of 1964, he was welcomed twice to Liu Shaoqi's private residence to reminisce about the vice-chairman's revolutionary experiences. Having participated in the 1922 strike and served as a general representative of the workers' club at Little Moscow, Yuan was well suited to the task of attesting to Liu's Anyuan credentials. His recent fame as the inspiration for the character of the fiery martial arts adept Yi the Fierce in the movie *Prairie Fire* further enhanced his credibility as supporting actor to the chief of state.

In their well-publicized reunion in the leadership compound of Zhongnanhai, Liu greeted Yuan Pin'gao with a jocular query that underscored the militant reputation of his former bodyguard, "Do you still have two fists?" Yuan answered with a swift martial arts move, bringing a smile to the vice-chairman's usually taut face. After updating Liu on his activities since the two men last saw each other in the mid-1920s, Yuan mentioned that he had spent much of the past year in Hunan and Hubei giving talks. Liu inquired, "Who invited you to give these talks?" When Yuan replied that Liu Shaoqi's old comrade-in-arms, Yuan Xuezhi of the Hunan trade union, had arranged the speaking tour, Liu commented, "Very good." Reassured that his own supporters were behind this effort to publicize his Anyuan experience, Liu proceeded to take personal credit for Yuan's progressive past: "You entered the league, entered the party, and went to the Guangzhou Peasant Training Institute because of my introduction. Do you still remember?" Yuan, who had actually been recruited to the league and party by Li Lisan, dutifully responded, "I remember." Liu then recalled the success of his tenure at Anyuan, as indicated by the lack of bloodshed during his time at the coal mine: "When we led the strike, there were no losses. Only after I left the place were some comrades sacrificed."[123]

Ten days later, having toured Beijing and paid a private courtesy call on Li Lisan, Yuan Pin'gao was again received by Liu Shaoqi. In the

Figure 10. Liu Shaoqi (left) welcomes former Anyuan bodyguard Yuan Pin'gao to his residence in Beijing in May 1964.

excerpts of their conversation that were later made public, Liu repeatedly emphasized that the Anyuan strike had concluded in "victory, not defeat," and that it had produced many cadres. Conceding that he had not arrived at Anyuan until just a few days before the strike began, Liu nonetheless suggested that the victorious outcome was largely due to his own skill in manipulating the complicated contradictions that prevailed among the local elite. He recalled the challenge of maneuvering amid conflicts between the director and vice-director of the mine, between the vice-director and the general manager, among the Pingxiang gentry, and between the gentry and the military garrison.[124]

As their conversation drew to a close, Yuan Pin'gao—like Zhu Zijin before him—sought to take back to Anyuan some material result from the meeting. He requested permission from Liu Shaoqi for support in repairing various revolutionary sites around the coal mining town. The cagey vice-chairman, however, again refused to commit central funds: "It's okay to do some repairs but don't spend much money. Historical artifacts are better when they are older. Relax: after we're dead, people will repair them. And they'll do a better job of it." Liu then turned the discussion to a more cosmic plane. In contrast to the admiration of Soviet superiority that Liu had often expressed during his days at Little Moscow, the vice-chairman's parting words to Yuan Pin'gao now compared the Chinese revolution favorably to that of the Russians while sounding a cautionary note about the future: "The Chinese revolution has succeeded but the world revolution has not yet succeeded. In the Soviet Union, after forty years of revolution, the revisionism of Khrushchev appeared. Whether or not our successors will become revisionist depends upon one thing. We must rely on the masses to avoid revisionism."[125] Little did Liu know that he would soon be branded "China's Khrushchev," charged with irredeemable revisionist crimes traceable all the way back to his mismanagement of the Anyuan labor movement.

## EDUCATING THE NEXT GENERATION

Despite Liu Shaoqi's lukewarm response to Anyuan's requests for central support, local authorities continued to promote and publicize his revolutionary legacy. A few months after Yuan's return from Beijing, the Pingxiang party committee approved the establishment of a full-fledged museum, called the Anyuan Railway and Mine Workers' Labor Movement Memorial Hall, to be located inside the restored workers' club building. Zhu Zijin, the daughter of Zhu Shaolian who had been serving as director of the Anyuan workers' club, was named director of the newly established memorial hall while Yuan Pin'gao was made vice-director. The inauguration of the memorial hall was accompanied by the unveiling of a much larger and more politically self-conscious representation of the Anyuan labor movement than the display that had been assembled in the spring of 1957 to mark the thirty-fifth anniversary of the founding of the workers' club. It was, moreover, a representation that, while acknowledging the participation of Mao Zedong and Li Lisan, nevertheless credited Liu Shaoqi with the major milestones in Anyuan's revolutionary record. On September 14, 1965, the new museum—which offered a carefully crafted six-part exhibition on the history of the Anyuan labor movement from 1921 to 1930—opened its doors to the public. The first section depicted the suffering of the Anyuan miners and their spontaneous struggles of resistance. The second focused on the founding of the Anyuan party organization and workers' club. The third exhibit told the tale of the Anyuan Great Strike, spotlighting Liu Shaoqi's courageous stance as chief negotiator, and the fourth detailed the "deep development" of the Anyuan labor movement during the days of Liu Shaoqi's leadership of Little Moscow. The fifth exhibit examined the integration of the Anyuan labor movement with the peasant movement, and the sixth portrayed the Anyuan workers' participation in the Autumn Harvest Uprising and their contribution to the establishment of a worker-peasant revolutionary base area.[126]

In addition to the six-part exhibit inside the workers' club, thirteen outdoor "revolutionary sites" at Anyuan were opened to the public at this time. Deciding which sites merited museum-level status and then determining where they had actually been located proved complicated. In the course of numerous interviews with older workers, the director of the new memorial hall, Zhu Zijin, discovered that places once associated with Li Lisan were remembered more fondly and clearly by veteran workers than those connected to Liu Shaoqi. Reluctant to bother the head of state himself with such matters, Zhu wrote instead to Li Lisan to inform him of the undertaking and to ask if he could recall where Liu Shaoqi had first lived while at Anyuan:

> Respected Comrade Li Lisan:
>
> In order to educate the youth in the revolutionary tradition, Anyuan has already formally established a labor movement memorial hall and restored the club, the night school, and other old revolutionary sites. Of the three major leaders of the Anyuan labor movement, Chairman Mao's and your own Anyuan residences have already been restored and opened. It's only Chairman Liu Shaoqi's residence at Anyuan, despite extensive investigation, that we are still unable to determine. I wonder whether you might recall where Chairman Liu lived during his time at Anyuan. If so, could you kindly reply by return mail?
>
> Salutations!
> Anyuan Labor Movement Memorial Hall Director,
> Zhu Zijin

Li's reply, although polite, indicated his reluctance to become involved with what he correctly perceived to be an increasingly politicized exercise in historical reconstruction:

Comrade Zijin:

I have received your two letters. It's good that Anyuan has established a memorial hall and restored the club, night school, and places where Chairman Mao lived for people to view. This has educational value for the younger generation. As for where Comrade Shaoqi lived when he first went to Anyuan, I can no longer remember.

As far as I am concerned, I was just an ordinary worker who acted according to the instructions of Chairman Mao and the opinions of the worker masses. Please do not post any signs at my former place of residence or secret workstation. Please take down any signs that have already been posted. I hope you will explain this to the comrades at the memorial hall and will act accordingly. If there are differences of opinion, please share this letter of mine with the party committee at the mine. I hope they will agree with my opinion and instruct the memorial hall to act accordingly! Regards! And please give my best wishes to the elderly workers.

Li Lisan
August 30 [1965][127]

Unaware of the degree to which Li Lisan had fallen out of favor in Beijing, the staff of the Anyuan memorial hall initially interpreted Li's demurral as an expression of modesty.[128] Moreover, since all the revolutionary sites had been duly designated as provincial-level protected heritage units by the Jiangxi government, neither the memorial hall nor the party committee of the mining company possessed the authority to undo it. Nevertheless, when Zhu transmitted Li Lisan's request for anonymity to higher levels, it was quickly approved.[129]

As the Communist leader who deserved the most credit for pioneering Anyuan's "revolutionary tradition," Li Lisan's desire for disengagement was undoubtedly attributable to more than mere modesty; Li was well aware that others with far greater political power than he were actively laying claim to this contested history. In 1964–65 Mao Zedong and Liu Shaoqi held a series of conversations about the ongoing Socialist Education Movement in which the case of Anyuan was repeatedly invoked. At a small discussion group of the central work conference on December 20, 1964, Mao expressed irritation with what he saw as an overly cumbersome approach in carrying out the Four Cleanups stage of the campaign, complaining bluntly, "I don't approve of that many steps." Liu Shaoqi's response was to remind the Chairman of his own cautious modus operandi more than forty years earlier, citing the case of Anyuan as an example of patience and prudence in mobilization: "In the beginning at Anyuan you made contact with the lower staff members. . . . We strove for the majority, to isolate the minority, to avoid being duped." To Mao, however, Anyuan symbolized bold action rather than caution. He observed, in a blatant contradiction of the historical record, that he had sent Liu Shaoqi to Anyuan because Li Lisan had proved unwilling to carry out his strike orders: "Li Lisan was an old stalwart, yet at the critical moment he refused to do anything—that's why I asked our state chairman to go." Rather than correct the falsehood, Liu piled on insults directed toward his former colleagues: "Not only Li Lisan. Jiang Xianyun also took flight." Faced with the inconvenient but widely known fact that it was Li Lisan rather than Liu Shaoqi who had presided over the exuberant celebration of the strike victory, Liu explained away Li's leadership role as a matter of simple expedience: "A lot of people knew Li Lisan, so the victory announcement was made by him." Then Liu returned to his trademark stress on caution and discipline: "We prohibited people from killing anyone by saying that if you kill someone we will shut down the mine. If the mine were shut down, it would have filled with water in three days."[130]

Two weeks later Mao Zedong again vented his frustration with the slow, methodical way in which the Four Cleanups was being conducted and again raised the example of Anyuan to illustrate the advantages of a speedier and more effective form of revolutionary mobilization than the disciplined work teams advocated by Liu Shaoqi: "In the past, when the Anyuan coal mine established a union, we didn't know a single Anyuan worker. . . . After three months of effort, the strike began."[131] Ominously for the future fate of the head of state, this time Mao gave Liu Shaoqi no credit for having achieved victory at Anyuan. The "genuine" leader whom Mao praised in connection with the Anyuan struggle was not Liu Shaoqi but the long-deceased railroad engineer Zhu Shaolian:

> Genuine leaders and good people stand out only in a struggle. . . .
> One of them was Zhu Shaolian, who had two wives. He also wanted
> to make revolution because, as foreman, he was oppressed and his
> wage was too meager. This man was heroically sacrificed later. . . .
> When you go out to develop and engage in mass movement, or to lead
> a mass struggle, the masses will do what they want to in the struggle
> and they will then create their own leaders in the struggle. . . . Now
> that you have founded a party, entered cities, and become bureau-
> crats, you are no longer adept at launching mass movements. . . . In
> short, we must rely on the masses, not the work teams.[132]

Although Liu Shaoqi was prepared to parrot the party chairman's call for quick action ("One high tide follows another, and we must not procrastinate," he echoed), the underlying differences between the two top leaders over the proper way to carry out the Socialist Education Movement prefigured a serious rift that would explode the following year during the Cultural Revolution. Liu Shaoqi's attempt to construct from his Anyuan experience a revolutionary reputation as fearless leader of the Chinese proletariat and rightful successor to Chairman Mao was coming back to haunt him.

A further hint that Liu Shaoqi was about to be dethroned as the hero of Anyuan came with the release in 1965 of the monumental film *The East Is Red*. The film, which offered a pageant of the history of the Chinese revolution in dance and music, anticipated the extraordinary cult of personality that would soon envelop Mao Zedong.[133] In the film, which was based on a live performance staged the previous year, the curtain opens with a paean to Chairman Mao: "The East is red, the sun has risen; China has produced a Mao Zedong; He strives for the happiness of the people; he is the Great Savior of the people." The equation of Mao with the rising sun in the east makes clear that there is but one paramount leader of the Chinese revolution. Mao is henceforth to be acknowledged as the savior of proletariat and peasantry alike. After an introductory dance number in which a banner with the face of the young Mao dominates the stage (sidelining the banners depicting Marx and Lenin), attention turns to the labor movement. The choice of the "Song of the Anyuan Workers' Club" (sung in front of a likeness of the Anyuan coal mine by joyful miners holding up the thirteen-point Anyuan strike agreement) to symbolize the early Communist labor movement, immediately following the dance number deifying Chairman Mao, indicates that Mao Zedong is the rightful leader of the Chinese proletariat. Neither Li Lisan, who wrote the original lyrics to the Anyuan song, nor Liu Shaoqi, who was so closely identified with the development of the Anyuan workers' club, makes an appearance in the number. Instead a railway engineer, presumably a dramatic likeness of the deceased Zhu Shaolian, stands at the head of a column of dancing workers joyfully waving a signal light.[134]

## WORKING CONDITIONS

The establishment of a new Communist regime claiming to represent the interests of the proletariat was more than a matter of competing song and dance performances, of course. The initial decade and a half of Communist rule also brought certain concrete benefits to the workers of Anyuan. The end of the labor contract system and suppression of secret societies were among the most publicized, but a number of other improvements were perhaps even more appreciated by ordinary workers. To replace the squalid shantytowns that dotted the area, the mining company invested substantially in the building of new housing for workers.[135] Cafeterias and bathhouses, previously operated by labor contractors, were upgraded at considerable company expense.[136] When the mining company was converted to state ownership in 1953, it implemented a generous pension program that permitted workers to draw retirement paychecks equal to 60 to 90 percent of their wages, depending upon their seniority.[137] As with other state enterprises, a sum equivalent to 3 percent of the company's entire wage bill went to underwrite the labor insurance (designed by Li Lisan) that provided basic medical coverage for permanent workers and their dependents. The union also operated a small program of loans and subsidies for exceptionally needy workers and offered some compensation to families of those injured or killed in industrial accidents.[138]

These advances aside, the perils of coal mining remained extreme. Gas explosions, cave-ins, floods, and other workplace disasters took the lives of 341 workers at the Pingxiang coal mine between 1950 and 1965. During the Great Leap Forward and its immediate aftermath, as pressure to increase coal tonnage reached impossible heights, the fatalities were especially numerous; a total of 213 workers died in industrial accidents between 1958 and 1962. Work-related illnesses also continued to present serious problems. When the mine acquired its first X-ray machine in 1953, more than 70 percent of elderly workers tested positive for black lung disease. Although improved preventative measures resulted in a decline in this grim statistic over the years that followed, miners' health remained a major concern.[139]

The Communist party-state—despite its evident interest in Anyuan's "glorious revolutionary tradition" and its stated commitment to ameliorating the plight of the working class—obviously did not transform the grimy coal mining town into a proletarian utopia.[140] Yet working at Anyuan was widely regarded as a privilege, especially by those still closely tied to the countryside. As one former villager recalled his experience of being hired at Anyuan,

> In 1956 the mine put out a call for temporary workers. At that time I didn't dream I could become a worker with a pension, let alone enjoy the benefits of labor insurance. I just hoped to make a little money, whether paid by the day or the month. . . . When I first went down into the coal pits I was supposed to haul coal, but because I was not

well nourished I was not strong enough to move the load. I could hardly bear it and I cried. But I kept at it and things got better. . . . The first time I wore the blue uniform, hat, and leather shoes issued by the mine I felt incredibly happy. I still remember how the uniform was embroidered with red characters that said "Chinese miner." . . . The mine gave you a household registration *(hukou)* and the cadres said to us, "Now you've become a miner. Work hard and be grateful to Chairman Mao." . . .

At that time cadres' wages and bonuses were less than those of workers and miners' wages were higher than those of engineers. Because there was no gap between masses and cadres, relations were good and workers were very motivated. A lazybones would be criticized by the entire work shift.

Whenever I returned home I always wore my miner's uniform, including the hat and shoes, and I felt very proud. At that time coal miners were considered "elder brothers." In 1957 (at age twenty-two), I got married. My wife was just seventeen. In the 1950s whenever a coal miner wore his uniform everyone was envious. . . . In the 1950s and 1960s it was very easy for coal miners to marry. Women were looking for a good meal ticket.[141]

Pride in being a member of the proletariat translated into support for the new Communist order, a sentiment that was not limited to the Anyuan coal miners. Steve Smith observes of China as a whole that "compared with the Soviet Union, it does seem that worker loyalty to Mao and enthusiasm for the goals of the party-state was widespread."[142]

The concrete benefits (and coercive constraints) that characterized workplace relations under Mao go some distance toward explaining the general support that the regime evidently enjoyed among permanent workers at state enterprises.[143] But the Communist party-state, like Little Moscow thirty years earlier, was not content to rule by carrots and sticks alone. It also appreciated and actively employed the power of cultural representation.

The system of cultural patronage that developed under the new order reflected the agendas of many different actors operating at multiple levels of the system. As we have seen in the case of Anyuan, local residents and officials made repeated attempts to parlay their revolutionary legacy into special attention and assistance from the central government. To some degree they were successful in this endeavor. The enthusiasm that higher-level leaders displayed for fostering the Anyuan revolutionary tradition through various cultural media resulted in certain tangible benefits, from the restoration of the rail line to a retirement home for veteran workers. Although the Anyuan workers' club, which reopened in 1956, was designed as a memorial hall to publicize the revolutionary exploits of party leaders rather than as a labor union to promote workers' welfare, its displays helped to attract distinguished visitors and tourist revenues to the impoverished coal mining town. Other cultural products focused on the history of Anyuan—stories, plays, paintings, films, and so on—redounded to the mutual advantage of local boosters and elite protagonists alike.

Nevertheless, the motivations underlying the practices of cultural patronage often diverged significantly among the various parties involved. The benefits were also unevenly distributed. These discrepancies became especially pronounced when individual leaders actively rewrote history to promote their own standing at the expense of others. With Liu Shaoqi's appointment as head of state in 1959, the spate of accounts and images of his "courageous" deeds as a young man at Anyuan began to assume cultlike proportions. Although these efforts paled in comparison to the "Anyuan aura" that soon would surround the chairman of the Chinese Communist Party himself, they pointed toward a disturbing and deepening trend: China's revolutionary heritage was being stretched and skewed to suit the personal and political agendas of its rulers.

Contestation over historical interpretation was a key ingredient in the strife that culminated in the Cultural Revolution. As Robert Jay Lifton observed at the height of the Cultural Revolution in 1968, "From 1962 onward, and especially since 1965 (when the preliminaries to the Cultural Revolution took place), the regime has been struggling to reassert the confident relationship to history it had possessed in earlier days. The split among Party leaders has had much to do with the image held of just how one should go about doing this."[144] As had been true in imperial China, rendering authoritative verdicts on history and historical scholarship was central to the exercise of political power.[145] Debates over the correct reading of the Anyuan legacy were part of a larger process of historical reconstruction conducted via a complicated cultural patronage system that involved prominent roles for scholars and artists as well as government officials.

The cult of Liu Shaoqi drew heavily on the vice-chairman's historical connection to Anyuan. Like the cult of Comrade Stalin, the cult of Comrade Shaoqi used heroic images of Liu striding alongside coal miners to assert his claim as leader of the proletariat. Mao, by implication, was relegated to leader of the peasantry—a less advanced and less revolutionary class, according to Marxist theory. When Maoists fought back with all the weapons of cultural representation at their disposal to invent an elaborated version of the Chairman's own cult of personality, they would not only portray him as the actual savior of the Anyuan labor movement, but they would also credit him with transmitting the Anyuan experience to the Hunan peasant associations, the Autumn Harvest Uprising, and the Red Army. In short, Chairman Mao was heralded as the paramount leader of workers, peasants, and soldiers alike.

The tendency to tamper with historical facts, already visible by the time of the Great Leap Forward, assumed even more absurd proportions during the Cultural Revolution, when the rift between Mao Zedong and his erstwhile comrades—most notably Liu Shaoqi—was framed as a violent class struggle to safeguard the true meaning of proletarian revolution against the dangers of revisionist retrenchment. Largely ignored in this struggle were the aspirations of those in whose name the revolution was waged: the once and still downtrodden proletariat. With the onset of Mao Zedong's ultimate crusade, the rallying cry of Little Moscow, "Long live the workers!" (*gongren wansui*), would be drowned out by another refrain, "Long live Chairman Mao!" (*Mao zhuxi wansui*). Forty years earlier, the revolutionary workers of Anyuan had proudly embraced a salutation of immortality traditionally reserved for emperors; now the authoritarian ruler, with the assistance of the People's Liberation Army, was seizing the mantle of imperial legitimacy for himself.

# 6   Mao's Final Crusade

*Purifying the Revolutionary Tradition*

In the spring of 1966, Mao Zedong launched the Great Proletarian Cultural Revolution.[1] Intended to cultivate "revolutionary successors" by giving young people a taste of the hardships that the rapidly aging revolutionary generation had endured in the course of its battle for power, the new mass campaign was supposed to prevent Soviet-style revisionism by promoting authentic proletarian culture. Millions of student Red Guards from across the country streamed to the sites where Mao and his comrades had once engaged in revolutionary struggle in hope of thereby acquiring their own proletarian bona fides. As a cradle of the Chinese Communist labor movement, Anyuan was a natural focal point for the campaign. The state-orchestrated attack on Communist Party vice-chairman Liu Shaoqi as "China's Khrushchev," charged with having committed counterrevolutionary crimes dating back to his days at Anyuan, further ensured that the coal mining town would be a touchstone of national political contention and controversy.

If the early years of the PRC had left any doubt, however, the unfolding of the Cultural Revolution made clear that outsiders' interest in Anyuan had less to do with advancing the aspirations of the proletariat than with using (and misusing) their history to serve other agendas. Despite its ostensibly proletarian objectives, the Cultural Revolution brought the workers of Anyuan few tangible benefits aside from increased national (and international) notice. And yet, paradoxically, that era has been seared into the collective consciousness of Anyuan residents as a moment of immense pride, as a time when Chairman Mao reasserted the dignity and revolutionary authority of the Chinese working class in general and the Anyuan workers in particular. The nostalgia that many local inhabitants today express openly for that (now officially discredited) period, and for the man whose machinations lay behind it, speaks no doubt to dissatisfaction with aspects of the post-Mao reforms. It also points, however, to the powerful impact of effective cultural patronage on popular memories and mentalities. Although the cult of personality developed for Mao Zedong during the Cultural Revolution mirrored the earlier Stalinist cult of Liu Shaoqi in many respects, it drew from deeper and more diverse sources of inspiration. The Mao worship seen in China today reflects—albeit in refracted form—the lasting impact of Cultural Revolution rituals.

The fervor of the Cultural Revolution evinced a distinctly religious quality. Spearheaded by sanctimonious Red Guard students and PLA soldiers, Mao's final crusade bore more than a passing resemblance to a fundamentalist revival. Like other "great awakenings" in history, the movement was led by a messiah seeking to purify and preserve his true faith against the dual dangers of complacency and heresy. Haiyan Lee observes of Mao, "a godhead figure, he mobilized the Red Guards to 'reproletarianize' the Party like a prophet calling on the salt of the earth to rechristen a corrupt world in a millenarian uprising."[2] The impact of the experience, again like other religious revivals, long outlived the high tide of evangelical zeal.[3]

## RED GUARD RAMPAGES

Anyuan was introduced to the turbulence of the Cultural Revolution by Red Guard emissaries from the capital. In October 1966 the first Red Guard contingent, from the Beijing Mining Academy, arrived in Pingxiang County to "exchange revolutionary experiences" (*chuanlian*) and spearhead a "destroy the old, establish the new" (*pojiu lixin*) campaign. The first mission of these evangelists was to exorcise "false gods." After putting up a big-character poster proclaiming that "Liu Shaoqi is a scab who sold out the workers," the Red Guards ordered all Anyuan residents to remove any pictures or other images of Liu Shaoqi within twenty-four hours. At first Anyuan workers were reluctant to accept direction from these callow outsiders. Unwilling to turn their backs on a man whom many regarded as their benefactor, locals gathered in front of the workers' club to debate the student zealots from Beijing. One incensed old miner, to the crowd's amusement, pointed out that the Red Guards had not even been born in the 1920s and thus could not possibly know much about Liu's activities at Anyuan. He thundered, "We order *you* to get the hell out of Anyuan within twenty-four hours!"[4]

Like the rest of the country, however, Anyuan could not swim against the national tide for long. Liu's defenders at Anyuan were silenced, and the northern Red Guards recruited local malcontents to engage in joint attacks on "revisionist" strongholds. With Liu Shaoqi having been fingered as "the number one party person in authority taking the capitalist road," the initial targets were predictable. The Red Guards—in concert with rebel organizations that had emerged among some of the younger workers at the coal mine—smashed a statue of Liu Shaoqi and sealed off various revolutionary sites associated with Liu's 1920s activities: the Anyuan workers' club, the building where the 1922 strike negotiations had been conducted, and so forth. The offensive quickly spread beyond historic symbols to affect current power holders as well. By year's end the combined student Red Guard–worker rebel force had subjected cadres at all administrative levels of the mining company to brutal "bombardment" *(paoda)* and "grilling" *(huoshao)* on the grounds of having followed a "bourgeois reactionary line." Management of the mine was effectively paralyzed as a result.[5]

After the so-called January Storm of 1967, when worker rebels in the city of Shanghai toppled the municipal party committee, a new infusion of Red Guards from Shanghai and elsewhere in south-central China descended on Anyuan intent upon seizing power from local authorities. Even more destructive than the earlier group from Beijing, the second wave of radical youths ruined many of the artifacts that had previously been assembled for the labor movement exhibit in the Anyuan workers' club and dynamited a section of the club where Liu Shaoqi had once lived. An older worker, appalled by this display of vandalism, confronted the rebels: "Liu Shaoqi also lived in Zhongnanhai. Why don't you go and blow up Zhongnanhai? Liu Shaoqi received foreign guests in the Great Hall of the People. Will you be blowing it up, too?"[6] Again, however, national trends rendered local resistance futile.

While this drama was unfolding on the ground in a pattern of Red Guard power seizure not unlike that of many industrial enterprises at the time, high-level decisions in Beijing would soon put the coal mine in a special position. The fact that Liu Shaoqi alone had become so closely identified with Anyuan in the public mind, even though multiple leaders of the Chinese Communist Party could stake a plausible claim to its "glorious revolutionary tradition," rendered the history of the Anyuan labor movement of unusual political interest. For central officials seeking to link the current struggle to past transgressions and achievements, Anyuan was a rich lode to mine. On November 19 and again on December 13,

1966, Mao's wife, Jiang Qing, drew attention to the possibilities in meetings with students from the Beijing Aeronautics Academy: "Chairman Mao was the first to go to the Anyuan coal mine. He walked, step by step. He talked to anyone he bumped into along the way. He walked. He didn't ride a train or boat. The transportation was difficult. Today we live in the world of the proletariat. To exercise a bit is not a big deal. In the past we walked. I think you, too, can walk."[7] Jiang Qing's emphasis on walking was surely intended to highlight a contrast with Liu Shaoqi's arrival at Anyuan by train, an image made popular by the movie *Prairie Fire*. Her remarks highlighting Mao's allegedly arduous trek generated instant interest in the coal mining town as a prime destination for revolutionary pilgrimages. Despite the admonition to sally forth on foot, however, Red Guards generally preferred to take advantage of the free train rides made available to "exchange revolutionary experiences," thereby snarling up the national transportation system for months. The convenience afforded by the recently reopened rail line from Pingxiang was no doubt a factor in Anyuan's rapid rise to prominence as a major node in the Cultural Revolution New Long March pilgrimage route.[8]

Anyuan was not only touted as a positive Maoist model for revolutionary observation and emulation. Whether he had first made his way to the coal mine by foot or by rail, Chairman Mao had indeed been actively involved in the early Anyuan labor movement—but so too had Vice-Chairman Liu Shaoqi. Moreover, the Chinese public had been made acutely aware of Liu's Anyuan exploits through the recent raft of cultural products, from children's stories to dramas, paintings, and motion pictures. Anyuan's previous role in promoting the reputation of the now disgraced head of state made it an ideal setting for a new religious allegory pitting the saintly Mao against the satanic Liu.[9]

The criticism of Liu Shaoqi's allegedly demonic behavior at Anyuan had the air of a nationwide morality play. Central documents likened Liu's attempts to burnish his reputation as the savior of the Chinese proletariat to a "heterodox sect" headquartered at Anyuan. The reopened Anyuan workers' club was mocked as Liu's "ancestral temple," and local followers were accused of having fueled a heretical cult of Liu Shaoqi: "In some places they really worship them [Liu and his associates]. For example, in Anyuan they display only images of Liu Shaoqi and don't display Chairman Mao."[10]

With Anyuan depicted as a mecca for the vice-chairman's apostasy during the first seventeen years of the PRC, the colliery was subject to a particularly nasty backlash when "revolutionary" forces sought to cleanse the area of its "revisionist" legacy. The crusade to purge Anyuan of Liu Shaoqi's pernicious influence reached heights of hysteria from which not even the local vegetation was immune. In February 1967, Red Guards chopped down the two beautiful old gum trees that had long framed the entrance to the Anyuan workers' club, claiming (erroneously) that they had been planted by Liu Shaoqi.[11] The misunderstanding could be traced back to Liu's former bodyguard, Yuan Pin'gao, who had stubbornly insisted—in contradiction of the historical evidence—that the trees had been planted by Liu himself. Yuan had even arranged to have an official plaque installed at the base of the trees identifying them as his benefactor's handiwork. It was at this very site that for years Yuan had recounted stories of Liu Shaoqi's revolutionary achievements for the edification of the youth of Anyuan. Unfortunately for the gum trees, Liu Shaoqi had failed to correct the record during his well-publicized meeting with Yuan in Beijing in 1964 (see chapter 5.) When Yuan informed Liu that the two trees he had planted at the entrance to the workers' club had already grown thick and tall, Liu did not demur, instead replying with a smile and exclaiming, "Ah! Still there, eh?"[12] Three years later the Red Guard mob, determined to eliminate any trace of the reviled Liu Shaoqi, dug deep into the ground to pull out all the roots. From roots to branches, the trees were then chopped up, doused with kerosene, and burnt to ashes to purify the site.[13] In a follow-up ritual intended to sanctify Anyuan with the spirit of the "true" savior of the proletariat, cypress saplings collected from Chairman Mao's nearby birthplace of Shaoshan were transported to Anyuan, where they were solemnly transplanted in place of the uprooted gum trees.[14]

People as well as trees were viciously attacked for their alleged association with Liu Shaoqi. Zhu Zijin, the daughter of railway engineer Zhu Shaolian who had been received by Liu in 1957 and who later became director of the Anyuan Labor Movement Memorial Hall, was now branded a "running dog" of Liu Shaoqi, and Liu's erstwhile bodyguard, Yuan Pin'gao, was denounced as a "big traitor." Both Zhu and Yuan were cursed, beaten, and repeatedly paraded through the streets in tall dunce caps, a repertoire of protest made known to the Red Guards through Mao's famous "Report on an Investigation of the Peasant Movement in Hunan," written forty years earlier at the height of the Red Terror in this very region.[15] In a latter-day rendition of the "costume lectures" of Little Moscow fame, the rebels also staged satirical political skits in which Yuan Pin'gao, attired in "bourgeois" Western clothing, was publicly mocked as the quintessential "labor aristocrat." The subsidy that the former general representative of the Anyuan workers' club had been receiving in recognition of his revolutionary record was suspended, and Yuan spent the next three years condemned to hard labor at a nearby coal pit.[16] The four-person writing group at the coal mine led by Peng Yonghui, which was responsible for creating the factory history *Red Anyuan* and the script of the movie *Prairie Fire*, was derided as a "Four Family Village"—a takeoff on the infamous "Three Family Village" of senior party propagandists in Beijing accused of having written veiled criticisms of Chairman Mao.[17] Peng, too, was subjected to humiliating public criticism.[18]

## ARMED STRUGGLE

Although shaped by particular historical circumstances, the unrest in Anyuan reflected the political strife that afflicted much of Jiangxi at the outset of the Cultural Revolution, when the top party and government leaders in the province, Yang Shangkui and Fang Zhichun, were both removed from their posts, accused of having followed Liu Shaoqi's revisionist line. The intense struggle that ensued between a faction still loyal to the former provincial leadership, led by the Jiangxi military district commander, and various local constellations of rebel alliances resulted in thousands of casualties.[19]

The confusing political conflict in the provincial capital of Nanchang was replicated with even less clarity at lower levels of the administrative hierarchy. In early 1967, rebel organizations at Anyuan split into two rival factions known as the Pingxiang Mining Company Revolutionary Rebel United Command Post and the Pingxiang Mining Company Proletarian Class Revolutionary General Headquarters. The two factions engaged in pitched battles, with each accusing the other of being secret supporters of Liu Shaoqi. Production ground to a standstill. To restore order, PLA troops were dispatched to occupy the coal mine.[20] This military occupation, however, did not end the deadly conflicts. For months, armed struggles resulting in a significant number of fatalities and injuries exploded across Pingxiang. Several schools, train stations, and other public buildings in the county, municipality, and surrounding countryside were burned to the ground during the mayhem that ensued.[21]

The violence in Pingxiang was sufficiently severe to attract top-level concern. Premier Zhou Enlai raised the matter at a meeting with representatives from Jiangxi on July 28. The premier at first tried to pin the rampant violence on rural residents who had been permitted to enter Pingxiang city during the Cultural Revolution turmoil, suggesting that peasants from the surrounding countryside were responsible for having burned down municipal buildings and destroyed trains at city stations. Eyewitnesses, however, insisted that blame for the arson and bloodletting lay not with their rural neighbors but with members of the military itself. They offered a hair-raising account of PLA atrocities that shocked even Zhou Enlai: "An old worker from Anyuan told the premier with a very heavy heart that a small number of people from the Yichun military subdistrict and the Pingxiang armed forces department had planned to burn down the Pingxiang coal school. Furious, Zhou ordered Zhang Jincai of the Pingxiang armed forces department to step forward. The old worker continued to testify, saying that little generals of the Red Guards had been burnt alive, leaving the entire room silent. . . . Zhou accused the military district, subdistrict, and armed forces departments of mistakes."[22] Not since the Red and White Terror had Pingxiang experienced such callous cruelty at the hands of soldiers.

Rather than call an immediate halt to the hostilities, however, the central leadership continued to inflame them. When a few days later Premier Zhou met again with the representatives from Jiangxi, his comments about Liu Shaoqi's Anyuan connection offered further grist for vengeful mills:

> I'll give you a little material. Liu Shaoqi for the past two years has boasted about his history at Anyuan in front of the Chairman. The Chairman said nothing, allowing him to expose himself. The Chairman has great tolerance. Actually it was the Chairman who all along led the struggle at Anyuan. The Pingxiang coal mine, the Daye ironworks, the Hanyeping Company—at that time the Anyuan movement was under the leadership of the Hunan provincial committee, and the Chairman is very clear about that whole history. The Chairman said Liu Shaoqi was the third generation; Li Lisan was the second generation; who was the first generation? . . .
>   Liu Shaoqi was always boasting, having raised this with me a number of times. (Directed toward Yao Wenyuan) He also spoke about this several times with you, right? So I felt there was something wrong. The revolutionary history research center of the Chinese Academy of Sciences is correct to begin its criticisms in the 1920s. After Liu Shaoqi had run off to the USSR for less than a year, he returned and began to work at Anyuan. . . . (Yao Wenyuan interrupts: This is what he has stolen as his political capital. This must be exposed.) I listened to this at least five times and thought it very odd. I suspected there was some ulterior motive. . . . The roots of the criticism against Liu start in the 1920s. If one is going to really criticize Liu, there is much in the 1920s that deserves criticism.[23]

Fueled by such accusations, factional fighting in Pingxiang between rivals seeking to distance themselves from the disgraced Liu Shaoqi only intensified. On August 8 a major clash, facilitated by a break-in at the municipal arsenal that netted over a hundred guns, left five dead and fifty-one badly wounded. A few days later an even more serious confrontation resulted in over a dozen fatalities.[24] By month's end, armed battles in Pingxiang had claimed more than twenty-five lives and caused countless injuries.[25]

## CRITICIZING "REVISIONIST" CULTURE

Denunciations of Liu Shaoqi were directed not only at his own characterizations of his activities at Anyuan but also at the portraits of him produced by others. The products of cultural patronage sponsored by Liu's boosters within the Department of Propaganda and the Ministry of Culture in the 1950s and early 1960s were now attacked as incriminating evidence of counterrevolutionary "revisionism." One of the first such targets was the formerly popular movie *Prairie Fire*. On May 20, 1967, the Chinese Communist party's theoretical journal, *Red Flag*, published an article entitled "The Reactionary Movie *Prairie Fire* and China's Khrushchev." It began, "The number one party authority taking the capitalist road, in order to attain his criminal aim of usurping party and state control, extended his demonic claws into the ideological arena, into the realm of art and literature. Ignoring Chairman Mao's warnings, he and a small handful of his counterrevolutionary revisionist associates . . . put forward the reactionary movie *Prairie Fire*. This movie is criminal evidence of his manipulating public opinion to launch a counterrevolutionary restoration."[26]

Liu Shaoqi was not the only prominent political figure to be attacked for his connection to the film. The *Red Flag* article also implicated another former Anyuan pioneer, Li Lisan, for his role in having identified the main character of the movie as Liu Shaoqi: "That old opportunist Li Lisan published one article after another publicly proclaiming that 'Lei Huanjue' [the protagonist of the movie] was a certain person. The certain person was never a Marxist but was always very much an old opportunist, a revisionist."[27] The implication was that Li had conspired with Liu to rob the true hero of Anyuan of his rightful recognition.

Aware of the dangers of being linked in this way to the main target of the Cultural Revolution, Li Lisan tried to defend himself. The day after the *Red Flag* accusation appeared, Li wrote a letter to Zhou Enlai pleading ill health and asking that the premier intervene to postpone an impending Red Guard struggle session against him. Zhou did not answer, and a series of brutal criticism sessions ensued. Repeatedly pressed to confess to the crime of acting as a "secret agent of Soviet revisionism," Li Lisan adamantly refused to accept the accusation. On May 31, when ordered to write down his crimes, Li scribbled defiantly, "The facts will show that I am not a counterrevolutionary revisionist element."[28]

A few days later, having suffered more Red Guard attacks than he could bear, Li wrote a long letter to Jiang Qing to explain the background behind his 1963 *People's Daily* critique of the movie *Prairie Fire*. Li pointed out that, contrary to the recent article in *Red Flag*, his identification of Liu Shaoqi as the chief protagonist in the movie had not been intended as praise for Liu Shaoqi. He insisted, moreover, that he had had nothing to do with the making of the movie and had first seen a draft of the script around the summer of 1960, when it was still entitled "The Anyuan Great Strike." At that time the party secretary of the Anyuan coal mine had paid Li a visit to ask for his reaction. Although he could not remember precisely what he had said on that occasion, Li thought it was probably quite similar to the newspaper review that he wrote three years later, soon after the movie opened. Just before the public release of the movie, Li recalled, he was invited to a private viewing by reporters from the *Beijing Daily* seeking his response. His verdict, he emphasized to Jiang Qing, was that the movie had "serious shortcomings and mistakes," especially with respect to Chairman Mao's "great leadership role" in the Anyuan strike, of which there was no mention at all in the film. Li stressed that he had thereupon written a critical movie review, but when it appeared in the *Beijing Daily* many of the negative passages had been removed. Displeased by this tampering with his original wording, Li then submitted his review to the *People's Daily*, which, however, also published a censored version in which a key sentence pointing out the film's grave error in omitting all mention of Mao's leadership role had been substantially softened. Li emphasized in his letter to Jiang Qing that "this revision not only completely changed my original meaning but also misled the audience and readership into thinking [I had] praised this big poisonous weed, the movie *Prairie Fire*." Li conceded that at the time he wrote the review he had not yet fully appreciated "Chairman Mao's enormous contribution to the Chinese and world revolutions," but he stressed that he had already become suspicious that Liu Shaoqi was using the movie as a means of promoting himself at the expense of the Chairman. For this reason, Li explained, he had noted in his review that greater emphasis on the leadership role of Mao Zedong Thought was needed in order for the audience to understand why a "certain person" (that is, Liu Shaoqi) had managed to accomplish things at Anyuan.[29]

No answer was forthcoming from Jiang Qing, and the relentless Red Guard criticism sessions continued unabated. Abandoned by the Cultural Revolution leadership to suffer a steady stream of orchestrated attacks from hostile groups of workers and students, Li Lisan enjoyed few comforts aside from the knowledge that at Anyuan itself he was still remembered fondly as a proletarian hero:

> People came from all over to question Li Lisan, to "investigate," by *danwei* or by campus, the past of the Communist Party. . . . His only consolation came one day in the form of a visit from a man who had arrived from Anyuan. He had traveled fifteen hundred miles to make the acquaintance of the man about whom the miners still talked so much. A middle-aged schoolteacher, the man spent two hours talking with Li. He brought him the news that down there the miners were still proud of him, and that the old men were perpetuating his memory.[30]

Reassuring as the thought of his loyal Anyuan admirers may have been to Li Lisan, it could not protect him from the gathering political storm. The problem for Li Lisan was not only the (surely unwarranted) allegation of his complicity in promoting Liu Shaoqi as the paramount leader of the Anyuan strike. Having spent fifteen years in the Soviet Union, and married to a Russian woman whom he had met in Moscow, Li was an easy target for the accusation of having sold out to Soviet revisionism. The Red Guards' questioning of his patriotism as a "conniver with foreign countries" proved particularly painful to Li Lisan. His wife, Lisa, had in fact recently been granted Chinese citizenship, and their two daughters also lived in Beijing. On June 22, a few hours prior to a massive struggle session scheduled for that afternoon, Li died while writing a final letter:

> Most, most beloved Chairman Mao:
>
> I am now embarking on the antiparty path of suicide. I have no way of expiating this crime. Save for one thing: neither I nor any member of my family has ever connived with foreign countries. On this one point I hope the central authorities will undertake a thorough investigation to reach an accurate conclusion.
>
> I have written another letter to you, which is still unfinished, kept under a quilt in my home. Please have someone find it and send it to you for your inspection.
>
> Best wishes for the Cultural Revolution.
>
> Li Lisan[31]

Whether or not Li Lisan actually committed suicide by taking an overdose of the sleeping pills that he took every night remains something of a mystery.[32] But that he died under tragic circumstances on June 22, 1967, accused of antirevolutionary revisionist crimes that he denied to his death, is certain.

Meanwhile, strident criticisms of that other Anyuan "traitor and scab," Liu Shaoqi, appeared in a string of high-profile articles in the major newspapers. From the spring of 1967 through the summer of 1968, *People's Daily*, *Liberation Daily*, and *Wenhui bao* all carried multiple spreads featuring detailed accounts of Liu's alleged crimes of having suppressed the Anyuan labor movement and then falsely claimed full credit for its development.[33] Those who had been connected to the production of the movie *Prairie Fire*—editors, actors, directors, and cameramen alike—were subject to house searches and public attack.[34] The former vice-minister of culture, Xia Yan, who had played a central role in approving and editing the final version of the screenplay, wrote in his diary entry for April 4, 1968, "Today an entire page of *People's Daily* was devoted to criticizing *Prairie Fire*. Even though there were all sorts of objective reasons behind this matter, I had to shoulder a major part of the responsibility. At the time I really had wanted to make a good movie in order to glorify Liu Shaoqi."[35] Although *Prairie Fire* came in for particular criticism as a blatant example of the falsification of Liu's revolutionary credentials, it was not the only product of cultural patronage to suffer this fate.

The popular factory history *Red Anyuan* was condemned as a reactionary work and withdrawn from circulation. On April 30, 1967, those responsible for its publication, from the vice-chairman of the Jiangxi Propaganda Department to local party historians, were paraded through the streets of Pingxiang in dunce caps that identified them as "loyal running dogs" of Liu Shaoqi.[36] Unable to withstand the criticism, one former member of the *Red Anyuan* editorial committee, Huang Zenghui, wrote his own big-character poster to express remorse for his earlier involvement in the factory history project. Proclaiming his firm commitment to Chairman Mao's revolutionary line, Huang proceeded to cast aspersions on Liu Shaoqi's most incontrovertible character trait—his discipline. Although he had been just seventeen or eighteen years old when he had encountered Liu at Anyuan some forty-five years earlier, Huang now offered graphic "eyewitness" accounts of Liu's alleged weakness for gluttony, gambling, and prostitution.[37]

Other formerly prevalent images of Liu Shaoqi were also called into question at this time. Hou Yimin's widely reproduced oil painting of Liu

Shaoqi leading the Anyuan strikers was deemed the "earliest evidence in the field of literature and art of Liu's attempt to change party history" and was labeled a "poisonous weed."[38] The artist was hung by his arms and severely beaten by Red Guards.[39] Hou's painting, *Liu Shaoqi and the Anyuan Miners*, was unceremoniously removed from the Museum of Revolutionary History to make way for a major new exhibition entitled *The Brilliance of Mao Zedong Thought Illuminates the Anyuan Labor Movement*.

### EXHIBITING "PROLETARIAN" CULTURE

The new exhibit at the Museum of Revolutionary History, which opened in the fall of 1967, was the brainchild of a young instructor in party history at People's University named Zhang Peisen. Zhang's in-depth research on the early Chinese Communist labor movement, which had included lengthy interviews conducted several years earlier with Li Lisan, convinced the budding historian that Liu Shaoqi was guilty of having falsified his Anyuan record. With the onset of the Cultural Revolution, Zhang Peisen realized that his ongoing research on Anyuan could be of more than arcane academic interest.[40] The exhibition that Zhang and his colleagues put together, explains Julia Andrews, "sought to redefine the iconography of China's revolutionary history by replacing Liu with Mao as the primary organizer of the important 1922 coal miners' strike."[41] Well-publicized remarks by party theoretician Qi Benyu shortly before the opening of the exhibit stressed the significance of Anyuan in the leadership struggle: "Even since the Anyuan coal mine, Liu Shaoqi was always engaged in a rival performance [*changduitaixi*] to Chairman Mao. Your criticisms . . . should focus on all aspects, beginning with the Anyuan coal mine."[42]

Zhang Peisen's Anyuan exhibit, like the "rival performance" it sought to discredit, was the product of deliberate cultural patronage. Although ostensibly a grassroots effort sponsored by an alliance of rebel organizations from Beijing and Jiangxi, the exhibition received crucial behind-the-scenes support from the Cultural Revolution Small Group and other top leaders, especially Premier Zhou Enlai. When Premier Zhou met with the Jiangxi delegation in July 1967 to discuss the bloody factional fighting that had claimed so many lives in the province, the delegate from Anyuan—the elderly worker who shocked the premier with his account of PLA atrocities—succeeded in securing the premier's pledge of assistance for the exhibit.[43] This high-level sponsorship allowed the construction of a large six-part exhibit housed in the main galleries of the Museum of Revolutionary History. Artifacts from the Anyuan workers' club that had not already been destroyed in rebel attacks on Liu Shaoqi's "ancestral temple" were shipped to Beijing for use in the new anti-Liu exhibit. The artifacts were supplemented by materials gathered by teams of party historians during special fact-finding expeditions to Anyuan (paid for with funds personally approved by Premier Zhou Enlai) and to the central party archives (also authorized by Premier Zhou).[44] Although the aim of the exhibit was clearly political rather than aesthetic, artwork was an integral part of it. The famous woodblock artist Yang Xianrang completed a set of prints to depict the events surrounding the Great Strike of 1922. The traditional watercolor painter and calligrapher Fan Zeng, who would later become one of China's most celebrated artists, was commissioned to draw a series of cartoons lampooning Liu Shaoqi's actions at Anyuan—including a historically inaccurate sketch of Liu (in place of Li Lisan) conducting a blood brotherhood ritual with the local secret-society chieftain.[45] To fill the spacious walls of the Museum of Revolutionary History, a sequence of paintings intended to portray Chairman Mao's various journeys to Anyuan was also specially prepared.[46]

Among these paintings of Chairman Mao's successive visits to Anyuan, one stood out for its simplicity and grandeur: Liu Chunhua's *Chairman Mao Goes to Anyuan*. Purporting to depict Mao Zedong's maiden journey to the coal mine in the fall of 1921, the large oil painting, 2.2 meters high and 1.8 meters wide, presented a stirring image of the young revolutionary. Standing majestically alone atop the scenic Wugong Mountains, clad in a long scholar's gown and holding a simple Hunan oiled-paper umbrella, Mao is portrayed in romantic—even religious—tones. As Andrews notes, the painting "possesses clear devotional appeal."[47] In interviews with art historians after the Cultural Revolution, Liu Chunhua revealed that his inspiration for the painting—the first oil painting he had ever completed—came in part from the religious paintings of Raphael.[48]

Forty years later Liu Chunhua offered the following account of the political origins of his painting:

> I painted this work in 1967, the second year of the Great Cultural Revolution. The political background of that time was largely defined by the campaign to criticize Liu Shaoqi. Many people were aware that in the past Liu Shaoqi had led workers' strikes in Anyuan. But a group of young teachers and students at universities in the capital who had conducted in-depth research on [Chinese Communist] party history

Figure 11. *Chairman Mao Goes to Anyuan,* oil painting by Liu Chunhua, 1967.

had a more complete understanding of that period, and in their opinion the true leader of the Anyuan workers movement was Chairman Mao—prior to the Cultural Revolution, most reports mentioned only Liu Shaoqi. This group felt that Chairman Mao's [role] in the revolutionary movements at Anyuan should be positively portrayed and disseminated, with the ultimate aim of criticizing Liu Shaoqi. They planned to organize an exhibition [entitled] "Mao Zedong's Thought Illuminates the Anyuan Workers Movement." Because all of the organizers were Red Guards, it was really an unofficial exhibition. Zhang Peisen, a professor in the Department of [Chinese Communist] Party History at People's University, brought along a group of students to prepare the exhibition and he also recruited a number of able painters from the various art academies in Beijing. When they came to the Central Academy of Fine Arts looking for people, they found me.[49]

Considering the painting's role in the attack on Liu Shaoqi, it is noteworthy that the depiction of Mao in Liu Chunhua's oil painting was in fact remarkably similar to the depiction of Liu Shaoqi (under the fictional name Lei Huanjue) in the opening scene of *Prairie Fire*, when he arrives at Anyuan garbed in a long Mandarin gown, holding a Hunan oiled-paper umbrella, with the sun breaking through above his head. The one difference—a point presaged by Jiang Qing in her talks with Red Guards—is that Mao is shown making his way through the mountainous terrain on foot rather than by train. The artist, a twenty-four-year-old Red Guard art student at the time, had almost certainly viewed the once-popular movie about Liu Shaoqi before putting his brush to canvas to compose a fitting image for a rival cult of personality. In any case, the possibility of Liu Chunhua's painting serving as a central pillar in the emerging cult surrounding Chairman Mao was not lost on Jing Qing when she first saw a photograph of the work. She requested a special viewing of the painting in Zhongnanhai, after which she concluded that it was indeed a suitable model for veneration and emulation. On the day before the anniversary of the founding of the Chinese Communist Party, Jiang declared, "Tomorrow is the party's birthday. We are thinking of two works of art as presents. One is the oil painting *Chairman Mao Goes to Anyuan*, the other is the piano score for *Red Lantern*. . . . The ideological level of *Chairman Mao Goes to Anyuan* is quite high and the artistic level is also quite good. . . . These two works of art are an inspiration to the entire nation."[50]

The next day, July 1, 1968, the front pages of *People's Daily, Liberation Army Daily, Red Flag*, and other major newspapers and journals were devoted to full-spread color reproductions of the painting. The fact that oil painting was a Western art form, and therefore open to criticism as an expression of "bourgeois culture," was conveniently ignored in light of Jiang Qing's endorsement. An editorial in Shanghai's *Wenhui bao* emphasized that *Chairman Mao Goes to Anyuan* enjoyed "the personal support and sponsorship of Comrade Jiang Qing" and justified the use of an alien art form as an example of "making foreign things serve China."[51] Thanks to Jiang Qing's high praise, Liu's portrait of the Chairman was revered as the epitome of artistic perfection, worthy of adoration and capable of triggering an emotional response in the viewer akin to a religious conversion. A young artist later recalled, "When Jiang Qing hailed the oil painting *Chairman Mao [Goes] to Anyuan* as a 'revolutionary masterpiece,' we hung a copy on the wall and took turns commenting on its 'profound spirituality' and 'perfect artistry.' Some people's voices trembled and others had tears in their eyes."[52] That religious conviction was indeed the prescribed reaction to the painting was made clear in newspaper editorials at the time. *Guangming ribao*, for example, characterized Liu's painting as "a hymn in praise of Chairman Mao's revolutionary line having vanquished China's Khrushchev's counterrevolutionary revisionist line."[53] *Liberation Army Daily* summed up the meaning of the painting: "From then on, Anyuan workers found their savior, the Chinese working class had its own leader, the toiling masses harbored hope for liberation."[54] Replicas of the iconic image soon appeared on posters, Mao buttons, cigarette tins, plates, vases, embroidery, and other media. The most common postage stamp during the Cultural Revolution, with a run of fifty million, was the eight-cent likeness of *Chairman Mao Goes to Anyuan*. It was also the only stamp exempted from postal cancellation, in order to avoid the desecration of its sacred image.[55]

In 1968 factories and communes around the country organized ritualized ceremonies to welcome the arrival of their own copies of Liu Chunhua's painting, which is said to be the most reproduced painting in history, with some nine hundred million copies in circulation at one time.[56] A reproduction of the painting was the only work of art on display in Premier Zhou Enlai's private residence for the remainder of the Cultural Revolution. Both Jiang Qing and Lin Biao frequently sported Mao badges with the Anyuan image. On October 1, 1968, a parade float carrying a giant likeness of the painting made its way past the Tiananmen reviewing stand (from where Chairman Mao and other top party leaders waved to the crowd) as part of the National Day celebration.[57] The appeal of Liu Chunhua's painting extended well beyond the borders of China. So sublime was the image of the young Mao's arrival at Anyuan that one reproduction, by an Italian artist, hung in the halls of the Vatican in Rome for several months above the caption "Young Chinese Missionary," until its true provenance was discovered and the beatific likeness of Chairman Mao was hastily removed![58]

More orchestrated, intense, and inspirational than earlier efforts at cultural patronage, this cult of personality was nonetheless familiar in many respects. The parallels to the previous project to build up Liu Shaoqi's Anyuan image were striking. Like Hou Yimin before painting his rendition of Comrade Liu Shaoqi, Liu Chunhua made the canonical pilgrimage to Anyuan to conduct obligatory interviews with elderly workers before painting Chairman Mao. Again like Hou, Liu later wrote of the tremulous emotion that he and his fellow Red Guards at the Anyuan exhibition had experienced in undertaking this sacred assignment, painting round the clock and even neglecting to eat in the process of "correcting" the historical record to reflect the true sentiments of the Chinese masses:

For a long period, China's Khrushchov arrogantly distorted history by claiming that he, and not Chairman Mao, had led the Anyuan workers' struggle. He made arrangements with a group of class enemies to produce expensive paintings and films and fabricate stories which portrayed himself, a scab and clown, as "the hero who led the Anyuan workers in struggle." These intolerable crimes aroused our intense hatred. We, the Red Guards of Chairman Mao, vowed to do our part to correct this distortion of history. . . . I painted day and night. In the grip of creation, I often forgot to eat. . . . Anyuan workers who took part in the struggles of early days volunteered to be our advisors. . . . Our painting was more than a fruit of collective wisdom, it was a crystallization of the love of millions for Chairman Mao.[59]

"Correcting" history required that Liu Chunhua and his Red Guard associates produce an image of Chairman Mao that represented him as even more godlike than the previous representation of Liu Shaoqi: "We placed Chairman Mao in the forefront of the painting, tranquil, far-sighted and advancing toward us like a rising sun bringing hope to the people. . . . In our mind, we seemed to be living in Anyuan during the 1920s, seeing with our own eyes the miserable plight of the miners, the wrath in the hearts of the suffering masses, hearing their cries for the early arrival of the great liberator. We seemed to see them looking eagerly toward the east, waiting for the sunrise."[60] Considering that the painter claimed to have channeled the yearnings of the downtrodden Anyuan miners, it is striking that no workers appear in his painting. Although Hou Yimin's portrayal of Liu Shaoqi leading the striking miners out of the coal pits had emphasized the distinction between the leader and the masses, with Liu placed in the center of the scene and the Anyuan miners serving largely as backdrop, in Liu Chunhua's painting of Chairman Mao the masses are missing altogether, and the savior of the working class stands alone on the mountaintop.[61]

In addition to its religious import, Liu Chunhua's painting of Chairman Mao's journey to Anyuan signaled several complementary political intentions. On one level, it was a direct attack on Liu Shaoqi, making clear that Mao was the lone hero of Anyuan and thus the undisputed leader of the Chinese proletariat. On another level, by highlighting the importance of the labor movement in Chinese revolutionary history, the painting served notice that henceforth workers rather than students would be the main foot soldiers of the Cultural Revolution. The painting played a hortatory role in the demobilization of the Red Guard student movement as part of the "Up to the Mountains and Down to the Villages" campaign.[62] In Shanghai, for example, students and teachers at all the major academies and universities gathered in the summer of 1968 to view copies of the painting and, "inspired by the great image of Chairman Mao forty-seven years ago, going to Anyuan to light the fires of revolution," pledged their own commitment to "become Chairman Mao's successors, following Chairman Mao's call to go to the villages, the border regions, the factories, the grass roots."[63] In the cities, Mao Zedong Thought propaganda teams composed of workers replaced student Red Guards as the central force charged with continuing Mao's crusade.

The multivalent implications of Liu Chunhua's oil painting helped account for its remarkably wide distribution. Ellen Laing explains:

> *Chairman Mao Goes to Anyuan* obliquely conveys two messages: Mao as undisputed leader of the strike (and the CCP), and the shift of his reliance to the workers. Art is now truly a political weapon. To guarantee that the dual messages were properly understood, millions of copies of the painting were distributed throughout China. Peasants planted seedlings with the painting posted nearby; Red Guards walked to Inner Mongolia with the portrait carried in the vanguard; study sessions in Xinjiang were held under the shadow of this picture. In September 1968 it was hailed as a "Great and Noble Image" and, along with the piano music for the Beijing opera *The Red Lantern*, became one of the "two gems of art," thus putting it on the same footing with the eight model operas.[64]

As millions of reproductions of the painting were being distributed to schools, communes, factories, and other work units, the exhibition for which Liu Chunhua's painting had originally been commissioned, *The Brilliance of Mao Zedong Thought Illuminates the Anyuan Labor Movement,* was also being reproduced in museums around the country. During the nearly two years (October 1967 to August 1969) that the exhibit remained open at the Museum of Revolutionary History in Beijing, it received more than two and a half million visitors. Among them were representatives of 267 cultural work units whose assignment was to duplicate parts of the Beijing exhibit for local edification.[65] Soon copycat displays were mounted at provincial and municipal museums from Shanxi to Yunnan.[66]

To reinforce the centrally approved political message, viewers of these local exhibits were offered the short written guide *From Anyuan to Jinggangshan.* Akin to a religious tract, the pamphlet chronicled milestones in the Anyuan labor movement as a testament to Chairman Mao's revolutionary miracles. The guide focused on Mao's six reputed visits to

Anyuan between the fall of 1921 and the fall of 1930, which corresponded to the six main displays of the exhibition.[67] Although the printed guides differed from one museum to another, varying in size and the illustrations and introductory political material included (most, but not all, contained a foreword by Defense Minister Lin Biao praising Mao as "the greatest Marxist-Leninist of the current age"), they all offered identical descriptions of Mao's six visits.[68] The first section, entitled "The Rays of Sunlight First Shine on Anyuan," for which Liu Chunhua's painting served as the pictorial representation, described Mao's initial trip to the coal mine in the fall of 1921. On the day of Mao's arrival, according to the exhibition guide, "claps of thunder rocked heaven and earth and a red sun illuminated Anyuan mountain."[69] The last section of the guide, entitled "The Jinggang Road Shines Brightly," highlighted Mao's final visit to Anyuan in the fall of 1930 to recruit soldiers for the Red Army. Anyuan was praised as the source of a Maoist revolutionary force that had liberated China and would eventually liberate the whole world: "The heroic workers of Anyuan have engraved Chairman Mao's teachings in their heart . . . rising up from the ground to follow Chairman Mao's revolutionary road. . . . The Anyuan workers closely followed the great leader Chairman Mao and established eternal revolutionary merit. . . . Follow Mao Zedong; continue the revolution forever! Follow Mao Zedong, until the whole world turns red!"[70] As Mao's chosen people, the workers of Anyuan were exalted as the faithful proletariat whose unswerving loyalty to their savior pointed the way toward worldwide redemption. "Correcting" the history of the Anyuan labor movement by purging it of the sins of "Soviet revisionism" would put China back on track to complete its sacred revolutionary mission.

Central to this project was the elimination of any competing Anyuan "deities." While the first half of the exhibition focused on events leading up to the strike of September 1922, including the establishment of a workers' school, party cell, and workers' club, no mention was made of the now deceased and discredited Li Lisan, let alone the Soviet inspiration that underlay the Anyuan experiment. Liu Shaoqi did make an appearance in the exhibit, but as a bestial figure whose evil machinations threatened to derail the proper course of the revolution:

> Two days before the explosion of the Great Strike, China's Khrushchev, Liu Shaoqi, scurried to Anyuan to take advantage of the revolution. As soon as this capitalist running dog got to Anyuan, he carried out a thoroughly capitulationist line . . . conniving with the capitalist factory director . . . to resist Chairman Mao's clear-sighted policies

and trying his best to oppose and repress the workers' rising up in a strike struggle. Liu Shaoqi, this Khrushchev-style careerist, repeatedly trumpeted himself as "leader of the Anyuan strike," saying, "At Anyuan, the one who did the hard work was myself." Hah! What strike "leader"? A complete and total big scab![71]

Complementing these museum exhibits was the publication of a flurry of popular books extolling the brilliance of Chairman Mao's correct leadership at Anyuan and excoriating the "counterrevolutionary" sins of Liu Shaoqi.[72] A new version of the narrative folk song about the 1922 Anyuan strike was also issued, this one filled with praise of "Mao Runzhi" (the name that the young Mao had used during the period when he visited Anyuan), despite the fact that no mention of Mao had been made in any of the original 1925 versions of the song.[73] As the supposed exemplification of "two-line struggle" between Mao's revolution and Liu's revisionism, the history of the Anyuan labor movement was being doctored and distorted almost beyond recognition.

The outpouring of attention placed upon Anyuan evidently piqued Mao Zedong's own curiosity about the past. In October 1968, during the twelfth plenum of the Eighth Central Committee, Mao pulled aside one of the delegates, Naval Commander Xiao Jinguang, to inquire about his days at Anyuan. After Xiao explained that he had been assigned to the coal mine as a labor organizer by the Hunan District party committee in 1924, right after completing a three-year study program in the Soviet Union, Mao asked whether the commander had known the celebrated Anyuan martyrs Zhu Shaolian and Huang Jingyuan. When Xiao answered in the affirmative, Mao waxed wistful, "What wonderful comrades. Such a pity they died so young, in the prime of life."[74] Left unspoken were any thoughts Mao may have harbored about the comrade responsible for overall operations at Anyuan at that time, the now disgraced Liu Shaoqi.

## CAPITALIZING ON "HISTORY"

The Cultural Revolution reinterpretation of the Anyuan labor movement had important repercussions at the coal mine itself. Party historians, elderly workers, and union and government cadres most closely associated with the earlier effort to promote Liu Shaoqi's Anyuan credentials were sidelined under a cloud of suspicion. A competing cohort of self-declared "radicals" eagerly stepped forward to carry on the business of bolstering ties to Beijing. Their predecessors having spent the previous seventeen years attempting to curry favor with Liu Shaoqi, the new contingent of local officials, most of whom had been replaced in the Red Guards' "power seizure," rushed to renounce all connections to the former head of state in hopes of winning the approval of an even more powerful patron in Zhongnanhai.

The Anyuan workers' club, sealed up by Red Guards in the fall of 1966, continued to serve as a focal point for local activism. Independent efforts by rebel groups in early 1967 to mount a new anti-Liu exhibition at the club were initially rebuffed by the Jiangxi provincial authorities, who were still uncertain about how to portray the sensitive topic of Anyuan's revolutionary history.[75] Six months later, however, a reopened workers' club issued an invitation to "all revolutionary organizations and the broad revolutionary masses" to view an officially approved exhibit that had been prepared in concert with the one being assembled at the Museum of Revolutionary History in Beijing.[76]

The fact that the Anyuan workers' club was so closely associated with Liu Shaoqi rendered it a problematic setting for a display focused on Mao Zedong's revolutionary contributions, and soon major changes in the Jiangxi political scene would permit a more expansive expression of cultural patronage. In January 1968, the Jiangxi Provincial Revolutionary Committee was established under the direction of Cheng Shiqing, commander of the 60th Army and a protégé of Defense Minister Lin Biao. Cheng and his troops had been assigned to Jiangxi the previous fall to restore order in the face of the armed factional fighting that had caused so many casualties across the province.[77] Within a few weeks of being named head of the provincial revolutionary committee, Cheng convened the first meeting of a special task force to publicize Mao's revolutionary footprint in the province. At the meeting it was proposed that Pingxiang municipality, the Pingxiang Mining Company, and the Pingxiang Railway Authority should assume joint responsibility for constructing a brand-new memorial hall designed to commemorate Chairman Mao's accomplishments at Anyuan. Soon afterward, the director of the Pingxiang Municipal Revolutionary Committee formed a local steering committee to oversee the work, with instructions that the new memorial hall should reflect the spirit of the ongoing exhibition at the Museum of Revolutionary History, *The Brilliance of Mao Zedong Thought Illuminates the Anyuan Labor Movement*, a complete duplicate of which had already been sent from Beijing to Anyuan.[78]

Inexperienced in putting together such a large-scale (and politically fraught) exhibition, the Pingxiang steering committee sought help from a seasoned party historian in Changsha, a man by the name of Ma

Yuqing, who had previously served as curator for the exhibit at Chairman Mao's birthplace of Shaoshan. Ma agreed to act as senior advisor to the project. After spending some time at Anyuan and immersing himself in materials concerning Mao's activities there, Ma came up with a bold plan for the new museum. To be situated prominently on the hilltop once occupied by the St. James Episcopal Church, directly above the site of Liu Shaoqi's old workers' club, the huge new Memorial Hall to Chairman Mao's Revolutionary Activities at Anyuan would tower over the much smaller club building below. As befitted such a grand undertaking, the cost of this capacious new museum would also be substantial—approximately two hundred thousand yuan according to Ma's initial estimate.[79]

Faced with such an expensive proposition, however, differences of opinion surfaced within the oversight committee. Although no one doubted the need for a memorial hall dedicated to the veneration of Chairman Mao that would supplant Liu Shaoqi's old "ancestral temple," some argued that there simply was not enough money to support a building on the proposed scale and that the project should therefore be postponed at least until the following year. Several officials in Pingxiang city, including the head of the revolutionary committee, agreed with Ma's insistence on a large exhibition space but suggested that this could be achieved by renovating a dilapidated workers' "cultural palace" located in the Pingxiang county seat at the site of a former Confucian temple. Once this proposal was made public, however, it generated an outcry from unhappy Anyuan residents who questioned how a memorial hall to commemorate Chairman Mao's activities at Anyuan could be situated in Pingxiang city rather than at the coal mine itself. Critics also pointed out the inappropriateness of locating a memorial hall to Chairman Mao on the premises of an old Confucian temple. Convinced by these arguments, city officials agreed to the idea of constructing a large new building at Anyuan so long as the district and provincial governments would take major responsibility for the financing. In June the Pingxiang officials presented the plan, for which they doubled Ma's estimated price tag, to provincial authorities in Nanchang.

Somewhat to the surprise of the Pingxiang officials, the director of the Jiangxi Provincial Revolutionary Committee, Cheng Shiqing, enthusiastically approved the proposal and readily agreed to allocate the requested four hundred thousand yuan to accomplish it. As he put it, "Anyuan is a very important place. Money is not an issue. Spare no expense. Construct a world-class exhibition hall as quickly as possible." Cheng, it seems, saw this undertaking as a means of ingratiating himself with his patron in Beijing, Defense Minister Lin Biao, whose (extremely brief) visit to Anyuan in 1930 would also be highlighted as part of the display. Cheng issued provincial-level permission to commission the top experts in museum construction from across the country. More than two thousand curatorial specialists, sculptors, and other artisans, recruited from Beijing, Nanjing, Hangzhou, Guangzhou, and other distant locales, were invited to Anyuan to work on the project. The approved price tag for the project, which enjoyed the full backing of the provincial government, soared, first to 800,000 yuan, then to 1.2 million yuan, and eventually to a whopping 2 million yuan.[80]

On the same day that Liu Chunhua's painting *Chairman Mao Goes to Anyuan* was plastered across the front pages of all the major newspapers, July 1, 1968, thousands of soldiers and workers gathered in Anyuan to mark the forty-seventh anniversary of the founding of the Chinese Communist Party and to conduct a groundbreaking ceremony for the new memorial hall in honor of Mao. Over the next month some ninety work units in the area mobilized more than fifty-four thousand "volunteers" to contribute their labor to the construction effort. Shouldering their own tools, the workers streamed in from neighboring coal mines and factories to the celebratory sound of firecrackers and revolutionary music.

A few days after the groundbreaking, another ceremony was held at Anyuan to herald the arrival of a gigantic replica of the original oil painting, which was also painted by the artist Liu Chunhua. As was the case with similar observances at factories and communes across the country, the ritual to welcome the reproduction of the iconic painting resembled a religious service. First the painting was received reverently by a PLA artillery brigade that had been stationed at the coal mine to "support the left." Waving red flags and singing a paean to Mao known as "Sailing the Seas Depends on the Great Helmsman" to the accompaniment of drums, cymbals, and firecrackers, the soldiers solemnly transported the painting to a makeshift altar directly in front of the construction site for the new memorial hall.[81] Having been alerted to the imminent arrival of the painting by the Mao Zedong Thought propaganda team at the coal mine—which, in a fashion not unlike the lion dancers of pre-1949 Anyuan temple festivals, had paraded from the coal pits to workshops to dormitories and through the town streets, performing celebratory dances and singing hymns of praise—workers poured out of the mine to greet the painting. They proceeded, in a manner not unlike that of the Triads or early Communist Party members, to pledge collective loyalty oaths in front of the painting: "Forever true to Chairman Mao, forever follow

Chairman Mao in revolution!" Elderly workers who had participated in the 1922 strike and the Autumn Harvest Uprising were called upon to bear witness that the painting looked just like the Mao they had seen with their own eyes almost half a century earlier. Invectives were then hurled at the "traitor and revisionist" Liu Shaoqi for tampering with the glorious history of Anyuan in order to advance his counterrevolutionary schemes. To conclude the ceremony, the deputy director of the Anyuan Revolutionary Committee intoned a creed to the painting on behalf of the entire Anyuan workforce:

> Chairman Mao, ah, Chairman Mao! We Anyuan miners are forever loyal to you, forever loyal to your brilliant thought, forever loyal to your revolutionary line. Seas may dry up and boulders turn to pebbles, but our red hearts loyal to you will never change! Heads may be smashed and blood may flow, but your brilliant thought will never be lost. We live to fight for your revolutionary line. We die to sacrifice for your revolutionary line. Chairman Mao, ah, Chairman Mao! We will always remember your great teaching, "Carry forth the revolutionary tradition, strive for greater glory."[82]

The construction of a memorial hall to the greater glory of Chairman Mao was tackled with zeal. For the next five months building proceeded at a frenetic pace. By the end of the year, an imposing structure 24.5 meters high and with 3,245 square meters of interior space had been completed. The exterior walls were finished in yellow brick, while the roof shone with yellow glazed tiles. Atop the roof, 6 meters in diameter and composed of 428 tiles, was a replica of Mao's head exactly as it was depicted in Liu Chunhua's oil painting. Ten red flags and ten torchlights made of tile adorned the roof eaves. Flanking the entrance to the building was Mao's famous slogan in his distinctive calligraphy, "A single spark can light a prairie fire." Although Mao had come up with that signature phrase while at Jinggangshan rather than at Anyuan, the (now banned) movie *Prairie Fire* had linked it permanently to Anyuan in the popular imagination. By placing the adage prominently at the entrance to this temple to Mao, the curators made clear that henceforth the slogan should be associated with the true savior of Anyuan rather than with the demonic imposter, Liu Shaoqi. Beneath Mao's calligraphy was a deferential phrase written by his disciple and presumed successor, Defense Minister Lin Biao: "Sailing the seas depends on the Great Helmsman; carrying out revolution depends on Mao Zedong Thought."

Just as the Anyuan workers' club under Liu Shaoqi had once served as a cultural hub for disseminating revolutionary propaganda to the

Figure 12. Memorial Hall to Chairman Mao's Revolutionary Activities at Anyuan, constructed in 1968. Note Mao's head on the rooftop.

surrounding area, so now the Memorial Hall to Chairman Mao's Revolutionary Activities at Anyuan, as it was officially named, undertook a similar mission. To herald the public opening, a drama troupe connected to the memorial hall performed nearly a hundred renditions of "The Red Sun Shines on Anyuan Mountain," a newly composed tea-picking opera celebrating Chairman Mao's leadership of the Anyuan strike, to audiences across Jiangxi Province. Lecture groups attached to the hall also traveled widely, delivering more than two hundred orations on the "correct" history of the Anyuan labor movement to audiences totaling more than 250,000 people. On April 4, 1969, after a final inspection tour by provincial authorities, the memorial hall officially opened its doors to the public.[83]

The inauguration of the memorial hall, generally considered the grandest of the several museums erected during the Cultural Revolution to honor Chairman Mao's revolutionary achievements, evoked much excitement at Anyuan. It also attracted a stream of domestic and international revolutionary pilgrims, who were drawn to the site made famous by Liu Chunhua's oil painting. A local resident who was a schoolboy at the time later recalled:

> That winter we sat in our freezing cold classroom, shivering as we studied the January 1 editorial "Welcome the Great 1970s" while

watching cars of all sizes gather in front of the memorial hall plaza. We were extremely excited because the memorial hall had opened to the revolutionary people of the whole world! As a beacon of European socialism, a delegation of our Albanian brothers came to Anyuan. We students felt the force of the saying "We have friends all over the world!" Later, delegations from Vietnam and the Japan Communist Party as well as domestic delegations of advanced workers from Daqing, Dazhai, and Lin County arrived to observe and study. At this time, Uncle Yuan [Pin'gao] was replaced by an older worker named Xu Shengyuan as the official storyteller. Holding a copy of *Quotations from Chairman Mao* and dressed in a blue Mandarin-style cotton jacket, he informed the visitors with deep emotion, "It was in the fall of 1921 that the great leader Chairman Mao, wearing a long blue Mandarin gown and holding a Hunan umbrella in his hand, walking along the railway tracks, proceeded step-by-step to Anyuan."[84]

Visitors to the Memorial Hall to Chairman Mao's Revolutionary Activities at Anyuan were greeted in the foyer by the gigantic replica of Liu Chunhua's *Chairman Mao Goes to Anyuan*, painted by the artist himself, which was surrounded by four large banners with the exalted titles that Defense Minister Lin Biao had ascribed to Chairman Mao: "Great Teacher," "Great Leader," "Great Supreme Commander," and "Great Helmsman." Like the exhibition at the Museum of Revolutionary History in Beijing, which had been replicated in the Anyuan workers' club, the display at the new Anyuan memorial hall was comprised of six sections, each featuring Mao's contributions to the Anyuan labor movement.[85] But even more than its predecessor, this exhibit presented the history of Anyuan as a pageant of violent class struggle. The third section, entitled "Beneath Anyuan Mountain, the Clouds and Rivers Rage," made no mention of Mao's call for restraint in the 1922 strike; rather, the Chairman is quoted as steeling the strikers' resolve with a stern reminder that "revolution does not fear bloodshed!" One woodblock print in this section depicted workers' picket Xie Huaide (Liu Shaoqi's old adversary, "Xie the Fierce") delivering a sound thrashing to the Anyuan railway station-master in order to "protect working-class interests." Another woodblock portrayed the workers beating up "old opportunist" Li Lisan when he tried to prevent the wildcat strike of 1923. Yet another woodblock print showed the Anyuan workers hurling buckets of night soil at mine director Shu Xiutai and a Japanese advisor.[86] This was accompanied by "black material" offering "ironclad evidence" that "China's Khrushchev" was a "loyal running dog of capitalists": excerpts from the 1956 letter from former Pingxiang Mining Company director Shu Xiutai to Liu Shaoqi.

Another departure from the previous exhibit was that, instead of concluding the Anyuan story in 1930 with the recruitment of soldiers for the Red Army, the final section of the new exhibit, entitled "The Workers of Anyuan Wish Chairman Mao Long Life without End," focused on the Cultural Revolution itself. The section began with the famous photograph of Mao atop Tiananmen in a military uniform attaching an armband offered by a young female Red Guard. The caption described his leadership of "the first Great Proletarian Cultural Revolution in the history of mankind" as "more momentous for the future of China and the destiny of the world than either the Paris Commune or the October Revolution." There followed several photographs of Mao and his "close comrade-in-arms" Lin Biao receiving Red Guards at Tiananmen and meeting with members of the Cultural Revolution Small Group. Then came an oil painting of Red Guards walking to Anyuan, "following in the footsteps of Chairman Mao," to exchange revolutionary experiences. Next was a photo of the first big-character poster of the Cultural Revolution in Pingxiang, a condemnation of Liu Shaoqi by railway workers. This was followed by photographs of Anyuan workers attacking the former party secretary of the mine at a mass struggle session. The caption explained the scene as "carrying on the glorious revolutionary tradition" of the Anyuan workers in response to Mao's call to "bombard the headquarters." Next came photographs of Red Guards and Anyuan workers "applying Chairman Mao's writings" by jointly engaging in such "revolutionary" acts as smashing a statue of Liu Shaoqi, sealing up the workers' club, ripping to shreds the newspaper *Pingxiang Miners' Journal,* whose masthead carried Liu's calligraphy, chopping down the gum trees in front of the workers' club that "symbolized China's Khrushchev," and so on. A photograph of Liu Shaoqi receiving the "traitor" Yuan Pin'gao at Liu's private residence was said to epitomize his vain attempt to portray himself as the hero of the Anyuan labor movement.

The prior provincial leadership came in for heavy criticism in the memorial hall exhibit. Incriminating "black materials" included a July 1957 directive from the previous governor of Jiangxi, Fang Zhichun, which had designated places once associated with Liu Shaoqi as protected cultural heritage sites. Liu's statements over the years embroidering his Anyuan achievements were prominently featured. Among the items in this category was Liu's remark to Anyuan's Zhu Zijin during their 1957 meeting: "As soon as I arrived, I actively advocated a strike, whereas Li Lisan still had some reservations and couldn't make up his mind." Also included was a statement that Liu had made about Anyuan at a cadres' conference in

Hunan in 1964: "After the strike began, all the other party members went into hiding, leaving only me." The caption noted that such boasts were patently false inasmuch as Chairman Mao deserved sole credit for the strike of 1922. These "black materials" were followed by pictures of Anyuan workers, described as "the best judges of history," denouncing Liu Shaoqi at mass struggle meetings. Then followed evidence of Liu Shaoqi's altering of his 1923 articles to render them suitable for republication thirty-five years later, a photograph of Anyuan workers criticizing the movie *Prairie Fire*, a shot of an elderly Pingxiang railway worker, Liu Xisheng, giving a talk in Tianjin to expose Liu Shaoqi's crimes, and a photo of relatives of Xie Huaide—the former vice-captain of the Anyuan pickets—denouncing Liu for having persecuted Xie during the 1920s at Anyuan. A substantial section was devoted to photographs showing the formation of revolutionary committees at the mine and railway company and the involvement of "support the left" PLA troops in providing assistance to the new power holders. Toward the end was an imposing oil painting of Chairman Mao and Vice-Chairman Lin Biao meeting with miners in the Great Hall of the People. The final segment was devoted to *Chairman Mao Goes to Anyuan*, Liu Chunhua's iconic oil painting. Here one could find Jiang Qing's high praise of the work along with poster renditions and other reproductions. The exhibition concluded with photographs of joyous Anyuan workers welcoming the huge replica of the oil painting that was currently hanging on display in the museum foyer.

## THE DEMISE OF MAO'S "SUCCESSORS"

Photographs of reproductions of a historically inaccurate painting were now the central stuff of political discourse. Anyuan's "glorious revolutionary tradition" had devolved into a caricature of itself, with layers of falsifications and fabrications substituted for serious attention to the plight of the proletariat.[87] But such inaccuracies and ironies did not render debates surrounding the interpretation of the Anyuan past any less politically charged—or perilous. Each of Chairman Mao's putative successors, Liu Shaoqi and Lin Biao, embellished his Anyuan resume, and each would in turn suffer a fatal fall from grace over the course of the Cultural Revolution.

In November 1969 Liu Shaoqi, like Li Lisan two years earlier, died an ignominious death. And similar to Li's death, the exact circumstances of Liu's death remain unclear. Suffering from either medical neglect or torture, a lifeless Liu was found lying on the floor of a makeshift prison in Kaifeng drenched in vomit and feces. His corpse was stuffed into a jeep and transported unceremoniously to a crematorium, where it was disposed of under a false name. The cause of death was recorded simply as "illness"; the family was not notified for three years, and the general public remained in the dark for another decade.[88] Keeping Liu alive in the public imagination as the country's chief "traitor, revisionist, and scab" was useful to Mao and his lieutenants in sustaining the artificial class struggle that animated the Cultural Revolution.

The constant drumbeat of criticism directed against Liu Shaoqi as a "scab" *(gongzei)* who had sold out the Chinese working class meant that the history of the Anyuan labor movement continued to feature as a salient issue in the national media. Posthumously, Liu Shaoqi (and, less prominently, Li Lisan) remained the target of unremitting attacks, as Mao continued to be the object of absurdly exaggerated adulation. But the roles of other characters in the Anyuan morality play were recast during the remaining years of the Cultural Revolution in tandem with larger political shifts.

The newly constructed Anyuan memorial hall was a bellwether for reinterpretations of the history and legacy of the Chinese revolution. In 1969, several months after the Ninth Party Congress at which Defense Minister Lin Biao was officially designated as Mao's successor, the Jiangxi provincial party secretary took advantage of the changing political winds to ensure that his patron enjoyed the exalted status befitting his recent promotion. A major reorganization of the Anyuan memorial hall saw increased space devoted to Lin Biao's brief sojourn at Anyuan in 1930, as well as to his over-the-top praise of Mao Zedong. Prominently featured in the center of the new display was Lin's effusive endorsement, "Chairman Mao's kind of genius appears in the world only once in several centuries and in China only once in several millennia. Chairman Mao is the world's greatest genius." Despite Lin Biao's tenuous connection to the Anyuan labor movement, four large paintings of Lin at Anyuan were specially commissioned and exhibited in the memorial hall. The place where Lin Biao had supposedly slept during his short visit to Anyuan was also opened to the public as a provincial-level cultural heritage site.[89] Keeping pace with the politically correct message of the day, the Anyuan memorial hall continued to draw international as well as domestic attention. In 1970 the museum hosted delegations from Japan, France, Norway Vietnam, Thailand, and other parts of Southeast Asia. Early the next year it welcomed delegations from Australia, Indonesia, Albania, North Korea, Vietnam, Thailand, and Japan.[90]

Lin Biao's Anyuan record was soon to be dramatically rewritten, however. In May 1971 the party secretary of the Memorial Hall to Chairman Mao's Revolutionary Activities at Anyuan, Lian Mingde, was suddenly summoned to a meeting in Beijing of revolutionary museum representatives, the purpose of which turned out to be an attempt to mitigate the influence of the Lin Biao faction.[91] At the meeting Premier Zhou Enlai made two cryptic reports in which he instructed the attendees to study Mao's December 18, 1970, conversation with the American journalist Edgar Snow. Although no direct mention was made of Lin Biao, Lian suspected that the defense minister must be in some kind of political trouble since Mao had complained to Snow that the so-called "four great" titles accorded to Mao by Lin Biao—Great Teacher, Great Leader, Great Supreme Commander, Great Helmsman—were now "a nuisance" that had contributed to an "overdone" cult of personality. In his conversation with Snow, Mao did not name Lin Biao in connection with the "four greats," but he stressed that he wanted to retain only one of the four titles that Lin had bestowed upon him: teacher.[92] When Premier Zhou arranged for the museum curators to tour the Great Hall of the People, Lian noticed the absence of any quotations from Lin Biao, further confirming his suspicions of an impending shake-up in the leadership lineup.

Upon his return to Anyuan, Lian Mingde ordered several changes at the memorial hall intended to reflect what he had gleaned from his trip to Beijing. The "four greats" banners that had previously adorned the museum foyer were taken down. Inside the hall, the most questionable quotations from Lin Biao were replaced with portraits of Marx, Engels, Lenin, and Stalin. Three of the four paintings of Lin Biao and seven of eight of Lin's quotations were removed. Although Lian felt confident that he had captured the spirit of Zhou Enlai's meeting, his renovations did not sit well with Lin Biao's chief local protégé and promoter, Cheng Shiqing, the head of the Jiangxi Provincial Revolutionary Committee. When Cheng caught wind of the alterations, he sent emissaries to the Anyuan memorial hall to admonish Lian for having changed the displays without provincial authorization and to demand that Lin Biao's prominence in the exhibition be restored at once.

Calculating that Premier Zhou Enlai was a more reliable political weather vane than officials in Nanchang, Lian was slow to comply with Cheng's directive, a foot-dragging tactic that would soon be vindicated by national developments.[93] When Jiangxi provincial authorities learned the stunning news of Lin Biao's alleged assassination plot against Chairman

Mao and his fatal plane crash over Mongolia, they ordered an immediate halt to the previously demanded alterations and sent armed military guards to surround the museum. Now it was Lin Biao's turn to suffer posthumous attacks for having faked his revolutionary credentials. Shortly after Lin's death, a study group of elderly revolutionary cadres toured the various museums in Jiangxi Province, including the Anyuan memorial hall, and reported on having encountered "much propaganda about Lin Biao that was all pretty much the same and whose contents were largely fabricated and exaggerated."[94] The politically loaded term "prairie fire" (liaoyuan), which had been inscribed outside the front entrance to the Anyuan labor museum as a symbol of Mao's repossession of his rightful revolutionary inheritance, was now invoked against Lin Biao as evidence of his "extreme negative pessimism." According to the recollection of Marshall Chen Yi, it was Lin Biao's skepticism toward Mao Zedong's effort to build the Red Army in Jiangxi that had prompted Mao in January 1930 to write a long letter in which he sought to dispel Lin's negativism by pointing out that "a single spark can light a prairie fire."[95]

After the Lin Biao study group had submitted its report, Lian Mingde, along with the directors of the Jinggangshan and the Red Army revolutionary museums, was summoned to the provincial capital of Nanchang to receive a briefing from the deputy political commissar of the military region. Informed of Lin Biao's abortive assassination attempt, the museum directors were instructed to dispose of their many Lin Biao–related displays. Lian was gratified that Anyuan, in contrast to the two other major Jiangxi revolutionary museums, had already taken care of most of the problem. Nevertheless, there were still several Lin Biao–related items that required further attention: one large statue, one oil painting (Anyuan Workers and Peasants Welcome the Red Army in 1930), one quotation, and the residence where Lin had allegedly stayed when he came to recruit soldiers for the Red Army. Lian gathered all the party members on the museum staff to participate in the demolition work. After everyone lent a hand in smashing the statue, they divided into three groups. The first worked on altering the oil painting so that the figure of Lin Biao was eliminated from the scene. The second focused on the written explanations that accompanied the displays in the museum, excising all mention of Lin Biao. The third sealed up Lin's 1930 residence. The following day, when the party secretary of Pingxiang city conducted an inspection of the memorial hall, he expressed complete satisfaction with the renovations.

REVERSING COURSE

In May 1972 Lin Biao's loyal lieutenant in Jiangxi, Cheng Shiqing, was purged. The next month provincial leaders personally reviewed the Anyuan exhibits to ensure compliance with the "correct" central line. During the review process, the new head of the Jiangxi standing committee, Huang Zhizhen, raised the sensitive question of the name of the Anyuan museum. On grounds that the name, Memorial Hall to Chairman Mao's Revolutionary Activities at Anyuan, had been chosen by Lin Biao's followers on the Jiangxi Revolutionary Committee, Huang proposed renaming the museum. The suggestion was controversial inasmuch as it involved the name of Chairman Mao. However, noting that Mao himself had recently called for scaling down his cult of personality, provincial authorities agreed after several months of deliberation to restore the name of the museum that had been located in the old Anyuan workers' club before the Cultural Revolution: the Anyuan Railway and Mine Workers' Labor Movement Memorial Hall. At the same time, the gigantic replica of Liu Chunhua's *Chairman Mao Goes to Anyuan* was removed from the museum foyer on the pretext that it had begun to mildew.[96]

The decision to dislodge the iconic oil painting was in part a product of rumors suggesting that Chairman Mao himself was displeased with the image. A year earlier, during a visit to the museum at Mao's birthplace of Shaoshan, Vice-Premier Zhang Chunqiao, upon encountering another copy of Liu's painting, told the curators that Mao Zedong had expressed reservations about the painting, considering the image to be both hackneyed and historically inaccurate. According to Zhang, Mao remembered having worn a shirt and trousers—not a long scholar's gown—on his maiden journey to Anyuan![97] On October 1, 1972, the renamed and refurbished Anyuan memorial hall, purged of the huge oil painting that had once graced its foyer, reopened to the public.[98]

Despite its new name, which underscored the contributions of the workers themselves in the development of the Anyuan labor movement, the memorial hall still featured Chairman Mao as central protagonist. The display that opened in 1972 was comprised of five sections, four of which highlighted Mao Zedong's leadership role: 1) The Anyuan workers' history of blood and tears; 2) Chairman Mao personally lights the fires of revolution at Anyuan; 3) Chairman Mao personally leads the Anyuan workers' Great Strike; 4) Chairman Mao leads the Anyuan workers to launch the peasant movement; 5) Chairman Mao leads the Anyuan workers on the revolutionary road to the seizure of armed power.[99] Muted in this exhibition, however, were the attacks on Mao's enemies and the glorification of violence that had figured so prominently in recent iterations. The only references to Liu Shaoqi in the entire display consisted of a few brief excerpts from his writings that urged "cooperation between labor and capital," thereby supposedly revealing his early opposition to Mao's revolutionary line. Entirely gone from this rendition of the Anyuan story was the section on the Cultural Revolution that had served as the climax of the 1969 exhibit. Rather, as was true of earlier displays, the 1972 version ended with the formation of the Red Army in 1928–30. Although a small copy of Liu Chunhua's famous painting could still be found sandwiched in the middle of the second section, the arresting image of the young Mao on his way to Anyuan was no longer the visual focal point of the entire exhibit. Also gone were the throngs of revolutionary pilgrims who had once flocked to the Anyuan museum.

Many years later, Liu Chunhua would insist that the sudden downturn in the popularity of his previously ubiquitous painting had less to do with Mao's disapproval of it than with the artist's conflict with Jiang Qing. Liu explained that after he had expressed negative opinions about some of Jiang Qing's statements at an expanded meeting of the Beijing party committee in the spring of 1972, he was under constant surveillance as an alleged "member of the Lin Biao clique" for the duration of the Cultural Revolution.[100] According to Liu, the precipitous decline in the status of his once-sacred painting at this time was the direct result of his own political misfortune. Whatever the precise reasons, the appeal of *Chairman Mao Goes to Anyuan*—and, not coincidentally, the popularity of Anyuan as a revolutionary pilgrimage site—began to ebb markedly soon after revelations surrounding the Lin Biao incident started to surface.

Another local indication of the shifting political tide was the rehabilitation of Liu Shaoqi's former bodyguard, Yuan Pin'gao. Following an investigation by the party organization of the Pingxiang coal mine, in 1972—after three years of "labor reform" at a small nearby coal pit—Yuan was cleared of all political charges. His party membership was restored, as was his "revolutionary" stipend. The next year Yuan retired and returned home to nearby Liling. Until his death at age eighty in 1975, Yuan made frequent visits back to Anyuan at the invitation of the memorial hall to share recollections of his earlier experiences.[101] Thus, several years prior to the official conclusion of the Cultural Revolution decade in 1976, contestation over the interpretation of the Anyuan revolutionary tradition had come almost full circle with the exoneration of Liu Shaoqi's most ardent and outspoken advocate.

Mao Zedong himself, perturbed by the factional strife that persisted well after the death of Lin Biao, seemed inclined to draw increasingly conservative implications from the history of Anyuan. Although his memory grew hazy toward the end of his life, in the year before his death Mao mentioned the lessons he had learned as a young labor organizer at Anyuan on several occasions. In May 1975, presumably as an oblique criticism of his wife and her three Shanghai colleagues for their propensity to act as a "gang of four," Mao recalled that his time at Anyuan—where workers from different native places formed competing gangs—had taught him the dangers of factionalism: "Don't form any gangs, whether a Guangdong gang or a Hunan gang."[102] Considering how Mao and his colleagues had favored their fellow Hunanese while at Anyuan, and, more to the point, how the history of Anyuan had recently been deployed to promote competing claims among warring factions of the Chinese Communist leadership, Mao's admonition was more than a little ironic.

## WORKERS' CONDITIONS

Despite the dramatic fluctuations in political climate that occurred over the course of the Cultural Revolution, an issue of abiding interest to workers—the condition of their livelihood—remained largely unimproved. The Cultural Revolution saw a significant rise in the ideological status of the working class in general, and the revolutionary reputation of the Anyuan proletariat in particular. But this heightened symbolic importance did not translate into commensurate gains in worker welfare, in Anyuan or elsewhere.[103]

Although coal production at Anyuan enjoyed an average annual increase of 4.8 percent over the Cultural Revolution decade, workers' wages were stagnant.[104] Welfare benefits also suffered. For four years, from 1966 through 1969, the Pingxiang Mining Company contributed nothing to the labor insurance fund that provided medical coverage to its workforce.[105] State investment in workers' housing declined markedly as well. Whereas annual investment in residential units for workers at the coal mine had averaged 530,000 yuan for the ten years prior to the Cultural Revolution, during the decade of the Cultural Revolution the amount plummeted by 70 percent to an annual average of 160,000 yuan.[106] Educational opportunities at the mine also largely evaporated. From 1966 through 1972, all schools and extracurricular classes for workers at Anyuan—previously operated by the culture and education department of the coal mining district union, which was itself dissolved during the Cultural Revolution—were discontinued.[107]

Not only did the Great "Proletarian" Cultural Revolution bring few economic gains to Anyuan workers; it also saw a reorganization of workplace administration along the lines of a military model that called for greater discipline and sacrifice. Martial nomenclature was introduced. The factory director was addressed as "regiment commander" (*tuanzhang*), the district directors as "battalion commanders" (*yingzhang*), and the work shifts were known as "companies" (*lian*), which were led by "platoon leaders" (*paizhang*). Party secretaries were referred to as "political commissars" (*zhengwei*) and technicians as "staff officers" (*canmou*). To encourage greater enthusiasm for the dangerous work of coal mining, descending into the pits was likened to "entering battle" and workers were urged to "fear no sacrifice."[108]

One might expect such regimentation to have engendered resentment and resistance among the poorly compensated labor force. Yet the Cultural Revolution is remembered fondly by many elderly miners, who recall the practice of emulating the army as part of a meaningful mission to revive an endangered revolutionary spirit. As one elderly worker recalled of that era, "Month after month we waged battle, singing a refrain from *Quotations from Chairman Mao:* 'Be resolute, don't fear sacrifice.' We went down into the pits at 3:45 in the morning and came up after 3 in the afternoon, on average working more than twelve hours a day. But we miners had no complaints and worked furiously."[109] Despite the martial discipline and material deprivation that characterized working-class life during the Cultural Revolution, the experience evokes nostalgic reflections from those who look back on it as a heady period of proletarian pride when Anyuan workers played a starring role on the national political stage.

The heightened ideological regard for the proletariat did afford some Anyuan workers new political opportunities over the course of the Cultural Revolution. In 1969, for example, three out of six chairmen of the Pingxiang Mining Company Revolutionary Representative Congress were workers rather than administrative cadres, who had formed the previous party committees. A coal miner by the name of Pan Shigao served on the central committees of both the ninth and tenth Chinese Communist Party Congresses, and also served for a time as deputy party secretary of Jiangxi Province. In April 1971, Pan headed a delegation of Chinese workers on an official visit to Albania. Many ordinary miners were also politically engaged in this period; among a total workforce of

2,900 at the main Anyuan coal pit, nearly one thousand were officially designated as "activists" in the study and application of Mao Zedong Thought.[110]

In later years, buffeted by the layoffs that accompanied Deng Xiaoping's market reforms, the Cultural Revolution would be remembered appreciatively for its provision of cradle-to-grave security. An elderly worker recalled of the period, "In those days . . . the work unit took care of everything. . . . Most important, the work unit guaranteed children's education and job placement. In our mine even baths and haircuts were provided for free. . . . These days? There's nothing at all."[111] As one veteran worker put it, "The reforms haven't done much good for workers. Wages are at a bare subsistence level."[112] If pressed, informants would concede that the post-Mao reforms brought higher living standards for the majority of Anyuan workers. At the same time, however, the loss of workplace security was bitterly resented.[113] Although in fact the guarantee of lifetime employment at state enterprises predated the Cultural Revolution by more than a decade, and owed far more to Li Lisan's labor insurance law than to Mao's last crusade, it had become linked in the popular mind with "Chairman Mao's revolution." When Mao passed away on September 9, 1976, among the floral wreaths sent to Beijing to mourn his death was one from the workers of Anyuan.[114]

If Anyuan workers were prone to romanticizing the revolutionary past, they were not alone in this tendency. The nostalgia for mass campaigns, and the Cultural Revolution in particular, has been detected in other places, among peasants as well as workers.[115] These sentiments undoubtedly reflect dissatisfaction with elements of present policies more than any genuine desire to return to the (often grim) realities of the past. However, they also speak to the powerful symbolic appeal of Mao's revolution to many Chinese, and especially its promise of dignity for the downtrodden.

The Great Proletarian Cultural Revolution was instigated, and to some extent orchestrated, by Chairman Mao himself. It was by no means simply an elite power struggle, however. Mao did not require the services of inexperienced Red Guards (or the Mao Zedong Thought propaganda teams who replaced them) to dispose of competitors within the party hierarchy; he was more than capable of handling such challenges without the help of naive students and workers.[116] At the heart of Mao's ultimate crusade lay a quest to cultivate reliable successors who would embrace "a new mass culture."[117] Only by imbuing the youth of China with an unshakable commitment to the ideals of proletarian revolution could the aging leader rest assured that his life's cause would not die with him.

The abiding concern for cultural transformation was reminiscent of the early Communist movement, when the young Mao Zedong, Li Lisan, and Liu Shaoqi devoted such attention to fostering a new revolutionary consciousness among young workers in Anyuan and other industrial centers. But whereas in the early 1920s Mao and his comrades conducted their efforts through local grassroots organizations such as workers' clubs and night schools, now powerful national state institutions—from the Central Propaganda Department to the People's Liberation Army— directed the process. And while party leaders remained committed in principle to a socialist project that privileged the proletariat, the tenor of the message had changed noticeably. China had embarked on a sacred revolutionary crusade to save the nation and the world from the perils of Soviet "revisionism." Unlike the pedagogical enterprise that had animated the Anyuan Great Strike and the operations of Little Moscow, this latter-day promotion of "proletarian culture" elevated the *wu* of the warrior over the *wen* of the scholar. The point was brought home by Chairman Mao himself at the beginning of the Cultural Revolution when he greeted throngs of Red Guard admirers in Tiananmen Square on August 18, 1966. As Mao, dressed in a PLA uniform, accepted an armband from a female student named Song Binbin, he advised the young woman to change her name to reflect the militarized spirit of the times:

> After learning her given name, "Binbin," meaning "refined" or "urbane," he reportedly declared this was a name suited for a high-class lady, not a young revolutionary. "Is that the 'bin' in 'wenzhi binbin' (soft and gentle)?" she recalled Mao inquiring of her. "I said, 'Yes.' Then he told me kindly: 'You want to be militant.'" He then conferred on her the now more fashionable name "Yaowu," or "seeking violence."[118]

Mao's recommended name change, designed to better match the young Red Guard to a new revolutionary mission, signaled that his Cultural Revolution was to draw upon the military, more the literary, tradition of Chinese authority. The culture that took shape during the Cultural Revolution, on stage as in the street, "expressed a rejection of the reliance on the cultivated mind of traditional intellectuals and a need for physical endurance and risk taking."[119] In this new version of proletarian culture, the refinement of *wen* (*wenzhi binbin*) would be replaced by the roughness of *wu* (*yaowu*). By selecting a bespectacled female Red Guard on whom to bestow such an obviously masculine name, Mao made clear that the martial ideal was intended to apply to students of both sexes.[120] The lesson was readily absorbed. As Emily Honig observes of the female perpetrators of Red Guard violence, "women invariably dressed as men, or more precisely, as male army combatants."[121]

The military was appealing as a model for emulation not only because it represented martial strength, but also because the army enjoyed substantial moral authority by virtue of its intimate connection to the history of the Chinese revolution. Mao's revolution had seemingly reversed the Confucian superiority of the scholar over the soldier as a source of cultural and political power. To be sure, the ascendance of the PLA in the early years of the Cultural Revolution was the result of personal and bureaucratic factionalism, reflecting the triumph of Defense Minister Lin Biao over party vice-chairman Liu Shaoqi as Mao's anointed successor. But the prominence of the military had a symbolic meaning, as well. Robert Lifton observes that the PLA connoted "revolutionary purity—with combined psychic and material power." The army was thus an appropriate vehicle for carrying out Mao's final crusade for "revolutionary immortality."[122]

The emotional blend of militancy and religiosity that characterized mass participation in Mao's Cultural Revolution, especially among the youth, helps to explain the continuing hold of this experience on the popular imagination. At Anyuan, a concrete expression of this blend was the construction of the grandiose memorial hall to commemorate Chairman Mao's revolutionary activities. Directed by the military, the ritualistic process was replete with devotional fervor. The inaugural exhibit within the new hall, modeled on that of the Museum of Revolutionary History in Beijing, emphasized in exaggerated terms the martial implications of the Anyuan story. Liu Shaoqi's injunctions against violence were rejected as a reflection of his "revisionist" sins; Mao Zedong's contributions to the Red Terror, the rise of the Red Army, and the Cultural Revolution "class struggle" were praised as nothing short of miraculous.

It is therefore all the more striking that a central icon of worship—in the memorial hall as in the Mao cult sweeping the rest of the country at the time—was the manifestly nonviolent image of Chairman Mao en route to Anyuan, dressed in a flowing scholar's gown and armed only with a paper umbrella, standing contemplatively amid the mountain clouds. The androgynous figure of the young intellectual, which resonated so powerfully not only with his wife, Jiang Qing, but also with adoring followers of both sexes and all ages all across China, drew its symbolic appeal not from the *wu* of the warrior but from the *wen* of the literatus.

To be sure, this soothing image announced the vicious annihilation of Mao's rival claimant to the legacy of Anyuan. When the deified portrait was unveiled, Liu Shaoqi was unmasked as the demonic "China's Khrushchev" who had attempted to plunder the sacred revolutionary treasury for his own nefarious ends. Henceforth Chairman Mao alone was to be revered as savior of proletariat and peasantry alike. But there was more to it than that. Presented in the attire of a literatus, Mao exudes the wisdom and authority of a Confucian teacher. Jiang Qing, who had a fondness for traditional Chinese dress herself, surely appreciated the sartorial significance of the painting that she so energetically promoted, understanding that a paramount leader must project pedagogical as well as military prowess.[123] In early 1971, Jiang exclaimed to her confidantes, "The Chairman's power is literary."[124] On the floral wreath that she prepared for her husband's funeral, Jiang's dedication made clear that Mao should be remembered, above all, as a teacher: "In deep mourning of the revered master teacher Chairman Mao Zedong, from your student and comrade in arms Jiang Qing."[125] The designation of Mao as teacher was consistent with his self-assessment. Edgar Snow, in explaining Mao's decision to accept only one of the "four great" titles that Lin Biao had bestowed upon him, that of teacher, wrote shortly before the Chairman's death, "Mao had always been a schoolteacher and still was one. He was a primary schoolteacher in Changsha even before he was a Communist. All the rest of the titles would be declined."[126]

The captivating appeal of the Anyuan image suggested that, despite the bloody road Mao's revolution had traversed, the allure of the "red literati" remained powerful. In depicting Mao on his way from Changsha to teach revolution to the miners, the painting also served as a reminder that the Great Proletarian Cultural Revolution was supposed to be about the proletariat. Although no workers appear in Liu Chunhua's painting, Mao's gaze is directed toward the coal mine. The release of the painting signaled that the time had come for student Red Guards to step aside in favor of workers' propaganda teams. Demobilized and dispatched "up to the mountains and down to the villages," the urban youth of China were enjoined to cease their factional strife and learn from the revolutionary experience of the peasants and workers.

The coal miners of Anyuan, who embodied a near perfect blend of the idealized social composition of the Chinese revolution—workers, peasants, and soldiers—and whose mobilization had drawn inspiration from both pillars of Chinese political authority (literary and military), were catapulted to the exalted status of the "revolutionary elect." Blessed by a special bond to the messianic prophet himself, and sanctified by the blood of countless martyrs along the way, the Anyuan labor movement symbolized sacrifice and loyalty to the revolutionary faith. This was a heady formula that proved exhilarating not only to the protagonists themselves but also to pilgrims, artists, intellectuals, and officials from around the country and beyond. As one veteran coal miner summarized the gospel of Anyuan in a feature article in *China Pictorial*,

> In those days of hard revolutionary struggle, the Anyuan coal mine was a hell where imperialism, feudalism and bureaucratic-capitalism co-operated to suck the blood of the miners. The miners then led a life worse than beasts of burden. . . . In the midst of our suffering Chairman Mao, the red sun in our hearts, arrived in Anyuan. . . . Chairman Mao's words lit our hearts and we miners . . . were awakened. . . . We who were no better than cattle in the old society have become the masters of the country. When we contrast the new with the old, we feel that dear as our parents are to us still dearer is Chairman Mao. We veteran miners are resolved to be thoroughly loyal to the great leader Chairman Mao, the great thought of Mao Tse-tung and his revolutionary line and follow him forever in making revolution.[127]

The redemptive religiosity that infused the Cultural Revolution reading of the Anyuan story was part of a nationwide cult that blurred the distinction between older rituals and new Communist practices. At the instigation of workers' propaganda teams, factories across China set up altars that displayed Mao's writings, behind which a portrait of Mao (usually the Anyuan image, but sometimes Mao in PLA uniform) was hung. Workers would gather there to "seek guidance" in the morning and to "report back" in the evening, as they might do before an ancestral tablet or bodhisattva idol in a family shrine.[128] The practice soon spread to the villages. In his memoir of the Cultural Revolution, Liang Heng describes how his father—an urban intellectual sent down to the countryside for "reeducation"—conveyed city rituals to his new peasant neighbors. After converting an old ancestor shrine into a place of adulation for Mao Zedong,

> He put up fresh posters of Chairman Mao and [Defense Minister] Lin Biao. . . . "Fellow countrymen," he announced to the fascinated crowd, "from now on we are going to be like the people in the city. In the morning we are going to ask for strength, in the evening make

reports." . . . Then he turned to face the Great Helmsman and the Revolutionary Marshal and bowed, with utmost gravity, three times to the waist. There was a general titter of nervous laughter. Father looked so serious, and the peasants had never seen anyone bow to anything except the images of their own ancestors. But they were eager learners, for they loved Chairman Mao. At last they had an earnest teacher to show them how to express their love.[129]

Mao worship took place within families as well. Anita Chan and her coauthors describe Cultural Revolution routines in a South China village: "Before every meal, in imitation of the army (where the Mao rituals were reaching extraordinary proportions), Chen Village families began performing services to Mao. Led by the family head, they intoned in unison a selection of Mao quotations; sang "The East is Red"; and as they sat to eat they recited a Mao grace."[130]

The intense religiosity of Mao's final crusade distinguished it from previous exercises in cultural patronage under the PRC. Although the Cultural Revolution perpetuated many features of the preceding seventeen years of Communist rule, it was a "great awakening" of such magnitude as to dwarf the campaigns that preceded it.[131] To be sure, efforts to burnish Liu Shaoqi's Anyuan reputation, especially once he was publicly acknowledged as Mao's putative successor in 1961, had also bordered on cultish devotion. But the earlier projects, although actively promoted by the state propaganda system, did not elicit anywhere near the levels of mass participation and fervent adulation witnessed in the Cultural Revolution. Liu's cult of personality, modeled on those of Lenin and Stalin, was designed to strengthen the prestige of the Communist Party and its leadership. Mao's, by contrast, was part of a cultural revolution intended to imbue the youth of the nation with a new proletarian spirit that would preserve his revolution for posterity.[132] For that purpose, didactic textbooks and propaganda movies were insufficient. Nothing less than a religious revival capable of stirring the national soul would do.

The adaptation of religious beliefs and practices to the service of a Maoist cult of personality was not just an instrumentalist ploy manufactured by cynical state leaders. For one thing, popular worship of Mao predated the establishment of the Communist party-state.[133] For another, as anthropologist Emily Martin Ahern reminds us of Chinese folk religion more broadly, "Any simple claim that Chinese ritual and religion served the ends of those with political authority must be misleading unless it admits the possibility that the religion also served some useful purpose for those with no political authority."[134] Seeking before his death to purify his congregation and restore the true faith by purging it of the revisionism of "China's Khrushchev" and his Soviet masters, Mao, with the assistance of the People's Liberation Army, called upon the Chinese people to follow him in reclaiming their own revolutionary heritage and in so doing to recoup their national pride. As a key staging ground in this spiritual crusade, Anyuan—in the eyes of its own residents as well as in the national media—attained unprecedented significance. Once hailed as China's Little Moscow, the coal mine had renounced its Soviet lineage in favor of a Maoist revolutionary line. No longer a symbol of deference to foreign precedent, it had come to connote a distinctively Chinese revolutionary path. The resonance of the Cultural Revolution rendition of the Anyuan morality play, with its triumph of national salvation over foreign apostasy, struck a powerful emotional chord that reverberates to this day.

# 7 Reforming the Revolutionary Tradition

With the death of Chairman Mao and the dramatic arrest of his widow, Jiang Qing, and other members of her radical so-called Gang of Four in the fall of 1976, the Cultural Revolution decade drew to an official close. Three years later, Deng Xiaoping announced his historic program of "reform and opening" to revitalize the economy and reconnect China to the international community. The resulting commercialization and globalization brought major changes in the system of cultural patronage that had developed under Mao. A longtime scholar of Chinese cultural politics, Richard Kraus, observes that "a new politics of culture has taken shape, with greater openness, vastly diminished state supervision, and increased professionalism by artists."[1] But this is not to say that the post-Mao state has abandoned an interest in shaping and controlling the thoughts of its citizens. The propaganda apparatus, now using to full advantage powerful new forms of mass media such as television, cellular technology, and the Internet, continues actively to promote state priorities. Indeed, communications scholar Zhao Yuezhi characterizes the contemporary system as a "pervasive regime of coercive, regulatory, bureaucratic, technological, and normative power that penetrates every facet of public communication."[2]

The combination of a comparatively open cultural arena with an opaque yet omnipresent propaganda effort has generated numerous ironies and inconsistencies in the reform-era presentation and preservation of China's revolutionary legacy. The upscale Xintiandi bar and restaurant complex in Shanghai, located at the site of the First National Congress of the Chinese Communist Party, is a well-known architectural illustration of the multivalent messages surrounding the revolutionary tradition.[3] Less familiar, but perhaps even more revealing, are competing reinterpretations of the history of the Anyuan labor movement.

## REVERSING VERDICTS

In the immediate post-Mao period, the retelling of the Anyuan story took place quite deliberately under official auspices. For example, the once reviled artist Hou Yimin, who was persecuted for his "reactionary" painting *Liu Shaoqi and the Anyuan Miners*, which had been displayed in the Museum of Revolutionary History at its opening in 1961, reentered the limelight in 1977 with an oil painting entitled *Chairman Mao and the Anyuan Miners*. Hou's new painting showed a casual Mao, clad in shirt and pants, down in the coal pits, squatting and chatting amid a group of mesmerized but grubby miners. In sharp contrast to the iconic Cultural Revolution era portrait by Liu Chunhua, *Chairman Mao Goes to Anyuan*, which had depicted a deified Mao Zedong standing majestically alone on the mountaintop, Hou's new painting—like his earlier rendition of Liu Shaoqi—placed the leader among the masses. Although completed more than a decade apart under vastly different political circumstances, Hou's two paintings were now regarded as companion pieces that correctly depicted both Liu Shaoqi and Mao Zedong as parallel leaders of the Anyuan labor movement.[4] The latter painting was hung in the Museum of Revolutionary History (later to be subsumed within the National Museum of China) shortly after the conclusion of the Cultural Revolution.[5]

Practicing artists were not the only beneficiaries of the post-Mao reversal of political verdicts. A wave of prominent rehabilitations among the political elite also occurred. Among the most noteworthy was the posthumous rehabilitation of the principal victim of the Cultural Revolution, Liu Shaoqi. In the spring of 1980, at a televised ceremony viewed by millions of Chinese, the former head of state was officially cleared of all political crimes. At Anyuan itself, more than twenty thousand people crowded into the open field in front of the workers' club to watch the live broadcast.[6]

As we have seen, Liu Shaoqi's alleged "rightist" errors at Anyuan figured significantly in the charges leveled against him during the Cultural Revolution. Not surprisingly, then, a major reinterpretation of Anyuan revolutionary history accompanied his subsequent political acquittal. A few months prior to Liu Shaoqi's official rehabilitation ceremony, his widow, Wang Guangmei, wrote an open letter to the editors of two major national periodicals, *China Youth* and *Workers Daily*, with the aim of setting straight Liu's Anyuan record. By selecting these two particular conduits, Wang signaled that her message was directed toward the two

Figure 13. *Mao and the Anyuan Miners,* oil painting by Hou Yimin, 1977. Photo courtesy of Eugene Wang.

principal participants in the Cultural Revolution mass mobilization that had pilloried her husband: the youth and the proletariat. Channeling the voice of her late husband, Wang Guangmei offered a spirited defense of his tactics in the Anyuan strike of 1922, justified in terms of the workers' own interests:

Comrades:

You have repeatedly asked me what Comrade Shaoqi said about the Anyuan Great Strike. I will now make some brief comments.

In the early Cultural Revolution period, many distortions of the Anyuan strike appeared in big-character posters and critical essays. After Comrade Shaoqi read them, he declared, "Concrete historical facts cannot be denied!" At that time I asked him, "Was there no better way to have carried out the struggle? Could you not have persisted in the strike until the mine and railway authorities agreed to every last demand?" Comrade Shaoqi replied, "Too risky. If the machine room were destroyed, the pits would have flooded with water and it would have been years before production could resume. What would the more than ten thousand workers have done? What would several tens of thousands of people have done for food, clothing, and livelihood? After the worker masses were mobilized and the strike reached a climax, through negotiations the authorities approved almost all of the workers' demands and a victory was achieved. We strove for the immediate interests of the Anyuan workers while also representing the long-term interests of the working class. The Anyuan Great Strike had a good result, improving the workers' livelihood, raising the workers' consciousness and political position, demonstrating the power of workers' unity, and encouraging the broad workers of the whole country." . . .

Comrade Shaoqi's emotional attachment to Anyuan was extremely deep. He repeatedly promised the elderly workers of Anyuan and the martyrs' children that he would definitely return to Anyuan for a look. Once, when Comrade Shaoqi was taking a train south to attend a meeting, in the middle of the journey he paced back and forth on the Pingxiang railway station platform for nearly half an hour. He promised the local cadres that in the future he would make a special trip to Anyuan to see his Anyuan comrades, view developments at the mine, and find out how the elderly workers were doing, whether the night school continued to operate. . . . The Anyuan scenery held an immense attraction for him.

This dream of Comrade Shaoqi's could never be realized! However, he can be comforted that the true face of history has been recovered. This is the victory of Marxism–Leninism–Mao Zedong Thought!

With a firm hand shake!
Wang Guangmei
January 25, 1980[7]

The rehabilitation of Liu Shaoqi had a number of repercussions at Anyuan itself. Responding to the changed political climate, local authorities first approved a series of symbolic steps, in the name of righting past wrongs, that partially restored the status quo ante. The local newspaper, for example, placed Liu Shaoqi's calligraphy back on its masthead.

When Wang Guangmei received a complimentary copy of the *Pingxiang Miners' Journal* bearing her late husband's calligraphy, as it had in pre–Cultural Revolution days, she sent an appreciative reply to the editors of the newspaper. Hailing the pivotal role of the Anyuan workers in resuscitating her husband's reputation, Wang stressed the importance of the Anyuan chapter in the subsequent success of the Chinese revolution:

Comrades:

I have received your kind letter and the copy of the *Pingxiang Miners' Journal*. When I saw that you had restored the masthead with Comrade Shaoqi's 1955 calligraphy, I was deeply moved. I felt that the

Anyuan worker comrades and I must share the same feelings.

Anyuan is the famous place where Comrade Shaoqi engaged in revolutionary work in his early years. Here he expended tremendous energy and deep emotion. More important, it was here that he gained much valuable knowledge and garnered much experience. This knowledge and experience had great influence and meaning for the later revolutionary struggles of Comrade Shaoqi and the party.

The exoneration of Comrade Shaoqi demonstrates the pragmatic spirit of the party. It is the result of the united struggles of the working class and the broad people. The workers of Anyuan have shown their power.

Please convey my regards to the workers and cadres of Anyuan!

Wang Guangmei
March 8, 1980[8]

Wang Guangmei, like generations of party leaders before her, invoked the purported will of the Anyuan workers to establish the rectitude of her (and her husband's) own political stance. As China's "chosen proletariat," Anyuan workers still possessed a spiritual power that political leaders found tempting to claim as evidence for their own revolutionary legitimacy. The workers of Anyuan, Wang suggested, shared her unbounded affection and unqualified approval of the revolutionary efforts of Liu Shaoqi.

Less than two weeks later, however, another political rehabilitation indicated that the Anyuan workers reserved fonder feelings still for that other leader of the 1922 strike, Li Lisan. On March 20, at a state ceremony attended by more than seven hundred people, including Deng Xiaoping and Hu Yaobang as well as Li Lisan's Russian-born widow, Lisa Kishkin, Li Lisan's contributions to the revolution—including his role at Anyuan—received long overdue recognition. The official resolution on Li Lisan read in part:

> In 1922 he and Comrade Liu Shaoqi were directed by the Hunan party organization and Comrade Mao Zedong to go to Anyuan to undertake labor mobilization. Because he opened the Anyuan school for workers, founded the Anyuan workers' club, fostered workers' cultural activities, used basic Marxist theory to educate the workers, and developed a party organization, even today any mention of Li Longzhi (the name used at that time by Comrade Lisan) evokes deep feelings of familiarity and intimacy from the older workers of Anyuan. Together with Liu Shaoqi and others, he led the Anyuan railway and mine workers in a strike struggle that had a major impact in advancing the labor movement at that time in Jiangxi, Hunan, and the whole country.[9]

With the political rehabilitation of both Liu Shaoqi and Li Lisan, grass-roots cadres and cultural workers had the green light to undertake a thorough reconsideration of the Anyuan labor movement.

In 1981, the formerly banned factory history *Red Anyuan* was reprinted in a new edition (still in the name of the Pingxiang Mining Company Propaganda Department) that featured as part of its front matter Wang Guangmei's March 1980 letter extolling her husband's Anyuan experience. The writer Peng Yonghui, who had been the lead author of earlier editions of *Red Anyuan* as well as the scriptwriter of the previously condemned movie *Prairie Fire*, reemerged with a sequel to *Prairie Fire* entitled *Eminences of the Great Marsh (Dazelongshe)*, which opened to large and appreciative audiences in 1982. The new movie continued the Anyuan story through the Northern Expedition and the Autumn Harvest Uprising to the formation of the Red Army in 1928. It followed the fate of Liu Shaoqi's bodyguard, Yuan Pin'gao (known in the movie as Yi the Fierce), from his capture by the Nationalists to his escape from prison and reconnection with the Communists. Filmed on location at Anyuan under the supervision of one of China's most famous movie directors, *Eminences of the Great Marsh* brought a flurry of welcome media coverage to the coal mining town.[10]

The rehabilitation of previously disgraced national leaders directly benefited their local clients in political terms as well. Peng Yonghui's return to literary prominence was rewarded with administrative office; in the early reform period he was named the director of the trade union at the Anyuan coal mine.[11] The labor model Guo Qingsi, who had procured central funding via Liu Shaoqi for the restoration of the Anyuan workers' club back in the early 1950s, also resurfaced at this time as vice-chairman of the Anyuan party committee.[12]

## EXHIBITING THE REFORMED TRADITION

The Anyuan Railway and Mine Workers' Labor Movement Memorial Hall, which continued to serve as a local gauge of shifting political winds, was overhauled in the early reform period to reflect the changed situation. In 1980 a major renovation of the exhibits replaced the Cultural Revolution era's deification of Chairman Mao with a more balanced picture. The displays were altered and augmented to acknowledge the contributions of other early Communist leaders, especially Li Lisan and Liu Shaoqi, in mobilizing the Anyuan strike and its aftermath. New, comparatively understated titles for the canonical six sections into which the exhibit was still divided indicated greater respect for the historical record: 1) Hardships of Anyuan workers and spontaneous struggles; 2) Establishment of the Anyuan party organization and workers' club; 3) The Great Strike; 4) The deepening development of the labor movement; 5) Combining the Anyuan labor movement with the peasant movement; 6) Anyuan workers' participation in the Autumn Harvest Uprising and embarkation on the road to a rural armed base area. Whereas previous displays had often cited recently conducted (and sometimes notoriously unreliable) interviews with elderly workers, now every item on display was meticulously documented with written sources culled from libraries and historical archives around the country.[13]

The refurbishing of the Anyuan memorial hall was not confined to the interior; the façade also received attention. Even though Mao Zedong's name had been dropped from the name of the memorial hall in 1972, the towering hilltop museum still bore the huge ceramic head of Chairman Mao, modeled on Liu Chunhua's 1967 painting of the young Mao going to Anyuan, on its rooftop. When Liu Shaoqi's widow, Wang Guangmei, announced her intention to pay her first visit to Anyuan in 1983, local cadres worried that the looming visage of her husband's Cultural Revolution nemesis might offend her. Anxious to provide their distinguished guest a hospitable reception, Pingxiang officials, after obtaining higher-level authorization, ordered the head removed prior to Wang's arrival. Chairman Mao was duly "decapitated" and the space formerly occupied by his head was filled by a replica of the old 1920s logo of the Anyuan workers' club, a sledgehammer and pickax superimposed upon a train wheel, which represented the club's dual constituency of miners and railroad workers. In keeping with its 1972 name change, the museum was presented as a monument to the achievements of the Anyuan workers rather than those of any single revolutionary leader.

Another symbolically significant exterior upgrade that indicated that Anyuan had not lost its knack for attracting cultural patronage from top leaders came in 1984, when Deng Xiaoping contributed his calligraphy for the nameplate above the front door of the museum, duly designating it the Anyuan Railway and Mine Workers' Labor Movement Memorial Hall.[14] Enlisting Deng Xiaoping's involvement had required years of patient and concerted efforts on the part of curators and cadres. In the late 1970s, with the turn away from Maoism in favor of "reform and opening," there had even been calls for closing the memorial hall as an outdated relic of a repudiated revolutionary past. In the early 1980s, local agencies began to survey the large expanse of prime land that the museum occupied with the intent to raze the memorial hall and replace it with workers' dormitories. Alarmed by this threat to their rice bowl, curators at the memorial hall got together in the spring of 1983 to discuss how best to ensure the museum's survival. They agreed that the most effective method would be to persuade some highly respected central official, preferably Deng Xiaoping himself, to contribute his brushwork in the form of an inscription for the name plaque. But they were uncertain how to go about enlisting Deng's support. Initial inquiries to the Pingxiang party committee elicited no response.

The impending visit to Anyuan of Wang Guangmei in December 1983 gave the museum staff a new idea. Aware of the value of personal connections to high-level officials in procuring cultural patronage for local projects, the memorial hall leadership asked Wang to transmit a letter directly to Deng Xiaoping. The response of Liu Shaoqi's widow to this request was, however, disappointingly noncommittal. As her late husband was wont to do, she demurred on grounds of party discipline: "Of course I can carry a letter, but for me personally to deliver this letter to Comrade Deng Xiaoping would not really be in keeping with party protocol." Although Wang took the letter back with her when she returned to Beijing, the museum waited for months with no reply. In May of 1984, however, the curators read newspaper reports of Deng having written inscriptions for the name plaques of several other revolutionary memorial halls. They thereupon drafted another letter to Deng Xiaoping, which, after being reviewed and edited (albeit not officially endorsed) by the Pingxiang party committee, was mailed to Beijing the following month. Nearly three months later, on August 31, 1984, Deng put ink brush to paper and crafted the eleven characters for the name of the museum. Soon after, the central office of the Communist Party express mailed the valuable calligraphy to the Jiangxi provincial party office in Nanchang. After retaining the original for its own archives, the provincial office sent a copy to Pingxiang for use at Anyuan. In late September, nearly a thousand people, including local party and government representatives as well as workers, peasants, soldiers, and students, gathered at the Anyuan memorial hall for a ceremonial unveiling of the new plaque written in Deng Xiaoping's own hand.[15]

The external alterations to the memorial hall were matched by changes in the interior displays. In 1987 another major reorganization occurred in preparation for the ninetieth anniversary of the establishment of the Anyuan coal mine the following year. The renovation sought to modernize what were characterized as "1950s-standard" displays. New lighting and audiovisual effects were introduced to render the exhibit more appealing to a contemporary audience. In terms of content, the guidelines for the 1987 alterations—while reaffirming the 1980 changes as having "restored the true face of the history of the Anyuan workers"—nevertheless stressed the need to highlight the peculiarities of Anyuan's own local experience (rather than present a generic account of Chinese revolutionary history) and to offer a more balanced view of the twists and turns of the history of the Anyuan labor movement (rather than present only the victories). In this more nuanced iteration, the goal was to devote due attention to the contributions of labor movement leaders while at the same time avoiding "the idealization of certain historical figures." The focus of the exhibition was centered on the "classic" period between 1921 and 1930, when the Anyuan labor movement was judged to have made its chief contributions to the development of the Chinese revolution.[16]

Among the many new artifacts displayed for the first time in 1987 was a fascinating photograph taken nearly ninety years earlier to mark the opening of the Anyuan coal mine in 1898. Donated to the museum by the son of the former director of the mining company, Li Shouquan, the group photo depicts Li and several of his Chinese colleagues together with chief engineer Gustavus Leinung and several of his German colleagues. Surprisingly, all the Chinese are dressed in Western coats and ties, whereas the Germans are all wearing mandarin Chinese gowns! In contrast to the monochromic "Western imperialism" narrative of earlier periods, the "reform and opening" of the post-Mao period permitted a more subtle and sympathetic acknowledgment of the international cooperation that had in fact surrounded the origins of the Anyuan coal mine.[17]

The son of the former coal mine director was not the only noteworthy descendant of Anyuan protagonists to lend support to the new, more cosmopolitan exhibit. The renovation of 1987 attracted distinguished visitors from around the country, including Mao Zedong's only surviving son, Mao Anqing. Having been born at just the time when his father was actively involved in the Anyuan labor movement, the younger Mao had grown up with stories about the coal mine and had long wished to pay a visit. After examining the displays, Mao Anqing was asked to record his impressions in the memorial hall guest book. Educated in the Soviet Union in the 1930s and 1940s, and unversed in the Chinese calligraphy that his father had wielded to such effect, Mao Anqing wrote his obligatory comments in Russian: "The Anyuan workers were the first to raise the banner of the Chinese revolution; the Anyuan workers were the vanguard of the Chinese revolution."[18]

Other cosmopolitan relatives of Anyuan notables were also called upon for their endorsements of the new exhibit. Li Lisan's Russian-born widow, Lisa, was interviewed at her home in Beijing for the occasion. Her poignant statement alluded to the ambivalent implications of Anyuan for her late husband: "Comrade Lisan spoke often to me of Anyuan. He had deep feelings toward Anyuan and wanted very much to return to take a look. But whenever he went south to convalesce, he always bypassed Anyuan. I think you can understand these contradictory emotions of his." Asked to contribute her own congratulatory calligraphy for the anniversary exhibit, she dutifully penned (in Russian) a politically correct statement: "The Anyuan labor movement wrote a glorious page in the history of the Chinese revolution! I hope the workers of Anyuan today will make an even bigger contribution to socialist construction!—written in remembrance of the ninetieth anniversary of the establishment of the Anyuan coal mine. Lisa."[19]

Four years later, in honor of the seventieth anniversary of the Anyuan Great Strike, another renovation of the memorial hall exhibits took place. Although the basic organizational and ideological framework of the previous rendition was retained, the 1992 iteration added more life to the Anyuan pageant by providing information about a wider and more complicated cast of characters than had been included in earlier displays. Li Lisan's successful effort to win over the Triad secret-society chieftain was now an acceptable part of the story. Even Chiang Kai-shek made a cameo appearance in the new exhibition, with a favorable caption that read, "On September 14, 1926, National Revolutionary Army Generalissimo Chiang Kai-shek arrived at Anyuan, welcomed by a mass gathering of more than fourteen thousand people. During the welcome assembly, Chiang Kai-shek highly praised the Anyuan workers and suggested joint management of the mine by the union and the mining company."[20] Now that the PRC was reaching across the Taiwan Straits in an effort to enlist the goodwill of its erstwhile Nationalist foes, the once vilified archenemy could be portrayed as having played a positive role in the Anyuan revolutionary drama.

## UNOFFICIAL INTERPRETATIONS

Although official reinterpretations of the Anyuan labor movement evidenced a more pluralistic plotline, the popular imagination remained centered on Mao Zedong. Elderly veterans of the 1922 strike might credit Li Lisan as the leader most deserving of recognition, but for the majority of workers who had come of age during the Cultural Revolution, Mao was the savior of the Anyuan working class. The reverence that workers felt for Chairman Mao surfaced during the preparations for the visit of Liu Shaoqi's widow, Wang Guangmei, in 1983. When locals caught wind of the official plan to demolish the face of Chairman Mao that had served since 1968 as the rooftop logo of the Anyuan memorial hall, not a single worker was willing to participate in what was widely perceived as an act of revolutionary sacrilege. As a result, three outsiders had to be recruited at considerable expense to tackle the job of smashing Mao's ceramic countenance. Within less than a year, so the local lore goes, all three of the hired laborers who participated in the controversial demolition work had died of unnatural causes. An Anyuan worker later insisted, "You mustn't doubt this. I'm telling you, this is the absolute truth. Anyone who dares to displace Mao Zedong will surely come to no good end."[21]

A rumor that swept Pingxiang city in 1993, recounted by the Communist Party secretary at the time, indicated the charismatic aura that continued to shroud the memory of Mao Zedong:

> Whether the tale was true or not was never established, but most people evidently preferred to believe it. According to the story, on the eve of Chairman Mao's one hundredth birthday on December 26, 1993, a bronze statue of Mao Zedong to be erected in the Shaoshan square was being transported through Pingxiang when the driver decided to take a short break before proceeding to Shaoshan. But, once the truck stopped in the city of Pingxiang, try as the driver might he could not start it up again. For hours he tried to determine the problem without success. He had no choice but to spend the night in Pingxiang. Early the next morning the driver called in a mechanic who was also unable to repair the truck. But as soon as the driver climbed into his rig and stepped on the accelerator, the truck started moving again. Later people said that there had been nothing wrong with the truck; it was that Mao Zedong was emotionally attached to Pingxiang—to Anyuan—and had especially wanted to spend the night there to see his old haunts and visit with his old friends. Then gradually many people came forward to say that that night Mao Zedong had appeared in their dreams. . . . Some even heard Mao Zedong's voice, with its thick Hunan accent.[22]

Ten years later Anyuan received its own bronze statue of Mao. As part of the commemoration of the eightieth anniversary of the 1922 strike, a large statue of Mao Zedong—modeled on Liu Chunhua's oil painting of the young Mao on his way to Anyuan—was erected just inside the front gate of the coal mine.[23] The local newspaper reported on the public excitement generated by the occasion:

When the escort vehicle for the bronze statue of Chairman Mao crossed Leap Forward Avenue . . . on its way to Anyuan, the crowds lining the route—including merchants as well as factory workers—spontaneously set off firecrackers in celebratory welcome. Some people who had gotten the news late rushed to rent motorcycles to go to Anyuan to welcome the bronze statue of Chairman Mao. After the statue had safely reached the plaza, the people still lingered for a long time, reluctant to leave. It was a very moving scene. It showed us what it means to live forever in the hearts of the people.[24]

Local residents clearly welcomed the outside attention that the unveiling of the statue attracted, but not everyone who attended the proceedings was so impressed. The American journalist Philip Pan wrote scornfully of his visit to Anyuan on this occasion:

In 2002, I traveled to Anyuan to attend a ceremony marking the eightieth anniversary of the miners' strike. On a warm, overcast afternoon, in a plaza near one of the old coal mines, a small crowd gathered as party functionaries unveiled a bronze statue of Mao just as he had been depicted in the Cultural Revolution portrait. Even by the standards of the Communist Party, there was something especially shameless about the event. It wasn't just that these officials were putting up a new statue of Mao years after most cities had had the decency to quietly take theirs down. It wasn't just that they were perpetuating the historical fraud about Mao's role in the Anyuan strike—a fraud designed to obscure the fact that Mao later persecuted to death the party men who had done the most to organize the miners. It was the cynical attempt to present the Communist Party as a champion of the working class. There was a time when the state seemed committed to the proletariat, when workers were promised an "iron rice bowl" of job security and benefits. But a quarter century after Mao's death, only fools and liars still claimed the party was building a workers' paradise and looking out for people like the coal miners of Anyuan.[25]

Although few Anyuan workers credited the post-Mao party-state with promoting their interests, even fewer of them—unlike Philip Pan—seemed prepared to cast aspersions on the still-sacred memory of Mao Zedong.

## REFRAMING ANYUAN

Competing interpretations of the Anyuan revolutionary tradition were not only evident at the coal mine itself. A lightning rod for contestation on a national level was the original archetype for the controversial bronze statue installed at the coal mine in 2002: Liu Chunhua's famous Cultural Revolution painting *Chairman Mao Goes to Anyuan*. In sharp contrast to officially sponsored interpretations, which continued to rely upon familiar practices of patronage, the debate surrounding Liu's oil painting proceeded in a fashion that demonstrated the growing influence of new cultural voices—art auctioneers, copyright claimants, television muckrakers, and avant-garde critics—in the cacophonous public discourse of the post-Mao period.

Decades earlier, when the exhibition for which Liu Chunhua's oil painting had been created was closed in Beijing, the painting was designated a "first-class national treasure" to be retained at the Museum of Revolutionary History as part of its permanent collection. Once the Cultural Revolution ended, however, the work began to draw criticism. In March 1979, the well-known cartoonist Ye Qianyu emerged from a decade of imprisonment with an article in *People's Daily* that highlighted the religious connotations of Liu Chunhua's painting. Ye condemned the work both for the adulatory inspiration that underlay its creation and for the devotional cult in which it played a central part: "Experts who saw the painting all remarked that in its conception, design, and even its use of color it was slavishly indebted to the religious paintings of the Italian renaissance. The 'Gang of Four' declared this painting to be a model artistic product, ordering its massive reproduction so that it would hang in every hall and auditorium, every public and private residence."[26] Perhaps stung by such criticism, the artist—brandishing an official letter from the Beijing painting academy—in 1980 reclaimed his youthful creation from the Museum of Revolutionary History.

For the next fifteen years Liu quietly kept the controversial painting in his private collection, but eventually the lure of profits to be made in the rapidly commercializing cultural market of the reform era proved irresistible. As the demand for Cultural Revolution art soared amid the "Mao craze" of the 1990s, Liu Chunhua decided to cash in on his prized possession.[27] In 1995, Liu, who was now director of the Beijing Painting Academy, sold *Chairman Mao Goes to Anyuan* at a public auction to the Guangzhou branch of the Chinese Bank of Construction for the astronomical price of 5.5 million yuan. The result was an outcry in the Chinese news media; articles, newspaper editorials, and television broadcasts roundly condemned the sale of the iconic painting as a crass misuse of state property. The influential China Central Television news program *Focus Interview* featured the incident as a cause célèbre. In a broadcast that attracted widespread public notice, the program showcased former Red Guards connected to the 1967–69 Anyuan exhibit at the Museum of Revolutionary History, *The Brilliance of Mao Zedong Thought Illuminates the Anyuan Labor Movement*, for which the painting had been commissioned, who fumed that the auction of the painting was a national scandal. "Man-in-the-street" interviews concurred in this assessment: "That was a painting that we all saw in elementary school. The influence of this painting across the entire country and even overseas was enormous. Looked at from the history of the Cultural Revolution, from the background of that time, it really does belong to the state."[28]

Thus made aware of the symbolic and material value of its former "national treasure," the Museum of Revolutionary History was prompted to recover it. But in the reform era state agencies are supposed to operate according to law rather than by fiat, so in 1998 the museum filed a lawsuit in the Beijing Intermediate Court against Liu Chunhua and the Bank of Construction claiming that *Chairman Mao Goes to Anyuan* was state property and should be returned. As part of its case, the museum produced a letter from the State Resources Management Bureau verifying that the painting in question was indeed state property. The following month Liu Chunhua filed a countersuit against the Ministry of Finance (into which the State Resources Management Bureau had just been incorporated) insisting that the painting had been his personal creation and was thus his own property to dispose of as he wished. Stymied by the sensitive political issues and unable to iron out the competing ownership claims, the court announced indefinite suspensions for both cases. At this point the former Red Guards who had organized the national Anyuan exhibit in 1967, angered by what they saw as a gross miscarriage of justice, filed their own lawsuit against Liu Chunhua in which they insisted that the oil painting was actually a collective work of revolutionary political art rather than Liu's individual creation. Liu's personal profit from the sale of the painting, they argued, violated what was in reality a group copyright. The plaintiffs offered the following explanation of their motives in an open letter to the press in March 2000:

> *Chairman Mao Goes to Anyuan* was created in the unique historical period of the Cultural Revolution. Even if the contents of this painting accord with historical fact, it nevertheless served a special political function during the Cultural Revolution. It served to heap further abuse on the already persecuted Chairman Liu Shaoqi. Yet Liu Chunhua continues to this day to regard the painting as his special glory. Even worse, Liu Chunhua appropriated this collective product

as though it were his own, making a big show of auctioning it off. During the time of the Cultural Revolution, Liu Chunhua misused this painting as his political capital to become an official; today he is again relying on this painting to become rich.[29]

In effect, the former Red Guards argued that Liu Chunhua had benefited unduly both from the cultural patronage of the Mao era and from the cultural commercialization of the post-Mao era. At hearings in conjunction with the lawsuit, the presiding judge pointed out the difficulty of reaching a fair conclusion in this politically charged conflict: "This case is a historical matter that touches on many background historical issues. Some matters are not best handled through the courts because some problems do not necessarily have a resolution, and even if there is a resolution, it is not necessarily the appropriate one." On April 1, 2002, after years of media attention and legal wrangling, the Beijing Intermediate Court finally delivered what one of the plaintiffs characterized as an "April Fool's Day surprise." In a convoluted and controversial verdict, the court ruled that although Liu Chunhua alone held the copyright to the painting, and thus could retain the full proceeds from his sale of it, the right of ownership actually rested with the state. However, since the purchaser of the painting—the Guangzhou branch of the Bank of Construction—was technically also a state agency, state property had remained in state hands. Liu Chunhua was rebuked for having sold a painting that he did not really own, but due to a statute of limitations the court further ruled that the Museum of Revolutionary History could no longer legally reclaim its rightful possession.[30]

The tortuous history of Liu Chunhua's painting can be read as a metaphor for the fate of the Chinese revolution. Created by idealistic students yearning to advance the cause of progressive social and political change, this romantic image became a vehicle for the state-orchestrated deification of a tyrannical despot, the crushing of his enemies in a vicious reign of terror, the disillusionment of millions of young people, and eventually the devolution of China's revolutionary tradition into a commercialized caricature of its original aims. Absurd as the court's adjudication of this case struck many critical observers, it reflected the near impossibility of rendering a widely accepted verdict on the meaning of the Chinese revolution.

Despite (or perhaps because of) its checkered history, Liu's painting continues to inspire political criticism. And, under the relatively relaxed cultural policies of the contemporary period, this criticism has been marked by considerable inventiveness. Throughout the reform period, avant-garde artists have redrawn the familiar image of *Chairman Mao Goes to Anyuan* in a variety of arresting and amusing ways.[31] In 1991, for example, Liu Dahong elaborated upon the religious flavor of Liu Chunhua's original painting in a revisionist rendition entitled *Spring*. Liu Dahong's work depicts the young Mao—with a halo over his head and a red sun rising behind his back—delivering a Buddhist equivalent of the Sermon on the Mount atop the Wugong Mountains. In Liu Dahong's fanciful version, Mao, still dressed in his scholar's gown, has laid down his Hunan umbrella and wields in its place a magical beam of light. While Liu Dahong's use of religious iconography underscored the devotional dimensions of the original work, in time the repainting of the Anyuan image came to reflect more commercial concerns. In 1995, the year that the original painting was auctioned to the Bank of Construction, Wang Xingwei's *The Way to the East* depicted a contemporary Mao—dressed in flashy business attire and carrying a new Western umbrella in place of his old Hunan one—striding across the Wugong Mountains with his back turned *away* from Anyuan. Clearly, Wang's picture suggested, the revolutionary project was being abandoned in favor of new economic opportunities. Wang Xingwei's 1996 *Blind* showed the same contemporary Mao, now tapping his Western umbrella as a blind man's cane, apparently in an attempt to find his way down from the mountaintop. Another eerie painting by Wang Xingwei in 2000, entitled *X-ray*, features the young Mao and the old Mao meeting on the mountaintop en route to Anyuan, while a crumpled body—the corpse of the Chinese revolution, perhaps?—collapses between them. Even foreign artists have gotten in on the act of redrawing the Anyuan image. Erro Gudmundur's 2003 *Mao's Last Visit to Venice* positions the young Mao, still wearing his scholar's gown and clutching his Hunan umbrella, against an Italian cityscape.

More recently, Chinese artists have injected a note of irony by adding or subtracting figures from the archetype. Yin Zhaoyang's 2005 painting titled, like Liu's original, *Chairman Mao Goes to Anyuan* inserts into a blurry rendering of the familiar scene atop the Wugong Mountains a young worker waving at Mao—whether to attract the Chairman's attention or to bid him a final farewell remains unclear. In Yue Minjun's 2005 painting, also entitled *Chairman Mao Goes to Anyuan*, we see a crystal clear Wugong mountainous landscape exactly replicating that of Liu Chunhua's original painting. But absent from Yue's canvas is any trace of a person, including Chairman Mao himself. Revolutionary leaders may fade away, perhaps, yet the beautiful landscape of China endures.

Figure 14. *The Way to the East,* oil painting by Wang Xingwei, 1995. The painting spoofs Liu Chunhua's *Chairman Mao Goes to Anyuan* by depicting a modern-day Mao Zedong, dressed in a business suit rather than a scholar's gown and clutching a Western umbrella instead of a Hunan umbrella, turning his back on Anyuan. Image courtesy of Hanart TZ Gallery.

A 2007 painting by Ma Baozhong, again entitled *Chairman Mao Goes to Anyuan,* presents a shadowy version of Chairman Mao atop the Wugong Mountains greeting that earlier practitioner of a cult of personality, Joseph Stalin, who is now garbed in a Mandarin scholar's gown himself. Communism has become Chinese!

Even more recently, digital technology has been employed to reconfigure the Anyuan image in ways that suggest its continuing power as a source of moral critique. A 2008 work by Wang Tong entitled *Chairman Mao Goes to Anyuan* superimposes the robed figure of Mao on a photograph of the palatial quarters of the Anyuan district government, a sprawling complex resented locally for its wasteful expenditure of public funds. An anonymous image entitled *Qian Yunhui Petitioning* replaces Mao's head with that of the upright local official Qian Yunhui, who lost his life in 2011 when he was run over by a truck—on government orders, it is rumored—after submitting a petition on behalf of villagers who had been dispossessed of their land. Inserted into the familiar Wugong landscape just behind the unsuspecting Qian, who stands serenely in his scholar's gown, holding a Hunan umbrella, is a large red truck.[32]

When the creator of the original *Chairman Mao Goes to Anyuan* was asked in 2007 about the meaning of his influential painting, Liu Chunhua's answer was predictably guarded: "This is an extremely sensitive question. In reality the Cultural Revolution was a political struggle. The history of political struggles is always a case of 'either you or me.' Today, the Cultural Revolution is considered to have been a catastrophe. . . . Looking at the history of the proletarian revolution from a sociological perspective, whether it has furthered the interests of the proletariat is a question I believe will need to be evaluated through future discussion of the history of the Cultural Revolution."[33] Evasive as the artist's response was, it captured the ambiguities of a ruthless mass movement that nonetheless still has defenders today, especially among the workers of Anyuan.

## WORKERS' MENTALITIES

In contrast to the ironic critiques of American journalists and avant-garde artists, many Anyuan workers continue to express unabashed admiration toward Mao Zedong, revering the party chairman for his revolutionary achievements and regarding the market reforms of the post-Mao era with considerable ambivalence. Although the living standards of most Anyuan residents have visibly improved under the economic policies of the reform period, emotional attachments toward Mao and his legendary accomplishments—particularly his contributions to the dignity of the Anyuan workers—remain strong nonetheless. A tendency to compare the (reformist) present unfavorably with the (revolutionary) past has emerged as a central theme in local discourse.[34]

Working-class partiality toward the Mao era reflects, among other things, appreciation for the "iron rice bowl" of employment security that state workers enjoyed in prereform days. The loss of jobs that accompanied market reform is interpreted as a betrayal of the promise of Mao's revolution. A retired coal miner explained,

During the time of "eating from one big rice pot," our livelihood was secure. At least we had jobs. If the cadres didn't like you, the most they could do was assign you a slightly worse job. Without an iron-clad reason, they couldn't fire you. Now it's different. Didn't they say they were going to reform things? Under this so-called reform, the power of the cadres has increased and they can lay off anyone they want without giving any reason. . . . Back in the days when Chairman Mao led us Anyuan workers on strike, it was in order to gain power for the workers. Today it's the Communist Party's world, and they use the reforms to steal power from us workers.[35]

Even more galling than the loss of job security, it would seem, is the growing inequality that has accompanied the market reforms. A veteran miner reminisced, "If you look back you'll see that the best period for cadre-mass relations was the 1960s and 70s. As difficult as the 60s were, there was no cadre banqueting. Everyone was equal. Today the gap is huge."[36] The perceived decline in workers' status is as much social and political as economic. As a sixty-nine-year-old retired miner reflected in 2001, after more than two decades of economic reform,

During Mao Zedong's day, workers' standing was high. . . . Mao Zedong cared about the worker masses. We workers were the leading class. Had it not been for Chairman Mao's revolution I never would have survived this world. Let me give an example. If you visit the homes of the older workers you'll see that anyone over fifty years of age has a good-looking wife and that some husbands are more than ten years older than their wives. This is because workers then enjoyed high standing and many good women sought to marry them. This was particularly the case at the Anyuan coal mine because Chairman Mao had worked here, and so it was attractive for women to marry in. But now it's different. The workers can't find wives. In the past a fifty-year-old miner could find a twentysomething wife. Now a twenty-something worker can't find any wife. . . . For us workers, the Mao era was good. Speaking of the Cultural Revolution, I've always believed that Chairman Mao's thinking was correct. He wanted to send this country down the socialist road. It was just that there were some bad people around him and those bad people messed things up.[37]

Misguided though the miner's impression of Mao Zedong may be, it reflects a widely shared belief among many Anyuan workers in the basic rectitude of the Chinese revolution. Above all, Mao's revolution is credited with having bestowed a newfound dignity upon the working class.

Especially unpopular among the workers are the wage reforms, first implemented in the latter part of 1994, which substantially increased the paychecks of cadres as compared to those of workers. As one worker summed up the outcome, "In China, worst off are the people sentenced to labor reform, and next worse off are the coal miners. The grassroots workers really, really suffer, and the wage gap is enormous: those who work get low pay, and those who do not work get lots of money. The foremen and party secretaries don't work and just go down into the pits once or twice a week to command you to work faster, work faster."[38] A laid-off Anyuan worker complained bitterly, "The enterprise leaders today are worse than the capitalists of bygone days. The old Anyuan workers would never have made a revolution if they'd known that the Communists' world would turn out like this."[39] Even a union cadre at the mine ruefully remarked, "I can say for sure that if some people today wanted to come to Anyuan to organize a night school like Mao Zedong and Li Lisan did at the time of the Anyuan strike, they would definitely be considered counterrevolutionaries and thrown in jail."[40]

The sense of injustice is pervasive. Summing up more than a year of ethnographic research at Anyuan, anthropologist Mei Fangquan observes, "In my investigation of the mining district, no matter what issues I asked about, in the end the miners would always return to questions of fairness and trust" (*gongping wenti, xinren wenti*). To reinforce his point, Mei quotes an Anyuan miner who is also a party member: "In the past, when Chairman Mao spoke there was no one who didn't trust what he said. Now there's freedom of speech and you can swear as you like and speak out as you like, but this doesn't solve problems."[41]

For many, Mao and his revolution represent a lost world of moral certitude in which the workers, and Anyuan workers in particular, were esteemed as the leading class. Summed up in the watchword of the 1922 strike, "Once beasts of burden, now we will be men," a sense of hard-earned dignity was central to their pride as inheritors of the Anyuan tradition. In the post-Mao era, increased wages and improved material conditions notwithstanding, market reforms also brought a precipitous decline in the social and political position of the proletariat. The broken promise of Mao's revolution could be seen in the unseemly ascendancy of a "Communist Party's world" in lieu of the anticipated "workers' world" for which they and their forefathers had sacrificed.

The nostalgia that residents express toward symbols of the revolution is not directed only to Chairman Mao. It was evident as well in the outpouring of public sympathy at the time of Zhu Zijin's death in 1987, when the former director of the Anyuan memorial hall, who had gained recognition for her 1957 audience with Liu Shaoqi, succumbed to liver cancer at age sixty. The daughter of the leading worker-Communist, Zhu Shaolian, at the time of the Great Strike, Zhu Zijin was regarded as a living link to the revolutionary fame of Anyuan. As her son described the poignant scene at the return of his mother's ashes for burial:

> It was already noon when the car arrived at Anyuan. There were many people from Anyuan waiting on the side of the road. As we entered the intersection, both sides of the main street were packed with people. Mother had worked most of her life at Anyuan, and the people of Anyuan had not forgotten her. They had come out to bid her farewell. The sound of firecrackers was everywhere, heating up the whole street. People said that Zhu Zijin must be smiling in paradise to see so many people showing so much feeling toward her.
>
> It had been twenty years since Anyuan had witnessed this kind of public excitement; the last time was to welcome the arrival of the oil painting *Chairman Mao Goes to Anyuan*. But on that occasion people came as part of leading organizations while this time people just came by themselves. The people hung a large banner that proclaimed, "Born in Anyuan, buried in Anyuan—a life devoted to Anyuan. A revolutionary in good times and bad times—a life sacrificed to revolution."[42]

With the daughter of railway engineer Zhu Shaolian transported to her final resting place on a hilltop overlooking the coal mine, a chapter in the history of Anyuan drew to a close. The public mourning for Zhu Zijin bespoke an abiding appreciation among the Anyuan populace for those who had propelled their otherwise obscure hometown and its workers to national prominence.

## REFORM AND OPENING

Despite persistent efforts to garner greater national (and international) recognition based on its revolutionary past, Anyuan languished in the post-Mao era. The coal mine had never fully recovered its previous economic importance after the devastation of the September Massacre of 1925. During the Cultural Revolution, however, the area had enjoyed something of a spiritual rebirth thanks to the throngs of Red Guards and other revolutionary evangelists and pilgrims who visited the mining town and its memorial hall on "new long marches" intended to connect them to the sacred sites of the revolution. In 2001, a retired cadre remarked ruefully, "Since the reform and opening, everything is based on economic construction. The political glory of Anyuan has disappeared. The memorial hall is still open, but no pilgrims come to pay homage.

It's like a temple with no spiritual power, where no one comes to burn joss sticks to the Buddha. . . . These days people in Anyuan feel like they've been forgotten both economically and politically. . . . With the contribution that Anyuan made to the liberation of the Chinese people, it shouldn't be forgotten."[43]

The sense of relative deprivation has generated not only grumbling but also protest. The official yearbook of Pingxiang acknowledges, "Poverty among the miners is deep, and they are a major source of complaints and petitions."[44] In the spring of 1998, as local authorities prepared to celebrate the centennial of the opening of the Anyuan coal mine, they were faced with a discordant challenge by workers claiming to have been left behind in the economic reforms:

> Thousands of laid-off workers from the famous Anyuan coal mining district marched to Pingxiang City centre to petition the government. Their demands included the right to adequate welfare and the right to work. After a two-day standoff, during which local government leaders refused to negotiate with workers' representatives, frustration boiled over and the workers marched to the train station and blocked the line. They demanded that a train take them to Beijing so they could alert the central government to their plight.
>   The authorities promptly sent in a squadron of armed riot police to disperse the demonstrators. . . . Jiangxi PSB [Public Security Bureau] and provincial party committee sent teams to investigate the situation and ordered that the workers and pensioners be paid one month's welfare payment of Rmb 120.[45]

The protest of 1998 was not an isolated incident. But workers' complaints did not reverse the momentum of industrial reform. In July 2002, nearly a century after the Hanyeping Coal and Iron Company had registered as one of China's first limited liability joint-stock companies so as to expand its modern mining operations at Anyuan, the coal mine, now known formally as the Pingxiang Mining Limited Liability Company, listed shares on the Shanghai Stock Exchange—this time, however, as a prelude to shifting out of coal mining into the manufacture of trucks, buses, glass products, and other more profitable items.[46]

Philip Pan offered a grim assessment of the economic reform effort based upon his 2002 visit to the coal mine:

> If the party's version of socialism had failed the miners of Anyuan, its take on capitalism brought them only further misery. The government was restructuring the coal industry, and shares of the Anyuan mine, one of the largest in the nation, had been listed on the Shanghai

stock exchange. Mass lay-offs had followed, and more were planned. The miners who kept their jobs saw their pay fall precipitously in real terms, even as coal prices and production climbed. Among the worst off were the retirees, old men who suffered lung diseases from a lifetime of digging coal for the glory of the state, and who now complained that the officials were looting their pensions and denying them proper health care. Some men spoke of wives working as prostitutes in the big cities to help their families make ends meet.[47]

Although it is difficult to gauge the extent to which such complaints reflected objective, as opposed to subjective, grievances, there is no doubt that a large number of miners blamed the post-Mao economic reforms for their troubles. Between 2003 and 2007 the Letters and Visits Bureau of Pingxiang municipality recorded an annual average of more than thirteen thousand officially registered complaints, many of them involving multiple complainants. The principal cause of these complaints was the privatization of state-owned enterprises, which generated massive layoffs among the workforce.[48]

In late 2004, several hundred elderly workers staged a sit-down protest in front of the Pingxiang Company headquarters to demand an increase in pension payments. When the demonstration ended with a fifty-yuan monthly increase for the retirees, one of the protest leaders remarked bitterly, "We got the type of treatment that is for class enemies."[49] In follow-up interviews about the underlying motivation behind the protest, one participant frankly observed, "As far as livelihood is concerned, we can get by all right. But these days the gap between rich and poor is too great, and that's what upsets us."[50]

Anyuan workers were not alone in feeling disadvantaged by the reforms. A similarly gloomy outlook could be found in many of the former revolutionary sites. Increasingly worried about the potential for social unrest (as well as political embarrassment) triggered by the simmering discontent in these locales, the central leadership began to devote special attention to their predicament. Both Premier Wen Jiabao and President Hu Jintao made a number of highly publicized visits to the former revolutionary base areas in which they emphasized the continuing importance of carrying on the revolutionary tradition. As President Hu Jintao stressed in a speech delivered at the site of the former Jiangxi Soviet in 2003, "Comrade Mao Zedong and other revolutionaries of the elder generation . . . bequeathed to us precious spiritual wealth."[51] The failure to specify what this "spiritual wealth" involved did not prevent the Chinese government from trying to convert it into a more tangible form of wealth.

Under the officially sponsored "red tourism" program, launched in 2005, travel to the sites of Mao's revolution was vigorously encouraged as a vehicle both for promoting state legitimacy and for pumping tourist dollars into what remain some of the poorest regions of the Chinese countryside.[52]

## RED TOURISM

In September 2004, when the Central Office of the Chinese Communist Party invited applications for its new red tourism initiative, Anyuan was the first place in the country to submit a bid. The selection of the Anyuan memorial hall as one of the one hundred officially designated top national red tourism sites acknowledged its value as a "red resource" capable of promoting "patriotic education."[53] Credited with having drawn more than five million Chinese visitors and eight thousand foreign visitors from more than seventy countries since its inaugural exhibit in 1956, the memorial hall was hailed as a tourist attraction of both domestic and international significance.[54]

The prominent place of Anyuan in the emerging red tourism program was made clear on October 17, 2005, with the opening at the Great Hall of the People in Beijing of a photographic exhibition to mark the beginning of "Anyuan week." Drawing nearly ten thousand visitors on opening day, the exhibit was intended to highlight the attractiveness of Anyuan as both a "red" educational and a "green" recreational tourist site. Photographs featured Anyuan's history as a cradle of the Chinese labor movement along with its lush mountain scenery. To further enliven the exhibition and entertain the throngs of viewers, a cultural troupe from Pingxiang performed spirited song and dance routines on the theme of "red Anyuan."[55] Red tourism contributed to a rise in Anyuan's revolutionary reputation that found expression that same year in the curriculum of the newly established national cadre training academy on Jinggangshan. The inclusion of a lesson entitled "The Theoretical Exploration and Practical Meaning of Our Party's Early Leaders during the Anyuan Labor Movement," prepared by a researcher at the Anyuan memorial hall, marked the first time that the history of Anyuan had been made a required subject of study at a central-level training program for government and party officials.[56]

Red tourism, as a new form of cultural patronage that seeks to tap the economic power of the consumer market for state-designated projects, has brought palpable benefits to the struggling coal mining district. In

Figure 15. Contemporary view of Anyuan Railway and Mine Workers' Labor Movement Memorial Hall. Note that Mao's head has been replaced by the old logo of the Anyuan workers' club on the rooftop. A statue of the young Mao looms in front. Photo by the author.

the fall of 2005 the Anyuan district government reported a 55 percent annual increase in the number of tourists, along with an 84 percent increase in tourism income. In total, some fifty-three thousand sight-seers were credited with having generated over six million yuan in red tourism revenues during the previous year. The effort was aided by state-sponsored television commercials featuring a "golden line" of sightseeing from Shaoshan (Mao's birthplace) to Anyuan to Jinggangshan (the site of Mao's first rural base area). By 2006 the annual number of red tourists reportedly had soared to over a million, and the income generated by them had reached an impressive 232 million yuan.[57] The main attraction for these tourists was the Anyuan memorial hall, which in addition to charging an entrance fee also opened a souvenir shop that offered a variety of objects connected to the revolutionary history of the area. The most popular souvenirs were small statues and other renditions of the *Chairman Mao Goes to Anyuan* image in bronze, crystal, ceramic, and gold-plated versions.[58]

The release around this time of the movie *Mao Zedong Goes to Anyuan,* two popular television serials titled *Chairman Mao Goes to Anyuan* and *The Young Pioneers of Anyuan,* and an MTV program titled *Anyuan Is a Good Place* further boosted the popularity of Anyuan as a tourist destination.[59] Significantly, a key theme of the movie and television serials is Mao's exceptional feel for the power of local cultural practice. Mao is depicted as winning over the workers with his earthy Hunan aphorisms, of softening Liu Shaoqi's reserved personality with his boisterous rendition of Hunan folk songs, and of correcting what he criticizes as Li Lisan's "foreign" approach to labor organizing (learned in France) with his own superior understanding of the indigenous inclinations of Chinese workers. The movie, which highlights (and exaggerates) Mao Zedong's contributions to the Great Strike of 1922, was awarded the national prize for films in the historical fiction category.

Although Anyuan's tourist appeal draws above all on its revolutionary connection to Mao Zedong, current cultural representations allow some room for the distinctive contributions of all three of the famous early Communist leaders. In movies as well as in the memorial hall displays, Mao is celebrated for having identified Anyuan as a promising site for mobilization and for providing overall leadership to the fledgling labor movement; Li Lisan is recognized for establishing the first night school for workers as well as the first party cell and workers' club; and Liu Shaoqi is credited with negotiating the strike victory and building Little Moscow into a center of proletarian cultural activity. However, lest there be any doubt as to the relative importance of the three, recently erected concrete statues at the coal mine make clear the official Communist party verdict on their comparative standing: a towering statue of the young Mao Zedong is located directly in front of the imposing stairway leading up the mountain to the memorial hall, a three-quarter-sized statue of the young Liu Shaoqi is located next to the workers' club that he rebuilt, and a half-sized bust of the young Li Lisan is tucked away in a corner. Although this official hierarchy is arguably in the opposite order of the actual contributions of the three men to the early Anyuan labor movement, it accurately reflects their fame and popularity among the contemporary sightseeing public.

Thanks to the growing success of red tourism, the eightieth anniversary of the Autumn Harvest Uprising in 2008 triggered a major state investment in the town of Anyuan that dwarfed previous investments. The memorial hall was closed for three months to permit what was advertised as the biggest renovation of its displays since it had first opened back in 1956, at a cost of more than three million yuan. A new children's museum, which highlights the role of Anyuan in the development of the Young Pioneers, and a new museum dedicated to "clean governance" (*lianzheng*), which focuses on the anticorruption measures of Liu Shaoqi and his colleagues during the days of Little Moscow, were opened within a few minutes' walk of the memorial hall. More than thirty million yuan in central and provincial funds went toward constructing a thirteen-kilometer "red expressway" to connect Anyuan to the national highway system. A large gate demarcating the Anyuan red tourism theme park was erected, and a number of older buildings associated with the revolutionary history of the area were restored to their earlier grandeur.[60]

## ECONOMIC OUTLOOK

Successful as the red tourism initiative has been in attracting both public and private money, local officials worry that it is an insufficient and unsustainable source of support for the future development of Anyuan. The director of the Anyuan district tourist bureau readily concedes that popular interest in the history of the labor movement is fading and looks to other areas of potential growth: temple renovation to encourage Buddhist and Daoist religious pilgrimages, a national museum on coal mining to attract those interested in industrial and business history, a new cinema with regular screenings of the many famous movies filmed on location at Anyuan, and so forth.[61]

Grateful for the renewed national attention that red tourism has recently brought them, workers in Anyuan also express anxiety about the future: "Now Anyuan is famous. The government and Communist Party stress politics so we still have rice to eat. The Communist Party cannot let the workers of Anyuan starve or it would lose face. But we worry about what might happen if one day the Communist Party no longer stresses politics. . . . How long can the workers of Anyuan continue to eat political rice?"[62] The general depoliticization and ebbing enthusiasm for revolutionary history among public and party alike is seen as cause for concern: "We often remark that because the CCP relied on us Anyuan workers to take over the realm, now they can't let us starve to death. To tell the truth, if Anyuan hadn't been able to play the history card it would have gone under long ago."[63]

Waning interest in the Anyuan labor movement coincides with a general decline in the position and prestige of the Chinese working class.[64] But the situation at Anyuan is particularly problematic, not only because of the acute sense of relative deprivation compared to its earlier revolutionary aura, but also because its coal deposits are nearly depleted. In 1985 the Pingxiang Mining Company ranked thirty-third in the country in terms of annual coal output; in 1990 its position dropped to forty-fifth; and by 2008 it had declined to seventy-fifth out of a total of 108 state-owned key point coal mines.[65] With the process of extraction becoming more difficult and dangerous as reserves dwindle, coal production increasingly resembles a throwback to the prerevolutionary scene. Unlike in the Mao era, when Anyuan miners were permanent state employees who enjoyed an impressive package of welfare provisions, today, as in the presocialist period, the labor force consists largely of villagers from the surrounding countryside who work under short-term contracts that afford few securities or benefits. The wages of these peasant-workers are low, amounting to less than 40 percent of an average wage in Pingxiang.[66] With many formerly state-owned enterprises having declared bankruptcy, most of the mining in the Pingxiang area is again being carried out at small, primitive, unsafe (and often illegal) pits that are privately owned and operated.[67] The number of injuries and fatalities from mining accidents is alarmingly high.[68]

The resurgence of premodern patterns of coal mining has been accompanied by a revival of religious practices that prevailed during the pre-Communist era. Ethnographer Mei Fangquan reports of his fieldwork in the Anyuan area, "In the neighborhood of the mining district there are many small private coal pits. On the whole safety measures are not satisfactory, hidden dangers are many, and the risks are immense. The owners of the small coal mines, seeking psychological solace, frequently burn incense and pray to Buddha before commencing operations. I have often seen ceramic statues of bodhisattvas such as the Goddess of Mercy and the God of Wealth at the entrances of the private coal mines."[69] The fear of accidents is not misplaced. China has the worst mining safety record, measured by the number of deaths per million tons of coal mined, of any country in the world, a record that is ten times worse than that of India and 160 times worse than that of the United States.[70] These comparisons are based on official Chinese statistics, which by most accounts severely underrepresent the extent of the problem. Moreover, with the remarkable upsurge of the Chinese economy being fueled in large measure by coal, mines across the country have become magnets for labor abuse by unscrupulous private entrepreneurs.[71] In short, Chinese coal mining is the most dangerous in the world, and coal miners are again among the most downtrodden of the Chinese labor force.

## LITERARY REPRESENTATION

Miners are not alone in noticing the recent retreat from revolutionary promises. The poignant reversals that punctuate the contemporary history of Anyuan have inspired impressive literary and academic interpretations by a number of gifted Chinese writers and scholars. In 2001 the novelist Zhang Xuelong published *Anyuan Past (Anyuan wangshi)* in honor of the eightieth anniversary of the founding of the Chinese Communist Party. A work of historical fiction, the novel begins with Mao Zedong's first visit to Anyuan in the fall of 1921 and ends with the factory director Li Shouquan's departure from Anyuan two years later. As Director Li prepares to board the train that will take him away from the coal mine he has managed for more than two decades, he reflects on the contrast between the reformist objectives that drew him to Anyuan and the revolutionary aims of the Communists who had appeared on the scene more recently: "More than twenty years ago I came here hoping to do what little I could to enrich the people and strengthen the nation through industry and commerce. They [Mao, Liu, and Li] came here hoping to use political methods to transform China. My efforts have already evaporated into thin air. Perhaps theirs was the right choice?"[72]

Zhang's novel, published nearly a century after the events it describes, appeared at a time when the Chinese Communist Party had largely disavowed political mobilization in favor of economic modernization. Highlighting the tensions and tradeoffs between "Communist" revolution and "capitalist" reform, the novel leaves unanswered the question of which strategy will prove more effective in the long run. In December 2008 the novel, with its title changed to *Coal City Storm (Meidu fengbao)*, was reprinted as part of a trilogy in which the first volume, initially published in 2005, chronicled the late-nineteenth-century founding of the coal mine as a beachhead of modern industry, while the third volume continued the story into the contemporary era of industrial restructuring under market reform. Anyuan, in other words, was being repackaged as a story of successful economic development rather than revolutionary triumph. In 2009 the first volume of Zhang's trilogy, entitled *Foreign Mine in the Qing Dynasty (Daqing yangkuang)*, was awarded the annual Jiangxi provincial level prize for outstanding literary and artistic merit in recognition of its illuminating account of the origins of modern Chinese industrial development.[73]

In 2002, the recently retired Communist Party secretary of Pingxiang city, Liu Nanfang, published his own novel on the Anyuan strike, titled

*Eastern Thunderbolt (Dongfang jinglei)*. Unlike Zhang Xuelong's trilogy, Liu's book focuses squarely on the revolutionary era. It does so, however, with an unusual literary sensibility. A graduate of the Chinese Literature Department of Jiangxi University, Liu confesses in the epilogue to his novel that he had always wanted to be a writer even though his career took him in the direction of party-state administration instead. During his nine-year tenure as party secretary of Pingxiang, he explains, he developed deep feelings toward the revolutionary history of Anyuan. He expresses the hope that his novel will help to correct the common misconceptions about that history that exist all over the country as a result of previous propaganda. Before the Cultural Revolution, he notes, the movie *Prairie Fire* had provided an "artistic" rendering of Liu Shaoqi, derived from the textbook lesson "Brave From Head to Toe," that misled many people into thinking that the Anyuan labor movement was entirely Liu Shaoqi's achievement. During the Cultural Revolution, he observes, the oil painting *Chairman Mao Goes to Anyuan* generated a kind of religious devotion around the country that misled many into believing that the Anyuan labor movement was entirely Mao Zedong's achievement. In the process, he concludes, Li Lisan's important leadership and organizational accomplishments were entirely neglected.[74]

In his novel, Liu Nanfang highlights the distinctive yet complementary contributions of all three major leaders of the Anyuan labor movement. Mao is depicted as the grand strategist, Li as the energetic activist, and Liu as the conscientious organizer. But Liu Nanfang is not content to limit his interpretation to this familiar plotline. One characteristic that all three of these quite different personalities shared, he shows, was a love of Chinese literature and a penchant for expressing their revolutionary aims in classical phrases. Applying his own erudition in Chinese literature to obvious effect, Liu directs his readers' attention to the many poems, songs, and literary allusions that the young Communist intellectuals employed to impress the local elite and to educate and inspire the workers of Anyuan. In short, cultural positioning is acknowledged as a critical factor in the success of the early revolutionaries.

## SCHOLARLY INTERPRETATIONS

Among contemporary Chinese intellectuals, the fate of the Anyuan coal mine has attracted not only an outpouring of avant-garde art and high-quality historical fiction but outstanding academic analyses as well. In addition to a steady stream of careful work by party historians (still heavily oriented toward determining the relative contributions of Mao Zedong, Liu Shaoqi, and Li Lisan), two scholarly monographs stand out for their illuminating and sympathetic treatment of the Anyuan miners themselves: Yu Jianrong's *The Plight of China's Working Class: Annals of Anyuan (Zhongguo gongren jieji zhuangkuang—Anyuan shilu)* and Mei Fangquan's *The Miners of Anyuan: A Study of Change in a Time of Transition (Anyuan kuanggong zhuanxingqi de bianqian yanjiu)*. These two books, both based on extended ethnographic research in Anyuan and published in 2006, offer complementary accounts of contemporary labor discontent at the coal mine. Mei's study was written as a doctoral dissertation at Zhongshan University; Yu's is the work of a seasoned scholar at the Chinese Academy of Social Sciences known for his pathbreaking studies of peasant protest in Hunan. Although the two books report similar findings, Mei is more guarded in his conclusions. As a consequence, Mei's book was published by a mainstream press in Beijing, whereas Yu was forced to take his to a Hong Kong publisher. In 2011, an abridged version of Yu's study, with a more politically correct title and the more incendiary quotes from Anyuan workers excised, was published by Jiangsu People's Press in Nanjing.[75] Within a few days of printing, however, even this watered-down version was withdrawn from circulation on orders from the Central Propaganda Department.[76]

Yu Jianrong's book is a remarkable study that is at once a carefully researched and cogently argued monograph, a colorful and entertaining travelogue, a revealing journalistic report, and an impassioned interpretation of the plight of the contemporary Chinese working class. Based on years of interviews and documentary research, his book provides a rich chronicle of the changing circumstances of the Anyuan workers, from the Great Strike of 1922 to present-day pensioners' protests. Rather than impose abstract concepts or models on his research subjects, Yu allows the workers of Anyuan to speak for themselves. The result is a rare firsthand glimpse of working-class subjectivities in contemporary China. Among the many aspects of workers' mentality that Yu Jianrong explores is their positive assessment of the Maoist era in general and the Cultural Revolution in particular. Although Yu is definitely no fan of the Cultural Revolution himself, he faithfully reports his respondents' answers to his probing questions. Again and again the workers express a longing for the days when they enjoyed higher political status and greater social respect. The miners' painful sense of loss—despite a rise in income for many of them—underscores the discrepancy between objective economic conditions and subjective political perceptions.[77]

Relations between workers and intellectuals, today as in the past, are an underlying theme of Yu Jianrong's book. Despite his demurrals, the bespectacled "Dr. Yu" (as the miners refer to him) is accorded great respect and welcomed as a conduit of workers' grievances to the outside world. This, of course, is an issue that resonates with the earlier history of Anyuan, and indeed of the Chinese revolution as a whole. Without the devoted attention of intellectuals such as Mao Zedong, Li Lisan, and Liu Shaoqi, the Anyuan strike of 1922 would not have occurred, let alone achieved a spectacular victory. Li Lisan's ability to compose Confucian aphorisms in classical Chinese earned him the respect of the Pingxiang County magistrate and the local elite, which allowed him to open a school for workers with their active support. It was through education that the Communists gradually convinced the hardened miners that the workers' club could offer them more than the Red Gang upon which they had long relied for assistance. The first worker who helped Mao and Li establish a Communist party cell at Anyuan, Zhu Shaolian, was himself something of a worker-intellectual, having received several years of education before becoming a railway engineer. Moreover, intellectual authority translated into spiritual power. The miners' reverence for Li Lisan, who dressed in academic attire and who had come to Anyuan after a work-study experience in France, bordered upon deification. Today, workers hope for similar assistance from intellectual intermediaries. Yu Jianrong, who happens to be a practicing lawyer as well as a prolific scholar, tells of being repeatedly approached for help in framing and presenting workers' protest demands. When Yu declined on the grounds that he is neither an official nor an activist, his new friends were clearly disappointed. Moreover, their frustrations accelerated over the course of Yu's research project.

The climax of Yu Jianrong's book is a protest movement by retired miners in which they justify their contemporary claim to a decent pension in terms of a proud revolutionary tradition that includes both historical contributions and cultural reconstructions: "We are retired employees of the Pingxiang Mining Company, the descendants and successors to the Anyuan railway and mine workers. Chairman Mao came to Anyuan to lead the Great Strike of the railway and mine workers. The older generation of revolutionaries spilled their blood in sacrifice for us, writing a glorious chapter in the history of the Pingxiang miners. The movie *Prairie Fire* praised Anyuan, allowing everyone in the country to see how a single spark ignited a revolution. . . . We are proud of this."[78]

Mei Fangquan's ethnography of Anyuan, although less richly researched and less passionately presented than Yu's, paints a parallel portrait that also underscores the miners' identification with their revolutionary heritage and their wistful longing for the bygone Mao era. He summarizes his interviewees' attachment to the prereform period: "The miners didn't necessarily understand the overall state policies regarding industry at that time, but they could certainly feel the elevation in workers' status as well the importance that workers enjoyed in state propaganda."[79] Mei is particularly intrigued by the popular culture of the miners. His informants express belief in a range of supernatural deities, from the particular gods associated with local exorcism *(nuo)* temples to more commonly acknowledged bodhisattvas such as the Goddess of Mercy. State strictures against folk religion may have changed the way in which locals talk about the supernatural, but they have not necessarily changed how they actually practice their beliefs: "Because of a long history of attacks on feudal superstitious activities as well as ideological education, the residents of the mining district on the one hand will disavow any belief in superstition, saying 'there are no gods and ghosts in the world, everything is caused by people,' and on the other hand will burn incense, pray to the Buddha, and voluntarily donate to temples."[80] As in the past, religious devotion is connected to protection against mining disasters: "If a certain person escapes injury during a mining accident, bystanders will remark, 'His mother believes in the bodhisattva and worships faithfully; merit has accumulated and the bodhisattva provides protection.'"[81] These religious beliefs, moreover, are seen by Mei Fangquan's informants as perfectly compatible with a continuing reverence for Chairman Mao. As one miner explains, "The bodhisattva will protect good-hearted people. . . . As the *Quotations from Chairman Mao* say, 'Evil is repaid with evil, and good is repaid with good.' . . . It's the same thing."[82]

Considering the exceptional risks inherent in coal mining, it is not surprising that those who engage in this dangerous occupation are inclined to seek otherworldly assistance. Religious beliefs and rituals were an important element of Anyuan miners' lives long before the arrival of Communist intellectuals. Much of Li Lisan's success in mobilizing the workers lay in the appropriation and adaptation of popular religious practices, from temple festivals to Triad rites, for revolutionary purposes. Despite the avowed atheism of the Chinese Communist Party, the introduction of a new Communist political order in 1949 did not obviate the miners' search for supernatural sources of solace and security. The cult of Mao that developed during the Cultural Revolution (a central ritual of which included adoration of the image of the young Mao arriving at Anyuan) was indicative of this continuing quest. Today, as coal mining increasingly resembles the primitive practices of an earlier era, the grafting of the Cultural Revolution reverence for Chairman Mao onto pre-Communist religious beliefs provides an extra layer of spiritual protection for those desperate to enlist whatever divine intervention may be available.

The adulation of Mao Zedong so prevalent among the workers of Anyuan is not an isolated phenomenon. Anthropologist Mobo Gao reports of his recent investigations in the North China countryside, "through all my travel and work in rural China . . . I have heard expressions of admiration and even love of Mao everywhere, but hardly any enthusiasm for Deng. . . . Mao's portrait can still be seen in the average household, but one can hardly find a portrait of Deng Xiaoping anywhere."[83] The preference of many rural dwellers for Mao Zedong over Deng Xiaoping is no doubt attributable to a number of things, including the fact that Deng did not encourage a cult of personality to buttress his own leadership. Yet the reverence toward Mao is more than the residual effect of a past personality cult. It also reflects continuing admiration for Mao's revolutionary ambitions and achievements, as well as a longing for a seemingly simpler and purer past, unsullied by the commercialization, cynicism, and corruption so evident in today's China.

Under Deng Xiaoping and his successors, China's sharp (re)turn to policies of marketization and globalization, while still retaining a powerful party propaganda apparatus, has generated social and political tensions and contradictions. The combination of an open cultural arena with an ossified communications system would at first glance seem like a dysfunctional and volatile mix, conducive neither to the public interest nor to political stability. Indeed, according to one analyst, post-Mao China can be characterized as "public sphere praetorianism," where the cultural realm has undergone excessive commercialization without a commensurate concern for public political goals.[84]

This type of system—in which a basically unreformed propaganda apparatus presides over a freewheeling cultural arena "awash not in serious political discussion but in meretricious entertainment"[85]—might appear inherently unstable. But if we compare the arrangement in place today to that of imperial China—one of the most resilient political systems in world history—we find some intriguing parallels. The cultural world of the Ming dynasty was also highly commercialized and cosmopolitan, while at the same time the state employed a range of (more or less effective) coercive, administrative, and normative instruments directed toward eliciting popular compliance and enhancing its own power and authority.[86] Viewed in this historical light, the contemporary pattern may look a little less tenuous.

As contemporary treatments of the Anyuan tradition attest, the cultural production of artists and academics in today's China is replete with bitter irony and biting critique. But it is not clear that such work poses a threat to the survival of the political system. By allowing considerable (albeit always ambiguous and precarious) room for creativity, the state responds to demands on the part of intellectuals and entrepreneurs for greater latitude in cultural and commercial expression. And by simultaneously maintaining and modernizing its relentless propaganda machine, the party-state also continues to proclaim the politically acceptable parameters of public belief and behavior. For better or worse, such a combination may be surprisingly well suited to sustaining authoritarian rule.

More problematic for the long-term future of the Communist party-state than the dissent of intellectuals could be the discontent of the dispossessed. To date, the widespread protests sweeping both urban and rural China have proven more stabilizing to the system than subversive.[87] Even so, the challenge of the revolutionary tradition looms as a continuing concern for the party leadership. That interpretations of this complex tradition remain tightly controlled yet contested and contradictory contributes to its incendiary potential.

# Conclusion

The common characterization of Mao's revolution as a struggle against Chinese culture, originating with the iconoclasm of the May Fourth era and culminating with Red Guard rampages against the "Four Olds"—Old Customs, Old Culture, Old Habits, and Old Ideas—has until quite recently discouraged serious investigation of the culture of the revolution itself. Whether or not Mao Zedong and his comrades succeeded in delivering a deathblow to tradition was often debated, but that they fully intended to do so was less often questioned.[1]

In the influential interpretation of historian Joseph Levenson, traditional Chinese culture had lost all value for twentieth-century Chinese thinkers and activists. The intellectual and moral vacuum created by the exhaustion of the Confucian tradition, Levenson contended, was precisely what persuaded politically concerned Chinese to embrace a Marxist alternative. In comparing the course of the Russian and Chinese revolutions, Levenson stressed the more natural and culturally congruent origins of the Russian variant of Communism:

> Russians and Chinese . . . came to their revolutions from different points of departure. Russia was part of Europe; China was all of China. . . . [In China] Marxism had its appeal as a compensation for the lost values of Confucian civilization, not (like its Russian appeal) as the culmination of a civilization to which the intelligentsia subscribed. . . . And so in China, as a resolver of the dilemma of cultural malaise, Marxism was really a *deus ex machina;* while in Russia, a Marxist resolution might seem to issue from the logic of the drama.[2]

According to Levenson, then, Marxism in China was an artificial substitute for a discredited Confucian tradition rather than an organic outgrowth of indigenous cultural impulses, as had been the case in Russia.

Writing in 1965, Levenson presented his argument at a moment when China stood at the threshold of the Great Proletarian Cultural Revolution, poised, it seemed, to jettison any lingering remnants of its outmoded past. Today, however, a comparison of the trajectories of the Russian and Chinese Communist revolutions, with the hindsight afforded by an additional half century of history, has given rise to a rather different understanding. As Thomas Metzger observes of contemporary Chinese intellectual discourse, "it has become almost a cliché to view Maoism and the Confucian tradition as a single if evolving amalgam."[3]

Now that a Communist political system has persisted in China for decades after the dismantling of the Soviet Union, Chinese Communism appears less contrived than it once did. The durability of the Chinese Communist political system—when contrasted with the sudden collapse of Communism in Eastern Europe and the Soviet Union—lends credence to the possibility that its resilience may reflect the recognition and redirection, rather than the wholesale rejection and replacement, of China's rich cultural resources. Although one would be hard-pressed to find many (or perhaps even any) Communist "true believers" in China these days, the impact of generations of both top-down and bottom-up efforts to interpret Marxist-Leninist-Maoist ideas in terms of familiar frameworks should not be underestimated. This process of cultural translation was critical to the victory of the Communist revolution and remains central to the nationalist/revolutionary authority that underpins the political system today. It helps explain how a Communist party-state that was in fact an alien import both ideologically and institutionally—a deus ex machina, as Levenson so aptly put it—came to be accepted as recognizably "Chinese."

## "SOCIALISM WITH CHINESE CHARACTERISTICS"

Since the establishment of the PRC, a succession of state-sponsored initiatives and societal responses served to render the new order culturally consonant—or, to borrow the phrase that Deng Xiaoping applied to his economic reforms, to create "socialism with Chinese characteristics." The decision in 1949 to occupy, rather than eviscerate, the symbolic center of imperial Chinese power—Tiananmen and the Forbidden City that stretched behind it—acknowledged that the architecture of the past offered a supple scaffold on which to construct a very different political system.[4] Even the Cultural Revolution, despite its frontal attack on the Four Olds, drew power from both elite and popular traditions.[5] The intense religiosity of that era, moreover, bestowed upon Mao Zedong and his thought a sacred authority that is now worshipped in local temples across China in what Timothy Cheek characterizes as "an astonishing syncretism of twentieth-century ideological politics and long-standing Chinese religious folkways."[6]

The Beijing Olympics in 2008 provided a graphic demonstration of the PRC's self-presentation as the rightful inheritor and steward of a five-thousand-year-old civilization. From the eye-catching logo based on the ancient art of seal calligraphy to the breathtaking opening ceremony directed by cinematographer Zhang Yimou, the Beijing Olympics offered a spectacular display of the Communist Party's claim to be perpetuating and perfecting longstanding cultural traditions. The current effort to project Chinese soft power globally through the establishment of hundreds of government-sponsored "Confucius Institutes" around the world is further evidence of this impulse.

Although these days China is home to few committed Marxist-Leninists, it suffers no shortage of nationalists. This is not to say, however, that cultural nationalism has recently replaced Communism as the reigning ideology.[7] The Chinese revolution has consistently been framed as a nationalist revolution (with global aspirations and implications), whether in opposition to Western imperialism and Japanese militarism (during the 1920s–1940s) or in opposition to Soviet revisionism (during the Great Leap Forward and Cultural Revolution).[8] Reinvigorated and refashioned under the Patriotic Education Campaign of the post-Mao era, cultural nationalism has always been a cornerstone and touchstone of Chinese Communism. From the early revolutionary leaders' wearing of Mandarin gowns and writing of Confucian aphorisms in mobilizing the workers of Anyuan, to the carefully orchestrated denunciations of Liu Shaoqi's alleged Soviet-style revisionism during the Cultural Revolution, to the recent Olympic games and worldwide proliferation of Confucius Institutes, cultural positioning and patronage have played a critical role in the rise and resilience of Chinese Communism.

To underscore the role of a nationalistic brand of cultural mobilization is by no means to deny the decisive importance of international influences on the trajectory of the Chinese revolution. The Chinese Communist Party and the state it spawned were closely modeled on the Bolsheviks and the Soviet Union, just as today's Confucius Institute is indebted to the Alliance Française and the Goethe Institute. The argument here is definitely not that there was an essential or inescapable "traditional Chinese culture" that Mao and his successors simply dressed up in Communist garb. For one thing, past cultural practices were far too diverse and dynamic to dictate any single political outcome. For another, both the Marxist-inspired revolution and the Communist party-state that it brought into being were decidedly *untraditional* political forms imported from abroad. But, committed as Mao and his comrades were to introducing a radically new style of politics along with a new proletarian culture to sustain it, they appreciated the value of a broad range of cultural materials—literary and military, folk and foreign—in realizing their ambition.

Needless to say, not all CCP cadres were equally astute or adept in the practice of cultural positioning and patronage. Qu Qiubai's criticism of the European-educated members of the early Chinese Communist Party as acting like "foreigners" in their own country pointed to the difficulties that many of the returned students experienced in dealing with indigenous Chinese culture. Such problems, moreover, were not simply a matter of individual inhibitions or inabilities. A further complication was the inconsistency in official party policy with regard to the treatment of Chinese tradition. Not until Qu became minister of education for the Jiangxi Soviet did the CCP embrace an explicit policy of popularizing and indigenizing cultural activities. Disagreements resurfaced at Yan'an and were silenced (temporarily) only when Mao championed "national forms" *(minzu xingshi)* and called for an end to foreign stereotypes.[9] That "national forms" were themselves susceptible to official opprobrium was seen dramatically during the Cultural Revolution, first in assaults on the Four Olds and later in the Criticize Confucius, Criticize Lin Biao Campaign.

Communist Chinese cultural policy has been inconsistent and, on occasion, ineffective. A recent example was the sudden removal (unannounced and overnight) of the large bronze statue of Confucius that had been installed in front of the National Museum (formerly the Museum of Revolutionary History) in Tiananmen Square only three months earlier.[10] Whether the removal reflected nothing more than a belated realization that the statue looked bizarrely out of place amid the various monuments to the revolution, or whether it pointed to a resurgence of neo-Maoist sympathies among the political elite, was unclear. That the reversal was evidence of a botched attempt at cultural patronage, however, was obvious to all.

Efforts at cultural mobilization—even by as seasoned a practitioner as the Central Propaganda Department—may be ill considered and unsuccessful. But from the earliest days of the Chinese Communist Party down to the present, such efforts have been regarded as critical to the party's mission. And the accumulated experience of generations of party organizers on the ground has confirmed the wisdom of Li Lisan's inspired approach at Anyuan: the skillful reconfiguration of familiar tropes and traditions by cultural insiders can work to spark and sustain popular support. Successful cultural positioning and patronage renders the foreign familiar; a Russian recipe can be made to taste Chinese.

## CHINA AND RUSSIA COMPARED

As strongly influenced by the Russian paradigm as the Chinese revolution most assuredly was, it differed significantly in its appreciation and appropriation of both elite and folk culture. A historian of the Soviet propaganda state, Peter Kenez, has argued that the Bolsheviks were condescending and dismissive of Russian culture: "Lenin and his fellow revolutionaries . . . saw little that was valuable in the indigenous culture of the Russian people."[11] Similarly, "Stalin and his circle were known to be contemptuous of peasants and peasant beliefs."[12] By contrast, Mao Zedong, although every bit as radical and ruthless as his Russian counterparts, was nevertheless keenly attuned to the political power inherent in China's folk wisdom and cultural traditions. Mao referred frequently to his own peasant background as a point of pride and a source of political and philosophical insight. But his interest in Chinese culture did not stop there. As Mao enjoined his colleagues during the height of the war with Japan:

> Our national history goes back several thousand years and has its own characteristics and innumerable treasures. But in these matters we are mere schoolboys. Contemporary China has grown out of the China of the past; we are Marxist in our historical approach and must not lop off our history. We should sum up our history from Confucius to Sun Yat-sen and take over this valuable legacy. . . . [W]e can put Marxism into practice only when it is integrated with the specific characteristics of our country and acquires a definite national form. . . . Foreign stereotypes must be abolished, there must be less singing of empty, abstract tunes, and dogmatism must be laid to rest; they must be replaced by the fresh, lively Chinese style and spirit which the common people of China love.[13]

Brutal as it often was, Mao's revolution was built upon a keen awareness of the efficacy of cultural assets for political mobilization.

The revolutionary victory of the CCP, credited by its own people with having rescued their nation and civilization from the ignominy of international humiliation, provides a wellspring of pride and legitimation for the Communist state today. Likewise, Mao Zedong—as the paramount leader of that revolution—commands respect in both official and popular circles within China. Delia Davin observes, "No honest person who has studied the Maoist record would wish to be cast as an apologist for him. His utopian dreams, his periodic refusal to engage with reality, his ruthlessness and his determination to win resulted in terrible human suffering. But his revolution reunified China and made the country a force to be reckoned with in the world. The Chinese still remember these achievements and so should we."[14] Among the most important of Mao's many accomplishments was the selective adaptation of an arsenal of cultural armaments to solidify a new revolutionary order that owed much to the Russian exemplar yet was widely perceived as distinctly "Chinese" rather than an alien implant. Mao Zedong instinctively understood what it took several generations of scholars of social movements to grasp; namely, that the cultural realm is every bit as critical a terrain of struggle as that of the state and economy.[15] The construction of a sense of national identity and community, introduced through revolutionary rhetoric, art, drama, mass campaigns, and more, was at the heart of this transformative project.

The PRC was comparatively advantaged in the practice of cultural nationalism vis-à-vis the Communist competition by virtue of the fact that over 90 percent of the population identifies ethnically as Han Chinese.[16] It was a relatively straightforward matter to present a new Communist culture as being at the same time a Chinese culture, in contrast to the USSR, where a new Soviet culture could not so easily be passed off as a Russian culture, let alone as an authentic culture for the multitude of other ethnicities that comprised the Soviet Union.[17] When the Stalin regime promoted Russian nationalism for a time during World War II, it generated predictable tensions with other nationalities.[18] But even when nationalism was downplayed in favor of "Soviet" values, suspicions of Russian chauvinism were difficult to dispel. As Mark Beissinger observes, "The Soviet state never fully extricated itself from the perception that lurking behind its multicultural policies was an essential Russian dominance."[19]

Differences in cultural nationalism between the two Communist giants were more than a product of ethnic distribution, however. Political leadership was decisive. Mao and his comrades were unabashed patriots, drawn to Communism as a means to repair China's damaged national pride, and they framed their proletarian appeals in nationalist terms.[20] By contrast, "the socialists of populist and Marxist provenance who came to shape the culture of the Russian working class . . . explicitly repudiated the language of nationalism."[21] In China, the sentiment behind the cri de coeur "Once beasts of burden, now we will be men!" which had proved so arresting as a centerpiece of the Anyuan strike in 1922, was reiterated by revolutionaries and political leaders throughout the course of the twentieth century in reference to the entire Chinese nation (vis-à-vis the rest of the world) as well as to the poor and weak within China.[22]

China's cultural nationalism was forged at stupendous cost in the form of prolonged struggle and sacrifice and was fortified by the agonizing experience of the Great Proletarian Cultural Revolution. In China, as Maurice Meisner has shown, the birth of Chinese nationalism was intertwined with the concept of a "cultural revolution." But while early radicals such as Chen Duxiu and Lu Xun had called for an all-out rejection of the traditional cultural heritage in building a new Chinese nation, Mao came to the conclusion—as he put it in his talks on art and literature at Yan'an—that the cultural revolution for which his party had already been struggling for many years must take into account "the fine old culture of the people, which has a more or less democratic and revolutionary character."[23]

The idea of a cultural revolution was not a Chinese invention, of course. The Soviets, too, had periodically advocated the need for such a revolution.[24] Mao's understanding of the process was quite different from that of Lenin or Stalin, however. For Lenin, "cultural revolution was designed to instill the ABC's of knowledge, as well as to develop a work ethic and discipline."[25] In Lenin's view, a cultural revolution was conceived as a mass education initiative directed toward the needs of industrial modernization. Although the process involved extensive agitprop efforts, the goal was limited to instilling Communist loyalty in order to build an advanced economy. For Stalin, too, a cultural revolution was a means of promoting economic development by stressing "outward political compliance, together with economic discipline and effort."[26] The orthodox Soviet conception of a cultural revolution, intended to build support for Communism through workers' education, was precisely the recipe that Liu Shaoqi had followed at Anyuan during the period when it was known as China's Little Moscow. And Liu continued to espouse a limited, utilitarian understanding well after the establishment of the PRC, proclaiming in the spring of 1958 that "in order to meet the needs of technical revolution, we must also launch a cultural revolution."[27] The result, in Anyuan as elsewhere in China, was a massive literacy campaign of the sort that had been carried out previously in the Soviet Union.[28]

Mao Zedong came to envision a far more thoroughgoing and militant movement, the purpose of which was less to promote economic development than to inoculate his revolution against extinction by cultivating committed revolutionary successors among the younger generation. This goal could not be achieved by education and propaganda alone; it called for a religious awakening conducted through mass struggle. To be sure, Mao's stress on the need for class warfare against hidden enemies owed a significant debt to Stalin.[29] But Stalin's cultural revolution was orchestrated by Komsomol (the Communist Youth League) and other party-directed agencies, whereas Mao's campaign—once the work teams associated with Liu Shaoqi were withdrawn—was far less controlled and much longer lasting. Even Stalin's Terror, with its deadly purges, show trials, cult of personality, and conspiratorial mentality, did not approach the intensity of Mao's final crusade to save Chinese Communism from the fate of (post-Stalinist) Soviet revisionism. The Chinese Cultural Revolution, like the Chinese Communist revolution as a whole, dwarfed its Russian prototype in duration, magnitude, and ferocity. The differences with Eastern Europe, where Communism had been imposed by Soviet tanks, were even starker. And the implications for political authority were profound. In China, unlike in Poland or Czechoslovakia, Communist leaders were popularly regarded not as Soviet agents but as nationalist and revolutionary heroes.

Shortly before his death, Mao confided to his inner circle that his lifetime achievements could be boiled down to two: the Revolution of 1949 and the Cultural Revolution. He mused that although most people would acknowledge the success of the first revolution, the outcome of the second was less certain.[30] Could it really rescue China from the revisionist fate of the USSR? Now that a Communist political system has persisted in China for more than a generation after the collapse of the Soviet Union, Mao Zedong's parting words take on particular poignancy.

Whether one admires or abhors Mao's revolution, it is too soon to write its obituary. Contemporary Chinese nationalism has surged in tandem with renewed attention on the part of the Communist party-state to its revolutionary heritage, including the superhuman persona of Mao Zedong. The year 2009, which marked the sixtieth anniversary of the founding of the PRC, saw a veritable explosion of films and television programs featuring Mao Zedong's larger-than-life contributions. Two years later, preparations for the Chinese Communist Party's ninetieth anniversary in 2011 witnessed a nationwide "singing red" campaign, fueled by the enthusiasm of the former Red Guard generation and designed to strengthen support for the ruling party by reviving memories of Mao and his revolution. And the blockbuster movie *Beginning of the Great Revival: The Founding of a Party*, which featured a star-studded volunteer cast depicting a highly romantic (and nationalistic) portrait of Mao Zedong and his fellow revolutionary pioneers, played to sell-out crowds across the country.

It is not an accident that such exercises in cultural patronage have struck a chord with many Chinese citizens. In 1968, at the height of the Cultural Revolution, psychiatrist and historian Robert Jay Lifton wrote insightfully,

> One cannot predict future attitudes of Chinese leaders toward the Maoist image, but there is good reason to believe that for some time at least they will continue to hold the image on high even as they retreat from its excesses. . . . [O]ne must also consider the potential durability and flexibility of Chinese Communist culture. . . . [W]e may expect that the Cultural Revolution will leave its traumatic impact in more ways than can now be imagined. Yet I believe it would be very rash to assume that a regime which has so recently commanded so much psychic power would suddenly cease to possess any at all.[31]

Lifton's prescient prediction about the lingering emotional appeal of Mao and his revolutionary quest cautions against an overly simplistic understanding of the sources of support for the contemporary Chinese Communist state.

To assume, as many do, that the PRC survives only by virtue of an instrumental "performance legitimacy" that will dissipate as soon as its sizzling economy begins to sputter may well prove naive.[32] Important as economic stagnation was in hastening the fall of Soviet and East European Communism, it is not clear that an economic downturn would have the same effect in China. If, as this study of Anyuan has tried to suggest, Chinese Communism draws strength from deeper reservoirs than current GDP growth rates, its longevity is not easily predicted by the life spans of other Communist regimes. Complicated and conflicted as contemporary Chinese attitudes toward the political system are, they are not compromised by suspicions that the party or its founders are in any sense "un-Chinese."

Perry Anderson observes in his recent comparison of the two major Communist revolutions that the Chinese, unlike the Russians, have been aided by a "millennial self-confidence, battered for a century, but ultimately unbroken, of the world's oldest continuous civilization in the world. . . . In this historical self-assurance lay a fundamental difference between Russia and China."[33] The comparative advantage enjoyed by the Chinese Communists in staking cultural claims should not obscure the fact that the Soviet Union was once able to capture the emotional and cultural allegiance of many of its citizens as well. Yet, as Stephen Kotkin explains, the eventual decline of what had been a widespread popular faith in Soviet socialism reflected that system's evident inability to measure up to the capitalist competition. Having developed its socialist identity in explicit opposition to capitalism, the Soviet Union could not survive once it became clear to its own people (Russians and non-Russians alike) that it was lagging ever further behind the capitalist world in living standards and technology.[34] By contrast, the willingness of Deng Xiaoping and subsequent generations of post-Mao Chinese Communist leaders to embrace economic reform as a defining feature of "socialism with Chinese characteristics" has greatly alleviated, if not entirely eliminated, the sense of challenge from an alternative capitalist system. Whether or not the combination of a market economy with an authoritarian political order ultimately will prove unsustainable is an open question. After all, such a configuration calls to mind not only the relatively short-lived precedents of Park Chung-Hee's South Korea or Chiang Kai-shek's Taiwan; it also invites comparisons to China's millennial imperial past.[35]

## MINING THE REVOLUTIONARY TRADITION

The survival of Chinese Communist authoritarianism to date is a product of many complex factors. Not least among them is the continuing allegiance that the regime evidently enjoys from a broad cross-section of its citizenry.[36] This popular acceptance derives in part, no doubt, from objective improvements in living standards in the post-Mao reform era. In part it reflects the tremendous discursive and coercive power of the Communist party-state, which renders dissent both difficult and dangerous. Perhaps even more critical in explaining the PRC's staying power, as Perry Anderson suggests, is the vitality attached to the assertion of a uniquely proud and enduring historical identity. But this is not to say that the current polity, which departs in many respects from pre-Communist patterns, is without serious vulnerabilities. The legitimacy of Chinese Communism rests, after all, not simply on alleged connections to an ancient civilization, but also on a revolution that promised dignity for its most downtrodden citizens as well as for the nation as a whole. And that promise is susceptible to challenge not only by hypernationalists, but also by those who feel left behind by the post-Mao reforms. As a consequence, the symbol of Mao is not an unproblematic source of authority for the contemporary Chinese state. Ching Kwan Lee describes a demonstration by thirty thousand disgruntled factory workers in Liaoning who marched behind a gigantic portrait of Mao "because we wanted to show the contrast we felt between the past and the present." An elderly woman worker among the protesters "cried out loud lamenting that 'Chairman Mao should not have died so soon!'"[37]

Many materially disadvantaged (as well as advantaged) Chinese express tremendous pride in the accomplishments of their country under Communist rule, from throwing off the shackles of semi-imperialism more than sixty years ago to overtaking Japan as the world's second largest economy in 2010. But many also express bitterness at what they perceive as the Communist Party's retreat from the revolutionary promise of a better life for the oppressed. An Anyuan miner sums up the current plight of the proletariat: "Workers' wages are sinking. . . . Workers' rights are shrinking. . . . Workers' living conditions are stinking. . . . These days our Anyuan workers' slogan goes like this, 'Once beasts of burden, now we are still not men!'"[38]

Cognizant of the potential for political criticism inherent within its own history, the Communist Party's verdict on the meaning of its revolutionary tradition is notably vague. The official line on Anyuan is as fuzzy as it is formulaic: "The Anyuan spirit is the precious spiritual treasure bequeathed by the 1920s Anyuan labor movement led by Mao Zedong, Li Lisan, Liu Shaoqi, and others in the previous generation of revolutionaries; it is the crystallization of collective struggle."[39] "The Anyuan spirit is the cornerstone of the Chinese revolutionary spirit; it is an organic part of the endless flow of the magnificent revolutionary spirit of modern Chinese history."[40] The imprecision of the party's own formulation does not amount to tolerance for other interpretations, however. For example, my own attempt to summarize the meaning of the Anyuan revolutionary tradition, presented as a presidential address to the Association for Asian Studies in 2008, was deemed unacceptable by Communist Party censors. The abstract of the address, published as an article in the *Journal of Asian Studies*, read in part:

> At Anyuan, idealistic young Communist cadres led a highly successful nonviolent strike and launched a major educational program for workers, peasants, and their families. The result was a remarkable

outpouring of popular support for the Communist revolutionary effort. Although the meaning of the "Anyuan revolutionary tradition" has been obscured and distorted over the years to serve a variety of personal, political, and pecuniary agendas, the author seeks to recover from its early history the possibility of alternative revolutionary paths, driven less by class struggle and cults of personality than by the quest for human dignity through grassroots organization.[41]

The Chinese Communist Party, however, does not welcome alternative perspectives. A translation of the article was slated to appear in a respected Chinese academic journal until it came to the attention of party censors, who sent a blunt warning to the editor:

> The essay "Reclaiming the Chinese Revolution" has many "political problems." It is not in accordance with higher-level requirements. In the right-hand margin of the article itself we have noted a number of points, but those don't necessarily cover the whole problem.
>
> The most important problems: The essay uses forbidden materials, touches on the forbidden zone of the Cultural Revolution, and commits some taboos in its discussion of the Cultural Revolution. The discussion of the Chinese revolution does not accord with the party's interpretation.
>
> Taboos: the evaluation of the Chinese Communist leadership, including Mao; an uncomplimentary reference to Hu's speech.
>
> Things that touch upon the Chinese Communist leadership invite interrogation.
>
> Discussion of the livelihood and mentality of the Anyuan workers is a taboo.
>
> If all these things were revised or removed, there would be nothing left of the essay. There is really no way to salvage this.
>
> We definitely do not want to take these problems into publication or else the press and the journal will be reprimanded and closed down.[42]

The alarm set off by an unorthodox interpretation of the Anyuan legacy not only exposes the continued grip of the party-state on academic discourse, but it also indicates the intense political sensitivities that still surround the interpretation of China's revolutionary tradition.

In the immediate aftermath of June Fourth and the discrediting of Communism in Eastern Europe and the former Soviet Union, many Chinese intellectuals appeared more than ready to part with their revolutionary heritage. The sensation created by the publication of Liu Zaifu and Li Zehou's *Farewell to Revolution: Looking Back at Twentieth-Century China* was symptomatic of a widespread desire to move beyond the question of revolution in approaching the problems of modern Chinese history and thought.[43] Revolutionary traditions are not so easily cast aside, however. Mobo Gao cautions that "the Chinese 1949 revolution and Maoist legacy have become part of the Chinese environment and cannot simply be discarded."[44] With the history and meaning of that inheritance insulated from open and honest examination, the possibility of an unexpected (and unwelcome) recrudescence looms especially large.

Even those at the forefront of advocating for democratic change in China have found themselves stymied by the fetters of the revolutionary tradition. In a candid retrospective on the Tiananmen Uprising of 1989, democracy activist and now Nobel laureate Liu Xiaobo conceded that the participants in that movement, himself included, were thwarted by a mentality marked by past habits: "Most of the resources and methods we made use of to mobilize the masses were ones that the Communist Party itself had used many times before. . . . As soon as we began our revolution, we became extremely conceited—just as if we had reverted to the time of the Cultural Revolution and felt ourselves to be the most revolutionary. . . . [H]ad we not fasted for democracy and devoted ourselves to it and made sacrifices for it? . . . Our voice became the only truth."[45] Liu's reflections are a harsh indictment of the 1989 protest as an undemocratic movement that unwittingly re-created many of the negative features of China's revolutionary political culture.

With the upsurge in "singing red" and other remnants of Maoism popularized by the recently discredited "Chongqing model," we have seen the instrumental use of such cultural weapons to buttress the credentials of the so-called princelings—the children and grandchildren of the revolutionary generation—who are preparing to take their turn at the helm of the ship of state.[46] Having cut their political teeth as Red Guards during the Cultural Revolution, these "red scions" betray the influence of their adolescent socialization as they jockey for political position today. Factional divisions notwithstanding, the princelings share a common commitment (and personal interest) in revitalizing revolutionary culture as a vehicle for perpetuating Communist Party rule.

The future of revolution, in China as elsewhere, is uncertain. Some scholars have predicted that the twenty-first century, thanks to a recent wave of democratization across much of the formerly colonized world, will see a sharp decline in revolutionary movements.[47] Others, highlighting growing inequities between the winners and losers of neoliberal reforms, argue that revolutions are as likely as ever.[48] In any event, it is clear that the "color revolutions" that swept the former Soviet republics in the first decade of this century, followed by the Arab Spring of 2011, have stoked fears among Chinese leaders about the possibility of a revolutionary threat to their own political system.[49]

Whatever the future may hold, the revolutionary past continues to haunt the political present in many unsettling ways. This predicament is not unique to China. Jill Lepore writes of the contemporary United States, "A nation born in revolution will always eye its history warily, and with anxiety. It's good that it happened once; twice could be trouble."[50] In China, where revolutions have occurred repeatedly over the course of the past century (in 1911, 1927, 1949, 1966, and—according to Deng Xiaoping—1979), anxieties are that much more intense. And yet in China as in America, critics as well as defenders of the political order claim justification for their positions by reference to their national revolutionary tradition, because, in the end, "nothing trumps the Revolution."[51] The challenge for future generations is not to forget or falsify the past but to mine the revolutionary inheritance in ways that encourage its inspiring vision to triumph over its appalling violence.

# Notes

INTRODUCTION

1. Robert Alexander, *Re-writing the French Revolutionary Tradition* (New York: Cambridge University Press, 2003).

2. Jill Lepore, *The Whites of Their Eyes: The Tea Party's Revolution and the Battle over American History* (Princeton, NJ: Princeton University Press, 2010).

3. Perry Anderson, "Two Revolutions," *New Left Review* 61 (January–February 2010): 59–96.

4. "Maoist Revival Gathers Pace in Chongqing," *Financial Times*, May 24, 2011.

5. For example, a blog by the respected economist Mao Yushi, posted in the spring of 2011, was highly critical of Mao Zedong, charging him with the deaths of some fifty million Chinese in the 1960s. The commentary, quickly removed by state authorities, sparked a barrage of hostile responses.

6. Li Xiangping, "Xinyang, quanli, shichang—Mao Zedong xinyang de jingjixue xianxiang" [Faith, power, and the market—The economics of Mao worship], January 28, 2011, Zhongguo zongjiao xueshu wang [Academic website on Chinese religion], http://iwr.cass.cn/zjyjj/201101/t20110128_6030.htm (accessed February 2, 2012).

7. Mobo Gao, *The Battle for China's Past: Mao and the Cultural Revolution* (London: Pluto Press, 2008).

8. For the impact of Maoism on contemporary policies, see Sebastian Heilmann and Elizabeth J. Perry, eds., *Mao's Invisible Hand: The Political Foundations of Adaptive Governance in China* (Cambridge, MA: Harvard University Press, 2011).

9. On the costs of the revolution, see, for example, Rana Mitter, *A Bitter Revolution: China's Struggle with the Modern World* (New York: Oxford University Press, 2004); and Peter Zarrow, *China in War and Revolution* (New York: Routledge, 2005). On Mao's own role, see Delia Davin, *Mao Zedong* (Stroud, UK: Sutton, 1997); Jonathan D. Spence, *Mao* (New York: Viking,

297

1999); Ross Terrill, *Mao: A Biography* (Stanford, CA: Stanford University Press, 1999); Philip Short, *Mao: A Life* (New York: Henry Holt, 2000); Lee Feigon, *Mao: A Reinterpretation* (Chicago: Ivan R. Dee, 2002); Timothy Cheek, *Mao Zedong and China's Revolutions* (Boston: St. Martin's, 2002); Michael Lynch, *Mao* (London: Routledge, 2004); Maurice Meisner, *Mao Zedong* (Cambridge: Polity Press, 2007); Roderick MacFarquhar and Michael Schoenhals, *Mao's Last Revolution* (Cambridge, MA: Harvard University Press, 2006). These works differ considerably in emphasis and evaluation, yet taken as a whole they offer a bleak picture of Mao and his revolution.

10. Jung Chang and Jon Halliday, *Mao: The Unknown Story* (London: Jonathan Cape, 2005).

11. Cao Shuji, *Da Jihuang* [The great famine] (Hong Kong: Times International Press, 2005); Yang Jisheng, *Mubei: Zhongguo liushi niandai dajihuang jishi* [Tombstone: Annals of China's Great Famine] (Hong Kong: Heaven and Earth Book Company, 2008); Ralph A. Thaxton Jr., *Catastrophe and Contention in Rural China: Mao's Great Leap Forward Famine and the Origins of Righteous Resistance in Da Fo Village* (New York: Cambridge University Press, 2008); Frank Dikotter, *Mao's Great Famine: The History of China's Most Devastating Catastrophe* (London: Bloomsbury, 2010).

12. There were, of course, also many important similarities between the two revolutions. See S. A. Smith, *Revolution and the People in Russia and China: A Comparative History* (New York: Cambridge University Press, 2008).

13. Richard Louis Walker, *China under Communism: The First Five Years* (New Haven, CT: Yale University Press, 1955); Alexander Pantsov, *The Bolsheviks and the Chinese Revolution, 1919–1927* (Honolulu: University of Hawai'i Press, 2000).

14. Benjamin I. Schwartz, *Chinese Communism and the Rise of Mao* (Cambridge, MA: Harvard University Press, 1966); Lucien Bianco, *Origins of the Chinese Revolution* (Stanford, CA: Stanford University Press, 1971).

15. For a small sampling of alternative approaches, see Chalmers A. Johnson, *Peasant Nationalism and Communist Power: The Emergence of Revolutionary China* (Stanford, CA: Stanford University Press, 1962); Mark Selden, *The Yenan Way in Revolutionary China* (Cambridge, MA: Harvard University Press, 1971); Ilpyong J. Kim, *The Politics of Chinese Communism: Kiangsi under the Communists* (Berkeley: University of California Press, 1973); Roy Hofheinz Jr., *The Broken Wave: The Chinese Communist Peasant Movement, 1922–1928* (Cambridge, MA: Harvard University Press, 1977).

16. Sherry B. Ortner, "Theory in Anthropology since the Sixties," *Comparative Studies in Society and History* 26, no. 1 (January 1984); Ann Swidler, "Culture in Action: Symbols and Strategies," *American Sociological Review* 51, no. 2 (April 1986): 273–86; Lisa Wedeen, "Conceptualizing Culture: Possibilities for Political Science," *American Political Science Review* 96, no. 4 (December 2002): 713–28; William H. Sewell Jr., *Logics of History: Social Theory and Social Transformation* (Chicago: University of Chicago Press, 2005), 152–74.

17. For other aspects of revolutionary leadership, see Ronald Aminzade, Jack A. Goldstone, and Elizabeth J. Perry, "Leadership Dynamics and Dynamics of Contention," in *Silence and Voice in the Study of Contentious Politics,* ed. Ronald Aminzade et al. (New York: Cambridge University Press, 2001), 126–54.

18. For a small sampling of this influential work, see Lynn Hunt, *Politics, Culture and Class in the French Revolution* (Berkeley: University of California Press, 1984); Keith Michael Baker, ed., *The French Revolution and the Creation of Modern Political Culture* (New York: Oxford University Press, 1987); Mona Ozouf, *Festivals and the French Revolution* (Cambridge, MA: Harvard University Press, 1988); Keith Michael Baker, *Inventing the French Revolution: Essays on French Political Culture in the Eighteenth Century* (Cambridge: Cambridge University Press, 1990).

19. Alberto Melucci, *Nomads of the Present: Social Movements and Individual Needs in Contemporary Society* (Philadelphia, PA: Temple University Press, 1989).

20. Prasenjit Duara, *Culture, Power, and the State: Rural North China, 1900–1942* (Stanford, CA: Stanford University Press, 1988).

21. On China's protest culture as political theater, see Joseph W. Esherick and Jeffery N. Wasserstrom, "Acting out Democracy: Political Theater in Modern China," in *Popular Protest and Political Culture in Modern China,* ed. Jeffrey N. Wasserstrom and Elizabeth J. Perry (Boulder, CO: Westview Press, 1994), 32–69.

22. Richard Curt Kraus, *Brushes with Power: Modern Politics and the Chinese Art of Calligraphy* (Berkeley: University of California Press, 1991), 11.

23. Ellen R. Judd, "Revolutionary Drama and Song in the Jiangxi Soviet," *Modern China* 9, no. 1 (1983): 127–60; David Holm, *Art and Ideology in Revolutionary China* (New York: Oxford University Press, 1991); Chang-tai Hung, *War and Popular Culture: Resistance in Modern China, 1937–1945* (Berkeley: University of California Press, 1994); Paul Clark, *The Chinese Cultural Revolution: A History* (New York: Cambridge University Press, 2008); Chang-tai Hung, *Mao's New World: Political Culture in the Early People's Republic* (Ithaca, NY: Cornell University Press, 2011).

24. William Hinton, *Fanshen: A Documentary of Revolution in a Chinese Village* (New York: Random House, 1968); Hinton, *Shenfan* (New York: Random House, 1983); Jan Myrdal, *Report from a Chinese Village* (New York: Pantheon, 1965); Myrdal, *Return to a Chinese Village* (New York: Pantheon, 1984); Edward Friedman, Paul G. Pickowicz, and Mark Selden, *Chinese Village, Socialist State* (New Haven, CT: Yale University Press, 1991); and Friedman, Pickowicz, and Selden, *Revolution, Resistance, and Reform in Village China* (New Haven, CT: Yale University Press, 2005).

25. Lynda Shaffer, *Mao and the Workers: The Hunan Labor Movement, 1920–1923* (Armonk, NY: M.E. Sharpe, 1982).

26. Michael Herzfeld, *Cultural Intimacy: Social Poetics in the Nation-State,* 2nd ed. (New York: Routledge, 2005), explains "cultural intimacy" as

providing insiders with "their assurance of common sociality, the familiarity with the bases of power that may at one moment assure the disenfranchised a degree of creative irreverence and at the next moment reinforce the effectiveness of intimidation" (3). Herzfeld's study of Greece focuses on the nation-state, but in the case of China one must also take into consideration subnational variations.

27. Elizabeth J. Perry, "Red Literati: Communist Educators at Anyuan, 1921–1925," *Twentieth Century China* (April 2007): 123–60.

28. The dualism is discussed in Kam Louie and Louise Edwards, "Chinese Masculinity: Theorizing Wen and Wu," *East Asian History* 8 (1994): 138–94; and Kam Louie, *Theorising Chinese Masculinity: Society and Gender in China* (Cambridge: Cambridge University Press, 2002).

29. Emily Martin Ahern, *Chinese Ritual and Politics* (New York: Cambridge University Press, 1981), 92.

30. Memoirs of many of these individuals—e.g., Han Wei, Wang Yaonan, Wu Lie, Xing Yuanlin, and numerous others—can be found in Pingxiang Municipal Party Committee, ed., *Anyuan lukuang gongren yundong* [Anyuan railway and mine workers' movement] (Beijing: Communist Party Historical Materials Press, 1990), 2: 893–1120. This invaluable source provides a wealth of primary materials on the Anyuan labor movement between 1922 and 1930.

31. For the perspective of rural women, see Gail Hershatter, *The Gender of Memory: Rural Women and China's Collective Past* (Berkeley: University of California Press, 2011).

32. Ching Kwan Lee and Guobin Yang, eds., *Re-envisioning the Chinese Revolution: The Politics and Poetics of Collective Memories in Reform China* (Stanford, CA: Stanford University Press, 2007), 11.

33. For different perspectives, see, for example, Wen Tiejun, *Sannong wenti yu shiji fansi* [The three rural issues and centennial reflections] (Beijing: Sanlian Press, 2005); Yu Jianrong, *Diceng zhengzhi* [Subaltern politics] (Hong Kong: Chinese Cultural Press, 2009).

## 1. REHEARSING REVOLUTION

1. Today Pingxiang has been elevated administratively from a county *(xian)* to a municipality *(shi)*, with Anyuan designated as both a district *(qu)* and a township *(zhen)*. Although still under the jurisdiction of Jiangxi Province, it remains culturally closer to Hunan than to Jiangxi.

2. "Pingxiang caichaxi jianjie" [Brief introduction to Pingxiang's tea-picking opera], *Pingxiang gujin* 4 (December 1984): 297 ff.

3. Hua Wen and Luo Xiao, "Pingxiang meitan fazhan gaikuang" [Overview of the development of Pingxiang coal], *Pingxiang wenshi ziliao* 6 (January 1987): 2; Li Weiyang, "Li Shouquan yu Anyuan meikuang" [Li Shouquan and the Anyuan coal mine], *Pingxiang wenshi ziliao* 6 (January 1987): 58.

4. Huang Shiguo, ed., *Pingxiang shizhi* [Gazetteer of Pingxiang City] (Beijing: Gazetteer Press, 1996), 11–15.

5. Pingxiang City Education Research Office, ed., *Pingxiang lishi* [Pingxiang history] (Pingxiang: n.p., 1995), 21.

6. Although it had occurred half a century earlier, the Taiping Rebellion was still vividly recalled in the early twentieth century, as we learn from Zhang Guotao's autobiography. A native of Pingxiang, this founding member of the CCP as a youth was fascinated by tales recounted by an elderly school watchman who had once fought with the Taiping rebels: "We youngsters showed enormous respect for this 'Long Hair' warrior and treated him as an old hero." Chang Kuo-t'ao, *The Rise of the Chinese Communist Party, 1921–1927* (Lawrence: University Press of Kansas, 1971), 14.

7. *Gongchan dang* [Communist Party] 3 (April 27, 1921).

8. Huang, ed., *Pingxiang shizhi*, 697, 699.

9. *Pingxiang bianpao yanhua shiliao* [Historical materials on Pingxiang fireworks and firecrackers], special issue, *Pingxiang wenshi ziliao* 9 (September 1988).

10. Peng Yunhua and Zhang Zhenchu, "Jiefangqian de Pingxiang meikuang" [The Pingxiang coal mine before liberation], *Pingxiang wenshi ziliao* 6 (January 1987): 16–21.

11. The information on Li Shouquan is based primarily on Li Mengxing, "Li Shouquan yishi" [Tales of Li Shouquan], *Yangzhou minge*, July 2005, 1–16. This article, written by Li Shouquan's grandson, draws heavily from Li Shouquan's personal diary, memoirs, poems, and other writings.

12. Huang, ed., *Pingxiang shizhi*, 1185.

13. Jeff Hornibrook, "Local Elites and Mechanized Mining in China: The Case of the Wen Lineage in Pingxiang County, Jiangxi," *Modern China* 27, no. 2 (April 2001).

14. Hornibrook, "Local Elites and Mechanized Mining," 222.

15. Albert Feuerwerker, *China's Early Industrialization: Sheng Hsuan-huai and Mandarin Enterprise* (Cambridge, MA: Harvard University Press, 1958); Feuerwerker, "China's Nineteenth Century Industrialization: The Case of the Hanyeping Coal and Iron Company, Limited," in *The Economic Development of China and Japan*, ed. Charles Donald Cowan (New York: Praeger, 1964), 79–110; Wellington Chan, *Politics and Industrialization in Late Imperial China* (Singapore: Institute of Southeast Asian Studies, 1975).

16. Zhang Zhenchu, *Anyuan yishi* [Anyuan anecdotes] (Pingxiang: Anyuan Coal Mine, 1995), 62–65.

17. Ibid., 46.

18. Feuerwerker, "China's Nineteenth Century Industrialization," 84. Despite a basic continuity in Sheng Xuanhuai's own managerial style, the transformation from a bureaucratically supervised entity into a shareholding company converted the enterprise into a wholly commercial firm. Feuerwerker, *China's Early Industrialization*, 68.

19. Anyuan was outdone only by the British-controlled Kailuan mine in Hebei and the Japanese-owned Fushun mine in Manchuria. Tim Wright, *Coal*

*Mining in China's Economy and Society, 1895–1937* (New York: Cambridge University Press, 1984), 142–46.

20. Feuerwerker, *China's Early Industrialization,* 68.

21. Jiangxi Academy of Social Sciences History Institute, ed., *Jiangxi jindai gongkuang shiziliao xuanbian* [Compendium of historical sources on modern industry and mining in Jiangxi] (Nanchang: Jiangxi People's Press, 1989), 447–48.

22. In 1869 the population of Pingxiang County stood at 215,648; by 1906 it had more than doubled to 590,948. Huang, ed., *Pingxiang shizhi,* 1131.

23. The number of employees fluctuated in tandem with production. In 1916, when the Anyuan coal mine reached an annual output of some 950,000 tons, the work force soared to more than twenty thousand. Jiangxi Academy of Social Sciences History Institute, ed., *Jiangxi jindai gongkuang shiziliao xuanbian,* 387, 449.

24. Zhang, *Anyuan yishi,* 27, 55, 154.

25. Ibid., 60.

26. Chang, *The Rise of the Chinese Communist Party,* 16.

27. Hornibrook, "Local Elites and Mechanized Mining," 223.

28. *Pingxiang gujin* [Pingxiang past and present] 10 (1990): 10.

29. "Sheng Xuanhuai zhi Lai Long xuntiao" [Instructions from Sheng Xuanhuai to Leinung], *Pingxiang wenshi ziliao* 6 (January 1987): 118.

30. "The Pingsiang Colliery," *Far Eastern Review* 12, no. 10 (March 1916): 377.

31. Guy Puyraimond, "The Ko-lao Hui and the Anti-Foreign Incidents of 1891," in *Popular Movements and Secret Societies in China, 1840–1950,* ed. Jean Chesneaux (Stanford, CA: Stanford University Press, 1972), 113–24.

32. Pingxiang City History Gazetteer Office, ed., *Zhonggong Pingxiang difangshi* [Local history of the Chinese Communists in Pingxiang] (Beijing: Chinese Communist Party History Press, 2003), 1: 22.

33. Ibid.; Huang, ed., *Pingxiang shizhi,* 696.

34. Dian H. Murray, *The Origins of the Tiandihui: The Chinese Triads in Legend and History* (Stanford, CA: Stanford University Press, 1994).

35. Huang, ed., *Pingxiang shizhi,* 696.

36. Pingxiang City History Gazetteer Office, ed., *Zhonggong Pingxiang difangshi,* 23–24; Huang, ed., *Pingxiang shizhi,* 696; Propaganda Department of the Chinese Communist Party Committee of the Pingxiang Mining Company, ed., *Hongse Anyuan* [Red Anyuan] (Nanchang: Jiangxi People's Press, 1981), 27; Xue Shixiao, *Zhongguo meikuang gongren yundongshi* [Labor movement history of Chinese miners] (Kaifeng: Henan People's Press, 1989): 35.

37. Li Junchao, "Hongjianghui yu Ping-Liu-Li qiyi" [The Hongjiang hui and the Ping-Liu-Li Uprising], *Hunan jingji guanli ganbu xueyuan xuebao* [Journal of Hunan Economic Management College] 13, no. 1 (January 2003); Propaganda Department of the Chinese Communist Party Committee of the Pingxiang Mining Company, ed., *Hongse Anyuan,* 27; Xue, *Zhongguo meikuang gongren yundongshi,* 36.

38. Li Junchao, "Hongjianghui yu Ping-Liu-Li qiyi"; Joseph W. Esherick, *Reform and Revolution in China: The 1911 Revolution in Hunan and Hubei* (Berkeley: University of California Press, 1976), 62–63.

39. Harold Z. Schiffrin, *Sun Yat-sen and the Origins of the Chinese Revolution* (Berkeley: University of California Press, 1968), 357.

40. Chang, *The Rise of the Chinese Communist Party*, 3–4; Xue, *Zhongguo meikuang gongren yundongshi*, 39.

41. Li Mengxing, "Li Shouquan yishi" [Anecdotes about Li Shouquan], *Yangzhou minge* (January 2007): 11.

42. Samuel Yale Kupper, "Revolution in China: Kiangsi Province, 1905–1913," PhD diss., University of Michigan, 1973, 81.

43. Chang, *The Rise of the Chinese Communist Party*, 2.

44. Ibid., 4–6.

45. Ibid., 15.

46. Esherick, *Reform and Revolution in China*, 59.

47. Tang Xiangping, *Huashuo Pingxiang* [Tales of Pingxiang] (Nanchang: Jiangxi Educational Press, 2001), 60.

48. Xue, *Zhongguo meikuang gongren yundongshi*, 41.

49. A persistent theme in Li's poetry was the beauty of the Anyuan landscape. "Li Shouquan reai Anyuan" [Li Shouquan deeply loved Anyuan], *Jiangxi wenshi ziliao* 23 (1987): 115–17.

50. Li "Li Shouquan yu Anyuan meikuang," 53–94; "Li Shouquan he Huang Xing youshan" [The friendship of Li Shouquan and Huang Xing], *Jiangxi wenshi ziliao xuanji* 23 (1987): 112–13.

51. Zhang Zhenchu, Liu Jialin, and Liu Zongdao, *Anyuan da bagong qianhou* [Before and after the Anyuan Great Strike] (Changsha: Hunan People's Press, 1981), 15; Liu Shanwen, *Anyuan lukuang gongren yundongshi* [History of the Anyuan railway and mine workers' movement] (Shanghai: Shanghai Academy of Social Sciences, 1993), 41.

52. Zhang, *Anyuan yishi*, 98.

53. Pingxiang Municipal Party Committee, ed., *Anyuan lukuang gongren yundong* [Anyuan railway and mine workers' movement] (Beijing: Communist Party Historical Materials Press, 1990), 2: 1127 (hereafter cited as AYLKGRYD); Yang Fangping, "Anyuan kuangjingdui suotan" [Miscellany about the Anyuan mine police], *Pingxiang wenshi ziliao* 2 (December 1984): 84–86.

54. Xiao Xianfu, ed., *Pingxiang dashiji* [Chronology of Pingxiang] (Pingxiang: Pingxiang City Gazetteer Office, 1989), 28–29.

55. Pingxiang City History Gazetteer Office, ed., *Zhonggong Pingxiang difangshi*, 26–36; Tang, *Huashuo Pingxiang*, 62–63; Wright, *Coal Mining in China's Economy and Society*, 183.

56. Liu Minghan, ed., *Hanyeping gongsi zhi* [Gazetteer of the Hanyeping Company] (Wuhan: Central China Institute of Technology Press, 1990), 62.

57. AYLKGRYD, 2: 983.

58. Pingxiang City History Gazetteer Office, ed., *Zhonggong Pingxiang difangshi*, 17; Zhang *Anyuan yishi*, 202.

59. Xiao, ed., *Pingxiang dashiji*, 25–31; Zhang *Anyuan yishi*, 193–94.

60. Pingxiang Historical Gazetteer Office, ed., *Anyuan lukuang gongren yundongshi yanjiu wenhui* [Compilation of studies on the Anyuan railway and mine workers' movement] (Nanchang: Jiangxi People's Press, 2002), 412–13.

61. Zhang Zhenchu, "Wang Hongqing qiren" [The person of Wang Hongqing], *Pingxiang wenshi ziliao* 8 (December 1987): 157.

62. Propaganda Department of the Chinese Communist Party Committee of the Pingxiang Mining Company, ed., *Hongse Anyuan*, 20–21; Zhang *Anyuan yishi*, 181; Wang Yaonan, interview on August 21, 1967, in *Anyuan lukuang gongren yundongshi ziliao huibian* [Compilation of historical materials on the Anyuan railway and mine workers movement] 3, no. 1. This is a mimeographed compilation, marked "top secret," held at the Anyuan Railway and Mine Workers' Labor Movement Memorial Hall Archives.

63. In June 1906 miners had gone on strike to protest an increase in the length of shifts from eight to twelve hours. The walkout was repressed with military force, however, and the new regime remained in place. Xue, *Zhongguo meikuang gongren yundongshi*, 52.

64. AYLKGRYD, 1: 115; 2: 984, 1134; Jiangxi Academy of Social Sciences History Institute, ed., *Jiangxi jindai gongkuang shizilIao xuanbian*, 459.

65. Ci Fei, "Anyuan youji" [Record of a trip to Anyuan], *Da Gong Bao* (Changsha: June 10, 23, 25, 26, 1922).

66. AYLKGRYD, 2: 1010.

67. A comparable dualism can be found in other mining cultures. For a fascinating discussion of the culture of Bolivian tin miners, see June Nash, *We Eat the Mines and the Mines Eat Us: Dependency and Exploitation in Bolivian Tin Mines* (New York: Columbia University Press, 1993).

68. Wu Yunduo, *Son of the Working Class* (Peking: Foreign Languages Press, 1956), 5–6.

69. Huang, ed., *Pingxiang shizhi*, 221; Zhang *Anyuan yishi*, 35–36.

70. Huan Zhao, "Pingxi siyan wenhua de tese" [The characteristics of temple culture in western Pingxiang], in *Pingxiang zongjiao wenhua daguan*, ed. Chen Shiguo (Nanchang: Jiangxi People's Press, 2000), 119–24; Mei Fangquan, *Anyuan kuanggong: zhuanxingqi de bianqian yanjiu* [Anyuan miners: A study of change in a time of transition] (Beijing: Chinese Academy of Social Sciences, 2006), 48.

71. "Pingxiang caichaxi jianjie," 297–99.

72. Zhang, *Anyuan yishi*, 66, 101.

73. Charlton M. Lewis, "Some Notes on the Ko-lao Hui in Late Ch'ing China," in *Popular Movements and Secret Societies in China, 1840–1950*, ed. Jean Chesneaux (Stanford, CA: Stanford University Press, 1972), 97–112.

74. Ibid., 101.

75. Contradictory interpretations of Elder Brother Society origins can be found in Hirayama Shu, *Zhongguo mimishehui shi* [History of secret societies in China] (Shanghai: Commercial Press, 1912); Tao Chengzhang, "Jiaohui yuanliu kao" [Investigation of the origins of sects and societies], in *Jindai*

*mimishehui shiliao* [Historical materials on modern secret societies], ed. Xiao Yisan (Taipei: Wenhai Press, 1965), 5; Jerome Chen, "Rebels between Rebellions," *Journal of Asian Studies* 29, no. 4 (August 1970): 815; Lewis, "Some Notes on the Ko-lao Hui," 98–100; Xu Ankun, *Gelaohui de qiyuan ji qi fazhan* [The origins and development of the Elder Brothers Society] (Taipei: Taiwan Provincial Museum, 1989).

76. Xu, *Gelaohui de qiyuan ji qi fazhan*, 60–68. The jurisdiction of a particular lodge was known in Jiangxi as its "wharf" *(matou)*. This was not a well-defined territory but rather indicated the area surrounding a particular chieftain's residence and lodge. Zhou Hanseng, "Wo suo zhidao de Jiangxi Hongjiang hui" [The Jiangxi Hongjiang hui that I know], *Jiangxi wenshi ziliao xuanji* 4 (December 1982): 145.

77. On Triad rituals, see Barend J. ter Haar, *Ritual and Mythology of the Chinese Triads: Creating an Identity* (Leiden: Brill, 1998). The Elder Brothers did not require that new members pass under a bridge of swords or knives, as was standard in Triad initiations, for example.

78. Lewis, "Some Notes on the Ko-lao Hui," 104; Charlton M. Lewis, *Prologue to the Chinese Revolution: The Transformation of Ideas and Institutions in Hunan Province, 1891–1907* (Cambridge, MA: Harvard East Asian Monographs, 1976), 76–77.

79. Tang, *Huashuo Pingxiang*, 123–24.

80. Xu, *Gelaohui de qiyuan ji qi fazhan*, 154.

81. Ibid., 153.

82. Lewis, "Some Notes on the Ko-lao Hui," 104; Chang *The Rise of the Chinese Communist Party*, 3–4.

83. AYLKGRYD, 2: 1127.

84. Barend J. ter Haar, "The Gathering of Brothers and Elders: A New View," in *Conflict and Accommodation in Early Modern East Asia*, ed. Leonard Blusse and Harriet T. Zurndorfer (Leiden: E.J. Brill, 1993), 259–84; Xu, *Gelaohui de qiyuan ji qi fazhan*, 102.

85. As G. William Skinner wrote of his field site in Sichuan, "During the republican period, the secret societies collectively known as the *Ko-lao hui* wielded supreme power at all levels of rural society." Skinner, "Marketing and Social Structure in Rural China (Part I)," *Journal of Asian Studies* 24, no. 1 (November 1964): 37.

86. One source lists female prostitution among the diverse occupations of Elder Brother members in Jiangxi, but all sources agree that the membership was overwhelmingly male. Zhou, "Wo suo zhidao de Jiangxi Hongjiang hui," 148.

87. The most detailed mid-nineteenth-century source on the Elder Brothers alleges that members kept young boys (whom they called "nephews") for their own sexual pleasure. It is possible that this was a false charge intended to discredit the society, but there is evidence of homosexual behavior among other Chinese secret societies, and it is not unlikely that some Elder Brother lodges—particularly those located in mining towns where women were in

very scarce supply—engaged in this practice as well. The allegation about the Elder Brothers can be found in "Gelao hui shuo" [A treatise on the Elder Brothers Society], in *Bixie jishi* [Annals of repressing heterodoxy] (1862), appendix. On homosexuality among the Triads, see Dian H. Murray, *Pirates of the South China Coast, 1790–1810* (Stanford, CA: Stanford University Press, 1987).

88. Xu, *Gelaohui de qiyuan ji qi fazhan*, 110.

89. Ibid., 102, 116; Li, "Hongjianghui yu Ping-Liu-Li qiyi."

90. Xu, *Gelaohui de qiyuan ji qi fazhan*, 155–59.

91. For a discussion of the Shanghai labor scene, see Elizabeth J. Perry, *Shanghai on Strike: The Politics of Chinese Labor* (Stanford, CA: Stanford University Press, 1993).

92. AYLKGRYD, 2: 983.

93. "The Pingsiang Colliery," 379.

94. Zhang Jun, "Mimi shehui yu diyici gongren yundong de gaochao" [Secret societies and the first high tide of the labor movement], *Shiqiu* 1 (2005): 190.

95. At the time of Mao's first visit to Anyuan, some two dozen religious organizations were said to be operating there. Exhibition, Anyuan Railway and Mining Workers' Movement Museum.

96. The following account of the Episcopal Church's activities at Anyuan is drawn from Ma Hanqin, "Pingxiang Jidujiao bainian shilue ji xianzhuang" [A brief hundred-year history and the current situation of Christianity in Pingxiang], *Pingxiang gaodeng zhuanke xuexiao xuebao* [Journal of Pingxiang College] 3, no. 1 (2004): 109.

97. In the case of the Episcopal Church, the Anyuan congregation was under the auspices of the Guangxi-Hunan diocese (headquartered in Changsha) during the years 1909–23, but it reported to Bishop Logan Roots in Hankou both before and after that period. I am grateful to Zhang Bo of Central China Normal University for this clarification.

98. AYLKGRYD, 2: 1133–34; Zhang, *Anyuan yishi*, 104–5; *Pingxiang gujin* [Pingxiang past and present] 1 (July 1982): 122.

99. Ma Hanqin, "Pingxiang Jidujiao bainian shilue ji xianzhuang."

100. Liu, *Anyuan lukuang gongren yundongshi*, 292.

101. Hornibrook, "Local Elites and Mechanized Mining," 226.

102. Chang, *The Rise of the Chinese Communist Party*, 27.

103. Ibid.

104. Clark Kerr and Abraham Siegel, "The Interindustry Propensity to Strike—An International Comparison," in *Labor and Management in Industrial Society*, ed. Clark Kerr (Garden City, NY: Doubleday, 1954).

105. On the "relative deprivation" generated by a sudden downturn, see Ted Robert Gurr, *Why Men Rebel* (Princeton, NJ: Princeton University Press, 1970); and James C. Davies, *When Men Revolt and Why* (New Brunswick, NJ: Transaction, 1997).

106. Kam Louie, *Theorising Chinese Masculinity: Society and Gender in*

*China* (Cambridge: Cambridge University Press, 2002). The dichotomy was reflected in local Pingxiang culture in two types of lion lanterns. One with a red face, known as a "civil lion," was hung at times of major celebrations and festivals; the other with a black face, known as a "martial lion" or "fighting lion," was hung during martial arts exhibitions. "Pingxiang shideng" [Lion lanterns of Pingxiang], *Pingxiang Gujin* [Pingxiang past and present], no. 4 (1984): 310–11. In many parts of China, popular religious worship was separated by "civil" and "military" altars, with Buddhists often responsible for the former and Daoists for the latter. John Lagerwey, *China: A Religious State* (Hong Kong: Hong Kong University Press, 2010), 103.

107. Louie, *Theorising Chinese Masculinity*, 17.

108. Nash, *We Eat the Mines and the Mines Eat Us*, 169.

109. On the obstacles that an entrenched tradition of protest presented for the Communist revolutionaries in another geographical setting, see Elizabeth J. Perry, *Rebels and Revolutionaries in North China, 1845–1945* (Stanford, CA: Stanford University Press, 1980).

## 2. TEACHING REVOLUTION

1. John H. Kautsky, *Political Change in Underdeveloped Countries: Nationalism and Communism* (New York: Wiley, 1962); Edward Shils, *The Intellectuals and the Powers* (Chicago: University of Chicago Press, 1972); and Theda Skocpol, *States and Social Revolutions* (New York: Cambridge University Press, 1979).

2. John Fitzgerald, *Awakening China: Politics, Culture and Class in the Nationalist Revolution* (Stanford, CA: Stanford University Press, 1996).

3. All-China Federation of Trade Unions, ed., *Zhonggong zhongyang guanyu gongren yundong wenjian xuanbian* [Compilation of central Communist Party documents concerning the labor movement] (Beijing: Archives Press, 1985), 1.

4. Ibid., 2.

5. Wen-Hsin Yeh, *The Alienated Academy: Culture and Politics in Republican China* (Cambridge, MA: Harvard University Press, 1990); Helen R. Chauncey, *Schoolhouse Politicians: Locality and State during the Chinese Republic* (Honolulu: University of Hawai'i Press, 1992).

6. Charles W. Hayford, *To the People: James Yen and Village China* (New York: Columbia University Press, 1990).

7. Donald J. Munro, *The Concept of Man in Early China* (Stanford, CA: Stanford University Press, 1969); *The Concept of Man in Contemporary China* (Ann Arbor: University of Michigan Press, 2000).

8. Benjamin A. Elman, *A Cultural History of Civil Examinations in Late Imperial China* (Berkeley: University of California Press, 2000).

9. Benjamin A. Elman and Alexander Woodside, eds., *Education and Society in Late Imperial China, 1600–1900* (Berkeley: University of California Press, 1994).

10. Deng Zhongxia, "Zhongguo gongchandang zuo zhigong yundong de qidian" [The starting point of the Chinese Communist Party's labor movement], in *Erqi dabagong ziliao xuanbian* [Selected materials on the Great Strike of February 7] (Beijing: Workers' Press, 1983), 21–23.

11. Lynda Shaffer, *Mao and the Workers: The Hunan Labor Movement, 1920–1923* (Armonk, NY: M. E. Sharpe, 1982), 42–49.

12. A reprint and analysis of the authorship of the letter can be found in Liu Shanwen, "'Gao Zhongguo de nongmin' yiwen zuozhe yingshi Mao Zedong" [The author of the "Open Letter to the Peasants of China" was surely Mao Zedong], in *Mao Zedong zai Pingxiang* [Mao Zedong in Pingxiang], ed. Pingxiang Party History Work Office (Pingxiang: Pingxiang Miners Journal, 1993), 135–50; Pingxiang City History Gazetteer Office, ed., *Zhonggong Pingxiang difangshi* [Local history of the Chinese Communists in Pingxiang] (Beijing: Chinese Communist Party History Press, 2003), 1: 36.

13. Sources conflict on exactly when and how many times Mao visited Anyuan, as well as on who exactly accompanied him on each trip. Even the same author sometimes offers contradictory accounts. See, for example, Li Rui, *Mao Zedong tongzhi de chuqi geming huodong* [Comrade Mao Zedong's early revolutionary activities] (Beijing: China Youth Press, 1957), 179; and Li Rui, *Mao Zedong de zaoqi geming huodong* [Mao Zedong's early revolutionary activities] (Changsha: Hunan People's Press, 1980), 373. I have tried to piece together the most plausible picture from a number of different sources, relying especially on Liu Shanwen and Yang Guixiang, "Mao Zedong dao Pingxiang he Anyuan congshi geming huodong jiujing shi jici" [How many times did Mao Zedong actually go to Pingxiang and Anyuan to undertake revolutionary activities], in *Anyuan lukuang gongren yundongshi yanjiu wenhui*, [Compilation of studies on the Anyuan railway and mine workers' movement], ed. Pingxiang City History Gazetteer Office (Nanchang: Jiangxi People's Press, 2002), 199–209; and Liu Shanwen and Liu Yisheng, "Mao Zedong tongzhi 1921 nianqiu dao Anyuan shiliaokao" [An investigation of historical materials on Comrade Mao Zedong's autumn 1921 trip to Anyuan], *Jiangxi gongyunshi yanjiu ziliao* 3 (August 10, 1982): 22–36. For an alternative account that argues that Mao's first visit did not take place until December 1921 in the company of Li Lisan, see *Pingxiang jingu* 3 (September 1982): 15–22.

14. Pingxiang Mining Company Editorial Committee, ed., *Pingxiang kuangwuju zhi* [Pingxiang Mining Company gazetteer] (Pingxiang: n.p., 1998), 65.

15. *Mao Zedong nianpu* [Mao Zedong chronicle] (Beijing: Central Documents Press, 2002), 91; Dan Shilian, "Anyuan san ren xing" [Three men at Anyuan], *Difang wengeshi jiaoliu wang* [Web exchange for local Cultural Revolution history], February 28, 2011.

16. The memory of Mao carrying a traditional Hunan umbrella and dressed in a long blue scholar's gown can be found in many interviews conducted with elderly workers in the 1950s to 1970s. See, for example, Pingxiang

Party History Work Office, ed., *Mao Zedong zai Pingxiang*, 46, 51, 53; and Anyuan Railway and Mine Workers' Movement Memorial Hall, ed., *Anyuan lukuang gongren yundongshi ziliao huibian* [Compilation of historical materials on the Anyuan railway and mine workers' movement] 3, no. 1 (1975).

17. "Zheng Dongguo yu Mao Zhuxi" [Zheng Dongguo and Chairman Mao], *Wen Hui Bao*, January 13, 1985.

18. Memoir of Zhu Zijian, September 15, 1967, in Anyuan Railway and Mine Workers' Movement Memorial Hall, ed., *Anyuan lukuang gongren yundong shiziliao huibian* 3, no. 1.

19. *Mao Zedong nianpu*, 91.

20. Zhang Liquan had already established contacts with four Hunanese railway mechanics at Anyuan, former students of his at the Jiazhong Industrial School, to whom he regularly sent twenty or so copies of the secretariat journal to distribute to fellow workers. *Pingxiang jingu* 3 (September 1982): 4, 19.

21. Propaganda Department of the Chinese Communist Party Committee of the Pingxiang Mining Company, *Hongse Anyuan* [Red Anyuan] (Nanchang: Jiangxi People's Press, 1981), 41, 319.

22. Li Lisan, interview on August 8, 1963, Anyuan Memorial Hall Archives, file no. 1451.

23. Ibid.

24. Pingxiang Municipal Party Committee, ed., *Anyuan lukuang gongren yundong* (Anyuan railway and mine workers' movement) (Beijing: Chinese Communist Party Historical Materials Press, 1990), 2: 899, 902, 1059 (hereafter cited as AYLKGRYD); and Li Sishen and Liu Zhikun, *Li Lisan zhi mi* (The puzzle of Li Lisan) (Beijing: People's Press, 2005), 38.

25. Li Lisan, interview on January 10, 1959, Anyuan Memorial Hall Archives, file no. 1450; AYLKGRYD, 1: 415; 2: 1133; Zhang Zhenchu, *Anyuan yishi* [Anyuan anecdotes] (Pingxiang: Anyuan Coal Mine, 1995), 104.

26. Memoir of Chen Chaichu, in Anyuan Railway and Mine Workers' Movement Memorial Hall, ed., *Anyuan lukuang gongren yundong shiziliao huibian* 3, no. 1.

27. AYLKGRYD, 2: 902; Propaganda Department of the Chinese Communist Party Committee of the Pingxiang Mining Company, ed., *Hongse Anyuan*, 45.

28. Pingxiang City History Gazetteer Office, ed., *Zhonggong Pingxiang difangshi*, 49–51.

29. AYLKGRYD, 2: 936.

30. Propaganda Department of the Chinese Communist Party Committee of the Pingxiang Mining Company, ed., *Hongse Anyuan*, 45.

31. Elizabeth J. Perry, *Shanghai on Strike: The Politics of Chinese Labor* (Stanford, CA: Stanford University Press, 1993).

32. Memoir of Wu Yousheng, April 24, 1971, in Anyuan Railway and Mine Workers' Movement Memorial Hall, ed., *Anyuan lukuang gongren yundong shiziliao huibian* 3, no. 1.

33. Propaganda Department of the Chinese Communist Party Committee of the Pingxiang Mining Company, ed., *Hongse Anyuan*, 61.

34. Ibid., 49.

35. AYLKGRYD, 2: 903.

36. Propaganda Department of the Chinese Communist Party Committee of the Pingxiang Mining Company, ed., *Hongse Anyuan*, 47.

37. Memoir of Zhu Zijian, July 9, 1968, in Anyuan Railway and Mine Workers' Movement Memorial Hall, ed., *Anyuan lukuang gongren yundong shiziliao huibian* 3, no. 1.

38. Initially used at Anyuan in stencil format, the first three volumes of Li Liuru's reader appeared in print in October 1922; the final volume came out in May 1923. Within less than a year, more than four reprints of the Mass Reader had been published to supply the huge demand for the texts in CCP-sponsored workers' schools that sprang up across Jiangxi, Hunan, Hubei, and Guangdong. *Zhonggong dangshi renwuzhuan* [Biographies of figures in Chinese Communist Party history] (Beijing: Central Documents Press, 1999), 69, 131.

39. The two hundred yuan needed to launch the school, along with the first few months of operating expenses (which came to a little over forty yuan per month) were from these two sources. AYLKGRYD, 1: 172.

40. Zhang Zhenchu, "Chen Shengfang qiren qishi" [Chen Shengfang, the man and his deeds], *Pingxiang wenshi ziliao* 12 (December 1990): 134. After serving for more than a decade as a foreman at the mine, Chen had amassed enough capital to purchase a sizable expanse of paddy fields back in his home county of Liling and to open a number of stores in the Hunan-Jiangxi area. As both a major landlord and capitalist, Chen Shengfang wielded considerable economic and social influence, which he sometimes used for Li Lisan's benefit. Zhang Zhenchu, Liu Jialin, and Liu Zongdao, *Anyuan da bagong qianhou* [Before and after the great Anyuan strike] (Changsha: Hunan People's Press, 1981), 9–10.

41. Propaganda Department of the Chinese Communist Party Committee of the Pingxiang Mining Company, ed., *Hongse Anyuan*, 64–66; AYLK-GRYD, 2: 1288; Deng Qipei, "Anyuan gongyun shi wodang jiti fendou de guanghui fanli" [The Anyuan labor movement is a glorious example of our party's collective struggles], in *Anyuan lukuang gongren yundong shi yanjiu wenhui*, ed. Pingxiang Historical Gazetteer Office, 28.

42. Propaganda Department of the Chinese Communist Party Committee of the Pingxiang Mining Company, ed., *Hongse Anyuan*, 68–70.

43. Pingxiang City History Gazetteer Office, ed., *Zhonggong Pingxiang difangshi*, 53.

44. Liu Shanwen, *Anyuan lukuang gongren yundongshi* [History of the Anyuan railway and mine workers' movement] (Shanghai: Shanghai Academy of Social Sciences Press, 1993), 95.

45. AYLKGRYD, 1: 161–62.

46. Fernando Galbiati, *Peng Pai and the Hai-Lu-Feng Soviet* (Stanford, CA: Stanford University Press, 1985), 122.

47. Pingxiang City History Gazetteer Office, ed., *Zhonggong Pingxiang difangshi*, 47; Propaganda Department of the Chinese Communist Party Committee of the Pingxiang Mining Company, ed., *Hongse Anyuan*, 71–77.

48. Propaganda Department of the Chinese Communist Party Committee of the Pingxiang Mining Company, ed., *Hongse Anyuan*, 76.

49. Memoir of Wu Yousheng, April 24, 1971, in Anyuan Railway and Mine Workers' Movement Memorial Hall, ed., *Anyuan lukuang gongren yundong shiziliao huibian* 3, no. 1.

50. Pingxiang City History Gazetteer Office, ed., *Zhonggong Pingxiang difangshi*, 54; Liu, *Anyuan lukuang gongren yundongshi*, 97; AYLKGRYD, 2: 978.

51. Chang Kuo-t'ao, *The Rise of the Chinese Communist Party, 1921–1927* (Lawrence: University Press of Kansas, 1971), 411.

52. AYLKGRYD, 2: 939. On Elder Brother chieftains' supernatural authority, see Xu Ankun, *Gelaohui de qiyuan ji qi fazhan* [The origins and development of the Elder Brothers Society] (Taipei: Taiwan Provincial Museum, 1989), 116–17.

53. Yi Youde, interview on March 20, 1967, Anyuan Memorial Hall Archives, file no. 1070; Patrick Lescot, *Before Mao: The Untold Story of Li Lisan and the Creation of Communist China* (New York: HarperCollins, 2004), 38–39.

54. Huang Aiguo, "Anyuan lukuang gongren xiaofei hezuoshe faxing de gupiao" [The stocks issued by the Anyuan railway and mine workers' consumer cooperative], in *Anyuan lukuang gongren yundong shi yanjiu wenhui*, ed. Pingxiang City History Gazetteer Office, 377; Pingxiang City History Gazetteer Office, ed., *Zhonggong Pingxiang difangshi*, 55; Liu Shaoqi and Zhu Shaolian, "Anyuan lukuang gongren julebu lueshi" [Brief history of the Anyuan railway and mine workers' club], in *Liu Shaoqi yu Anyuan gongren yundong* [Liu Shaoqi and the Anyuan labor movement] (Beijing: Chinese Academy of Social Sciences Press, 1981), 5.

55. Propaganda Department of the Chinese Communist Party Committee of the Pingxiang Mining Company, ed., *Hongse Anyuan*, 294–303; AYLK-GRYD, 2: 1384.

56. Huang Aiguo, "Geming de ying gutou: ji Anyuan meikuang lao gongren Yuan Pin'gao" [Ironman of the revolution: Notes on old Anyuan miner Yuan Pin'gao], in *Anyuan lukuang gongren yundong shi yanjiu wenhui*, ed. Pingxiang History Gazetteer Office, 359–62.

57. Yi Youde, interview on March 20, 1967, Anyuan Memorial Hall Archives, file no. 1070.

58. Yi Youde, interview on October 20, 1973, Anyuan Memorial Hall Archives, file no. 1103.

59. Jean Chesneaux, *The Chinese Labor Movement, 1919–1927* (Stanford, CA: Stanford University Press, 1968), chapter 8; Chen Weimin, "1922nian

Shanghai bagong yundong de xingqi" [The rise of the strike movement in Shanghai in 1922], *Shilin* 1–2 (1986): 126–35.

60. Pingxiang City History Gazetteer Office, ed., *Zhonggong Pingxiang difangshi*, 56–59.

61. Ibid., 60–61; *Mao Zedong nianpu*, 98.

62. Memoir of He Guilan, August 9, 1971, in Anyuan Railway and Mine Workers' Movement Memorial Hall, ed., *Anyuan lukuang gongren yundong shiziliao huibian* 3, no. 1.

63. Zhang, Liu, and Liu, *Anyuan da bagong qianhou*, 28–29.

64. *Mao Zedong nianpu*, 99.

65. Years later Mao would remark that, from the time he first met Li Lisan in Changsha, he never really warmed to him. Edgar Snow, *Red Star Over China* (New York: Grove Press, 1968), 146.

66. Guo Chen, "Anyuan douzheng shiling" [Miscellany about the Anyuan struggle], in *Liu Shaoqi yu Anyuan gongren yundong*, 182–83.

67. In an 1896 letter to bureaucrat capitalist Sheng Xuanhuai, an emissary sent to Pingxiang to help negotiate the purchase of land for the new coal mine, referred to the Anyuan miners as "worse off than beasts of burden." Zhang, *Anyuan yishi*, 8. For more on this metaphor, see S.A. Smith, *Like Cattle and Horses: Nationalism and Labor in Shanghai, 1895–1927* (Durham, NC: Duke University Press, 2002).

68. Pingxiang City History Gazetteer Office, ed., *Zhonggong Pingxiang difangshi*, 64–65.

69. Qiang Fang, "Hot Potatoes: Chinese Complaint Systems from Early Times to the Late Qing," *Journal of Asian Studies* 68, no. 4 (November 2009): 1105–35.

70. AYLKGRYD, 1: 41.

71. Huang Zenghui and Liu Jialin, "Yongfu kaitang" [Going bravely to the lodge rite], *Jiangxi gongyunshi yanjiu ziliao* 3 (August 10, 1982): 85–91. Publication for internal circulation by the Jiangxi Trade Union Party Committee.

72. Changsha Revolutionary Memorial Sites Office and Anyuan Labor Museum, eds., *Anyuan lukuang gongren yundong shiliao* [Historical materials on the Anyuan railway and mine workers' movement] (Changsha: Hunan People's Press, 1980), 697.

73. Liu Shanwen, Hu Ziguo, Gao Fei, and Huang Aiguo, eds., "Lao gongren huiyi Anyuan da bagong" [Elderly workers recall the Anyuan Great Strike], *Jiangxi gongyunshi yanjiu ziliao* 3 (August 10, 1982): 55–58.

74. Zhang, Liu, and Liu, *Anyuan da bagong qianhou*, 29.

75. AYLKGRYD, 1: 122–23.

76. Ibid., 2: 939; Propaganda Department of the Chinese Communist Party Committee of the Pingxiang Mining Company, ed., *Hongse Anyuan*, 104–5; Zhang, "Chen Shengfang qiren qishi," 135.

77. AYLKGRYD, 1: 43.

78. Deng Zhongxia, *Zhongguo zhigong yundong jianshi* [A brief history

of the Chinese labor movement] (Harbin: Northeast Book Company, 1948). Reprint, Changsha: Hunan People's Press, 1980, 158–59.

79. T.Y. Chang, "Five Years of Significant Strikes," *Chinese Students Monthly* 21, no. 8 (June 1926): 19.

80. AYLKGRYD, 1: 897.

81. Ibid., 1: 128.

82. *Pingxiang meitan fazhan shilue* [Brief history of the development of the Pingxiang coal industry], combined issue of *Jiangxi wenshi ziliao xuanji* 23 and *Pingxiang wenshi ziliao* 6 (1987): 177.

83. AYLKGRYD, 1: 45.

84. Ibid., 1: 129.

85. Ibid., 2: 901.

86. Pingxiang Mining Company Party Committee, ed., *Mao Zedong, Liu Shaoqi, Li Lisan zai Anyuan de gushi* [Stories of Mao Zedong, Liu Shaoqi, and Li Lisan at Anyuan] (Beijing: Chinese Communist Party History Press, 1998), 68.

87. AYLKGRYD, 2: 901.

88. Pingxiang Mining Company Party Committee, ed., *Mao Zedong, Liu Shaoqi , Li Lisan zai Anyuan de gushi*, 69.

89. Liu Shaoqi and Zhu Shaolian, "Anyuan lukuang gongren julebu lueshi" [A concise history of the Anyuan railway and mine workers' club], in AYLKGRYD, 1: 124.

90. Ibid., 1: 122.

91. Ibid., 1: 126. Although Director Li designated the head of the documents division, Shu Jijun, as official negotiator for the mining company, Director Li himself called the shots from behind the scenes. Liu, *Anyuan lukuang gongren yundongshi*, 131.

92. Zou Pei and Liu Chen, *Zhongguo gongren yundong shihua* [Historical tales of the Chinese labor movement] (Beijing: Chinese Workers' Press, 1993), 1: 217–18.

93. "Comrade Li Lisan Chats about the Anyuan Labor Movement," in *Liu Shaoqi yu Anyuan gongren yundong*, 150.

94. *Pingxiang meitan fazhan shilue*, 78; Pingxiang Mining Company Party Committee, ed., *Mao Zedong, Liu Shaoqi, Li Lisan zai Anyuan de gushi*, 77.

95. Tan Jiuru, "Pingxiang jidujiao de lishi yu xianzhuang" [The history and current situation of the Christian church in Pingxiang], in *Pingxiang zongjiao wenhua daguan*, ed. Chen Shiguo (Nanchang: Jiangxi People's Press, 2000), 112–16; Ma Hanqin, "Pingxiang jidujiao bainian shilue ji xianzhuang" [A brief hundred-year history and current situation of the Pingxiang Christian church], *Pingxiang gaodeng zhuanke xuexiao xuebao* 3 (2004): 109–10; Zhan Hailie, "Jiangxi jidujiao shenggonghui shihua" [Historical tales of the Episcopal Church in Jiangxi], *Wenshi daguan* 1 (1995): 40–45.

96. John Fitzgerald, "Nationalism, Democracy and Dignity in Twentieth-Century China," in *The Dignity of Nations: Equality, Competition and Honor*

*in East Asian Nationalism*, ed. Sechin Y.S. Chien and John Fitzgerald (Hong Kong: Hong Kong University Press, 2006), 93–114.

97. S.A. Smith, *Like Cattle and Horses: Nationalism and Labor in Shanghai, 1895–1927* (Durham, NC: Duke University Press, 2002), 268.

98. On the involvement of local gentry, see *Liu Shaoqi yu Anyuan gongren yundong*, 150; Li Liuru, *Liushinian de bianqian* [Sixty years of transformation] (Beijing: Writers' Press, 1961), 2: 184; *Liling Xianzhi* [Liling county gazetteer], Republican edition, ed. Ling Enfeng. Reprint, Liling: Liling City Gazetteer Committee, 1987, 901.

99. John Gaventa, *Power and Powerlessness: Quiescence and Rebellion in an Appalachian Valley* (Urbana: University of Illinois Press, 1980), 116.

100. AYLKGRYD, 2: 940.

101. Ibid., 2: 840–59.

102. This very brief (and very loose) translation summarizes but a few stanzas of what is a long rhymed folksong.

103. Quoted in Robert Marks, *Rural Revolution in South China: Peasants and the Making of History in Haifeng County, 1570–1930* (Madison: University of Wisconsin Press, 1984), 225–26. On "Bodhisattva Peng," see Marks, *Rural Revolution in South China*, 186; and Galbiati, *Peng Pai and the Hai-Lu-Feng Soviet*, 121.

104. Liu, *Anyuan lukuang gongren yundongshi*, 207.

## 3. CHINA'S LITTLE MOSCOW

1. Liu Shanwen, *Anyuan lukuang gongren yundongshi* [History of the Anyuan railway and mine workers' movement] (Shanghai: Shanghai Academy of Social Sciences Press, 1993), 2.

2. *Pingxiang gujin* [Pingxiang past and present] 5 (1985): 52.

3. Pingxiang Municipal Party Committee, ed., *Anyuan lukuang gongren yundong* [Anyuan railway and mine workers' movement] (Beijing: Chinese Communist Party Historical Materials Press, 1990) 2: 940–41 (hereafter cited as AYLKGRYD).

4. One impediment may have been Liu's own limited grasp of what he studied during his year in Moscow. His Russian language skills were reportedly less than adequate. Chang Kuo-t'ao, *The Rise of the Chinese Communist Party, 1921–1927* (Lawrence: University of Kansas Press, 1971), 201.

5. The initiation fees, equivalent to a day's wage, brought the club more than 1,500 yuan, while the monthly dues (also pegged to wages) garnered an additional 480 yuan per month.

6. Liu, *Anyuan lukuang gongren yundongshi*, 227.

7. AYLKGRYD, 2: 1060.

8. Ibid., 2: 900.

9. Rex A. Wade, *Red Guards and Workers' Militias in the Russian Revolution* (Stanford, CA: Stanford University Press, 1984), 40, 159.

10. On the *baojia*, see Hsiao Kung-ch'uan, *Rural China: Imperial Control*

*in the Nineteenth Century* (Seattle: University of Washington Press, 1960); for the Ping-Li-Liu Uprising, see chapter 2 of this book; and for the May Fourth Movement, see Jeffrey N. Wasserstrom, *Student Protest in Twentieth-Century China: The View from Shanghai* (Stanford, CA: Stanford University Press, 1991), 66–67. On the parallel structures of "orthodox" and "heterodox" organizations in late imperial China, see Philip A. Kuhn, *Rebellion and Its Enemies in Late Imperial China* (Cambridge, MA: Harvard University Press, 1970), chapter 3.

11. AYLKGRYD, 1: 94–95, 141.

12. For the secret society parallel, see Li Junchao, "Hongjianghui yu Ping-liuli qiyi" [The Hongjiang hui and the Ping-Liu-Li Uprising], *Hunan jingji guanli ganbu xueyuan xuebao* 13, no. 1 (January 2002).

13. Pingxiang City History Gazetteer Office, ed., *Zhonggong Pingxiang difangshi* [Local history of the Chinese Communists in Pingxiang] (Beijing: Chinese Communist Party History Press, 2003), 1: 91.

14. Liu, *Anyuan lukuang gongren yundongshi*, 237.

15. AYLKGRYD, 1: 142–43.

16. Liu, *Anyuan lukuang gongren yundongshi*, 239.

17. AYLKGRYD, 1: 139.

18. Ibid., 1: 141.

19. On the role of the native place in Communist organizing in other parts of China, see, for example, Wen-hsin Yeh, *Provincial Passages: Culture, Space and the Origins of Chinese Communism* (Berkeley: University of California Press, 1996).

20. AYLKGRYD, 1: 202–3.

21. Zhang Zhenchu, Liu Jialin, and Liu Zongdao, *Anyuan da bagong qian-hou* [Before and after the great Anyuan strike] (Changsha: Hunan People's Press, 1981), 59.

22. Memoir of Han Wei, July 18, 1968, in Anyuan Railway and Mine Workers' Movement Memorial Hall, ed., *Anyuan lukuang gongren yundong shiziliao huibian* 3, no. 1; Pingxiang City History Gazetteer Office, ed., *Zhonggong Pingxiang difangshi*, 92; AYLKGRYD, 1:103.

23. Zhang Zhenchu, *Anyuan yishi* [Anyuan anecdotes] (Pingxiang: Anyuan Coal Mine, 1995), 166.

24. Pingxiang City History Gazetteer Office, ed., *Zhonggong Pingxiang difangshi*, 132–33; Zhang, *Anyuan yishi*, 167.

25. Pingxiang City History Gazetteer Office, ed., *Zhonggong Pingxiang difangshi*, 129.

26. AYLKGRYD, 2: 994–95.

27. Victoria Bonnell, *Iconography of Power: Soviet Political Posters under Lenin and Stalin* (Berkeley: University of California Press, 1997).

28. AYLKGRYD, 2: 939.

29. Lowell Dittmer, *Liu Shao-ch'i and the Chinese Cultural Revolution: The Politics of Mass Criticism* (Berkeley: University of California Press, 1974), 209.

30. Chang Kuo-t'ao, "Introduction," in *Collected Works of Liu Shao-ch'i* (Hong Kong: Union Research Institute, 1969), i; quoted in Dittmer, *Liu Shao-ch'i and the Chinese Cultural Revolution*, 10.

31. Pingxiang Mining Company Party Committee, ed., *Mao Zedong, Liu Shaoqi, Li Lisan zai Anyuan de gushi* [Stories of Mao Zedong, Liu Shaoqi, and Li Lisan at Anyuan] (Beijing: Chinese Communist Party History Press, 1998), 3.

32. AYLKGRYD, 1: 90.

33. Ibid., 1: 99.

34. Chinese Academy of Social Sciences and Anyuan Labor Movement Memorial Hall, eds., *Liu Shaoqi yu Anyuan gongren yundong* [Liu Shaoqi and the Anyuan labor movement] (Beijing: Chinese Academy of Social Sciences Press, 1981), 181.

35. Propaganda Department of the Chinese Communist Party Committee of the Pingxiang Mining Company, ed., *Hongse Anyuan* [Red Anyuan] (Nanchang: Jiangxi People's Press, 1981), 208–9.

36. AYLKGRYD, 1: 91.

37. Pingxiang Municipal Trade Union and Anyuan Labor Movement Memorial Hall, eds., *Anyuan lukuang gongren da bagong shengli liushi zhounian jinian huace* [Picture book to commemorate the sixtieth anniversary of the victory of the Anyuan railway and mine workers Great Strike] (Anyuan: n.p., 1982), 25, 29.

38. AYLKGRYD, 1: 221–22.

39. Ibid., 2: 920.

40. Chinese Academy of Social Sciences and Anyuan Labor Movement Memorial Hall, eds., *Liu Shaoqi yu Anyuan gongren yundong*, 156, 186; AYLKGRYD, 1: 326–29.

41. Li Lisan was repaid eighty of the ninety yuan he had loaned the club soon after its inauguration. AYLKGRYD, 1: 327–28.

42. Ibid., 2: 894

43. Ibid., 1: 93.

44. Nym Wales, *The Chinese Labor Movement* (New York: John Day, 1945), 40.

45. AYLKGRYD, 1: 178, 347. Percentages were recalculated from the raw figures provided.

46. Ibid., 1: 290–95.

47. Liu Jialin, "Ershi niandai Anyuan gongren jiaoyu" [Anyuan workers' education in the 1920s], *Jiangxi gongyunshi yanjiu ziliao* 3 (August 10, 1982): 48–49.

48. Huang Aiguo, "Anyuan lukuang gongren dushuchu" [Anyuan railway and mine workers' reading rooms], in *Anyuan lukuang gongren yundongshi yanjiu wenhui* [Compilation of studies on the Anyuan railway and mine workers' movement], ed. Pingxiang City History Gazetteer Office (Nanchang: Jiangxi People's Press, 2002), 294.

49. AYLKGRYD, 1: 179–81.

50. Pingxiang City History Gazetteer Office, ed., *Zhonggong Pingxiang difangshi,* 131–32; Deng Qipei, "Anyuan gongyun shi wodang jiti fendou de guanghui fanli" [The Anyuan labor movement is a glorious example of our party's collective struggles], in *Anyuan lukuang gongren yundongshi yanjiu wenhui,* 33; Yang Fangping and Huang Aiguo, "Liu Shaoqi lingdao Anyuan gongren yundong de lishi gongxian" [The historical contributions of Liu Shaoqi in leading the Anyuan labor movement], in *Anyuan lukuang gongren yundongshi yanjiu wenhui,* 38; AYLKGRYD, 1: 111 and 2: 1215.

51. Although virtually all the workers employed by the Anyuan railway and mining company were male, a number of them had wives living near the mine.

52. Propaganda Department of the Chinese Communist Party Committee of the Pingxiang Mining Company, ed., *Hongse Anyuan,* 199; Pingxiang City History Gazetteer Office, ed., *Zhonggong Pingxiang difangshi,* 131; AYLKGRYD, 1: 269, 342.

53. AYLKGRYD, 2: 1008.

54. Ibid., 2: 868–69.

55. Yang Fangping, "Lueshu Anyuan gongyunzhong dang dui gongren zhi jiaoyu" [A brief discussion of the party's education of workers in the Anyuan labor movement], *Dangshi tongxun* [Party history bulletin] 2 (1987): 12; AYLKGRYD, 1: 269. Compelling recalcitrant illiterate workers to attend classes was also Bolshevik policy, codified in Lenin's decree of December 1919. See Peter Kenez, *The Birth of the Propaganda State: Soviet Methods of Mass Mobilization* (New York: Cambridge University Press, 1985), 150.

56. AYLKGRYD, 2: 946–47.

57. Ibid., 1: 104.

58. Ibid., 2: 782. Huang Aiguo, "Anyuan lukuang gonghui jiaoyugu bianyin de 'xiaoxue guoyu jiaokeshu'" [The "Elementary Chinese Primer" edited by the education department of the Anyuan railway and mine workers' union], in *Anyuan lukuang gongren yundongshi wenhui,* 379–81.

59. As Wu explains in his autobiography, in 1925, at the age of ten, he studied in the fourth grade at one of the Communist Party's schools for Anyuan miners' children. Wu Yunduo, *Son of the Working Class* (Peking: Foreign Languages Press, 1956), 16. Pavel Korchagin was the central character in the famous Soviet novel *How the Steel Was Tempered,* written by Nikolai Ostrovsky (1904–36).

60. AYLKGRYD, 2: 828–38.

61. Ibid., 2: 821–22.

62. Ibid., 2: 1001.

63. On the importance of this standard in the PRC, see Donald J. Munro, "Egalitarian Ideal and Educational Fact in Communist China," in *China: Management of a Revolutionary Society,* ed. John M. H. Lindbeck (Seattle: University of Washington Press, 1971); Susan Shirk, *Competitive Comrades* (Berkeley: University of California Press, 1982); and Andrew G. Walder, *Communist Neo-Traditionalism: Work and Authority in Chinese Industry*

(Berkeley: University of California Press, 1986). I am indebted to Steve Smith for pointing out the lack of a Soviet equivalent.

64. Chinese Academy of Social Sciences and Anyuan Labor Movement Memorial Hall, eds., *Liu Shaoqi yu Anyuan gongren yundong,* 161.

65. Yan Ziming, "Zhonggong zuizao de difang dangxiao" [The earliest local Communist Party school], in *Anyuan lukuang gongren yundongshi yanjiu wenhui,* 292–93; Pingxiang City History Gazetteer Office, ed., *Zhonggong Pingxiang difangshi,* 130; Yang, "Lueshu Anyuan gongyunzhong dang dui gongren zhi jiaoyu," 14; Pingxiang Party School, ed., *Zhongguo gongchandang zui zao de dangxiao* [The Chinese Communist Party's earliest party school] (Pingxiang: Pingxiang Education Press, 2004). The last source was published for internal circulation only.

66. Liu, *Anyuan lukuang gongren yundongshi,* 214–19.

67. AYLKGRYD, 1: 186.

68. Vladimir Brovkin, *Russia after Lenin: Politics, Culture and Society, 1921–1929* (London: Routledge, 1998), 84–93.

69. Pingxiang City History Gazetteer Office, ed., *Zhonggong Pingxiang difangshi,* 133.

70. Liu, *Anyuan lukuang gongren yundongshi,* 256.

71. AYLKGRYD, 2: 919.

72. Wu Lie, "Yi Anyuan lukuang gongren geming yundong" [The revolutionary movement of the Anyuan railway and mine workers], *Pingxiang dangshi tongshi* [Pingxiang party history bulletin] 3 (1985): 16–17.

73. AYLKGRYD, 1: 332–33.

74. Ibid., 2: 1014.

75. Kenez, *The Birth of the Propaganda State,* 58.

76. AYLKGRYD, 2: 941.

77. Pingxiang City History Gazetteer Office, ed., *Zhonggong Pingxiang difangshi,* 132, 162.

78. Liu, *Anyuan lukuang gongren yundongshi,* 222.

79. AYLKGRYD, 2: 903.

80. Ibid., 2: 946.

81. Drawing attention to this continuity, David Holm notes that in the Yan'an period the CCP set out to lay claim to the Mandate of Heaven by staging massive public festivities reminiscent of those of earlier rebels. David Holm, *Art and Ideology in Revolutionary China* (New York: Oxford University Press, 1991), 333.

82. Kenez, *The Birth of the Propaganda State,* 139.

83. On Republican patterns, see Henrietta Harrison, *The Making of the Republican Citizen: Ceremonies and Symbols in China, 1911–1929* (New York: Oxford University Press, 2000).

84. AYLKGRYD, 2: 1172.

85. *Pingxiang gujin* 6 (May 1985): 8–9, 33; 8 (March 1987): 31.

86. *Pingxiang gujin* 6 (May 1985): 26.

87. Karl Gerth, *China Made: Consumer Culture and the Creation of the Nation* (Cambridge, MA: Harvard University Asia Center, 2003), 4.

88. Li Lisan would serve as chair and Liu Shaoqi as general manager of the Shanghai General Labor Union, which provided overall direction for the May Thirtieth Movement. On that occasion, Li made good use of his Anyuan experience by forging critical alliances with secret-society chieftains. See Elizabeth J. Perry, *Shanghai on Strike: The Politics of Chinese Labor* (Stanford, CA: Stanford University Press, 1993), 81.

89. AYLKGRYD, 1: 190.

90. Propaganda Department of the Chinese Communist Party Committee of the Pingxiang Mining Company, ed., *Hongse Anyuan*, 153.

91. Liu, *Anyuan lukuang gongren yundongshi*, 228–31.

92. AYLKGRYD, 1: 155. Nearly a hundred of those expelled were later reinstated.

93. Liu, *Anyuan lukuang gongren yundongshi*, 232–33.

94. Ibid., 233–34; AYLKGRYD, 1: 198.

95. *Pingxiang meitan fazhan shilue* [Brief history of the development of the Pingxiang coal industry], combined issue of *Jiangxi wenshi ziliao xuanji* 23 and *Pingxiang wenshi ziliao* 6 (1987): 79.

96. Zhang, Liu, and Liu, *Anyuan da bagong qianhou*, 45; Pingxiang City History Gazetteer Office, ed., *Zhonggong Pingxiang difangshi*, 85–86.

97. AYLKGRYD, 1: 363.

98. Liu, *Anyuan lukuang gongren yundongshi*, 245–46; AYLKGRYD, 2: 996–97.

99. AYLKGRYD, 1: 900.

100. Liu, *Anyuan lukuang gongren yundongshi*, 244–45.

101. *Pingxiang meitan fazhan shilue*, 77–84; AYLKGRYD, 2: 1272–88.

102. *Pingxiang meitan fazhan shilue*, 31.

103. Editorial Committee of Pingxiang Mining Company Gazetteer, ed., *Pingxiang kuangwuju zhi* [Gazetteer of Pingxiang Mining Company] (Pingxiang: n.p., 1998): 89.

104. *Hanyeping gongsi dang'an shiliao xuanbian* [Selection of archival materials of the Hanyeping Company] (Beijing: Chinese Academy of Social Sciences Press, 1992), 2: 262.

105. AYLKGRYD, 2: 866.

106. Propaganda Department of the Chinese Communist Party Committee of the Pingxiang Mining Company, ed., *Hongse Anyuan*, 149–50; Zhang, *Anyuan yishi*, 137–38; Pingxiang Propaganda Department, ed., *Liu Shaoqi zai Anyuan de gushi* [Stories of Liu Shaoqi at Anyuan] (Shanghai: Shanghai People's Press, 1980), 38–40.

107. Zhang, *Anyuan yishi*, 130.

108. Ibid., 133.

109. Editorial Committee of Pingxiang Mining Company Gazetteer, ed., *Pingxiang kuangwuju zhi*, 98.

110. Anyuan Labor Movement Memorial Hall, ed., *Anyuan lukuang gon-*

*gren yundong shiliao* [Historical materials on the Anyuan railway and mine workers' movement] (Changsha: Hunan People's Press, 1991), 769–71.

111. Memoir of Li Lisan, June 1963, in AYLKGRYD, 2: 904.

112. Pingxiang City History Gazetteer Office, ed., *Zhonggong Pingxiang difangshi*, 107.

113. AYLKGRYD, 2: 920.

114. Liu, *Anyuan lukuang gongren yundongshi*, 165; AYLKGRYD, 1: 135–36.

115. Liu Shanwen and Huang Aiguo, "Li Lisan zai Anyuan shiliao shulue" [Historical materials on Li Lisan at Anyuan], in *Anyuan lukuang gongren yundong yanjiu wenhui*, 276–77; *Liu Shaoqi lun gongren yundong* [Liu Shaoqi discusses the labor movement] (Beijing: Central Documents Press, 1988), 144.

116. *Liu Shaoqi lun gongren yundong*, 216.

117. AYLKGRYD, 1: 98.

118. Liu, *Anyuan lukuang gongren yundongshi*, 167; AYLKGRYD, 1: 134–35.

119. These details were relayed to Anyuan party historian Huang Aiguo in a series of interviews that he conducted with Yuan Pin'gao, Liu Shaoqi's former bodyguard and a member of the workers' pickets under Xie Huaide. Interview with Huang Aiguo at Pingxiang Communist Party School, October 23, 2009.

120. AYLKGRYD, 1: 97, 100.

121. Ibid., 1: 237–51.

122. Liu, *Anyuan lukuang gongren yundongshi*, 242–44.

123. AYLKGRYD, 1: 234.

124. Xie Jiajun, "Anyuan lukuang gongren julebu jindu" [The Anyuan railway and mine workers' club's gambling prohibition], *Pingxiang dangshi tongxun* [Pingxiang party history bulletin] 1 (1990): 40.

125. AYLKGRYD, 1: 235.

126. Ibid., 1: 159.

127. Ibid., 1: 198.

128. *Pingxiang meitan fazhan shilue*, 84–88. The gratitude that the Hunan gentry felt for Li Shouquan could be seen in their farewell gifts: a large ceramic bust in his likeness as well as numerous works of embroidery (for which this area of Hunan is renowned), including an enormous embroidered portrait, encased in glass, which required four men to lift and could not be hung on his wall at home because of its weight.

129. Propaganda Department of the Chinese Communist Party Committee of the Pingxiang Mining Company, ed., *Hongse Anyuan*, 200; Jiangxi Chinese Communist Party History Research Office, ed., *Liu Shaoqi zai Jiangxi* [Liu Shaoqi in Jiangxi] (Beijing: Chinese Communist Party History Press, 1998), 2.

130. For accounts suggesting cordial relations between the Episcopal rector and the strikers, see Ma Hanqin, "Pingxiang jidujiao bainian shilue ji

xianzhuang" [A brief hundred-year history and current situation of Christianity in Pingxiang], *Pingxiang gaodeng zhuanke xuexiao xuebao* 3, no. 1 (2004): 109; and Yan Hailie, "Jiangxi jidujiao shenggonghui shihua" [Historical tales of the Protestant Episcopal Church in Jiangxi], *Wenshi daguan* 1 (1995): 40.

131. Walworth Tyng, "The Miners' Church at Peaceful Spring: Among the Collieries and Coke Ovens at Anyuen—A Vivid Picture of Our Work in a Little Known Part of the District of Hankow," *The Spirit of Missions* 90 (1925): 477.

132. Propaganda Department of the Chinese Communist Party Committee of the Pingxiang Mining Company, ed., *Hongse Anyuan*, 201–3.

133. Liu Jialin, "Ershi niandai Anyuan gongren jiaoyu" [Anyuan workers' education in the 1920s], *Jiangxi gongyunshi yanjiu ziliao* 3 (August 10, 1982): 50–51. Liu's anti-Christian effort was part of a larger, joint CCP-KMT nationalistic campaign against Christianity. See Jessie G. Lutz, "Chinese Nationalism and the Anti-Christian Campaigns of the 1920s," *Modern Asian Studies* 10, no. 3 (1976): 395–416. Similar campaigns, directed against the Russian Orthodox Church, were occurring at this same time in the USSR. See Brovkin, *Russia after Lenin*, 93–107; Daniel Peris, *Storming the Heavens: The Soviet League of the Militant Godless* (Ithaca, NY: Cornell University Press, 1998), 28.

134. Propaganda Department of the Chinese Communist Party Committee of the Pingxiang Mining Company, ed., *Hongse Anyuan*, 163–99.

135. AYLKGRYD, 2: 950.

136. Liu, *Anyuan lukuang gongren yundongshi*, 171–75; AYLKGRYD, 2: 941–42.

137. Letter from J. Calvin Huston (April 23, 1925), quoted in Lynda Shaffer, *Mao and the Workers: The Hunan Labor Movement, 1920–1923* (Armonk, NY: M. E. Sharpe, 1982), 104.

138. Liu, *Anyuan lukuang gongren yundongshi*, 178–91.

139. Ibid., 192–93; Yu Jianrong, *Yuecun zhengzhi* [The politics of Yue Village] (Beijing: Commercial Press, 2001), 142–70.

140. AYLKGRYD, 2: 1380.

141. Gong Yiqing, "Guanyu Andi gongzuo shibai hou tongzhi beibu jingguo de xiangxi qingkuang baogao" [Detailed situation report on comrades arrested after the failure of the work at Anyuan], *Pingxiang dangshi tongxun* [Pingxiang party history bulletin] 4 (1985): 7–8.

142. AYLKGRYD, 1: 526, 574.

143. Zhang, *Anyuan yishi*, 174; Liu, *Anyuan lukuang gongren yundongshi*, 258–62.

144. *Shen Bao*, October 21, 1925, in AYLKGRYD, 2: 1217–19.

145. AYLKGRYD, 2: 927.

146. Pingxiang City History Gazetteer Office, ed., *Zhonggong Pingxiang difangshi*, 166–72; Huang Aiguo, "Anyuan jiuyue can'an de jingguo" [The

September Massacre at Anyuan], in *Anyuan lukuang gongren yundong yanjiu wenhui*, 298–304; AYLKGRYD, 1: 574; 2: 913, 1340.

147. *Pingxiang meikuang fazhan shilue*, 31.

148. Pingxiang City History Gazetteer Office, ed., *Zhonggong Pingxiang difangshi*, 173; Zhang, *Anyuan yishi*, 183; Liu, *Anyuan lukuang gongren yundongshi*, 259.

149. Chang Kuo-t'ao, "Introduction," in *Collected Works of Liu Shao-ch'i* (Hong Kong: Union Research Institute, 1969), iv.

150. AYLKGRYD, 1: 909–10.

151. Liu, *Anyuan lukuang gongren yundongshi*, 231.

152. Dittmer, *Liu Shao-ch'i and the Chinese Cultural Revolution*.

153. V.I. Lenin, "On Cooperation," in *Collected Works*, 2nd English ed. (Moscow: Progress Publishers, 1965), 33: 467–75.

154. Peter Kenez points out that in some cases the Russian peasantry was so hostile to the directors of village reading rooms and their mission of political education that they and their families were subject to physical danger. Kenez, *The Birth of the Propaganda State*, 141. Vladimir Brovkin asserts that Russian villagers "detested the libraries as centers of anti-religious campaigns. . . . Campaigns of the 1920s on the ideological front, to overturn customs, traditions, way of life, and religiosity failed dismally." Brovkin, *Russia after Lenin*, 92, 107. James von Geldern observes of this same period that "there was a ceaseless struggle between what Bolsheviks thought should be read and what people wanted to read." James von Geldern, "Introduction," in *Mass Culture in Soviet Russia*, ed. James von Geldern and Richard Stites (Bloomington: Indiana University Press, 1995), xvi.

155. Kam Louie and Louise Edwards, "Chinese Masculinity: Theorizing Wen and Wu," *East Asian History* 8 (1994): 138–94.

156. Cheng–Hua Fang, "Power Structures and Cultural Identities in Imperial China: Civil and Military Power from Late Tang to Early Song Dynasties," PhD diss., Brown University, 2001.

157. Liu Shaoqi, "Er qi shibai hou de Anyuan gonghui" [The Anyuan union after the February 7 defeat] (April 1925), in AYLKGRYD, 1: 446.

158. Jung Chang and Jon Halliday, *Mao: The Unknown Story* (New York: Alfred A. Knopf, 2005).

159. "Di 'Hunan quansheng qingxiang zongbaogao shu' zhailu" [Excerpts from the enemy's "Hunan All-Province Village Pacification General Report"], in *Anyuan lukuang gongren yundongshi ziliao huibian* [Compilation of historical materials on the Anyuan railway and mine workers' movement], ed. Anyuan Railway and Mine Workers' Labor Movement Memorial Hall 2, no. 6 (1984): 26. This unpublished collection of primary sources, held at the Anyuan Memorial Hall Archives, is marked "top secret."

160. According to incomplete statistics, more than 3,280 workers, 3,180 children, and 100 women graduated from the Communists' schools at Anyuan in the period between 1921 and 1925. Yang, "Lueshu Anyuan gongyunzhong dang dui gongren zhi jiaoyu," 17.

4. FROM MOBILIZATION TO MILITARIZATION

1. Pingxiang Municipal Party Committee, ed., *Anyuan lukuang gongren yundong* [Anyuan railway and mine workers' movement] (Beijing: Chinese Communist Party Historical Materials Press, 1990), 1: 526–27 (hereafter cited as AYLKGRYD); Liu Shanwen, *Anyuan lukuang gongren yundongshi* [History of the Anyuan railway and mine workers' movement] (Shanghai: Shanghai Academy of Social Sciences Press, 1993), 261–62.

2. Liu, *Anyuan lukuang gongren yundongshi*, 265; Zhang Zhenchu, *Anyuan yishi* [Anyuan anecdotes] (Pingxiang: Anyuan Coal Mine, 1995), 180.

3. AYLKGRYD, 1: 539.

4. Ibid., 1: 542.

5. Ibid., 2: 915.

6. Ibid., 2: 921.

7. John W. Lewis, "Leader, Commissar and Bureaucrat: The Chinese Political System in the Last Days of the Revolution," in *China in Crisis*, ed. Ping-ti Ho and Tang Tsou (Chicago: University of Chicago Press, 1968), vol. 1, book A: 449–81; Lowell Dittmer, *Liu Shao-ch'i and the Chinese Cultural Revolution: The Politics of Mass Criticism* (Berkeley: University of California Press, 1974).

8. AYLKGRYD, 1: 532–33.

9. Liu, *Anyuan lukuang gongren yundongshi*, 268–70.

10. AYLKGRYD, 1: 574.

11. Ibid., 1: 659.

12. Zhang, *Anyuan yishi*, 149.

13. AYLKGRYD, 2: 1384. Numerous other coal miners who had studied at the Anyuan workers' schools followed a similar pattern of returning to their home villages in Hunan as part of the Northern Expedition, after receiving training in Guangzhou, to serve as military propagandists and founders of peasant associations. These included, among many others, Yuan Desheng, Yuan Dexi, Tang Zhenglun, Zhu Changyan, and Zhao Guocheng. Capsule biographies can be found in AYLKGRYD, 2: 1394–1405.

14. *Anyuan lukuang gongren julebu shihua* [Historical tales of the Anyuan railway and mining workers' club] (Nanchang: Jiangxi People's Press, 1983), 65.

15. Chiang Kai-shek referred to this incident in his diary entry for September 20, 1926, contained in the archives of the Hoover Institution at Stanford University. My appreciation to Matthew Sommer and Hsieh Mei-yu for their help in locating this entry. A report of Chiang's speech can be found in a November 13, 1926, letter from the vice–general manager of the Hanyeping Coal and Iron Company to its board of governors; see AYLKGRYD, 2: 1358. See also Liu, *Anyuan lukuang gongren yundongshi*, 284–85.

16. AYLKGRYD, 2: 928.

17. Pingxiang City History Gazetteer Office, ed., *Zhonggong Pingxiang*

*difangshi* [Local history of the Chinese Communists in Pingxiang] (Beijing: Chinese Communist Party History Press, 2003), 1: 199–200.

18. AYLKGRYD, 2: 1358; Zhang, *Anyuan yishi*, 182.

19. "Xiangqu shuji baogao" [Report of the party secretary of Hunan district], in *Zhonggong zhongyang wenjian xuanji* (October 22, 1926) (Beijing: Central Party School Press, 1982), 2: 297.

20. Hans J. van de Ven, *War and Nationalism in China, 1925–1945* (New York: Routledge Curzon, 2003), 95.

21. Mao Zedong, "Report on an Investigation of the Peasant Movement in Hunan," in *Selected Works of Mao Tsetung* (Beijing: Foreign Languages Press, 1967), 1: 28.

22. Ibid., 1: 46.

23. Zhang Baohui, "Communal Cooperative Institutions and Peasant Revolutions in South China, 1926–1934," *Theory and Society* 29, no. 5 (2000): 702.

24. Stephen C. Averill, *Revolution in the Highlands: China's Jinggangshan Base Area* (Lanham, MD: Rowman & Littlefield, 2006), 234–37.

25. Liu, *Anyuan lukuang gongren yundongshi*, 281–82.

26. AYLKGRYD, 2: 929.

27. Elizabeth J. Perry, *Patrolling the Revolution: Worker Militias, Citizenship and the Modern Chinese State* (Lanham, MD: Rowman and Littlefield, 2006), 80–82.

28. Liu, *Anyuan lukuang gongren yundongshi*, 282–83.

29. Ibid., 291–92.

30. Ibid.; Gao Fei, "Qiangbi da eba dizhu Ye Ziping" [Executing the big hegemonic landlord Ye Ziping], *Pingxiang wenshi ziliao* 2 (December 1984): 136–38; "Pingxiang renmin shenpan tuhao lieshen weiyuanhui ji tebie fating" [The Pingxiang people's committee and special court to try local bullies and evil gentry], *Pingxiang dangshi tongxun* 3 (1988): 42–44.

31. AYLKGRYD, 2: 1031.

32. Liu, *Anyuan lukuang gongren yundongshi*, 293.

33. Pingxiang City History Gazetteer Office, ed., *Zhonggong Pingxiang difangshi*, 215–16.

34. Christina K. Gilmartin, *Engendering the Chinese Revolution: Radical Women, Communist Politics, and Mass Movements in the 1920s* (Berkeley: University of California Press, 1995).

35. Zhang, *Anyuan yishi*, 191.

36. Pingxiang City History Gazetteer Office, ed., *Zhonggong Pingxiang difangshi*, 219.

37. "Pingxiang meikuang gongren guanli kuangshan" [The Pingxiang coal miners manage the mine], *Pingkuang gongren bao* [Pingxiang miners' journal], June 11, 1998. Reprinted in Pingxiang Historical Gazetteer Office, ed., *Anyuan lukuang gongren yundongshi yanjiu wenhui* [Compilation of studies on the Anyuan railway and mine workers' movement] (Nanchang: Jiangxi People's Press, 2002), 418–20.

38. AYLKGRYD, 2: 1243.

39. Chang Kuo-t'ao, *The Rise of the Chinese Communist Party, 1921–1927* (Lawrence: University Press of Kansas, 1971), 606–7. The accuracy of Zhang's account is questioned in Tang Chunliang, *Li Lisan quanzhuan* [Li Lisan's complete biography] (Hefei: Anhui People's Press, 1999), 103–5. Whatever the actual fate of Li Lisan's father, there is no doubt that the revolutionary terror in Hunan's Liling County was extreme.

40. For an account of the April 12 coup, see Nicholas R. Clifford, *Spoilt Children of Empire: Westerners in Shanghai and the Chinese Revolution of the 1920s* (Hanover, NH: Middlebury College Press, 1991), chapter 15.

41. Xing Yuanlin, "Anyuan gongren geming douzheng pianduan huiyi" [Memories of the Anyuan workers' revolutionary struggles], *Pingxiang dangshi tongxun* 6 (1985): 16.

42. Liu, *Anyuan lukuang gongren yundongshi*, 298–307.

43. Roy M. Hofheinz Jr., *The Broken Wave: The Chinese Communist Peasant Movement, 1922–1928* (Cambridge, MA: Harvard University Press, 1977), 53.

44. AYLKGRYD, 1: 636.

45. Ibid., 1: 324.

46. Jiangxi Cultural Office and Anyuan Labor Movement Museum, eds., *Qiushou qiyi zai Jiangxi* [The Autumn Harvest Uprising in Jiangxi] (Beijing: Wenwu Press, 1993), 24.

47. On this process, see Averill, *Revolution in the Highlands*.

48. Pingxiang City History Gazetteer Office, ed., *Zhonggong Pingxiang difangshi*, 275.

49. *Pingxiang meitan fazhan shilue* [Brief history of the development of the Pingxiang coal industry], combined issue of *Jiangxi wenshi ziliao xuanji* 23 and *Pingxiang wenshi ziliao* 6 (1987): 26–32.

50. Jiangxi Cultural Office and Anyuan Labor Movement Museum, eds., *Qiushou qiyi zai Jiangxi*, 31.

51. Ibid., 32

52. Walworth Tyng, "Difficult Days in Hunan: Veteran Missionary Gives Vivid Picture of Unrest in China as Governments Change," *The Spirit of Missions* 92 (1927): 71.

53. Liu, *Anyuan lukuang gongren yundongshi*, 333.

54. AYLKGRYD, 1: 644.

55. Liu, *Anyuan lukuang gongren yundongshi*, 334–37.

56. "Di 'Hunan quansheng qingxiang zongbaogao shu' zhailu" [Excerpts from the enemy's "Hunan All-Province Village Pacification General Report"), in *Anyuan lukuang gongren yundongshi ziliao huibian* [Compilation of historical materials on the Anyuan railway and mine workers' movement], ed. Anyuan Railway and Mine Workers' Labor Movement Memorial Hall, 2, no. 6 (1984): 26. This unpublished collection of primary sources, held at the Anyuan Memorial Hall Archives, is marked "top secret."

57. On the mutual imitation by the Communists and Nationalists in this period, see Perry, *Patrolling the Revolution*, chapter 3.

58. Zhang Dehan, "Wo suo zhidao de 'Anyuan gongren fangong weiyuanhui'" [What I know about the Anyuan workers' anti-Communist commission], *Pingxiang wenshi ziliao* 12 (December 1990): 109–10.

59. "Di 'Hunan quansheng qingxiang zongbaogao shu' zhailu," 136–37, 171–72.

60. Ibid., 170–71.

61. AYLKGRYD, 2: 1095–96.

62. Jianggangshan Revolutionary Base Area Party History Materials Compilation and Editorial Committee, ed., *Jinggangshan geming genjudi* [Jinggangshan revolutionary base area] (Beijing: Chinese Communist Party Historical Materials Press, 1987), 1: 121.

63. *Mao Zedong xuanji* [Selected works of Mao Zedong] (Beijing: People's Press, 1991), 4: 62.

64. Liu, *Anyuan lukuang gongren yundongshi*, 374.

65. Quoted in Pingxiang City History Gazetteer Office, ed., *Zhonggong Pingxiang difangshi*, 323–24.

66. *Shenggong hui bao* [The Chinese churchman] 24, no. 6 (March 15, 1931): 10–11.

67. Wang Yaonan, interview on August 21, 1967, in *Anyuan lukuang gongren yundongshi ziliao huibian* 3, no. 1.

68. Liu Ronghua, interview on May 24, 1969, Anyuan Memorial Hall Archives, file no. 1254.

69. Xu Guisheng, "Qinghongbang fazhan jiankuang ji qi zai Pingxiang de huodong" [The development and situation of the Red and Green gangs and their activities in Pingxiang], *Pingxiang wenshi ziliao* 12 (December 1990): 76.

70. *Pingxiang Anyuan meikuang diaocha baogao* [Investigative report on the Anyuan coal mine in Pingxiang] (Nanchang: Jiangxi Government Economic Commission, 1935), 168–72). Held in the Shanghai Municipal Library.

71. On the wartime takeover of other critical enterprises, see, for example, Mark W. Frazier, *The Making of the Chinese Industrial Workplace* (New York: Cambridge University Press, 2002); and Joshua Howard, *Workers at War: Labor in China's Arsenals* (Stanford, CA: Stanford University Press, 2004).

72. On the role of the NRC in economic administration at this time, see William C. Kirby, *Germany and Republican China* (Stanford, CA: Stanford University Press, 1984).

73. Propaganda Department of the Chinese Communist Party Committee of the Pingxiang Mining Company, ed., *Hongse Anyuan* [Red Anyuan] (Nanchang: Jiangxi People's Press, 1981), 451.

74. Ibid., 459.

75. Pingxiang City History Gazetteer Office, ed., *Zhonggong Pingxiang difangshi*, 478.

76. Propaganda Department of the Chinese Communist Party Commit-

tee of the Pingxiang Mining Company, ed., *Hongse Anyuan* [Red Anyuan] (Nanchang: Jiangxi People's Press, 1959), 504. For more on the various editions of *Hongse Anyuan*, see chapter 5.

77. Pingxiang Municipal Union Editorial Committee, ed., *Pingxiangshi gonghuizhi* [Pingxiang city union gazetteer] (Pingxiang: n.p., 1999), 38.

78. Pingxiang Party Committee Editorial Committee, ed., *Pingxiang renmin geming douzhengshi* [History of the people's revolutionary struggles in Pingxiang] (Pingxiang: n.p., 1962), 153. On the Pingjiang Incident, see Gregor Benton, *The New Fourth Army: Communist Resistance along the Yangtze and the Huai, 1938–1941* (Berkeley: University of California Press, 1999).

79. National History Archives (Taipei), file no. 003–010305–0205, contains NRC reports from August 1946 to March 1948 on the revival of illegal private mining in the Anyuan area.

80. Pingxiang Municipal Union Editorial Committee, ed., *Pingxiangshi gonghuizhi*, 38.

81. Pingxiang Mining Company Editorial Committee, ed., *Pingxiang kuangwuju zhi* [Pingxiang Mining Company gazetteer] (Pingxiang: n.p., 1998), 16.

82. Pingxiang Party Committee Editorial Committee, ed., *Pingxiang renmin geming douzhengshi*, 153–54.

83. Ibid., 155.

84. Ibid., 156.

85. Ibid., 156–57.

86. Ibid., 158, 166–67; *Anyuan meikuang shi* [History of the Anyuan coal mine] (Changsha: Hunan Normal College, 1958), 156.

87. Dittmer, *Liu Shao-ch'i and the Chinese Cultural Revolution*, 11–29.

88. A November 16, 1930, letter from the Comintern criticized Li Lisan for "adventurist" errors of "line" for blindly attacking cities without developing a consolidated rural revolutionary base. This criticism precipitated Li's resignation from the CCP Politburo on November 25 and his departure from China soon thereafter. Derek J. Waller, *The Kiangsi Soviet Republic: Mao and the National Congresses of 1931 and 1934* (Berkeley: University of California Center for Chinese Studies, 1973), 16.

89. Edgar Snow, *Red Star over China* (New York: Grove Press, 1968), 146.

90. Quoted in Liu Tao and Liu Yunzhen, "Kan Liu Shaoqi de qiu'e linghun" [See Liu Shaoqi's evil spirit], January 2, 1967, in *Zhongguo wenhua da geming wenku* [The Chinese Cultural Revolution database], ed. Song Yongyi (Hong Kong: University Services Centre, 2002).

91. Anna Louise Strong, *China's Millions* (New York: Coward-McCann, 1928), 100.

92. Ibid., 103–4.

93. Nym Wales, *The Chinese Labor Movement* (New York: John Day, 1945), 32–33.

94. Yu Jianrong, *Zhongguo gongren jieji zhuangkuang: Anyuan shilu* [The

plight of China's working class: Annals of Anyuan] (Hong Kong: Mirror Books, 2006), 67–68.

95. Chang-tai Hung, *War and Popular Culture: Resistance in Modern China, 1937–1945* (Berkeley: University of California, 1994), 221. On the contrast between the KMT and CCP, see 278–79.

96. Robert C. North, *Kuomintang and Chinese Communist Elites* (Stanford, CA: Stanford University Press, 1952).

97. As David Holm observes, the dramas and music of the Jiangxi Soviet, which formed the basis of Red Army cultural production for years to come, were inspired by southern Jiangxi-Hunan traditions. David Holm, *Art and Ideology in Revolutionary China* (New York: Oxford University Press, 1991), 28–29.

98. On the importance of "red theater" to the Communist revolution, see Snow, *Red Star over China*, 119–25.

99. For a description of workers' cultural palaces in the Soviet Union, see John Dewey, *Impressions of Soviet Russia and the Revolutionary World* (New York: New Republic, 1929). Although the Chinese institution was modeled on Soviet precedent, the cultural activities that took place inside evidenced an obvious local flavor.

100. Paul Pickowicz, *Marxist Literary Thought in China: The Influence of Ch'u Ch'iu-pai* (Berkeley: University of California Press, 1981), 107, 172–73.

101. Holm, *Art and Ideology in Revolutionary China*, 20.

102. Pickowicz, *Marxist Literary Thought in China*, 228–31.

103. Holm, *Art and Ideology in Revolutionary China*, 55.

104. Jack Belden, *China Shakes the World* (New York: Monthly Review Press, 1949), 63.

## 5. CONSTRUCTING A REVOLUTIONARY TRADITION

1. Pingxiang Mining Company Editorial Committee, ed., *Pingxiang kuangwuju zhi* [Pingxiang Mining Company gazetteer] (Pingxiang: n.p., 1998), 17.

2. Richard Curt Kraus, *The Party and the Arty in China: The New Politics of Culture* (Lanham, MD: Rowman & Littlefield, 2004), 37, 48–49.

3. Chang-tai Hung, *Mao's New World: Political Culture in the Early People's Republic* (Ithaca, NY: Cornell University Press, 2010), 257.

4. Julian Chang, "The Mechanics of State Propaganda: The People's Republic of China and the Soviet Union in the 1950s," in *New Perspectives on State Socialism in China*, ed. Timothy Cheek and Tony Saich (Armonk, NY: M. E. Sharpe, 1997), 76.

5. In January 1951 a woman by the name of Song Weijing was appointed to replace Guo as head of the Pingxiang Mining Bureau, but for some reason she did not actually take up the post, and Guo continued to exercise administrative authority. When a reorganized Communist Party committee was established at the mining bureau later that year, it eclipsed Guo's authority.

Even so, Guo remained in place for another year, until June 1952. Pingxiang Mining Company Editorial Committee, ed., *Pingxiang kuangwuju zhi*, 18, 711. Holdovers from the Nationalist era notwithstanding, the new order was hardly business as usual; in the four months after Liberation, according to the Pingxiang Public Security Bureau, more than 140 "evil hegemons" were arrested and 1,043 Nationalists, policemen, and "bandits" were either detained or executed. See Pingxiang City Public Security History Gazetteer Office, ed., *Pingxiang gong'an zhi* [Pingxiang municipal public security gazetteer] (Beijing: Police Education Press, 1991), 9. This is an internal-circulation publication.

6. Pingxiang Mining Company Editorial Committee, ed., *Pingxiang kuangwuju zhi*, 17; Hunan Normal College, ed., *Anyuan meikuan shi* [History of the Anyuan coal mine], mimeographed draft manuscript, Changsha, December 1958, 158.

7. Pingxiang City Public Security History Gazetteer Office, ed., *Pingxiang gong'an zhi*, 63.

8. Julia C. Strauss, "Paternalist Terror: The Campaign to Suppress Counterrevolutionaries and Regime Consolidation in the People's Republic of China, 1950–1953," *Comparative Studies in Society and History* 44, no. 1 (January 2002): 80–105; Yang Kuisong, "Reconsidering the Campaign to Suppress Counterrevolutionaries," *China Quarterly* 193 (2008): 102–21.

9. Hunan Normal College, ed., *Anyuan meikuang shi*, 158–59.

10. For a discussion of the campaign in Shanghai factories, see Elizabeth J. Perry, *Patrolling the Revolution: Worker Militias, Citizenship and the Modern Chinese State* (Lanham, MD: Rowman & Littlefield, 2006). In Pingxiang, just over 5 percent of the county's population was attacked during the campaign. Pingxiang City Public Security History Gazetteer Office, ed., *Pingxiang gong'an zhi*, 64.

11. For a revealing compilation of thousands of cases of sectarian-based opposition to the new Communist regime in virtually all regions of the country, see Gao Quanli, ed., *Zhongguo huidaomen shiliao jicheng* [Compilation of historical materials on Chinese sectarian groups] (Beijing: Chinese Academy of Social Sciences Press, 2004), 2 vols. Volume 1, pp. 599–600 discusses Pingxiang.

12. Wen Yuncheng and Shi Zongzheng, "Huazhong fangong jiuguojun de chansheng ji qi miewang" [The rise and demise of the Central China Anti-Communist National Salvation Army], *Pingxiang wenshi ziliao* 4 (1985): 7.

13. "Zhang Guangxin de zibai" [The confession of Zhang Guangxin], *Pingxiang wenshi ziliao* 4 (1985): 68–69.

14. Wen and Shi, "Huazhong fangong jiuguojun de chansheng ji qi miewang," 9–10; Wang Zhongmin, "Huazhong fangong jiuguojun zai Pingxiang meikuang de fumie" [The destruction of the Central China Anti-Communist National Salvation Army at the Pingxiang coal mine], *Pingxiang wenshi ziliao* 4 (1985): 46.

15. Huang Shiguo, ed., *Pingxiangshi zhi* [Pingxiang city gazetteer] (Bei-

jing: Gazetteer Press, 1996), 899; Pingxiang City Public Security History Gazetteer Office, ed., *Pingxiang gong'an zhi*, 72–73.

16. "Zhou Xuezhi de zibai" [The confession of Zhou Xuezhi], *Pingxiang wenshi ziliao* 4 (1985): 67; Huang Shiguo, ed., *Pingxiangshi zhi*, 898–99.

17. Wang "Huazhong fangong jiuguojun zai Pingxiang meikuang de fumie," 44.

18. Pingxiang City Public Security History Gazetteer Office, ed., *Pingxiang gong'an zhi*, 76.

19. Hunan Normal College, ed., *Anyuan meikuang shi*, 160.

20. Pingxiang City Public Security History Gazetteer Office, ed., *Pingxiang gong'an zhi*, 158–72.

21. According to the Public Security Bureau gazetteer, it was not until 1986 that Pingxiang experienced another attempted rebellion. That year a millenarian Buddhist group known as the Longhua Assembly, with forty-eight members in Hunan and Jiangxi, was suppressed on the grounds that they were organizing a "counterrevolutionary" insurgency. Ibid., 74–75.

22. Hunan Normal College, ed., *Anyuan meikuang shi*, 161–63.

23. Pingxiang Mining Company Editorial Committee, ed., *Pingxiang kuangwuju zhi*, 226.

24. Ibid., 463.

25. Zhu Xun, ed., *Zhongguo kuangye shi* [The history of Chinese mining] (Beijing: Geology Press, 2010), 192 ff.

26. Chinese Academy of Social Sciences Modern History Institute, ed., *Liu Shaoqi yu Anyuan gongren yundong* [Liu Shaoqi and the Anyuan labor movement] (Beijing: Chinese Academy of Social Sciences Press, 1981), 72. Although the date on Liu's reply letter did not indicate a year, and while some sources suggest that the exchange occurred in 1953 or even later, the 1952 dating is generally accepted by local party historians.

27. Ibid., 178.

28. Pingxiang Mining Company Party Committee, ed., *Mao Zedong, Liu Shaoqi, Li Lisan zai Anyuan de gushi* [Stories of Mao Zedong, Liu Shaoqi, and Li Lisan at Anyuan] (Beijing: Chinese Communist Party History Press, 1998), 204.

29. Pingxiang Mining Company Editorial Committee, ed., *Pingxiang kuangwuju zhi*, 22–23; Chinese Academy of Social Sciences, ed., *Anyuan gongren yundong de lishi burong diandao* [The history of the Anyuan labor movement must not be turned upside down] (Beijing: n.p., 1967), 17.

30. Feng Chongyi, "Jiangxi in Reform: The Fear of Exclusion and the Search for a New Identity," in *The Political Economy of China's Provinces: Comparative and Competitive Advantage*, ed. Hans Hendrischke and Feng Chongyi (London: Routledge, 1999), 256.

31. *Fandong yingpian Liaoyuan chulong ji* [A record of the launching of the reactionary film *Prairie Fire*], Cultural Revolution handbill produced by the Shanghai East Is Red Movie Company, n.d. Held in the Pingxiang City Library.

32. See Peng Jiangliu's account in *Pingxiang Gujin* [Pingxiang past and present] 2 (August 1982): 108.

33. Hunan Normal College, ed., *Anyuan meikuang shi*, 166–67; Propaganda Department of the Chinese Communist Party Committee of the Pingxiang Mining Company, ed., *Hongse de Anyuan* [Red Anyuan] (Beijing: Writers' Press, 1961), 357; *Pingxiang ribao* [Pingxiang daily], September 26, 2004.

34. Pingxiang Party Committee Party History Editorial Office, ed., *Pingxiang yinglie* [Heroic martyrs of Pingxiang] (Pingxiang: Pingxiang Press, 1986), 72–77.

35. Propaganda Department of the Chinese Communist Party Committee of the Pingxiang Mining Company, ed., *Hongse de Anyuan* (1961 edition), 357–58.

36. Hunan Normal College, ed., *Anyuan meikuang shi*, 167.

37. Zhu Peiyun, "Fang Anyuan meikuang" [A visit to the Anyuan coal mine], *Luxingjia* [Traveler] 3 (1956): 7–8.

38. *Hongan zhanbao* [Red An(yuan) Battle Bulletin], July 5, 1967. Red Guard newspaper held in the Pingxiang City Library.

39. Hunan Normal College, ed., *Anyuan meikuang shi*, 167–68.

40. Pingxiang Mining Company Party Committee, ed., *Mao Zedong, Liu Shaoqi, Li Lisan zai Anyuan*, 202.

41. *Renmin ribao* [People's daily], September 22, 1949.

42. Liu Shaoqi, in a March 1949 talk at Xibaipo, in *Liu Shaoqi xuanji* [Selected works of Liu Shaoqi] (Beijing: People's Press, 1981), 1: 421.

43. Elizabeth J. Perry, "From Native Place to Workplace: Labor Origins and Outcomes of China's Danwei System," in *Danwei: The Changing Chinese Workplace in Historical and Comparative Perspective*, ed. Lu Xiaobo and Elizabeth J. Perry (Armonk, NY: M. E. Sharpe, 1997).

44. Elizabeth J. Perry, "Masters of the Country? Shanghai Workers in the Early PRC," in *Dilemmas of Victory: The Early Years of the People's Republic of China*, ed. Jeremy Brown and Paul Pickowicz (Cambridge, MA: Harvard University Press, 2007), 59–79.

45. Shanghai Municipal Archives, file no. C1-2-240.

46. Tang Chunliang, *Li Lisan zhuan* [Biography of Li Lisan] (Harbin: Heilongjiang People's Press, 1989), 153.

47. Paul Harper, "The Party and the Unions in Communist China," *China Quarterly* 37 (1969): 96. See also Jackie Sheehan, *Chinese Workers: A New History* (New York: Routledge, 1998), chapter 1.

48. Liu Shaoqi, "Guoying gongchang neibu de maodun he gonghui gongzuo de jiben renwu" [Internal contradictions in state factories and the basic responsibilities of union work], in *Liu Shaoqi lun gongren yundong* [Liu Shaoqi discusses the labor movement], ed. Chinese Communist Party Central Documents Research Office (Beijing: Central Documents Press, 1988), 407.

49. Li Sishen, *Li Lisan zhi mi* [The puzzle of Li Lisan] (Beijing: Xinhua Press, 2005), 337–53.

50. On the origins and outcome of the strike wave, see Elizabeth J. Perry, "Shanghai's Strike Wave of 1957," *China Quarterly* 137 (March 1994).

51. Shanghai Municipal Archives, file no. C1-2-2255.

52. Pingxiang Mining Company Editorial Committee, ed., *Pingxiang kuangwuju zhi*, 24.

53. "Chedi qingsuan Liu Shaoqi zai Anyuan de fangeming zuixing" [Thoroughly eliminate Liu Shaoqi's counterrevolutionary crimes at Anyuan], *Xin Beida*, April 25, 1967, 6. Reprinted in Yuan Zhou, ed., *A New Collection of Red Guard Publications*, (Oakton, VA: Center for Chinese Research Materials, 1991), part I, vol. 15, 7195.

54. For various versions of the story, see Bai Yang, ed., *Anyuan gongren douzheng gushi* [Stories of the struggles of Anyuan workers] (Nanchang: Jiangxi People's Press, 1954), 15–20; *Mao Zhuxi diyici dao Anyuan* [Chairman Mao's first trip to Anyuan] (Beijing: Writer's Press, 1959), 36–42.

55. "Pingxiang caichaxi jianjie" [A brief introduction to Pingxiang's tea-picking opera], *Pingxiang gujin* [Pingxiang past and present] 4 (December 1984): 300.

56. Chen Huansheng, *Shuochang: 1922nian Anyuan da bagong* [Popular opera: The Anyuan Great Strike of 1922] (Nanchang: Jiangxi People's Press, 1956). A longer version of the opera, published in 1959, did make brief mention of Mao and Li, but the climax of the drama remains Liu Shaoqi's courageous negotiations on behalf of the workers. Xiao Song, *Anyuan da bagong* [The Anyuan Great Strike] (Beijing: China Drama Press, 1959).

57. Pingxiang Municipal Party Committee, ed., *Anyuan lukuang gongren yundong* [Anyuan railway and mine workers' movement] (Beijing: Chinese Communist Party Historical Materials Press, 1990), 2: 1270–72 (hereafter cited as AYLKGRYD).

58. Ibid., 2: 897.

59. *Fandong yingpian Liaoyuan chulong ji.*

60. Chinese Academy of Social Sciences, ed., *Anyuan gongren yundong de lishi burong diandao; Hongan zhanbao* 16 (June 30, 1967).

61. *Fandong yingpian Liaoyuan chulong ji.*

62. Pingxiang Mining Company Party Committee, ed., *Mao Zedong, Liu Shaoqi, Li Lisan zai Anyuan*, 205.

63. See, for example, the July 4, 1960, article by Zhang Zhenchu on workers' tales of Liu Shaoqi at Anyuan.

64. *Pingxiangshi zhengfu zhi* [Pingxiang city government gazetteer] (Beijing: Xinhua Press, 1992), 192.

65. Chinese Academy of Social Sciences Modern History Institute, ed., *Liu Shaoqi yu Anyuan gongren yundong*, 189–91.

66. Ibid., 216.

67. Pingxiang Mining Company Editorial Committee, ed., *Pingxiang kuangwuju zhi*, 24.

68. Chinese Academy of Social Sciences, ed., *Anyuan gongren yundong de lishi burong diandao*, 45.

69. Propaganda Department of the Chinese Communist Party Committee of the Pingxiang Mining Company, ed., *Hongse Anyuan* [Red Anyuan] (Nanchang: Jiangxi People's Press, 1959), 583.

70. For background on the Hundred Flowers Movement and the Anti-Rightist Campaign that followed, see Roderick MacFarquhar, *Contradictions among the People, 1956–1957* (New York: Columbia University Press, 1974); Merle Goldman, *China's Intellectuals: Advise and Dissent* (Cambridge, MA: Harvard University Press, 1981).

71. Hunan Normal College, ed., *Anyuan meikuang shi*, 178–82.

72. Ibid., 217.

73. Chinese Academy of Social Sciences, ed., *Anyuan gongren yundong de lishi burong diandao*, 23.

74. Xiao Jianping, "Dou shi *Liao Yuan* re de 'huo'" [The troubles were all caused by *Prairie Fire*], *Dazhong dianying* [Mass movies] 8 (2005).

75. Yuan's audiences were not limited to tourists. In 1962 the Pingxiang municipal union arranged for Yuan to visit local factories to recount tales of the 1922 strike to audiences of more than twenty thousand workers. *Pingxiangshi gonghui zhi* [Pingxiang city union gazetteer] (Pingxiang: Pingxiang Press, 1999), 192.

76. Hunan Normal College, ed., *Anyuan meikuang shi*, 209.

77. Ibid., 209–13.

78. Ibid., 188–202.

79. Ibid., 220.

80. Pingxiang Mining Company Editorial Committee, ed., *Pingxiang kuangwuju zhi*, 457–63.

81. "'Wenhua da geming' shiqi de Pingxiang meikuang" [The Pingxiang coal mine during the time of the 'Great Cultural Revolution'], *Pingkuang gongren bao* [Pingxiang miners' journal], September 24, 1998. Reprinted in Pingxiang City History Gazetteer Office, ed., *Anyuan lukuang gongren yundongshi yanjiu wenhui* [Compilation of studies on the Anyuan railway and mine workers' movement] (Nanchang: Jiangxi People's Press, 2002), 436.

82. *Pingxiang meitan fazhan shilue* [Brief history of the development of the Pingxiang coal industry], combined issue of *Jiangxi wenshi ziliao xuanji* 23 and *Pingxiang wenshi ziliao* 6 (1987): 140–41.

83. Nanchang Municipal Archives, (confidential file) no. 5018-18-1.

84. *Fanxiu zhanbao* [Antirevisionism battle bulletin] 1 (1967). Held in the Pingxiang City Library.

85. Paul Clark, *Chinese Cinema: Culture and Politics since 1949* (New York: Cambridge University Press, 1987), 63–64; and Paul Clark, *The Chinese Cultural Revolution: A History* (New York: Cambridge University Press, 2008), 13.

86. Author interview with Cai Shaoqing, former member of Beijing University's Anyuan labor movement research team, June 2006, Nanjing. The team also interviewed more than twenty army veterans in Beijing who had worked at Anyuan before enlisting and carried out documentary research in

personnel dossiers held in the central archives. According to Professor Cai, the draft manuscript was well received by Deng Tuo and other senior party cadres who reviewed it. Because of the volatile political climate, however, the project was never completed and no publication ensued. Anyuan Memorial Hall Archives, file no. 1450. A transcript of the team's interview with Li Lisan on January 10, 1959, can be found in AYLKGRYD 2: 896–901.

87. Hunan Normal College, ed., *Anyuan meikuang shi*.

88. "Chedi qingsuan Liu Shaoqi zai Anyuan de fangeming zuixing," 7.

89. *Hongse shuguang* [Red rays] 8 (April 30, 1967). Red Guard newspaper held in the Pingxiang City Library.

90. Propaganda Department of the Chinese Communist Party Committee of the Pingxiang Mining Company, ed., *Hongse Anyuan* (1959 edition), 5–10.

91. *Pingxiangshi gonghui zhi*, 283.

92. "Chedi qingsuan Liu Shaoqi zai Anyuan de fangeming zuixing," 8.

93. Propaganda Department of the Chinese Communist Party Committee of the Pingxiang Mining Company, ed., *Hongse de Anyuan* (1961 edition), 359–60.

94. Propaganda Department of the Chinese Communist Party Committee of the Pingxiang Mining Company, ed., *Hongse Anyuan* (1959 edition), 618–20.

95. On the roles of both Liu and Mao as architects of the Great Leap, albeit with characteristically different priorities (Liu stressing the need for party organization and Mao emphasizing mass spontaneity), see especially Roderick MacFarquhar, *The Great Leap Forward, 1958–1960* (New York: Columbia University Press, 1983).

96. *Zhongguo gongyun shiliao* [Historical materials on the Chinese labor movement] 2 (1958): 134.

97. *Hunan lishi ziliao* [Hunan historical materials] 1 (1958): 4.

98. AYLKGRYD, 1: 91–104 contains the original version of Liu's essay.

99. AYLKGRYD, 1: 139–43 contains the original version of this essay.

100. "Liu Shaoqi zai Zhonggong junwei kuoda huiyi shang jianghua" [Liu Shaoqi's speech to the enlarged conference of the Chinese Communist Military Commission], September 9, 1959,:10–12 (mimeograph held in Fung Library, Harvard University). Liu Shaoqi's admiration for a Stalinist style of leadership was indeed longstanding. In a March 4, 1937, letter to Zhang Wentian he wrote, "We don't yet have a Stalin in China. Conditions in China are still immature and we need to humbly study the Soviet example, while exercising collective leadership." *Liu Shaoqi wenti ziliao zhuanji* [Special collection of materials on the Liu Shaoqi problem] (Taipei: Institute for the Study of Chinese Communist Problems, 1970), 1.

101. In the early 1950s local historian and propagandist Peng Jiangliu had written another version of the folk song in which Li Lisan (Li Longzhi) was replaced with Mao Zedong (Mao Runzhi). It began, "In 1921, the clouds

suddenly parted and a superman named Mao Runzhi came from Hunan to Anyuan." *Pingxiang Gujin* [Pingxiang past and present] 2 (August 1982): 112.

102. "Chedi qingsuan Liu Shaoqi zai Anyuan de fangeming zuixing," 7–8. For the original 1925 versions, see AYLKGRYD, 2: 840–59; and Anyuan Labor Movement Memorial Hall, ed., *Anyuan lukuang gongren yundong shiliao* (Changsha: Hunan People's Press, 1980), 571. A 1955 version of the song, in which Liu Shaoqi is portrayed as playing a far larger role than in the 1925 versions yet still not a role as exaggerated as that in the 1959 version, can be found in Chinese Academy of Social Sciences Modern History Institute, ed., *Liu Shaoqi yu Anyuan gongren yundong*, 126–39.

103. *Liu Shaoqi zai Jiangxi* [Liu Shaoqi in Jiangxi] (Beijing: Chinese Communist Party History Press, 1988), 152–59.

104. Pingxiang Communist Party Committee People's Revolutionary Struggle History Editorial Committee, ed., *Pingxiang renmin geming douzhengshi* [Pingxiang people's revolutionary struggle history] (Pingxiang: n.p., 1962), 29.

105. Julia F. Andrews, *Painters and Politics in the People's Republic of China, 1949–1979* (Berkeley: University of California Press, 1994), 242–43.

106. Ellen Johnston Laing, *The Winking Owl: Art in the People's Republic of China* (Berkeley: University of California Press, 1988), 38.

107. *Meishu fenglei* [Art storm] 1 (1967): 10–14.

108. Andrews, *Painters and Politics in the People's Republic of China*, 240.

109. Victoria E. Bonnell, *Iconography of Power: Soviet Political Posters under Lenin and Stalin* (Berkeley: University of California Press, 1997), 162.

110. Ibid.,165.

111. Hou Yimin, "*Liu Shaoqi he Anyuan kuanggong* de gousi" [The conception of *Liu Shaoqi and the Anyuan miners*], *Meishu* 4 (1961): 21–22.

112. Andrews, *Painters and Politics in the People's Republic of China*, 328.

113. Pingxiang Mining Company Editorial Committee, ed., *Pingxiang kuangwuju zhi*, 28, 694.

114. Yang Gongmin, "Dianying 'Liaoyuan' paishe zhuiyi" [Memoir of filming the movie *Prairie Fire*], *Liu Shaoqi zai Shanghai* [Liu Shaoqi in Shanghai] (Beijing: Chinese Communist Party History Press, 1998), 326–28.

115. *Liaoyuan* [Prairie fire], Tianma studio, Shanghai, 1962.

116. "Chedi qingsuan Liu Shaoqi zai Anyuan de fangeming zuixing," 8.

117. *Fandong yingpian Liaoyuan chulong ji.*

118. David Brandenberger, "Stalin as Symbol: A Case Study of the Personality Cult and Its Construction," in *Stalin: A New History*, ed. Sarah Davies and James Harris (New York: Cambridge University Press, 2005), 250.

119. Ibid., 251–70.

120. Xiao Jianping, "Dianying *Liaoyuan* fengpo shimo: Lei Huanjue jiu shi Liu Shaoqi?" [The storm over the movie *Prairie Fire*: Was Lei Huanjue none other than Liu Shaoqi?], *Dazhong dianying* [Mass movies] 8 (2005).

121. *Gu Jiegang riji* [Gu Jiegang diary], vol. 10 (1964–67) (Taipei: Lianjing Press, 2007), 150.

122. AYLKGRYD, 2: 906–10.

123. Chinese Academy of Social Sciences Modern History Institute, ed., *Liu Shaoqi yu Anyuan gongren yundong,* 184–85.

124. AYLKGRYD, 2: 894–95.

125. Chinese Academy of Social Sciences Modern History Institute, ed., *Liu Shaoqi yu Anyuan gongren yundong,* 188.

126. *Anyuan lukuang gongren yundong jinianguan neirong jieshao* [Introduction to the contents of the Anyuan Railway and Mine Workers' Movement Memorial Hall]. There is no date or place of publication given, but from its contents, this pamphlet must have been published around the time of the opening of the hall in 1965. Held in the Harvard-Yenching Library.

127. Pingxiang Mining Company Party Committee, ed., *Mao Zedong, Liu Shaoqi, Li Lisan zai Anyuan de gushi,* 217, 218.

128. Thinking that Li Lisan was still minister of labor, Zhu Zijin had sent her first letter (in June 1965) to that address. It was not until August, when a central official visited the Anyuan memorial hall, that she learned of Li's demotion to the post of secretary of the North China Bureau and sent a follow-up letter to that address. Shortly upon his return to Beijing from a three-month rest at the seaside resort of Beidaihe, Li answered both letters. Ibid., 216.

129. Ibid., 218.

130. Mao Zedong, "Zai zhongyang gongzuo huiyi xiaoxing zuotanhui shang de jianghua" [Talk at the small-scale discussion group of the central work conference], December 20, 1964, in *Zhongguo wenhua da geming wen ku* [The Chinese Cultural Revolution database], ed. Song Yongyi (Hong Kong: University Services Centre, 2002).

131. Mao Zedong, "Guanyu siqing yundong de yici jianghua" [A talk about the Four Cleanups movement], January 3, 1965, in Song Yongyi, ed., *Zhongguo wenhua da geming wen ku.*

132. Mao Zedong, "Talk on the Four Cleanups Movement," *Long Live Mao Tse-tung Thought,* January 3, 1965.

133. Clark, *The Chinese Cultural Revolution: A History,* 158.

134. That Zhu Shaolian had been dead for decades was doubtless helpful to his revolutionary reputation in these vindictive times. It had long been rumored that Zhu, like many former Anyuan activists, went over to the Nationalist side during the White Terror. Li Lisan, when asked by a team of Peking University historians in January 1959 whether Zhu had betrayed the revolution, replied, "I've heard it said that after he was captured he was a turncoat, but to what degree I don't know. Maybe after being tortured he revealed a few names. I doubt that it was a major betrayal, but I don't know the actual circumstances." Anyuan Memorial Hall Archives, file no. A12-27-27 (1). This section was deleted from the various published versions of Li's interview.

135. The Pingxiang mining company reported spending nearly seven and a half million yuan between 1950 and 1965 to construct 181,921 square meters

of new residential housing for 7,665 workers and their families. In the same period, new dormitories were built to accommodate another 6,227 bachelor workers. Pingxiang Mining Company Editorial Committee, ed., *Pingxiang kuangwuju zhi*, 608, 612.

136. Ibid., 613–16.

137. Pingxiang Mining Company Party Committee, ed., *Mao Zedong, Liu Shaoqi, Li Lisan zai Anyuan de gushi*, 209.

138. Pingxiang Mining Company Editorial Committee, ed., *Pingxiang kuangwuju zhi*, 671–77.

139. Ibid., 302, 599.

140. On the failed effort to create industrial utopias in Mao's China, see Li Hou, "Urban Planning in Mao's China: The Rise and Fall of the Daqing Model," PhD diss., Harvard University, 2009.

141. Quoted in Mei Fangquan, *Anyuan kuanggong: zhuanxingqi de bianqian yanjiu* [Anyuan miners: A study of change in a transitional time] (Beijing: Chinese Academy of Social Sciences Press, 2006), 86.

142. S.A. Smith, *Revolution and the People in Russia and China: A Comparative Study* (New York: Cambridge University Press, 2008), 232–33.

143. Andrew G. Walder, *Communist Neo-Traditionalism: Work and Authority in Chinese Industry* (Berkeley: University of California Press, 1986).

144. Robert Jay Lifton, *Revolutionary Immortality: Mao Tse-tung and the Chinese Cultural Revolution* (New York: Vintage Books, 1968), 23.

145. R. Kent Guy, *The Emperor's Four Treasures: Scholars and the State in the Late Ch'ien-lung Era* (Cambridge, MA: Harvard East Asian Monographs, 1987).

## 6. MAO'S FINAL CRUSADE

1. For a political history of this period, see especially Roderick MacFarquhar and Michael Schoenhals, *Mao's Last Revolution* (Cambridge, MA: Harvard University Press, 2006).

2. Haiyan Lee, "The Charisma of Power and the Military Sublime in Tiananmen Square," *Journal of Asian Studies* 70, no. 2 (May 2011): 405.

3. Timothy L. Smith, *Revivalism and Social Reform* (Baltimore, MD: Johns Hopkins University Press, 1980); Marshall William Fishwick, *Great Awakenings: Popular Religion and Popular Culture* (New York: Haworth Press, 1995); Thomas S. Kidd, *The Great Awakening* (New Haven, CT: Yale University Press, 2007).

4. Chinese Academy of Social Sciences Modern History Institute, ed., *Liu Shaoqi yu Anyuan gongren yundong* [Liu Shaoqi and the Anyuan labor movement] (Beijing: Chinese Academy of Social Sciences Press, 1981), 213–14; Li Shaozhou, "Women de 'Anzhan'" [Our Anyuan exhibit], in *Shen xi feichang suiyue* [Living through extraordinary times], online oral history at www.boofan.com/ (accessed April 2009).

5. "'Wenhua da geming' shiqi de Pingxiang meikuang" [The Pingxiang

coal mine at the time of the "Great Cultural Revolution"], in *Anyuan lukuang gongren yundongshi yanjiu wenhui* [Compilation of studies on the Anyuan railway and mine workers' movement], ed. Pingxiang City History Gazetteer Office (Nanchang: Jiangxi People's Press, 2002), 436.

6. Chinese Academy of Social Sciences Modern History Institute, ed., *Liu Shaoqi yu Anyuan gongren yundong*, 215.

7. "Chen Boda, Jiang Qing dui Beijing hangkong xueyuan tongxue de jianghua" [Talk by Chen Boda and Jiang Qing to students at the Beijing Aeronautics Academy], November 19, 1966; "Chen Boda, Jiang Qing jiejian hangkong xueyuan hongqi zhanshi de jianghua" [Talk by Chen Boda and Jiang Qing while receiving the Red Flag warriors from Beijing Aeronautics Academy], December 13, 1966, both in *Zhongguo wenhua de geming wenku* [The Chinese Cultural Revolution database], ed. Song Yongyi (Hong Kong: University Services Centre, 2002).

8. Still, many of those who visited the coal mine, even if they arrived by train, continued by foot up the steep mountain paths to Jinggangshan. Personal communication in July 2009 with Professor Yue Daiyun of Beijing University, who visited Anyuan as part of the Beida May Seventh Cadre School contingent in 1970.

9. For a "theological" interpretation of Mao's revolutionary appeal, see Christian Sorace, "Saint Mao," *Telos* 151 (Summer 2010): 173–91.

10. Qi Benyu, "Qi Benyu dui 'pipan Tao Zhu lianluozhan' de zhishi" [Directive from Qi Benyu toward the "Criticize Tao Zhu Liaison Station"], February 9, 1967, in Song, ed., *Zhongguo wenhua de geming wenku*.

11. Chinese Academy of Social Sciences Modern History Institute, ed., *Liu Shaoqi yu Anyuan gongren yundong*, 215. The memoirs of longtime Anyuan residents make a convincing case that the trees had been planted well before the construction of the workers' club and originally had nothing to do with Liu Shaoqi. See Zhu Zijian, interview on December 15, 1967, in Anyuan Railway and Mine Workers' Movement Memorial Hall, ed., *Anyuan lukuang gongren yundongshi ziliao huibian* [Compilation of historical materials on the Anyuan railway and mine workers' movement] 3, no. 1 (1975).

12. Chinese Academy of Social Sciences, ed., *Anyuan gongren yundong de lishi burong diandao* [The history of the Anyuan labor movement must not be turned upside down] (Beijing: n.p., 1967), 47.

13. Xiao Jianping, "Dou shi *Liaoyuan* re de 'huo'" [All the trouble stemmed from *Prairie Fire*], *Dazhong dianying* [Mass movies] 8 (2005).

14. Chinese Academy of Social Sciences, ed., *Anyuan gongren yundong de lishi burong diandao*, provides photographic evidence of the tree cutting and replanting.

15. Chinese Academy of Social Sciences Modern History Institute, ed., *Liu Shaoqi yu Anyuan gongren yundong*, 215.

16. Huang Aiguo, "Geming de yinggutou: ji Anyuan meikuang laogongren Yuan Pin'gao" [Revolutionary iron man: Records of old Anyuan miner

Yuan Pin'gao], in Pingxiang City History Gazetteer Office, ed., *Anyuan lukuang gongren yundongshi yanjiu wenhui*, 368.

17. On the Three Family Village, see Roderick MacFarquhar, *The Origins of the Cultural Revolution: The Coming of the Cataclysm, 1961–1966* (New York: Columbia University Press, 1997), 3: chapter 11.

18. "Chedi qingsuan Liu Shaoqi zai Anyuan de fangeming zuixing" [Thoroughly eliminate Liu Shaoqi's counterrevolutionary crimes at Anyuan], *Xin Beida*, April 25, 1967, 8.

19. Feng Chongyi, "Jiangxi in Reform: The Fear of Exclusion and the Search for a New Identity," in *The Political Economy of China's Provinces: Comparative and Competitive Advantage*, ed. Hans Hendrischke and Feng Chongyi (London: Routledge, 1999), 257.

20. "'Wenhua da geming' shiqi de Pingxiang meikuang," 436–37.

21. Pingxiang City History Gazetteer Office, ed., *Pingxiang da shiji* [Annals of Pingxiang] (Pingxiang: Pingxiang Gazetteer Office, 1989), 86.

22. "Zhou Enlai, Yao Wenyuan jiejian Jiangxisheng sifang daibiao jianghua lilu" [Transcripts of talks by Zhou Enlai and Yao Wenyuan during a meeting with the four groups of representatives from Jiangxi Province], July 28, 1967, in Song, ed., *Zhongguo wenhua de geming wenku*.

23. "Zhongyang shouzhang jiejian Jiangxi sifangmian daibiao tanhua zhaiyao" [Excerpts from the central leadership's talks during a meeting with representatives from four groups in Jiangxi Province], August 3, 1967, in Song, ed., *Zhongguo wenhua de geming wenku*.

24. Pingxiang Party Committee Party History Work Office, ed., *Zhonggong Pingxiang dangshi dashiji* [Chronology of Chinese Communist Party history in Pingxiang] (Pingxiang: n.p., 1955), 179.

25. Pingxiang City History Gazetteer Office, ed., *Pingxiang da shiji*, 86.

26. *Hongqi* [Red Flag] 7 (May 20, 1967). Reprinted in Li Sishen, *Li Lisan hongse zhuanqi* [Red biography of Li Lisan] (Beijing: China Workers' Press, 2004), 2: 797.

27. Ibid.

28. Ibid., 2: 806.

29. Li Lisan's June 5 letter to Jiang Qing is reprinted in Li, *Li Lisan hongse zhuanqi*, 2: 806–9. In the fall of 1970, in reply to an inquiry from the Anyuan memorial hall, the *People's Daily* arts department claimed that nothing had been deleted or altered in the published version of the movie review that Li Lisan had submitted to them in 1963. However, noting that it was standard editorial policy not to retain original manuscripts, the *People's Daily* staff said it was impossible to locate Li's original submission. Anyuan Memorial Hall Archives, file no. A12-27-27 (2).

30. Patrick Lescot, *Before Mao: The Untold Story of Li Lisan and the Creation of Communist China* (New York: HarperCollins, 2004), 327.

31. This letter is reprinted in Li, *Li Lisan hongse zhuanqi*, 2: 817.

32. Li Lisan's family members insisted that he had not voluntarily con-

sumed the overdose of sleeping pills that killed him. See ibid., 2: 819–20; Lescot, *Before Mao*, 344–48.

33. *People's Daily*, May 8, 1967, August 5, 1967, and April 22, 1968; *Liberation Daily*, August 15, 1967, June 23, 1968, and July 1, 1968; *Wenhui bao*, May 21, 1967, August 22, 1967, and July 3, 1968. See also *Liberation Army Daily*, April 29, 1967; *Beijing Daily*, May 11, 1967; and *Jiangxi Daily*, October 20, 1967.

34. Yang Gongmin, "Dianying 'Liaoyuan' paishe zhuiyi" [Memoir of filming the movie *Prairie Fire*] (Beijing: Chinese Communist Party History Press, 1998), 328.

35. *Xia Yan quanji* [Collected works of Xia Yan], vol. 16 (Hangzhou: Zhejiang Art and Literature Press, 2005), 403.

36. *Hongse shuguang* [Red rays] 9 (May 11, 1967). This Red Guard newspaper, published in Pingxiang, is held in the Pingxiang City Library.

37. *Liansi haojiao* [United voice] 10 (September 14, 1967). This Red Guard newspaper is held in the Pingxiang City Library.

38. Ellen Johnston Laing, *The Winking Owl: Art in the People's Republic of China* (Berkeley: University of California Press, 1988), 68.

39. Julia F. Andrews, *Painters and Politics in the People's Republic of China, 1949–1979* (Berkeley: University of California Press, 1994), 328. Hou Yimin later recalled that this was actually the second time he had been forced to write a confession in connection with this painting. The first was when he had ripped up a bad reproduction of the painting in fury over its faulty reproduction of the original colors. On that occasion Hou was criticized for having shown a lack of proper respect to the head of state by destroying a copy of his likeness. Not long after, when Liu Shaoqi was named the number one capitalist roader, Hou was forced to write a second confession, this time to explain why he had painted Liu in the first place. Hou Yimin, *Paomoji* [Collection of bubbles] (Shenyang: Liaoning Fine Arts Press, 2006), 58.

40. Li, "Women de 'Anzhan.'" A transcript of one of Zhang Peisen's interviews with Li Lisan, conducted in June 1963, can be found in Pingxiang Municipal Party Committee, ed., *Anyuan lukuang gongren yundong* [Anyuan railway and mine workers' movement] (Beijing: Chinese Communist Party Historical Materials Press, 1990), 2: 902–5 (hereafter cited as AYLKGRYD).

41. Andrews, *Painters and Politics in the People's Republic of China*, 338.

42. Qi Benyu, "Qiyue ershiliu ri Qi Benyu tongzhi zai jiejian jiangong xueyuan xin bayi zhanshi de tanhua" [Comrade Qin Benyu's July 26 talk with the new August 1 Warriors of the Construction Academy], in *Anyuan gongren yundong de lishi burong diandao*, ed. Chinese Academy of Social Sciences.

43. The worker had previously been contacted by Zhang Peisen and other members of the exhibition committee, who had enlisted his assistance in seeking the premier's personal approval. Zhang Peisen, "Wo suo liaojie de 'Anzhan' ji youhua 'Mao zhuxi qu Anyuan' de chuangzuo" [What I know about the Anyuan exhibit and the creation of the oil painting *Chairman Mao Goes to Anyuan*], *Yanhuang chunqiu* 7 (1998): 32.

44. A two-month field investigation conducted in Hunan and Jiangxi by a combined team of "revolutionary" researchers from the Chinese Academy of Social Sciences, Beijing Normal University, and the Beijing Mining Academy together with local rebel organizations in Pingxiang and Anyuan provided the basis for much of the written material in the exhibition. Their findings were presented in a July 1967 mimeographed publication, Chinese Academy of Social Sciences, ed., *Anyuan gongren yundong de lishi burong diandao*.

45. Li, "Women de 'Anzhan.'"

46. Andrews, *Painters and Politics in the People's Republic of China*, 338; Li, "Women de 'Anzhan.'"

47. Andrews, *Painters and Politics in the People's Republic of China*, 339.

48. Ibid., 338–39.

49. Zheng Shengtian, "*Chairman Mao Goes to Anyuan:* A Conversation with the Artist Liu Chunhua," in *Art and China's Revolution*, ed. Melissa Chiu and Zheng Shengtian (New York: Asia Society, 2008), 119.

50. Jiang Qing, Chen Boda, and Kang Sheng, "Zhongyang wenge jiejian gangqin banchang 'hongdengji' yanyuandeng geming wenyi zhanshi de jianghua" [Talk during the meeting of the Central Cultural Revolution with the musicians, actors, and other revolutionary artistic warriors of the *Red Lantern*], June 30, 1968, in Song, ed., *Zhongguo wenhua de geming wenku*.

51. *Wenhui bao*, July 6, 1968.

52. Quoted in Wu Hung, *Remaking Beijing: Tiananmen Square and the Creation of a Political Space* (Chicago: University of Chicago Press, 2005), 80.

53. *Guangming ribao*, July 12, 1968.

54. *Jiefang junbao*, December 2, 1968.

55. Mei Fangquan, *Anyuan kuanggong: zhuanxingqi de bianqian yanjiu* [Anyuan miners: A study of change in a transitional time] (Beijing: Chinese Academy of Social Sciences, 2006), 58.

56. Andrews, *Painters and Politics in the People's Republic of China*, 339.

57. Huang Shiguo and Huang Aiguo, "'Mao Zhuxi qu Anyuan' de muhou fengbo yu lishi zhenshi" [The behind-the-scenes stir and historical truth of *Chairman Mao Goes to Anyuan*], *Nanfang zhoumo* [Southern weekend], April 20, 2006.

58. "Picture of Priest in Vatican Is of Mao," *New York Times*, December 24, 1969; Han Suyin, *The Morning Deluge: Mao Tsetung and the Chinese Revolution* (Boston: Little, Brown, 1972), 95.

59. Liu Chunhua, "Painting Pictures of Chairman Mao Is Our Greatest Happiness," *China Reconstructs* 17, no. 10 (October 1968): 5–6.

60. Ibid., 6. Since Mao came from Hunan, which is located to the west of Anyuan, the reference to workers looking eastward to the rising sun was obviously meant metaphorically rather than literally.

61. Hou's painting was criticized in a 1964 issue of the journal *Meishu* (vol. 1, no. 42) because the figures of the miners were so generic, although Hou himself in his 1961 article (vol. 4, no. 21) had noted that several of the

figures were based on photographs of actual Anyuan workers known to have had close connections to Liu Shaoqi.

62. For a general study of this campaign, see Thomas P. Bernstein, *Up to the Mountains and Down to the Villages: The Transfer of Youth from Urban to Rural China* (New Haven, CT: Yale University Press, 1977).

63. Shanghai Municipal Archives, file no. B105-4-302.

64. Laing, *The Winking Owl*, 69.

65. Zhang, "Wo suo liaojie de 'Anzhan' ji youhua 'Mao zhuxi qu Anyuan' de chuangzuo," 36.

66. Li, "Women de 'Anzhan.'"

67. According to Li Shaozhou's memoir, the exhibit originally was comprised of only five sections, apparently due to the belief at that time that Mao had visited Anyuan a total of five times. The five visits are chronicled in a January 20, 1967, Red Guard handbill held in the Pingxiang City Library, "The Brilliance of Mao Zedong Thought Forever Illuminates Red Anyuan." Subsequently, however, Mao was found to have visited Anyuan six times. Today the official party line is that Mao visited Anyuan eight times between 1921 and 1930, although several of the alleged visits are based on rather thin oral history evidence. Interview with Huang Aiguo, Pingxiang Communist Party School, October 2009.

68. The Harvard-Yenching Library holds six different versions of the pamphlet, from exhibitions held between 1968 and 1969 in Beijing, Guangzhou, Wenzhou, Dezhou, Xiangfan, and an unidentified location.

69. *Cong Anyuan dao Jinggangshan* [From Anyuan to Jinggangshan] (Beijing: July 1968), 2.

70. Ibid., 26.

71. Ibid., 11.

72. For a sampling of these hagiographic praises of Mao at Anyuan, see Shanghai Workers Revolutionary Literary Creation Troupe, ed., *Hong taiyang zhaoliang Anyuan shan* [The red sun lights up Anyuan mountain] (Shanghai: Shanghai Cultural Press, 1968); and Anyuan Worker-Peasant-Soldier Song and Poetry Editorial Small Group, ed., *Hongri zhao Anyuan* [The red sun shines on Anyuan] (Nanchang: Jiangxi People's Press, 1969). The former publication, the second printing of which was a run of three hundred thousand copies, stirred some controversy because the image on the book's cover—although modeled on Liu Chunhua's *Chairman Mao Goes to Anyuan*—seemed to show Chairman Mao's face peppered with black spots that looked like unshaven beard stubble! Noting that this breach of decorum suggested "the utmost disloyalty to Chairman Mao," the Shanghai revolutionary committee ordered a thorough investigation of the matter. The subsequent investigation revealed that the black spots were simply the result of having relied on a grainy woodblock print replica of Liu's painting. Although the spots had been successfully camouflaged by white powder for the first printing, the powder had fallen off by the second printing. The first printing had also raised concerns, however, when Zhang Chunqiao objected that the

use of gold paint on the cover image was unattractive and overly ostentatious; it was changed to the more dignified (imperial) yellow for the second edition. Shanghai Municipal Archives, file no. B167-3-99.

73. Li Sizhen and Liu Zhikun, *Li Lisan zhi mi* [The puzzle of Li Lisan] (Beijing: People's Press, 2005), 401.

74. Pingxiang Mining Company Party Committee, ed., *Mao Zedong, Liu Shaoqi, Li Lisan zai Anyuan de gushi* [Stories of Mao Zedong, Liu Shaoqi, and Li Lisan at Anyuan] (Beijing: Chinese Communist Party History Press, 1998), 222.

75. Red Guard handbill, January 20, 1967, held in the Pingxiang City Library.

76. *Hongan zhanbao* [Red Anyuan battle bulletin] 16 (June 30, 1967). The exhibit took a month to prepare, with the assistance of the Hunan Supreme Court and the Zhuzhou Railway Mechanics School.

77. Feng, "Jiangxi in Reform," 257.

78. Zhang, "Wo suo liaojie de 'Anzhan' ji youhua 'Mao zhuxi qu Anyuan' de chuangzuo," 35.

79. Huang Weiai and Huang Aiguo, "Mao Zhuxi zai Anyuan geming huodong jinianguan xingjian shimo" [The full story of the construction of the Memorial Hall of Chairman Mao's Revolutionary Activities at Anyuan], in *Anyuan lukuang gongren yundongshi yanjiu wenhui*, ed. Pingxiang City History Gazetteer Office, 391–93.

80. Ibid., 393–95.

81. "Qianwanke hongxin xiangzhe hong taiyang" [Tens of millions of red hearts face the red sun], in *Liberation Army Daily*, July 9, 1968. Reprinted in *Zan geming youhua "Mao zhuxi qu Anyuan"* [In praise of the revolutionary oil painting *Chairman Mao Goes to Anyuan*] (Xi'an: Shaanxi People's Press, 1970), 57.

82. "Mao Zhuxi a! Anyuan kuanggong yongyuan zhong yu ni!" [Chairman Mao, ah! The Anyuan miners are forever loyal to you!], *People's Daily*, July 11, 1968, reprinted in *Zan geming youhua*, 21–24.

83. Huang and Huang, "Mao Zhuxi zai Anyuan geming huodong jinianguan xingjian shimo," 395–98.

84. Xiao, "Dou shi *Liaoyuan* re de 'huo.'"

85. The following account is drawn from *Mao zhuxi zai Anyuan geming huodong jinianguan chenlie shuoming (chugao)* [Explanation of the displays at the Chairman Mao's Revolutionary Activities in Anyuan memorial hall (draft)], October 10, 1968, Anyuan Memorial Hall Archives, file no. A6/3-29-5.

86. The basis for this image was a newspaper article in the April 29, 1925, edition of *Minguo Ribao* [Republic daily], which reported on a visit to Anyuan the previous day by a Japanese advisor sent by the Hanyeping Coal and Iron Company, whom the workers mistakenly thought was going to resolve the problem of several months of withheld wages. When it became clear that the Japanese advisor had come only to inspect the construction projects being

completed with loans from Japan and was not authorized to provide relief for back pay, the workers erupted in fury and unleashed buckets of night soil on the inspection group, including Director Shu Xiutai. The newspaper account is reprinted in AYLKGRYD, 2: 1189–90.

87. For the official charges against Liu as foe of the Chinese working class, see, for example, *Da gongzei Liu Shaoqi shi gongren jieji de sidi* [Big scab Liu Shaoqi is the sworn enemy of the working class] (Hong Kong: Sanlian Press, 1968). A central piece in this propaganda tract is a November 22, 1968, editorial in *People's Daily* entitled "True Scab, Fake Leader." Attributed to the Anyuan coal mine revolutionary committee, the editorial accuses Liu of having betrayed the revolutionary inclinations of the Anyuan miners. The minister of public security, Kang Sheng, summarized the "evidence" implicating Liu Shaoqi as a "scab" at the Ninth Party Congress. See "Kang Sheng zai zhongyang zhishu jiguan chuanda 'jiuda' dahuishang jieda wenti" [Kang Sheng's transmission to the central agencies of questions and answers from the Ninth Party Congress], May 24, 1969, in Song, ed., *Zhongguo wenhua de geming wenku*.

88. Lowell Dittmer, "Death and Transfiguration: Liu Shaoqi's Rehabilitation and Contemporary Chinese Politics," *Journal of Asian Studies* 11, no. 3 (May 1981): 455–80.

89. *Mao Zhuxi zai Anyuan geming huodong jinianguan chenlie dagang* [Outline of displays in Memorial Hall to Chairman Mao's Revolutionary Activities at Anyuan], December 1, 1969, Anyuan Memorial Hall Archives, file no. 322-B4-4-26.

90. Pingxiang City History Gazetteer Office, ed., *Pingxiang da shiji*, 91–92.

91. The impact of the Lin Biao affair on the Anyuan memorial hall is discussed in detail in Huang Aiguo, "9.13 shijian qianhou de Anyuan jinianguan" [The Anyuan memorial hall before and after the September 13 incident], *Pingxiang gongren bao* [Pingxiang workers' daily], September 13, 2001.

92. Edgar Snow, *The Long Revolution* (New York: Vintage, 1973), 169.

93. On the Lin Biao incident, see Jin Qiu, *The Culture of Power: The Lin Biao Incident in the Cultural Revolution* (Stanford, CA: Stanford University Press, 1999); and Frederick C. Teiwes and Warren Sun, *The Tragedy of Lin Biao: Riding the Tiger during the Cultural Revolution, 1966–71* (London: Hurst, 1996).

94. "Comrade Xiao Ke exposes Lin Biao," in *Jielu dapantu, dahanjian, damaiguozei, dayexinjia Lin Biao zaonian de fandang cuowu he zuixing* [Expose the big traitor, renegade, careerist Lin Biao's early antiparty mistakes and crimes], May 20, 1972, in Song, ed., *Zhongguo wenhua de geming wenku*.

95. Chen Yi, in ibid.

96. Huang and Huang, "'Mao zhuxi qu Anyuan.'"

97. Anyuan Memorial Hall Archives, file no. C5-1-8 (July 20, 1971). Zhang Chunqiao also reported that "a comrade" (presumably Jiang Qing) suggested

to the Chairman that, due to the passage of time, he might simply have forgotten that he wore a scholar's gown.

98. Huang, "9.13 shijian."

99. Anyuan Memorial Hall Archives, file no. 329-B4-4-29 (July 1, 1972).

100. Liu Chunhua, "Ye tan 'Mao Zhuxi qu Anyuan' de muhou fengbo yu lishi zhenshi" [Further discussion of the behind-the-scenes stir and historical truth of *Chairman Mao Goes to Anyuan*], *Nanfang zhoumo* [Southern weekend], July 27, 2006.

101. Huang, "Geming de yinggoutou," 368–69.

102. Mao Zedong, "Tong zai Jing zhongyang zhengzhiju weiyuan de tanhua" [Chat with members of the Politburo in the capital], May 3, 1975, in Song, ed., *Zhongguo wenhua de geming wenku.*

103. On the impact of the Cultural Revolution on the workers of Shanghai, see Elizabeth J. Perry and Li Xun, *Proletarian Power: Shanghai in the Cultural Revolution* (Boulder, CO: Westview Press, 1997).

104. "'Wenhua da geming' shiqi de Pingxiang meikuang."

105. Pingxiang Mining Company Editorial Committee, ed., *Pingxiang kuangwuju zhi* [Pingxiang Mining Company gazetteer] (Pingxiang: n.p., 1998), 671.

106. Ibid., 608–9.

107. Ibid., 558–59.

108. Mei, *Anyuan kuanggong,* 92–93.

109. Ibid., 280.

110. Yu Jianrong, *Zhongguo gongren jieji zhuangkuang: Anyuan shilu* [The plight of China's working class: Annals of Anyuan] (Hong Kong: Mirror Books, 2006), 176–78; Pingxiang Historical Gazetteer Office, ed., *Pingxiang da shiji,* 88–89.

111. Ibid., 191.

112. Mei, *Anyuan kuanggong,* 281.

113. Yu, *Zhongguo gongren jieji zhuangkuang,* 202. My own interviews with Anyuan workers in the summers of 2005, 2006, and 2008 and the fall of 2009 elicited similar responses.

114. September 12, 1976, New China News Agency report on wreaths to commemorate death of Mao, in Song, ed., *Zhongguo wenhua de geming wenku.*

115. Kevin J. O'Brien and Lianjiang Li, "Campaign Nostalgia in the Chinese Countryside," *Asian Survey* 39, no. 3 (May–June 1999): 376–91; Ching-Kwan Lee, "The Revenge of History: Collective Memories and Labor Protests in Northeastern China," *Ethnography* 1, no. 2 (2000): 217–37.

116. MacFarquhar and Schoenhals, *Mao's Last Revolution.*

117. Paul Clark, *The Chinese Cultural Revolution: A History* (New York: Cambridge University Press, 2008), 3.

118. Emily Honig, "Maoist Mappings of Gender: Reassessing the Red Guards," in *Chinese Femininities Chinese Masculinities,* ed. Susan Brownell and Jeffrey N. Wasserstrom (Berkeley: University of California Press, 2002),

259. Note that the transliterations in this quotation were changed from Wade-Giles to pinyin for greater clarity.

119. Clark, *The Chinese Cultural Revolution*, 252–53. That women as well as men were expected to emulate the ideal of the bold revolutionary soldier was exemplified in the famous revolutionary ballet (and later model opera) of the period, *The Red Detachment of Women*.

120. Mao's call to seek violence was not figurative. Two weeks earlier students at an elite girls' school in Beijing had beaten their teacher to death. Wang Youqin, "1966: Xuesheng da laoshi de geming" [1966: The revolution of students beating teachers], *Ershiyi shiji*, August 1995, 36–42.

121. Honig, "Maoist Mappings of Gender," 257.

122. Robert Jay Lifton, *Revolutionary Immortality: Mao Tse-tung and the Chinese Cultural Revolution* (New York: Vintage Books, 1968), 50.

123. In the early 1970s Jiang Qing designed a new "national dress" for women based on imperial fashion from the Tang through the Ming dynasties. Honig, "Maoist Mappings of Gender," 256.

124. Ross Terrill, *Madame Mao: The White-Boned Demon* (Stanford, CA: Stanford University Press, 1999), 266.

125. Ibid., 325.

126. Snow, *The Long Revolution*, 169.

127. *China Pictorial* 9 (1968): 44.

128. Donald E. McInnis, *Religious Policy and Practice in Communist China* (New York: Macmillan, 1972), 338.

129. Liang Heng and Judith Shapiro, *Son of the Revolution* (New York: Vintage Books, 1983), 174.

130. Anita Chan, Richard Madsen, and Jonathan Unger, *Chen Village: The Recent History of a Peasant Community in Mao's China* (Berkeley: University of California Press, 1984), 170.

131. Lynn White points to the importance of pre–Cultural Revolution policies of campaigns, class labels, and clientelism in contributing to the violence of the Cultural Revolution. Lynn White III, *Policies of Chaos: The Organizational Causes of Violence in China's Cultural Revolution* (Princeton, NJ: Princeton University Press, 1989).

132. On the differences between Maoist and Leninist conceptions of cultural revolution, "which played no small part in molding the histories of the Soviet Union and the PRC," see Maurice Meisner, "Iconoclasm and Cultural Revolution in China and Russia," in *Bolshevik Culture*, ed. Abbott Glason, Peter Kenez, and Richard Stites (Bloomington: Indiana University Press, 1985), 279.

133. Jack Belden, *China Shakes the World* (New York: Monthly Review Press, 1949), 63; Maurice Meisner, *Marxism, Maoism and Utopianism* (Madison: University of Wisconsin Press, 1982).

134. Emily Martin Ahern, *Chinese Ritual and Politics* (New York: Cambridge University Press, 1981), 106.

7. REFORMING THE REVOLUTIONARY TRADITION

1. Richard Curt Kraus, *The Party and the Arty in China: The New Politics of Culture* (Lanham, MD: Rowman & Littlefield, 2004), viii.

2. Yuezhi Zhao, *Communication in China: Political Economy, Power, and Conflict* (Lanham, MD: Rowman & Littlefield, 2008), 20.

3. Peter G. Rowe and Seng Kuan, eds., *Shanghai: Architecture and Urbanism for Modern China* (New York: Prestel, 2004); and Anne Warr, *Shanghai Architecture* (Sydney: Watermark Press, 2007).

4. Although he did not finish until after the Cultural Revolution, Hou began painting Mao at Anyuan in 1962 shortly after completing his portrait of Liu. Hou Yimin, *Paomoji* (A collection of bubbles) (Shenyang: Liaoning Art Press, 2006), 5–7, 58.

5. Tianjin People's Art Press, ed., *Hou Yimin chuangzuo youhua "Mao zhuxi yu Anyuan gongren zai yiqi" meishu zuopin fenxi* [Artistic analysis of Hou Yimin's oil painting "Chairman Mao with the Workers of Anyuan"] (Tianjin: Tianjin People's Art Press, 1978).

6. Pingxiang City Historical Gazetteer Office, ed., *Pingxiang da shiji* [Annals of Pingxiang] (Pingxiang: Pingxiang Gazetteer Office, 1989), 103.

7. Reprinted in Chinese Academy of Social Sciences, ed., *Liu Shaoqi yu Anyuan gongren yundong* [Liu Shaoqi and the Anyuan labor movement] (Beijing: Chinese Academy of Social Sciences Press, 1981), 73–74.

8. Reprinted in Chinese Academy of Social Sciences, ed., *Liu Shaoqi yu Anyuan gongren yundong,* 75.

9. Reprinted in Li Sizhen and Liu Zhikun, *Li Lisan zhi mi* [The puzzle of Li Lisan] (Beijing: People's Press, 2005), 421.

10. Xiao Jianping, "Anyuan you 're' qilaile" [Anyuan gets "hot" again], *Dazhong dianying* [Mass movies] 8 (2005).

11. Pingxiang Mining Company Editorial Committee, ed., *Pingxiang kuangwuju zhi* [Pingxiang Mining Company gazetteer] (Pingxiang: n.p., 1998), 713.

12. Ibid., 718.

13. Anyuan Memorial Hall Archives, file no. 577-B4-4-43.

14. Pingxiang City History Gazetteer Office, ed., *Pingxiang da shiji,* 112.

15. "Deng Xiaoping wei Anyuan lukuang gongren yundong jinianguan tixie guanming de qianqian houhou" [The full story behind Deng Xiaoping's inscription for the name of the Anyuan Railway and Mine Workers' Labor Movement Memorial Hall], *Anyuan zhoukan* [Anyuan weekly], August 5, 2004, A1–2. The calligraphy evidently served the purpose of providing the protective cover for the museum that its curators had been seeking. Twenty years later, on the anniversary of Deng's hundredth birthday in August 2004, researchers at the memorial hall credited Deng's inscription with having bestowed "eternal luster" on the revolutionary history of Anyuan.

16. *Anyuan lukuang gongren yundong jinianguan chenlie dagang* [Outline of the displays in the Anyuan Railway and Mine Workers' Labor Movement

Memorial Hall], November 1987. Mimeographed document without file number in the Anyuan Memorial Hall Archives.

17. Anyuan Memorial Hall Archives, file no. 7-007 (July 15, 1987).

18. Liu Jialin, "Mao Anqing lai Anyuan canguan fangwen" [Mao Anqing visits Anyuan], *Pingxiang dangshi tongxun* [Pingxiang party history bulletin] 1 (1988): 89.

19. Liu Chuanzheng, "Fengyu tongzhou, qinggan ridu" [Sharing a boat through the storms, forever true], *Pingxiang dangshi tongxun* [Pingxiang party history bulletin] 1 (1988): 76–78.

20. Anyuan Memorial Hall Archives, file no. 029 (August–September 1991).

21. Yu Jianrong, *Zhongguo gongren jieji zhuangkuang: Anyuan shilu* [The plight of China's working class: Annals of Anyuan] (Hong Kong: Mirror Books, 2006), 67. The rumor was repeated in numerous interviews with Anyuan residents that I conducted in October 2009.

22. Liu Nanfang, *Dongfang jinglei* [Eastern thunderbolt] (Nanchang: Baihuazhou Arts Press, 2002), 2.

23. The eightieth anniversary of the strike also occasioned another major reorganization of the memorial hall displays, which opened to the public on September 18, 2002. Although this exhibit reaffirmed the political rectitude of the previous (1992) exhibit, it nevertheless took nearly a year to prepare. The refurbished display added more than fifty new items, including nineteenth-century railway equipment made in Germany and a boiler produced locally in 1921, intended to highlight the area's contribution to the development of China's modern industrial sector. In addition to the six familiar sections that chronicled the Anyuan story from the founding of the mine to the formation of a rural base area, the 2002 display appended a new concluding section featuring more than twenty military officers whose careers began as workers at Anyuan. *Anyuan lukuang gongren yundong jinianguan chenlie neirong dagang* [Outline of the contents of the displays at the Anyuan Railway and Mine Workers' Labor Movement Memorial Hall], January 11, 2002. Mimeographed document without file number in the Anyuan Memorial Hall Archives.

24. "Feiteng Anyuan" [Anyuan bubbling with excitement], *Pingkuang gongren bao* [Pingxiang mine workers' journal], September 18, 2002.

25. Philip P. Pan, *Out of Mao's Shadow: The Struggle for the Soul of a New China* (New York: Simon and Schuster, 2008), 114–15.

26. *Renmin ribao* [People's daily], March 14, 1979.

27. On the Mao craze, see Geremie Barmé, *Shades of Mao: The Posthumous Cult of the Great Leader* (Armonk, NY: M. E. Sharpe, 1996).

28. Li Shaozhou, "Weile guoyou zichan de zunyan jianzheng falu de jianjia—Canjia youhua 'Mao zhuxi qu Anyuan' quanyi su song zhaji" [Legal impediments in the testimony about state property—random recollections of participating in the copyright lawsuit concerning the oil painting *Chairman Mao Goes to Anyuan*], accessed at www.boofan.com/.

29. Ibid.

30. Accounts of the auction and attendant lawsuits can be found in *Nanfang zhoumo* [Southern weekend], July 27, 2006; *People's Daily Online*, December 4, 2006; and www.chinanews.com, October 22, 2007.

31. For a general treatment of avant-garde art in China, see Karen Smith, *Nine Lives: The Birth of Avant-Garde Art in New China* (New York: Prestel, 2006).

32. Copies of these and other paintings and digitally altered images based on the *Chairman Mao Goes to Anyuan* motif are all available online.

33. Zheng Shengtian, "*Chairman Mao Goes to Anyuan*: A Conversation with the Artist Liu Chunhua," in *Art and China's Revolution*, ed. Melissa Chiu and Zheng Shengtian (New York: Asia Society, 2008), 129.

34. The tendency to compare the present unfavorably with the past was part of a national trend, particularly pronounced at Anyuan (and presumably other places whose claim to fame was based on Mao's revolutionary activities), in which revolutionary nostalgia implied a critique of the post-Mao reforms. Geremie Barmé, *In the Red: On Contemporary Chinese Culture* (New York: Columbia University Press, 1999); Lu Hanchao, "Nostalgia for the Future: The Resurgence of an Alienated Culture in China, *Pacific Affairs* 75, no. 2 (Summer 2002): 169–86.

35. Yu, *Zhongguo gongren jieji zhuangkuang*, 62.

36. Mei Fangquan, *Anyuan kuanggong: zhuanxingqi de bianqian yanjiu* [Anyuan miners: A study of change in a transitional time] (Beijing: Chinese Academy of Social Sciences, 2006), 295.

37. Yu, *Zhongguo gongren jieji zhuangkuang*, 244.

38. Mei, *Anyuan kuanggong*, 283.

39. Yu, *Zhongguo gongren jieji zhuangkuang*, 122.

40. Ibid., 278.

41. Mei, *Anyuan kuanggong*, 297.

42. Chen Haiping, "Yinian ji" [A year's memorial ceremony], Kaidi media website, www.cat898.com.

43. Yu, *Zhongguo gongren jieji zhuangkuang*, 45–46.

44. Pingxiang Yearbook Editorial Committee, ed., *Pingxiang nianjian* [Pingxiang yearbook] (Beijing: Gazetteer Press, 2006), 116.

45. *China Labour Bulletin* (Hong Kong) 43 (July–August 1998).

46. www.china-project.com/en-end/july2f.html (accessed September 2009).

47. Pan, *Out of Mao's Shadow*, 114–15.

48. Compiled from various years of Pingxiang Yearbook Editorial Committee, ed., *Pingxiang nianjian* [Pingxiang yearbook] (Beijing: Gazetteer Press, 2003–2008).

49. Mei, *Anyuan kuanggong*, 299.

50. Ibid., 287–88.

51. For a description of Hu Jintao's visit to the Jiangxi revolutionary base areas, see *Renmin ribao* [People's daily], September 3, 2003.

52. Mollie Kirk, *Patriotism for Sale: Communist Apologetics in the Red*

*Tourism Program,* senior honors thesis, Harvard University, East Asian Studies, 2008.

53. The red tourism program was in some respects a continuation of the Patriotic Education Campaign launched in the early 1990s, in the wake of the Tiananmen Uprising of 1989, to raise national consciousness among the youth. In addition to including textbook reform, the earlier campaign designated sites associated with the revolution, including Anyuan, as worthy of state-sponsored study tours. Zhao Suisheng: "A State-led Nationalism: The Patriotic Education Campaign in Post-Tiananmen China," *Communist and Post-Communist Studies* 31, no. 3 (1998): 287–302; Wang Zheng, "National Humiliation, History Education, and the Politics of Historical Memory: Patriotic Education Campaign in China," *International Studies Quarterly* 52, no. 4 (December 2008): 783–806; http://tour.jxnews.com.cn/system/2004/09/17/000730857.shtml (accessed September 2009); www.jxay.gov.cn/zwdt/show.asp?id=2366; www.jxay.gov.cn/zwdt/show.asp?id=1828 (accessed September 2009).

54. *Pingkuang gongren bao* [Pingxiang miners' journal], August 5, 2004.

55. www.jxgdw.com/jxgd/news/jszt/2006jxhbh/hspx/userobject1ai 610374.html.

56. *Pingxiang ribao* [Pingxiang daily], June 7, 2005.

57. Pingxiang City Government, "Pingxiangshi hongse lvyou fazhan qingkuang huibao" [Situation report on the development of red tourism in Pingxiang city], unpublished report received from the Pingxiang Tourism Bureau, May 23, 2007.

58. Pingxiang Yearbook Editorial Committee, ed., *Pingxiang nianjian* [Pingxiang yearbook] (Beijing: Gazetteer Press, 2007), 243; author interviews conducted at Anyuan Memorial Hall (October 2009).

59. www.jxay.gov.cn/zwdt/show.asp?id+2366.

60. Pingxiang Yearbook Editorial Committee, ed., *Pingxiang nianjian* [Pingxiang yearbook] (Beijing: Gazetteer Press, 2008), 146.

61. Author interview with Tang Jiangqi, director of the Anyuan tourism bureau, October 29, 2009, Anyuan. About a dozen movies and television serials on the theme of Anyuan's revolutionary history have been filmed on location at the coal mine itself. Mei, *Anyuan kuanggong,* 59. A permanent movie set was recently built adjacent to the coal mine.

62. Quoted in Yu, *Zhongguo gongren jieji zhuangkuang,* 116.

63. Ibid., 212.

64. Anita Chan, *China's Workers Under Assault: Exploitation and Abuse in a Globalizing Economy* (Armonk: M. E. Sharpe, 2001); Pun Ngai, *Made in China: Women Factory Workers in a Global Workplace* (Durham, NC: Duke University Press; Hong Kong: Hong Kong University Press, 2005).

65. *Dangdai Zhongguo de meitan gongye* [Contemporary China's coal industry] (Beijing: Chinese Academy of Social Sciences Press, 1989), 281; *Zhongguo meitan zhi* [China coal gazetteer] (Beijing: Coal Industry Press,

1999), 151; *Zhongguo meitan gongye nianjian 2008* (China's coal industry yearbook 2008) (Beijing: Coal Industry Press, 2009).

66. Pingxiang Yearbook Editorial Committee, ed., *Pingxiang nianjian* (2006), 116.

67. Pingxiang Yearbook Editorial Committee, ed., *Pingxiang nianjian* (2005), 126–27.

68. In 2002–2007, 124 deaths from coal mining accidents were officially reported in Pingxiang. Pingxiang Yearbook Editorial Committee, ed., *Pingxiang nianjian* (2005–2008). By most accounts, the actual number of fatalities was considerably higher than the official statistics.

69. Mei, *Anyuan kuanggong*, 275.

70. Ibid., 324.

71. Coal currently supplies about two-thirds of China's primary energy needs. In 2005 China's coal output reached some 2.23 billion tons, nearly double that of the United States, the world's second largest coal producer. See *The Future of Coal: An Interdisciplinary MIT Study* (Cambridge, MA: Massachusetts Institute of Technology, 2007), chapter 5.

72. Zhang Xuelong, *Anyuan wangshi* [Anyuan past] (Nanchang: Hundred Flowers Literary Press, 2001), 402.

73. http://hi.pingxiang.gov.cn/archiver/?tid-316.html.

74. Liu, *Dongfang jinglei*, 427–28.

75. Yu Jianrong, *Anyuan shilu: yige jieji de guangrong yu mengxiang* (Annals of Anyuan: The glory and dreams of a class) (Nanjing: Jiangsu People's Press, 2011).

76. www.youtube.com/watch?v=SqN9GevrtDU (accessed August 23, 2011).

77. This theme has also been explored by other analysts of the contemporary Chinese working class. See, for example, Ching Kwan Lee, *Against the Law: Labor Protests in China's Rustbelt and Sunbelt* (Berkeley: University of California Press, 2007); and Chen Feng, "Privatization and Its Discontents in Chinese Factories," *China Quarterly* 185 (March 2006): 42–60.

78. Reprinted in Yu, *Zhongguo gongren jieji zhuangkuang*, 411.

79. Mei, *Anyuan kuanggong*, 88.

80. Ibid., 274.

81. Ibid., 271.

82. Quoted in ibid., 272.

83. Mobo Gao, *The Battle for China's Past: Mao and the Cultural Revolution* (London: Pluto Press, 2008), 198–99.

84. Daniel C. Lynch, *After the Propaganda State: Media, Politics, and 'Thought Work' in Reformed China* (Stanford, CA: Stanford University Press, 1999), 5.

85. Ibid., 9.

86. On commercialization of Ming culture, see Craig Clunas, *Superfluous Things: Material Culture and Social Status in Early Modern China* (Honolulu: University of Hawai'i Press, 2004); and *Empire of Great Brightness: Visual*

*and Material Cultures of Ming China* (Honolulu: University of Hawai'i Press, 2007). On the political system, see Charles O. Hucker, *The Ming Dynasty: Its Origins and Evolving Institutions* (Ann Arbor: University of Michigan Center for Chinese Studies, 1978).

87. Elizabeth J. Perry, "Popular Protest: Playing by the Rules," in *China Today China Tomorrow: Domestic Politics, Economy and Society,* ed. Joseph Fewsmith (Lanham, MD: Rowman & Littlefield, 2010), chapter 1.

CONCLUSION

1. For the familiar argument that Mao's revolution was in essence an attack on Chinese culture, see, for example, Richard H. Solomon, *Mao's Revolution and the Chinese Political Culture* (Berkeley: University of California Press, 1974).

2. Joseph R. Levenson, *Confucian China and Its Modern Fate: A Trilogy* (Berkeley: University of California Press, 1968), 3: 115–17.

3. Thomas A. Metzger, *"Transcending the West": Mao's Vision of Socialism and the Legitimization of Teng Hsiao-p'ing's Modernization Program* (Stanford, CA: Hoover Institution Press, 1996), 17.

4. Wu Hung, *Remaking Beijing: Tiananmen Square and the Creation of a Public Space* (Chicago: University of Chicago Press, 2005); Geremie R. Barmé, *The Forbidden City* (Cambridge, MA: Harvard University Press, 2007).

5. For an argument that the elite politics of the Cultural Revolution reflected elements of "traditional" Chinese political culture, see Jin Qiu, *The Culture of Power: The Lin Biao Incident in the Cultural Revolution* (Stanford, CA: Stanford University Press, 1999). For a discussion of the popular cultural origins of mass rhetoric, see Elizabeth J. Perry and Li Xun, "Revolutionary Rudeness: The Language of Red Guards and Rebel Workers in China's Cultural Revolution," in *Twentieth-Century China: New Approaches,* ed. Jeffrey N. Wasserstrom (New York: Routledge, 2003), 221–36.

6. Timothy Cheek, "Mao, Revolution, and Memory," in *A Critical Introduction to Mao,* ed. Timothy Cheek (New York: Cambridge University Press, 2010), 25.

7. Guo Yingjie, *Cultural Nationalism in Contemporary China* (New York: Routledge, 2004); Zhao Suisheng, *A Nation-State by Construction: Dynamics of Modern Chinese Nationalism* (Stanford, CA: Stanford University Press, 2004).

8. The nationalism of the pre-1949 period has been well explored. See, for example, Chalmers A. Johnson, *Peasant Nationalism and Communist Power: The Emergence of Revolutionary China* (Stanford, CA: Stanford University Press, 1962); Tetsuya Kataoka, *Resistance and Revolution in China* (Berkeley: University of California Press, 1974); George E. Taylor, *The Struggle for North China* (New York: AMS Press, 1978).

9. David Holm, *Art and Ideology in Revolutionary China* (New York: Oxford University Press, 1991), 24, 53.

10. "Confucius Statue Vanishes Near Tiananmen Square," *New York Times,* April 22, 2011.

11. Peter Kenez, *The Birth of the Propaganda State: Soviet Methods of Mass Mobilization, 1917–1929* (New York: Cambridge University Press, 1985), 6.

12. Jeffrey Brooks, *Thank You, Comrade Stalin! Soviet Public Culture from Revolution to Cold War* (Princeton, NJ: Princeton University Press, 2001), 67.

13. Mao Zedong, "The Role of the Chinese Communist Party in the National War" (October 1938), in *Selected Readings from the Works of Mao Tsetung* (Beijing: Foreign Languages Press, 1971), 155–56.

14. Delia Davin, "Dark Tales of Mao the Merciless," in *Was Mao Really a Monster,* ed. Gregor Benton and Lin Chun (New York: Routledge, 2010), 20.

15. Hank Johnston and Bert Klandermans, eds., *Social Movements and Culture* (Minneapolis: University of Minnesota Press, 1995).

16. Colin Mackerras, *China's Minorities: Integration and Modernization in the Twentieth Century* (New York: Oxford University Press, 1994).

17. This is not to say that efforts to create a new Soviet culture were futile. See Bruce Grant, *In the Soviet House of Culture: A Century of Perestroikas* (Princeton, NJ: Princeton University Press, 1995), for a fascinating study of the active participation of a small population of fishermen on Sakhalin Island, the Nivkhi, in the construction of Soviet culture. Russian workers were also key participants in this process, as detailed in Stephen Kotkin, *Magnetic Mountain: Stalinism as a Civilization* (Berkeley: University of California Press, 1995).

18. David Brandenberger, *National Bolshevism: Stalinist Mass Culture and the Formation of Modern Russian National Identity, 1931–1956* (Cambridge, MA: Harvard University Press, 2002), 233.

19. Mark Beissinger, *Nationalist Mobilization and the Collapse of the Soviet State* (New York: Cambridge University Press, 2002), 51.

20. S.A. Smith, *Like Cattle and Horses: Nationalism and Labor in Shanghai* (Durham, NC: Duke University Press, 2002); Kataoka, *Resistance and Revolution in China;* Suzanne Pepper, *Civil War in China* (Lanham, MD: Rowman & Littlefield, 1999); Jonathan Unger, ed., *Chinese Nationalism* (Armonk, NY: M.E. Sharpe, 1996).

21. S.A. Smith, *Revolution and the People in Russia and China: A Comparative History* (New York: Cambridge University Press, 2008), 167.

22. John Fitzgerald, "Nationalism, Democracy and Dignity in Twentieth-Century China," in *The Dignity of Nations: Equality, Competition and Honor in East Asian Nationalism,* ed. Sechin Y.S. Chien and John Fitzgerald (Hong Kong: Hong Kong University Press, 2006), 93–114.

23. Quoted in Maurice Meisner, "Iconoclasm and Cultural Revolution in China and Russia," in *Bolshevik Culture,* ed. Abbott Glason, Peter Kenez, and Richard Stites (Bloomington: Indiana University Press, 1985), 280–84.

24. Alfred G. Meyer, "Communist Revolutions and Cultural Change," *Studies in Comparative Communism* 5 (Winter 1972): 345–70; Sheila Fitzpatrick, ed., *Cultural Revolution in Russia, 1928–1931* (Bloomington: Indiana

University Press, 1978); Alfred G. Meyer, "Cultural Revolutions: The Uses of the Concept of Culture in the Comparative Study of Political Systems," *Studies in Comparative Communism* 16 (Spring–Summer 1983): 6.

25. Zenovia A. Sochor, *Revolution and Culture: The Bogdanov-Lenin Controversy* (Ithaca, NY: Cornell University Press, 1988), 228–29.

26. Ibid., 229.

27. *Anyuan meikuang shi* [History of the Anyuan coal mine] (Changsha: Hunan Normal College, 1958), 209.

28. Charles E. Clark, "Literacy and Labour: The Russian Literacy Campaign within the Trade Unions, 1923–1927," *Europe-Asia Studies* 47, no. 8 (December 1995): 1327–41.

29. During the First Five Year Plan (1928–33), Stalin had characterized cultural revolution as "class war" designed to create a new "proletarian intelligentsia" through overthrowing the old cultural authorities. Sheila Fitzpatrick, "Cultural Revolution as Class War," in *Cultural Revolution in Russia, 1928–1931*, ed. Sheila Fitzpatrick (Bloomington: Indiana University Press, 1978), 8.

30. Wang Nianyi, *Da dongluan de niandai* [A decade of turmoil] (Zhengzhou: Henan People's Press, 1988), 600–601.

31. Robert Jay Lifton, *Revolutionary Immortality: Mao Tse-tung and the Chinese Cultural Revolution* (New York: Vintage Books, 1968), 156–61.

32. Zhao Dingxin, *The Power of Tiananmen: State-Society Relations and the 1989 Beijing Student Movement* (Chicago: University of Chicago Press, 2001).

33. Perry Anderson, "Two Revolutions," *New Left Review* 61 (January–February 2010): 79.

34. Kotkin, *Magnetic Mountain*, 359–61. On the alienation of Russians as well as non-Russians, see Roman Szporluk, *Russia, Ukraine, and the Breakup of the Soviet Union* (Stanford, CA: Hoover Institution Press, 2000).

35. For two such comparisons, see Jae Ho Chung, "Central-Local Dynamics: Historical Continuities and Institutional Resilience," in *Mao's Invisible Hand: The Political Foundations of Adaptive Governance in China*, ed. Sebastian Heilmann and Elizabeth J. Perry (Cambridge, MA: Harvard University Press, 2011); and Elizabeth J. Perry, "Sixty Is the New Forty (Or Is It?): Reflections on the Health of the Chinese Body Politic," in *The PRC at Sixty: An International Assessment*, ed. William C. Kirby (Cambridge, MA: Harvard University Press, 2011).

36. Andrew J. Nathan, "Authoritarian Resilience," *Journal of Democracy* 14, no. 1 (January 2003): 13–14; Teresa Wright, *Accepting Authoritarianism: State-Society Relations in China's Reform Era* (Stanford, CA: Stanford University Press, 2010).

37. Quoted in Ching Kwan Lee, "What Was Socialism to Workers? Collective Memories and Labor Politics in an Age of Reform," in *Re-envisioning the Chinese Revolution: The Politics and Poetics of Collective Memories in Reform*

*China*, ed. Ching Kwan Lee and Guobin Yang (Stanford, CA: Stanford University Press, 2007), 158–59.

38. Quoted in Yu Jianrong, *Zhongguo gongren jieji zhuangkuang: Anyuan shilu* [The plight of China's working class: Annals of Anyuan] (Hong Kong: Mirror Books, 2006), 298.

39. Tan Gengbin and Huang Aiguo, "Anyuan jingshen de jicheng he fazhan" [Continuing and developing the Anyuan spirit], in *Anyuan lukuang gongren yundongshi yanjiu wenhui* [Compilation of studies on the Anyuan railway and mine workers' movement], ed. Pingxiang Historical Gazetteer Office (Nanchang: Jiangxi People's Press, 2002), 184.

40. Liu Jianmin, "Anyuan jingshen shi Zhongguo geming jingshen zhi yuan" [The Anyuan spirit is the source of the Chinese revolutionary spirit], in ibid., 193.

41. Elizabeth J. Perry, "Reclaiming the Chinese Revolution," *Journal of Asian Studies* 67 (November 2008): 1147–64.

42. August 31, 2010, email from party censor to journal.

43. Liu Zaifu and Li Zehou, *Gaobie geming: huiwang ershi shiji Zhongguo* [Farewell to revolution: Looking back at twentieth-century China] (Hong Kong: Tiandi Books, 1995).

44. Mobo Gao, *The Battle for China's Past: Mao and the Cultural Revolution* (London: Pluto Press, 2008), 201.

45. Liu Xiaobo, "That Holy Word, 'Revolution,'" in *Popular Protest and Political Culture in Modern China*, 2nd edition, ed. Jeffrey N. Wasserstrom and Elizabeth J. Perry (Boulder, CO: Westview Press, 1994), 315 ff.

46. *Nanfang zhoumo* [Southern weekend], March 10, 2011.

47. Jeff Goodwin, "Is the Age of Revolution Over?" in *Revolution: International Dimensions*, ed. Mark N. Katz (Washington, DC: CQ Press, 2001), 276 ff.

48. Eric Selbin, "Same as It Ever Was: The Future of Revolutions at the End of the Century," in Katz, ed., *Revolution: International Dimensions*, 285–86.

49. Jonas Parello-Plesner and Raffaello Pantucci, *China's Janus-Faced Response to the Arab Revolutions* (London: European Council on Foreign Relations, June 2011).

50. Jill Lepore, *The Whites of Their Eyes: The Tea Party's Revolution and the Battle over American History* (Princeton, NJ: Princeton University Press, 2010), 21.

51. Ibid., 14.

# Glossary

| Chinese characters | Pinyin |
|---|---|
| 哀而动人 | *ai er dongren* |
| 哀兵必胜 | *aibing bisheng* |
| 安源矿工转型期的变迁研究 | *Anyuan kuanggong zhuanxingqi de bianqian yanjiu* |
| 安源路矿工人俱乐部工人补习学校补习教科书 | *Anyuan lukuang gongren julebu gongren buxi xuexiao buxi jiaokeshu* |
| 安源往事 | *Anyuan wangshi* |
| 罢工歌 | *Bagong ge* |
| 百代表 | *bai daibiao* |
| 包 | *bao* |
| 包工制 | *baogongzhi* |
| 保甲 | *baojia* |
| 北岳农工会 | *Beiyue nonggonghui* |
| 表现 | *biaoxian* |
| 采茶戏 | *caichaxi* |
| 参谋 | *canmou* |
| 唱对台戏 | *changduitaixi* |
| 厂史 | *changshi* |
| 赤卫队 | *chiweidui* |
| 穿红鞋子 | *chuan hongxiezi* |
| 串连 | *chuanlian* |
| 春锣 | *chunluo* |
| 从前是牛马，现在要做人 | *congqian shi niuma, xianzai yao zuoren* |
| 大救星 | *dajiuxing* |

| | |
|---|---|
| 党史 | *dangshi* |
| 大请洋矿 | *Daqing yangkuang* |
| 大泽龙蛇 | *Dazelongshe* |
| 东方惊雷 | *Dongfang jinglei* |
| 动武 | *dongwu* |
| 放票 | *fangpiao* |
| 哥老会 | *gelaohui* |
| 革命斗争史 | *geming douzhengshi* |
| 革命史 | *gemingshi* |
| 宫 | *gong* |
| 公平问题 | *gongping wenti* |
| 工人 | *gongren* |
| 工人读本 | *gongren duben* |
| 工人俱乐部 | *gongren julebu* |
| 工人万岁 | *gongren wansui* |
| 工人周刊 | *Gongren zhoukan* |
| 工贼 | *gongzei* |
| 红十条 | *hong shitiao* |
| 红帮 | *hongbang* |
| 红家 | *hongjia* |
| 洪家 | *hongjia* |
| 洪江会 | *Hongjiang hui* |
| 化装讲演 | *huazhuang jiangyan* |
| 户口 | *hukou* |
| 火烧 | *huoshao* |
| 己 | *ji* |
| 件 | *jian* |
| 监察队 | *jianchadui* |
| 件工制 | *jiangongzhi* |
| 建立共和, 平均地权 | *jianligonghe, pingjundiquan* |
| 开山堂 | *kai shantang* |
| 开票 | *kaipiao* |
| 开山祖 | *kaishanzu* |
| 矿票 | *kuangpiao* |
| 劳工纪 | *Laogong ji* |
| 劳工周报 | *Laogong zhoubao* |
| 连 | *lian* |

| | |
|---|---|
| 廉政 | *lianzheng* |
| 燎原 | *Liaoyuan* |
| 刘少奇一身是胆 | *Liu Shaoqi yishen shi dan* |
| 龙头 | *longtou* |
| 毛主席万岁 | *Mao zhuxi wansui* |
| 煤都风暴 | *Meidu fengbao* |
| 民族形式 | *minzu xingshi* |
| 牛 | *niu* |
| 牛马 | *niuma* |
| 傩 | *nuo* |
| 排长 | *paizhang* |
| 炮打 | *paoda* |
| 萍矿工人报 | *Pingkuang gongren bao* |
| 平民读本 | *pingmin duben* |
| 破旧立新 | *pojiu lixin* |
| 十代表 | *shi daibiao* |
| 十分信仰 | *shifen xinyang* |
| 十人团 | *shirentuan* |
| 天 | *tian* |
| 同盟会 | *Tongmeng hui* |
| 通讯 | *tongxun* |
| 团长 | *tuanzhang* |
| 弯弓待发 | *wangong daifa* |
| 万岁 | *wansui* |
| 王爷 | *Wangye* |
| 维持委员会 | *weichi weiyuanhui* |
| 文 | *wen* |
| 文官 | *wenguan* |
| 文明婚礼 | *wenming hunli* |
| 文明戏 | *wenming xi* |
| 文人 | *wenren* |
| 文史馆 | *wenshiguan* |
| 文武双全 | *wenwu shuangquan* |
| 文艺 | *wenyi* |
| 文质彬彬 | *wenzhi binbin* |
| 武 | *wu* |
| 武官 | *wuguan* |

| | |
|---|---|
| 武人 | *wuren* |
| 武术 | *wushu* |
| 武艺 | *wuyi* |
| 先锋 | *Xianfeng* |
| 向导 | *Xiangdao* |
| 先师 | *xianshi* |
| 小学国语教科书 | *Xiaoxue guoyu jiaokeshu* |
| 谢猛子 | *Xie mengzi* |
| 新青年 | *Xin qingnian* |
| 信任问题 | *xinren wenti* |
| 宣传大队 | *xuanchuan dadui* |
| 要武 | *yaowu* |
| 营长 | *yingzhang* |
| 游乐部 | *youle bu* |
| 游学先生 | *youxue xiansheng* |
| 侦察 | *zhencha* |
| 政委 | *zhengwei* |
| 职工协济会 | *zhigong xiejihui* |
| 中国工人阶级状况—安源实绿 | *Zhongguo gongren jieji zhuangkuang—Anyuan shilu* |
| 总代表 | *zong daibiao* |

# Bibliography of English-Language Sources

Ahern, Emily Martin. *Chinese Ritual and Politics*. New York: Cambridge University Press, 1981.

Alexander, Robert. *Re-writing the French Revolutionary Tradition*. New York: Cambridge University Press, 2003.

Aminzade, Ronald, Jack A. Goldstone, and Elizabeth J. Perry. "Leadership Dynamics and Dynamics of Contention." In *Silence and Voice in the Study of Contentious Politics*, edited by Ronald Aminzade et al., 126–54. New York: Cambridge University Press, 2001.

Anderson, Perry. "Two Revolutions." *New Left Review* 61 (January–February 2010): 59–96.

Andrews, Julia F. *Painters and Politics in the People's Republic of China, 1949–1979*. Berkeley: University of California Press, 1994.

Averill, Stephen C. *Revolution in the Highlands: China's Jinggangshan Base Area*. Lanham, MD: Rowman & Littlefield, 2006.

Baker, Keith Michael, ed. *The French Revolution and the Creation of Modern Political Culture*. New York: Oxford University Press, 1987.

———. *Inventing the French Revolution: Essays on French Political Culture in the Eighteenth Century*. Cambridge: Cambridge University Press, 1990.

Barmé, Geremie. *The Forbidden City*. Cambridge, MA: Harvard University Press, 2007.

———. *In the Red: On Contemporary Chinese Culture*. New York: Columbia University Press, 1999.

———. *Shades of Mao: The Posthumous Cult of the Great Leader*. Armonk, NY: M.E. Sharpe, 1996.

Beissinger, Mark. *Nationalist Mobilization and the Collapse of the Soviet State*. New York: Cambridge University Press, 2002.

Belden, Jack. *China Shakes the World*. New York: Monthly Review Press, 1949.

Benton, Gregor. *The New Fourth Army: Communist Resistance along the*

Yangtze and the Huai, 1938–1941. Berkeley: University of California Press, 1999.

Bernstein, Thomas P. *Up to the Mountains and Down to the Villages: The Transfer of Youth from Urban to Rural China.* New Haven, CT: Yale University Press, 1977.

Bianco, Lucien. *Origins of the Chinese Revolution.* Stanford, CA: Stanford University Press, 1971.

Bonnell, Victoria E. *Iconography of Power: Soviet Political Posters under Lenin and Stalin.* Berkeley: University of California Press, 1997.

Brandenberger, David. *National Bolshevism: Stalinist Mass Culture and the Formation of Modern Russian National Identity, 1931–1956.* Cambridge, MA: Harvard University Press, 2002.

———. "Stalin as Symbol: A Case Study of the Personality Cult and its Construction." In *Stalin: A New History,* edited by Sarah Davies and James Harris, 249–70. New York: Cambridge University Press, 2005.

Brooks, Jeffrey. *Thank You, Comrade Stalin! Soviet Public Culture from Revolution to Cold War.* Princeton, NJ: Princeton University Press, 2001.

Brovkin, Vladimir. *Russia after Lenin: Politics, Culture and Society, 1921–1929.* London: Routledge, 1998.

Chan, Anita. *China's Workers Under Assault: Exploitation and Abuse in a Globalizing Economy.* Armonk, NY: M. E. Sharpe, 2001.

Chan, Anita, Richard Madsen, and Jonathan Unger. *Chen Village: The Recent History of a Peasant Community in Mao's China.* Berkeley: University of California Press, 1984.

Chan, Wellington. *Politics and Industrialization in Late Imperial China.* Singapore: Institute of Southeast Asian Studies, 1975.

Chang, Julian. "The Mechanics of State Propaganda: The People's Republic of China and the Soviet Union in the 1950s." In *New Perspectives on State Socialism in China,* edited by Timothy Cheek and Tony Saich, 76–124. Armonk, NY: M. E. Sharpe, 1997.

Chang, Jung, and Jon Halliday. *Mao: The Unknown Story.* New York: Alfred A. Knopf, 2005.

Chang, Kuo-t'ao. *The Rise of the Chinese Communist Party, 1921–1927.* Lawrence, KS: University Press of Kansas, 1971.

Chang, T. Y. "Five Years of Significant Strikes." *Chinese Students Monthly* 21, no. 8 (June 1926).

Chauncey, Helen R. *Schoolhouse Politicians: Locality and State during the Chinese Republic.* Honolulu: University of Hawai'i Press, 1992.

Cheek, Timothy. "Mao, Revolution, and Memory." In *A Critical Introduction to Mao,* edited by Timothy Cheek, 3–30. New York: Cambridge University Press, 2010.

———. *Mao Zedong and China's Revolutions.* Boston: St. Martin's, 2002.

Chen, Feng. "Privatization and Its Discontents in Chinese Factories." *China Quarterly* 185 (March 2006): 42–60.

Chen, Jerome. "Rebels between Rebellions." *Journal of Asian Studies* 29, no. 4 (August 1970): 807–22.

Chesneaux, Jean. *The Chinese Labor Movement, 1919–1927.* Stanford, CA: Stanford University Press, 1968.

*China Labour Bulletin* (Hong Kong) 43 (July–August 1998).

Chung, Jae Ho. "Central-Local Dynamics: Historical Continuities and Institutional Resilience." In *Mao's Invisible Hand: The Political Foundations of Adaptive Governance in China,* edited by Sebastian Heilmann and Elizabeth J. Perry, 297–320. Cambridge, MA: Harvard University Press, 2011.

Clark, Charles E. "Literacy and Labour: The Russian Literacy Campaign within the Trade Unions, 1923–1927." *Europe-Asia Studies* 47, no. 8 (December 1995): 1327–41.

Clark, Paul. *Chinese Cinema: Culture and Politics since 1949.* New York: Cambridge University Press, 1987.

———. *The Chinese Cultural Revolution: A History.* New York: Cambridge University Press, 2008.

Clifford, Nicholas R. *Spoilt Children of Empire: Westerners in Shanghai and the Chinese Revolution of the 1920s.* Hanover, NH: Middlebury College Press, 1991.

Clunas, Craig. *Empire of Great Brightness: Visual and Material Cultures of Ming China.* Honolulu: University of Hawai'i Press, 2007.

———. *Superfluous Things: Material Culture and Social Status in Early Modern China.* Honolulu: University of Hawai'i Press, 2004.

Davies, James C. *When Men Revolt and Why.* New Brunswick, NJ: Transaction, 1997.

Davin, Delia. "Dark Tales of Mao the Merciless." In *Was Mao Really a Monster,* edited by Gregor Benton and Lin Chun, 15–20. New York: Routledge, 2010.

———. *Mao Zedong.* Stroud, UK: Sutton, 1997.

Dewey, John. *Impressions of Soviet Russia and the Revolutionary World.* New York: New Republic, 1929.

Dikotter, Frank. *Mao's Great Famine: The History of China's Most Devastating Catastrophe.* London: Bloomsbury, 2010.

Dittmer, Lowell. "Death and Transfiguration: Liu Shaoqi's Rehabilitation and Contemporary Chinese Politics." *Journal of Asian Studies* 11, no. 3 (May 1981): 455–80.

———. *Liu Shao-ch'i and the Chinese Cultural Revolution: The Politics of Mass Criticism.* Berkeley: University of California Press, 1974.

Duara, Prasenjit. *Culture, Power, and the State: Rural North China, 1900–1942.* Stanford, CA: Stanford University Press, 1988.

Elman, Benjamin A. *A Cultural History of Civil Examinations in Late Imperial China.* Berkeley: University of California Press, 2000.

Elman, Benjamin A., and Alexander Woodside, eds. *Education and Society in Late Imperial China, 1600–1900.* Berkeley: University of California Press, 1994.

Esherick, Joseph W. *Reform and Revolution in China: The 1911 Revolution in Hunan and Hubei.* Berkeley: University of California Press, 1976.

Esherick, Joseph W., and Jeffery N. Wasserstrom. "Acting out Democracy: Political Theater in Modern China." In *Popular Protest and Political Culture in Modern China,* edited by Jeffrey N. Wasserstrom and Elizabeth J. Perry, 32–69. Boulder, CO: Westview Press, 1994.

Fang, Cheng–Hua. "Power Structures and Cultural Identities in Imperial China: Civil and Military Power from Late Tang to Early Song Dynasties." PhD diss., Brown University, 2001.

Fang, Qiang. "Hot Potatoes: Chinese Complaint Systems from Early Times to the Late Qing." *Journal of Asian Studies* 68, no. 4 (November 2009): 1105–35.

Feigon, Lee. *Mao: A Reinterpretation.* Chicago: Ivan R. Dee, 2002.

Feng, Chongyi. "Jiangxi in Reform: The Fear of Exclusion and the Search for a New Identity." In *The Political Economy of China's Provinces: Comparative and Competitive Advantage,* edited by Hans Hendrischke and Feng Chongyi, 249–76. London: Routledge, 1999.

Feuerwerker, Albert. *China's Early Industrialization: Sheng Hsuan-huai and Mandarin Enterprise.* Cambridge, MA: Harvard University Press, 1958.

———. "China's Nineteenth Century Industrialization: The Case of the Hanyeping Coal and Iron Company, Limited." In *The Economic Development of China and Japan,* edited by Charles Donald Cowan, 79–110. New York: Praeger, 1964.

Fishwick, Marshall William. *Great Awakenings: Popular Religion and Popular Culture.* New York: Haworth Press, 1995.

Fitzgerald, John. *Awakening China: Politics, Culture and Class in the Nationalist Revolution.* Stanford, CA: Stanford University Press, 1996.

———. "Nationalism, Democracy and Dignity in Twentieth-Century China." In *The Dignity of Nations: Equality, Competition and Honor in East Asian Nationalism,* edited by Sechin Y.S. Chien and John Fitzgerald, 93–114. Hong Kong: Hong Kong University Press, 2006.

Fitzpatrick, Sheila, ed. *Cultural Revolution in Russia, 1928–1931.* Bloomington: Indiana University Press, 1978.

Frazier, Mark W. *The Making of the Chinese Industrial Workplace.* New York: Cambridge University Press, 2002.

Friedman, Edward, Paul G. Pickowicz, and Mark Selden. *Chinese Village, Socialist State.* New Haven, CT: Yale University Press, 1991.

———. *Revolution, Resistance, and Reform in Village China.* New Haven, CT: Yale University Press, 2005.

*The Future of Coal: An Interdisciplinary MIT Study.* Cambridge, MA: Massachusetts Institute of Technology, 2007.

Galbiati, Fernando. *Peng Pai and the Hai-Lu-Feng Soviet.* Stanford, CA: Stanford University Press, 1985.

Gao, Mobo. *The Battle for China's Past: Mao and the Cultural Revolution.* London: Pluto Press, 2008.

Gaventa, John. *Power and Powerlessness: Quiescence and Rebellion in an Appalachian Valley.* Urbana: University of Illinois Press, 1980.

Gerth, Karl. *China Made: Consumer Culture and the Creation of the Nation.* Cambridge, MA: Harvard University Asia Center, 2003.

Gilmartin, Christina K. *Engendering the Chinese Revolution: Radical Women, Communist Politics, and Mass Movements in the 1920s.* Berkeley: University of California Press, 1995.

Goldman, Merle. *China's Intellectuals: Advise and Dissent.* Cambridge, MA: Harvard University Press, 1981.

Goodwin, Jeff. "Is the Age of Revolution Over?" In *Revolution: International Dimensions,* edited by Mark N. Katz, 272–83. Washington, DC: CQ Press, 2001.

Grant, Bruce. *In the Soviet House of Culture: A Century of Perestroikas.* Princeton, NJ: Princeton University Press, 1995.

Guo, Yingjie. *Cultural Nationalism in Contemporary China.* New York: Routledge, 2004.

Gurr, Ted Robert. *Why Men Rebel.* Princeton, NJ: Princeton University Press, 1970.

Guy, R. Kent. *The Emperor's Four Treasures: Scholars and the State in the Late Ch'ien-lung Era.* Cambridge, MA: Harvard East Asian Monographs, 1987.

Haar, Barend J. ter. "The Gathering of Brothers and Elders: A New View." In *Conflict and Accommodation in Early Modern East Asia,* edited by Leonard Blusse and Harriet T. Zurndorfer, 259–84. Leiden: E. J. Brill, 1993.

———.*Ritual and Mythology of the Chinese Triads: Creating an Identity.* Leiden: Brill, 1998.

Han, Suyin. *The Morning Deluge: Mao Tsetung and the Chinese Revolution.* Boston: Little, Brown, 1972.

Harper, Paul. "The Party and the Unions in Communist China." *China Quarterly* 37 (1969): 84–119.

Harrison, Henrietta. *The Making of the Republican Citizen: Ceremonies and Symbols in China, 1911–1929.* New York: Oxford University Press, 2000.

Hayford, Charles W. *To the People: James Yen and Village China.* New York: Columbia University Press, 1990.

Heilmann, Sebastian, and Elizabeth J. Perry, eds. *Mao's Invisible Hand: The Political Foundations of Adaptive Governance in China.* Cambridge, MA: Harvard University Press, 2011.

Hershatter, Gail. *The Gender of Memory: Rural Women and China's Collective Past.* Berkeley: University of California Press, 2011.

Herzfeld, Michael. *Cultural Intimacy: Social Poetics in the Nation-State,* 2nd ed. New York: Routledge, 2005.

Hinton, William. *Fanshen: A Documentary of Revolution in a Chinese Village.* New York: Random House, 1968.

———.*Shenfan.* New York: Random House, 1983.

Hofheinz, Roy M., Jr. *The Broken Wave: The Chinese Communist Peasant Movement, 1922–1928.* Cambridge, MA: Harvard University Press, 1977.

Holm, David. *Art and Ideology in Revolutionary China.* New York: Oxford University Press, 1991.

Honig, Emily. "Maoist Mappings of Gender: Reassessing the Red Guards." In *Chinese Femininities / Chinese Masculinities,* edited by Susan Brownell and Jeffrey N. Wasserstrom, 259–68. Berkeley: University of California Press, 2002.

Hornibrook, Jeff. "Local Elites and Mechanized Mining in China: The Case of the Wen Lineage in Pingxiang County, Jiangxi." *Modern China* 27, no. 2 (April 2001).

Hou, Li. "Urban Planning in Mao's China: The Rise and Fall of the Daqing Model." PhD diss., Harvard University, 2009.

Howard, Joshua. *Workers at War: Labor in China's Arsenals.* Stanford, CA: Stanford University Press, 2004.

Hsiao, Kung-ch'uan. *Rural China: Imperial Control in the Nineteenth Century.* Seattle: University of Washington Press, 1960.

Hucker, Charles O. *The Ming Dynasty: Its Origins and Evolving Institutions.* Ann Arbor: University of Michigan Center for Chinese Studies, 1978.

Hung, Chang-tai. *Mao's New World: Political Culture in the Early People's Republic.* Ithaca, NY: Cornell University Press, 2010.

———. *War and Popular Culture: Resistance in Modern China, 1937–1945.* Berkeley: University of California Press, 1994.

Hunt, Lynn. *Politics, Culture and Class in the French Revolution.* Berkeley: University of California Press, 1984.

Jin, Qiu. *The Culture of Power: The Lin Biao Incident in the Cultural Revolution.* Stanford, CA: Stanford University Press, 1999.

Johnson, Chalmers A. *Peasant Nationalism and Communist Power: The Emergence of Revolutionary China.* Stanford, CA: Stanford University Press, 1962.

Johnston, Hank, and Bert Klandermans, eds. *Social Movements and Culture.* Minneapolis: University of Minnesota Press, 1995.

Judd, Ellen R. "Revolutionary Drama and Song in the Jiangxi Soviet." *Modern China* 9, no. 1 (1983): 127–60.

Kataoka, Tetsuya. *Resistance and Revolution in China.* Berkeley: University of California Press, 1974.

Kautsky, John H. *Political Change in Underdeveloped Countries: Nationalism and Communism.* New York: Wiley, 1962.

Kenez, Peter. *The Birth of the Propaganda State: Soviet Methods of Mass Mobilization, 1917–1929.* New York: Cambridge University Press, 1985.

Kerr, Clark, and Abraham Siegel. "The Interindustry Propensity to Strike—An International Comparison." In *Labor and Management in Industrial Society,* edited by Clark Kerr, 105–47. Garden City, NY: Doubleday, 1954.

Kidd, Thomas S. *The Great Awakening.* New Haven, CT: Yale University Press, 2007.

Kim, Ilpyong J. *The Politics of Chinese Communism: Kiangsi under the Communists.* Berkeley: University of California Press, 1973.

Kirby, William C. *Germany and Republican China*. Stanford, CA: Stanford University Press, 1984.

Kirk, Mollie. "Patriotism for Sale: Communist Apologetics in the Red Tourism Program." Senior honors thesis, Harvard University, East Asian Studies, 2008.

Kotkin, Stephen. *Magnetic Mountain: Stalinism as a Civilization*. Berkeley: University of California Press, 1995.

Kraus, Richard Curt. *Brushes with Power: Modern Politics and the Chinese Art of Calligraphy*. Berkeley: University of California Press, 1991.

——. *The Party and the Arty in China: The New Politics of Culture*. Lanham, MD: Rowman & Littlefield, 2004.

Kuhn, Philip A. *Rebellion and Its Enemies in Late Imperial China*. Cambridge, MA: Harvard University Press, 1970.

Kupper, Samuel Yale. "Revolution in China: Kiangsi Province, 1905–1913." PhD diss., University of Michigan, 1973.

Lagerwey, John. *China: A Religious State*. Hong Kong: Hong Kong University Press, 2010.

Laing, Ellen Johnston. *The Winking Owl: Art in the People's Republic of China*. Berkeley: University of California Press, 1988.

Lee, Ching Kwan. *Against the Law: Labor Protests in China's Rustbelt and Sunbelt*. Berkeley: University of California Press, 2007.

——. "The Revenge of History: Collective Memories and Labor Protests in Northeastern China." *Ethnography* 1, no. 2 (2000): 217–37.

——. "What Was Socialism to Workers? Collective Memories and Labor Politics in an Age of Reform." In *Re-envisioning the Chinese Revolution: The Politics and Poetics of Collective Memories in Reform China*, edited by Ching Kwan Lee and Guobin Yang, 141–65. Stanford, CA: Stanford University Press, 2007.

Lee, Ching Kwan, and Guobin Yang, eds. *Re-envisioning the Chinese Revolution: The Politics and Poetics of Collective Memories in Reform China*. Stanford, CA: Stanford University Press, 2007.

Lee, Haiyan. "The Charisma of Power and the Military Sublime in Tiananmen Square." *Journal of Asian Studies* 70, no. 2 (May 2011): 397–424.

Lepore, Jill. *The Whites of Their Eyes: The Tea Party's Revolution and the Battle over American History*. Princeton, NJ: Princeton University Press, 2010.

Lescot, Patrick. *Before Mao: The Untold Story of Li Lisan and the Creation of Communist China*. New York: HarperCollins, 2004.

Levenson, Joseph R. *Confucian China and Its Modern Fate: A Trilogy*. Berkeley: University of California Press, 1968.

Lewis, Charlton M. *Prologue to the Chinese Revolution: The Transformation of Ideas and Institutions in Hunan Province, 1891–1907*. Cambridge, MA: Harvard East Asian Monographs, 1976.

——. "Some Notes on the Ko-lao Hui in Late Ch'ing China." In *Popular Movements and Secret Societies in China, 1840–1950*, edited by Jean Chesneaux, 97–112. Stanford, CA: Stanford University Press, 1972.

Lewis, John W. "Leader, Commissar and Bureaucrat: The Chinese Political System in the Last Days of the Revolution." In *China in Crisis*, edited by Ping-ti Ho and Tang Tsou, vol. 1, book A, 449–81. Chicago: University of Chicago Press, 1968.

Liang, Heng, and Judith Shapiro. *Son of the Revolution*. New York: Vintage Books, 1983.

Lifton, Robert Jay. *Revolutionary Immortality: Mao Tse-tung and the Chinese Cultural Revolution*. New York: Vintage Books, 1968.

Liu, Chunhua. "Painting Pictures of Chairman Mao Is Our Greatest Happiness." *China Reconstructs* 17, no. 10 (October 1968): 5–6.

Liu, Xiaobo. "That Holy Word, 'Revolution.'" In *Popular Protest and Political Culture in Modern China*, 2nd edition, edited by Jeffrey N. Wasserstrom and Elizabeth J. Perry, 309–24. Boulder, CO: Westview Press, 1994.

Louie, Kam. *Theorising Chinese Masculinity: Society and Gender in China*. Cambridge: Cambridge University Press, 2002.

Louie, Kam, and Louise Edwards. "Chinese Masculinity: Theorizing Wen and Wu." *East Asian History* 8 (1994): 138–94.

Lu, Hanchao. "Nostalgia for the Future: The Resurgence of an Alienated Culture in China." *Pacific Affairs* 75, no. 2 (Summer 2002): 169–86.

Lutz, Jessie G. "Chinese Nationalism and the Anti-Christian Campaigns of the 1920s." *Modern Asian Studies* 10, no. 3 (1976): 395–416.

Lynch, Daniel C. *After the Propaganda State: Media, Politics, and 'Thought Work' in Reformed China*. Stanford, CA: Stanford University Press, 1999.

Lynch, Michael. *Mao*. London: Routledge, 2004.

MacFarquhar, Roderick. *Contradictions among the People, 1956–1957*. New York: Columbia University Press, 1974.

———. *The Great Leap Forward, 1958–1960*. New York: Columbia University Press, 1983.

———. *The Origins of the Cultural Revolution: The Coming of the Cataclysm, 1961–1966*. New York: Columbia University Press, 1997.

MacFarquhar, Roderick, and Michael Schoenhals. *Mao's Last Revolution*. Cambridge, MA: Harvard University Press, 2006.

Mackerras, Colin. *China's Minorities: Integration and Modernization in the Twentieth Century*. New York: Oxford University Press, 1994.

Mao, Zedong. *Selected Readings from the Works of Mao Tsetung*. Beijing: Foreign Languages Press, 1971.

Marks, Robert. *Rural Revolution in South China: Peasants and the Making of History in Haifeng County, 1570–1930*. Madison: University of Wisconsin Press, 1984.

McInnis, Donald E. *Religious Policy and Practice in Communist China*. New York: Macmillan, 1972.

Meisner, Maurice. "Iconoclasm and Cultural Revolution in China and Russia." In *Bolshevik Culture*, edited by Abbott Glason, Peter Kenez, and Richard Stites, 279–94. Bloomington: Indiana University Press, 1985.

———. *Mao Zedong*. Cambridge: Polity Press, 2007.

———. *Marxism, Maoism and Utopianism*. Madison: University of Wisconsin Press, 1982.

Melucci, Alberto. *Nomads of the Present: Social Movements and Individual Needs in Contemporary Society*. Philadelphia, PA: Temple University Press, 1989.

Metzger, Thomas A. *"Transcending the West": Mao's Vision of Socialism and the Legitimization of Teng Hsiao-p'ing's Modernization Program*. Stanford, CA: Hoover Institution Press, 1996.

Meyer, Alfred G. "Communist Revolutions and Cultural Change." *Studies in Comparative Communism* 5 (Winter 1972): 345–70.

———. "Cultural Revolutions: The Uses of the Concept of Culture in the Comparative Study of Political Systems." *Studies in Comparative Communism* 16 (Spring–Summer 1983): 5–8.

Mitter, Rana. *A Bitter Revolution: China's Struggle with the Modern World*. New York: Oxford University Press, 2004.

Munro, Donald J. *The Concept of Man in Contemporary China*. Ann Arbor: University of Michigan Press, 2000.

———. *The Concept of Man in Early China*. Stanford, CA: Stanford University Press, 1969.

———. "Egalitarian Ideal and Educational Fact in Communist China." In *China: Management of a Revolutionary Society*, edited by John M. H. Lindbeck. Seattle: University of Washington Press, 1971.

Murray, Dian H. *The Origins of the Tiandihui: The Chinese Triads in Legend and History*. Stanford, CA: Stanford University Press, 1994.

———. *Pirates of the South China Coast, 1790–1810*. Stanford, CA: Stanford University Press, 1987.

Myrdal, Jan. *Report from a Chinese Village*. New York: Pantheon, 1965.

———. *Return to a Chinese Village*. New York: Pantheon, 1984.

Nash, June. *We Eat the Mines and the Mines Eat Us: Dependency and Exploitation in Bolivian Tin Mines*. New York: Columbia University Press, 1993.

Nathan, Andrew J. "Authoritarian Resilience." *Journal of Democracy* 14, no. 1 (January 2003): 6–17.

North, Robert C. *Kuomintang and Chinese Communist Elites*. Stanford, CA: Stanford University Press, 1952.

O'Brien, Kevin J., and Lianjiang Li. "Campaign Nostalgia in the Chinese Countryside." *Asian Survey* 39, no. 3 (May–June 1999): 376–91.

Ortner, Sherry B. "Theory in Anthropology since the Sixties." *Comparative Studies in Society and History* 26, no. 1 (January 1984): 126–66.

Ozouf, Mona. *Festivals and the French Revolution*. Cambridge, MA: Harvard University Press, 1988.

Pan, Philip P. *Out of Mao's Shadow: The Struggle for the Soul of a New China*. New York: Simon & Schuster, 2008.

Pantsov, Alexander. *The Bolsheviks and the Chinese Revolution, 1919–1927*. Honolulu: University of Hawai'i Press, 2000.

Parello-Plesner, Jonas, and Raffaello Pantucci. *China's Janus-Faced Response* to the Arab Revolutions. London: European Council on Foreign Relations, June 2011.

Pepper, Suzanne. Civil War in China. Lanham, MD: Rowman & Littlefield, 1999.

Peris, Daniel. Storming the Heavens: The Soviet League of the Militant Godless. Ithaca, NY: Cornell University Press, 1998.

Perry, Elizabeth J. "From Native Place to Workplace: Labor Origins and Outcomes of China's Danwei System." In Danwei: The Changing Chinese Workplace in Historical and Comparative Perspective, edited by Lu Xiaobo and Elizabeth J. Perry, 42–59. Armonk, NY: M. E. Sharpe, 1997.

———. "Masters of the Country? Shanghai Workers in the Early PRC." In Dilemmas of Victory: The Early Years of the People's Republic of China, edited by Jeremy Brown and Paul Pickowicz, 59–79. Cambridge, MA: Harvard University Press, 2007.

———. Patrolling the Revolution: Worker Militias, Citizenship and the Modern Chinese State. Lanham, MD: Rowman & Littlefield, 2006.

———. "Popular Protest: Playing by the Rules." In China Today China Tomorrow: Domestic Politics, Economy and Society, edited by Joseph Fewsmith, 11–28. Lanham, MD: Rowman & Littlefield, 2010.

———. Rebels and Revolutionaries in North China, 1845–1945. Stanford, CA: Stanford University Press, 1980.

———. "Reclaiming the Chinese Revolution." Journal of Asian Studies 67 (November 2008): 1147–64.

———. "Red Literati: Communist Educators at Anyuan, 1921–1925." Twentieth Century China (April 2007): 123–60.

———. "Shanghai's Strike Wave of 1957." China Quarterly 137 (March 1994): 1–27.

———. Shanghai on Strike: The Politics of Chinese Labor. Stanford, CA: Stanford University Press, 1993.

———. "Sixty Is the New Forty (Or Is It?): Reflections on the Health of the Chinese Body Politic." In The PRC at Sixty: An International Assessment, edited by William C. Kirby, 133–44. Cambridge, MA: Harvard University Press, 2011.

Perry, Elizabeth J., and Li Xun. Proletarian Power: Shanghai in the Cultural Revolution. Boulder, CO: Westview Press, 1997.

———. "Revolutionary Rudeness: The Language of Red Guards and Rebel Workers in China's Cultural Revolution." In Twentieth-Century China: New Approaches, edited by Jeffrey N. Wasserstrom, 221–36. New York: Routledge, 2003.

Pickowicz, Paul. Marxist Literary Thought in China: The Influence of Ch'u Ch'iu-pai. Berkeley: University of California Press, 1981.

"The Pingsiang Colliery." Far Eastern Review 12, no. 10 (March 1916): 377.

Pun, Ngai. Made in China: Women Factory Workers in a Global Workplace. Durham, NC: Duke University Press; Hong Kong: Hong Kong University Press, 2005.

Puyraimond, Guy. "The Ko-lao Hui and the Anti-Foreign Incidents of 1891." In *Popular Movements and Secret Societies in China, 1840–1950*, edited by Jean Chesneaux, 113–24. Stanford, CA: Stanford University Press, 1972.

Rowe, Peter G., and Seng Kuan, eds. *Shanghai: Architecture and Urbanism for Modern China*. New York: Prestel, 2004.

Schiffrin, Harold Z. *Sun Yat-sen and the Origins of the Chinese Revolution*. Berkeley: University of California Press, 1968.

Schwartz, Benjamin I. *Chinese Communism and the Rise of Mao*. Cambridge, MA: Harvard University Press, 1966.

Selbin, Eric. "Same as It Ever Was: The Future of Revolutions at the End of the Century." In *Revolution: International Dimensions*, edited by Mark N. Katz, 284–98. Washington, DC: CQ Press, 2001.

Selden, Mark. *The Yenan Way in Revolutionary China*. Cambridge, MA: Harvard University Press, 1971.

Sewell, William H., Jr. *Logics of History: Social Theory and Social Transformation*. Chicago: University of Chicago Press, 2005.

Shaffer, Lynda. *Mao and the Workers: The Hunan Labor Movement, 1920–1923*. Armonk, NY: M. E. Sharpe, 1982.

Sheehan, Jackie. *Chinese Workers: A New History*. New York: Routledge, 1998.

Shils, Edward. *The Intellectuals and the Powers*. Chicago: University of Chicago Press, 1972.

Shirk, Susan. *Competitive Comrades*. Berkeley: University of California Press, 1982.

Short, Philip. *Mao: A Life*. New York: Henry Holt, 2000.

Skinner, G. William. "Marketing and Social Structure in Rural China (Part I)." *Journal of Asian Studies* 24, no. 1 (November 1964): 3–43.

Skocpol, Theda. *States and Social Revolutions*. New York: Cambridge University Press, 1979.

Smith, Karen. *Nine Lives: The Birth of Avant-Garde Art in New China*. New York: Prestel, 2006.

Smith, S. A. *Like Cattle and Horses: Nationalism and Labor in Shanghai, 1895–1927*. Durham, NC: Duke University Press, 2002.

———. *Revolution and the People in Russia and China: A Comparative History*. New York: Cambridge University Press, 2008.

Smith, Timothy L. *Revivalism and Social Reform*. Baltimore, MD: Johns Hopkins University Press, 1980.

Snow, Edgar. *The Long Revolution*. New York: Vintage, 1973.

———. *Red Star over China*. New York: Grove Press, 1968.

Sochor, Zenovia A. *Revolution and Culture: The Bogdanov-Lenin Controversy*. Ithaca, NY: Cornell University Press, 1988.

Solomon, Richard H. *Mao's Revolution and the Chinese Political Culture*. Berkeley: University of California Press, 1974.

Sorace, Christian. "Saint Mao." *Telos* 151 (Summer 2010): 173–91.

Spence, Jonathan D. *Mao*. New York: Viking, 1999.

Strauss, Julia C. "Paternalist Terror: The Campaign to Suppress Counterrevolutionaries and Regime Consolidation in the People's Republic of China, 1950–1953." *Comparative Studies in Society and History* 44, no. 1 (January 2002): 80–105.

Strong, Anna Louise. *China's Millions.* New York: Coward-McCann, 1928.

Swidler, Ann. "Culture in Action: Symbols and Strategies." *American Sociological Review* 51, no. 2 (April 1986): 273–86.

Szporluk, Roman. *Russia, Ukraine, and the Breakup of the Soviet Union.* Stanford, CA: Hoover Institution Press, 2000.

Taylor, George E. *The Struggle for North China.* New York: AMS Press, 1978.

Teiwes, Frederick C., and Warren Sun. *The Tragedy of Lin Biao: Riding the Tiger during the Cultural Revolution, 1966–71.* London: Hurst, 1996.

Terrill, Ross. *Madame Mao: The White-Boned Demon.* Stanford, CA: Stanford University Press, 1999.

———. *Mao: A Biography.* Stanford, CA: Stanford University Press, 1999.

Thaxton, Ralph A., Jr. *Catastrophe and Contention in Rural China: Mao's Great Leap Forward Famine and the Origins of Righteous Resistance in Da Fo Village.* New York: Cambridge University Press, 2008.

Tyng, Walworth. "Difficult Days in Hunan: Veteran Missionary Gives Vivid Picture of Unrest in China as Governments Change." *The Spirit of Missions* 92 (1927): 71.

———. "The Miners' Church at Peaceful Spring: Among the Collieries and Coke Ovens at Anyuen—A Vivid Picture of Our Work in a Little Known Part of the District of Hankow." *The Spirit of Missions* 90 (1925): 477.

Unger, Jonathan, ed. *Chinese Nationalism.* Armonk, NY: M. E. Sharpe, 1996.

Van de Ven, Hans J. *War and Nationalism in China, 1925–1945.* New York: Routledge Curzon, 2003.

von Geldern, James. "Introduction." In *Mass Culture in Soviet Russia,* edited by James von Geldern and Richard Stites. Bloomington: Indiana University Press, 1995.

Wade, Rex A. *Red Guards and Workers' Militias in the Russian Revolution.* Stanford, CA: Stanford University Press, 1984.

Walder, Andrew G. *Communist Neo-Traditionalism: Work and Authority in Chinese Industry.* Berkeley: University of California Press, 1986.

Wales, Nym. *The Chinese Labor Movement.* New York: John Day, 1945.

Walker, Richard Louis. *China under Communism: The First Five Years.* New Haven, CT: Yale University Press, 1955.

Waller, Derek J. *The Kiangsi Soviet Republic: Mao and the National Congresses of 1931 and 1934.* Berkeley: University of California Center for Chinese Studies, 1973.

Wang, Zheng. "National Humiliation, History Education, and the Politics of Historical Memory: Patriotic Education Campaign in China." *International Studies Quarterly* 52, no. 4 (December 2008): 783–806.

Warr, Anne. *Shanghai Architecture.* Sydney: Watermark Press, 2007.

Wasserstrom, Jeffrey N. *Student Protest in Twentieth-Century China: The View from Shanghai.* Stanford, CA: Stanford University Press, 1991.

Wedeen, Lisa. "Conceptualizing Culture: Possibilities for Political Science." *American Political Science Review* 96, no. 4 (December 2002): 713–28.

White, Lynn, III. *Policies of Chaos: The Organizational Causes of Violence in China's Cultural Revolution.* Princeton, NJ: Princeton University Press, 1989.

Wright, Teresa. *Accepting Authoritarianism: State-Society Relations in China's Reform Era.* Stanford, CA: Stanford University Press, 2010.

Wright, Tim. *Coal Mining in China's Economy and Society, 1895–1937.* New York: Cambridge University Press, 1984.

Wu, Hung. *Remaking Beijing: Tiananmen Square and the Creation of a Public Space.* Chicago: University of Chicago Press, 2005.

Wu, Yunduo, *Son of the Working Class.* Peking: Foreign Languages Press, 1956.

Yang, Kuisong. "Reconsidering the Campaign to Suppress Counterrevolutionaries." *China Quarterly* 193 (2008): 102–21.

Yeh, Wen-Hsin. *The Alienated Academy: Culture and Politics in Republican China.* Cambridge, MA: Harvard University Press, 1990.

———. *Provincial Passages: Culture, Space and the Origins of Chinese Communism.* Berkeley: University of California Press, 1996.

Zarrow, Peter. *China in War and Revolution.* New York: Routledge, 2005.

Zhang, Baohui. "Communal Cooperative Institutions and Peasant Revolutions in South China, 1926–1934." *Theory and Society* 29, no. 5 (2000): 687–736.

Zhao, Dingxin. *The Power of Tiananmen: State-Society Relations and the 1989 Beijing Student Movement.* Chicago: University of Chicago Press, 2001.

Zhao, Suisheng. *A Nation-State by Construction: Dynamics of Modern Chinese Nationalism.* Stanford, CA: Stanford University Press, 2004.

———. "A State-led Nationalism: The Patriotic Education Campaign in Post-Tiananmen China." *Communist and Post-Communist Studies* 31, no. 3. (1998): 287–302.

Zhao, Yuezhi. *Communication in China: Political Economy, Power, and Conflict.* Lanham, MD: Rowman & Littlefield, 2008.

Zheng, Shengtian. "*Chairman Mao Goes to Anyuan:* A Conversation with the Artist Liu Chunhua." In *Art and China's Revolution,* edited by Melissa Chiu and Zheng Shengtian, 119–32. New York: Asia Society, 2008.

Zhou, Yuan, ed. *A New Collection of Red Guard Publications.* Oakton, VA: Center for Chinese Research Materials, 1991.

# Index

agitprop, 5, 95, 289
Ahern, Emily Martin, 9, 245
All-China Federation of Trade
   Unions, 154, 168
anarchists, 109, 110
Anderson, Perry, 1–2, 291–92
Andrews, Julia, 188, 216, 217
anti-Christian campaigns, 111,
   321n133
antiforeign hostility, 21–22, 22–23
anti-Manchu sentiment, 23, 35–36
Anti-Rightist Campaign (1957), 168,
   175–76, 178
Anyuan: Communist Party branch,
   10, 145; as conduit for communist
   movement, 7, 78, 140; known as
   "China's Little Moscow," 10–11, 78,
   118; literary and artistic works on,
   14, 275–76; symbolic power of, 8,
   208–9. *See also* Anyuan experiment; Anyuan labor movement;
   Anyuan mine; Anyuan revolutionary tradition; Anyuan workers
Anyuan Anti-Communism Commission, 139
Anyuan experiment, 7, 118, 120, 122–
   23, 124–25, 149. *See also* Anyuan
   revolutionary tradition
*Anyuan Great Strike, The* (opera),
   170–71, 332n56

*Anyuan Is a Good Place* (television
   program), 272
Anyuan labor movement: in the construction of Anyuan's revolutionary tradition, 163–64; cultural
   positioning in, 76; establishment
   of the workers' club, 57–58; gradual
   approach to mobilization, 60–61;
   histories of, 180–83, 333–34n86;
   reinterpretation of, 247–48. *See
   also* Anyuan workers' club
Anyuan martyrs, 166, 224
Anyuan mine: accidents and injuries at, 28, 101–2, 112, 201, 274, 279,
   351n68; centennial of, 268; closing of, in 1939, 145; conditions at,
   28–29, 29, 200–201; during the
   Cultural Revolution, 207, 231, 267;
   and decreased demand during Little Moscow period, 104; established
   by Pingxiang Mining Company,
   17–23; histories of, 180; under
   Nationalist control, 144–45, 146;
   occupied by PLA during Cultural
   Revolution, 210; original entrance
   to, 31*fig.*; police force of, 132–33,
   140, 147; production at, 138, 160,
   178–79, 238, 274; reactivation of,
   after the Communist takeover, 160;
   underground organization in